SCRAMBLING AND BARRIERS

LINGUISTIK AKTUELL

This series provides a platform for studies in the syntax,
semantics, and pragmatics of the Germanic languages
and their historical developments.
The focus of the series is represented by its German title
Linguistik Aktuell (Linguistics Today)
Texts in the series are in English.

Volume 5

Günther Grewendorf and Wolfgang Sternefeld (eds)

Scrambling and Barriers

SCRAMBLING
AND
BARRIERS

Edited by

GÜNTHER GREWENDORF and WOLFGANG STERNEFELD
J.W. Goethe University, Frankfurt

JOHN BENJAMINS PUBLISHING COMPANY
AMSTERDAM/PHILADELPHIA

1990

Library of Congress Cataloging-in-Publication Data

Scrambling and barriers / edited by Günther Grewendorf and Wolfgang Sternefeld.
    p.   cm. -- (Linguistik aktuell, ISSN 0166-0829 ; v. 5)
Includes bibliographical references.
1. Generative grammar. 2. German language -- Grammar, Generative. I. Grewendorf,
Günther. II. Sternefeld, Wolfgang, 1953-   . III. Series: Linguistik aktuell : Bd. 5.
P158.S37   1989
415--dc20   89-18427
ISBN 90 272 2725 X (alk. paper)   CIP

Table of contents

I. Introduction

Scrambling Theories

Günther Grewendorf and Wolfgang Sternefeld
Johann Wolfgang Goethe University, Frankfurt

The term *"Scrambling"* originates from Ross's famous dissertation on "Constraints on Variables in Syntax" (Ross 1967). Ever since this early period of restrictive syntax, generative grammarians have occasionally been interested in languages such as Latin, Russian, Czech, etc. whose order of major elements within a clause is free, within certain limits. In his dissertation, Ross proposed a universal *Scrambling Rule* to account for the variable word order in these so-called "free word order" languages. The "skeleton" of such a rule stated that two adjacent constituents can be permuted if they are clause-mates, i.e., constituents of the same minimal clause.

Language specific parameters of this universal rule had to account for idiosyncratic properties of *Scrambling*, e.g., whether or not certain constituents could be productively involved in this process. The *Scrambling Parameter* had to specify whether or not a prenominal adjectival phrase can be separated from its nominal head, a postpositional NP could be scrambled away from its postposition, or a specifier away from the head it specifies.

If a particular grammar chooses to apply the *Scrambling Rule*, it might be necessary to specify in addition *marked values* of the *Scrambling Parameter*. For example, in the particular grammars of Latin and Russian it would not only be necessary to note that *Scrambling* could apply, but in Latin, one would be required to specify in addition that (besides major constituents as unmarked values of the *Scrambling Parameter*) it is also possible to scramble verbs and adjectives, separating adjectives from their nominal heads and verbs from their arguments.

Although Ross's brief sketch of *Scrambling* anticipates many aspects of the principles-and-parameters theory of grammar, he was not overly concerned with an explicit statement of the parameter and its values in a particular language, "for the problems involved in specifying exactly the subset of the strings which will be generated ... are far too complicated for me to even mention them here, let alone to come to grips with them" (p. 52).

Meanwhile a considerable amount of work has been done, and a number of valuable studies on "free word order," especially in German, have appeared; to mention just a few, *vide* Engel (1972), Lenerz (1977), Etzensberger (1979), Hoberg (1981), Lötscher (1981), Höhle (1982), Abraham (1986) or Reis (1986).

Although the descriptive value of the cited work is unquestioned, only a few of these studies seem to bear on more theoretical issues of Generative Grammar. As for Ross himself, his actual concern was not the phenomenon as such, rather it was (*inter alia*) the observed *clause-boundedness* of *Scrambling*, a fact which has already been noticed in Bierwisch's detailed generative grammar of German, which appeared as early as 1963. While Bierwisch concentrated on descriptive details of his *Permutation Rule*, Ross's interest was entirely theory-internal: If indeed it is the case that *Scrambling* is bound to a particular domain, "free-word-order" languages provide us with a strong empirical test for justifying higher constituents in terms of domains for rule applications. On the other hand, they also justify — and this was one of the major topics of Ross's dissertation — (universal) rules that could *remove* these constituents in case the domain of *Scrambling* is larger than otherwise well-motivated principles of (Deep-Structure) syntax would predict.

Theory-internal arguments of this sort and the interaction of *Scrambling* with other rules of grammar became particularly relevant in the syntax of German: As will be exemplified further below, *Scrambling* turned out to be one of the major constituent tests in deciding whether or not infinitives in German are "*satzwertig*" (or "incoherent," to use another traditional term for the same phenomenon). Ross himself was, at the time, engaged in finding arguments for the rule of *Tree Pruning* (cf. also Ross 1969), trying to establish that the derivation of prenominal adjectives from a clausal source involves a rule which deletes S-nodes that do not branch.

Concerning the formal status of the rule of *Scrambling*, Ross remarked that "it seems to be wrong to use normal rules of derived constituent structure to assign trees to the output of this rule, for the number of trees that will be assigned to any sentence will be very large" (1967: 52). Since the rule could be re-applied to its own output, every sentence could have an infinite number of derivations. This formal peculiarity led Ross to conclude that rules like *Scrambling* "should be placed in the stylistic component, because they are formally so unlike other transformational rules" (ibid.).

Since then the question of where *Scrambling* applies has been answered in different ways. Following Ross, Williams (1984) and others have suggested that within the so-called T-model of grammar *Scrambling* applies between S-Structure and Phonological Form. Arguing against this assumption, Webelhuth (1984/85), among others, has pointed out that *Scrambling* is related to a certain weak (anti-)cross-over effect, cf. e.g.:

(1) a. **weil   seine$_i$ Lehrer   jeden$_i$ fürchten*
         because his$_i$ teachers   everyone$_i$ fear
     b. *weil   jeden$_i$ seine$_i$ Lehrer   fürchten*
         because everyone$_i$ his$_i$ teachers fear

Furthermore, *Scrambling* can be shown to have particular effects on the grammaticality of focussed NPs and of *wh*-phrases *in situ*, in that scrambling of such phrases will lead to ungrammatical results, cf.

(2) a. *weil   der Professor dem   Studenten DAS BUCH*
         because the professor to-the student   the   book
         ausgeliehen hat
         lent   has

     b. **weil   dem   Studenten DAS BUCH der Professor*
         because to-the student   the   book   the professor
         ausgeliehen hat
         lent   has

     c. *weil   dem   Studenten das Buch DER PROFESSOR*
         because to-the student   the book the   professor
         ausgeliehen hat
         lent   has

(3) a. *Was hat wer dem   Studenten ausgeliehen?*
         what has who to-the student   lent
     b. *Was hat der Professor wem   ausgeliehen?*
         what has the professor to whom lent
     c. *Wem   hat der Professor was ausgeliehen?*
         to whom has the professor what lent
     d. ??*Was hat wem   der Professor ausgeliehen?*
         what has to whom the professor lent

e. ?? *Wem   hat   was   der Professor ausgeliehen?*
to whom has what the professor lent

Given that *Scrambling* is adjunction to IP, these observations could be explained in terms of Chomsky's (1986) principle of adjunction which blocks adjunction of *wh*-elements to IP. However this may work out in detail, it should be clear that, within the T-model of grammar, *Scrambling* cannot take place in PF if it is related to restrictions which take effect at the level of LF. So, if it is correct that *Scrambling* has to be analyzed in terms of movement, then this movement rule should apply between D-Structure and S-Structure.

But even if that much is agreed, opinions diverge as to the question of what kind of movement is involved. If *Scrambling* is a case of *NP-movement*, as suggested by Fanselow (in this volume), we would expect the following characteristics of NP-movement to hold: (a) The landing site of *Scrambling* is a non-theta position which is assigned Case; (b) *Scrambling* originates from a theta position to which no Case is assigned; (c) *Scrambling* starts from an A-position and ends up in an A-position; (d) the empty element left behind by *Scrambling* is subject to principle (A) of the binding theory.

If *Scrambling* is analyzed as *wh*-movement, as suggested by Webelhuth (in this volume), we would expect it to be a kind of movement that originates from a Case position, that ends up in a A'-position, that is constrained by the subjacency condition, that licenses parasitic gaps, and that leaves behind a variable subject to the universal restrictions governing the distribution of this kind of empty category.

But as *Scrambling* does not fit completely in either of these well-known schemes, the question whether *Scrambling* is the result of movement at all, i.e. the question of *what form a general rule of Scrambling should take*, is far from being subject to general consensus. Another tradition within generative grammar, represented most prominently by the work of H. Haider, rejects the view that free constituent order is the result of a movement rule. According to this tradition, free word order is a base-structure phenomenon: the D-Structure base already provides us with all the various options of word order that show up at S-Structure.

As is obvious, the two accounts of free word order make different predictions with respect to the question of what kind of restrictions these phenomena are subject to. The movement hypothesis predicts that *Scrambling* will be constrained by those principles of Universal Grammar that restrict movement processes in general; in other words, this approach predicts that certain applications of *Scrambling* must be ruled out by exactly these principles. The base structure approach predicts either that there are no general restrictions on *Scrambling* that would not already follow from restrictions on D-Structure, or that additional restrictions will take a form quite different from restrictions on movement.

Let us schematically illustrate the different *Scrambling* theories we have mentioned so far:

(4) *Scrambling* theories

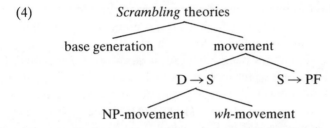

The most recent generative literature on *Scrambling* shows a strong preference for the view that *Scrambling* is very much like other transformational rules, in fact most authors seem to believe that *Scrambling* is an instance of move-α; see for instance Thiersch (1982), Koster (1987), Grewendorf (1988), Grewendorf (1989) or the contributions of Fanselow and Sternefeld in this volume.

Although it is agreed by now that the entire transformational framework of the "Constraints on Variables" period was mistaken in a number of fundamental respects, it is hardly surprising that many of Ross's problems are still relevant for any of the movement analyses of today: while trace theory and the principles of structure preservance have largely changed the form and style of syntactic representations, the programme of finding constraints for movement rules is still with us and has not yet been fully carried out with respect to the analysis of *Scrambling*; even the generative semanticist's analysis of prenominal adjectives as constituents having a full-fledged clausal source has not entirely been put in limbo (cf. Fanselow 1986). Very much in the spirit of Ross, there is also an enduring debate concerning a modern analogue of tree pruning: does the analysis of "verb-raising" structures (or so-called "coherent" infinitives) involve a rule of reanalysis which removes a clausal node, or should we directly generate these "coherent" infinitives as mono-clausal structures without involving a kind of S-bar deletion rule? See for instance Evers (1975), Rizzi (1982),

Riemsdijk (1985), Haegeman & Riemsdijk (1986), Grewendorf (1987), Fanselow (1987), Koster (1987) as some contributions to this lively debate. And should these rules apply on the road to PF or somewhere on the road from S-structure to LF (see v.stechow/Sternefeld (1988) for some discussion)? Or could we even do without mono-clausal structures and without S-bar deletion (cf. Baker (1988) and Sternefeld, this volume)?

As some of our remarks might already have suggested, there are different things that have been subsumed under the label of "scrambled structures." In addition to phenomena which have been considered characteristic of so-called "free word order" languages, a number of particular reordering processes that are not only found in typical free word order languages have also sometimes been analyzed in terms of "*Scrambling.*" For instance, many languages which cannot simply be labelled "free word order languages" allow for subjects to be postpositioned in the presence of so-called "ergative verbs" (see e.g. Burzio (1986)). The same kind of "subject inversion" has been observed with so-called "psych-verbs" (see e.g. den Besten (1982) for German and Dutch, and Belletti/Rizzi (1986) for Italian). Furthermore, as has already pointed out above, verb raising structures and the related problem of the sentential nature of a certain class of infinitives have also been analyzed in terms of a theory of *Scrambling* of verbs and verb projections.

The present volume unites a series of articles that deal with various phenomena which the notion of *Scrambling* was supposed to cover. Before we give a short summary of these contributions, pointing out how they can be grouped together with respect to the main problems and aspects of a "theory of *Scrambling*," we would like to present briefly a number of *descriptive generalizations* about *Scrambling* phenomena which, in the best of all possible worlds, should fall out as theorems of an explanatorily adequate theory of universal grammar. The purpose of this introductory section is to make the reader more familiar with an unwonted phenomenon which can hardly be found in the grammar of English. But we do not intend to develop a coherent theory of *Scrambling*: first steps towards an explanatorily satisfying treatment should be sought in the contributions themselves.

The following descriptive statements are largely drawn from v.Stechow/Sternefeld (1988), which in turn refers to still unpublished work by Webelhuth and to Fanselow's article in this volume. As has already been pointed out above, the first generalization about *Scrambling* is due to Haj Ross:

1ˢᵗ Generalization:
   Scrambling is clause-bound.

A clear illustrative example from German is the following:

(5)   a.   *daß den Max jeder* ——— *kennt.*
            that ART Max everyone   knows
      b.   **weil   den Max ich glaube [daß jeder* ——— *kennt].*
            because ART Max I   believe that everyone   knows

In (a) *Scrambling* has permuted the subject and the object of a single verb, in (b) *Scrambling* has moved the object into a higher clause. In case (b) the clausal character of the embedded complement is unproblematic. To illustrate the claim that *Scrambling* has become a valuable test for clause-mateness in the analysis of infinitival construction in German, we are to consider contrasts that arise from embeddings of "coherent" and "incoherent" infinitives:

(6)   a.   *weil   den Max jeder*$_{nom}$ *zu kennen glaubt*
            because ART Max everyone   to know   believes
      b.   **weil   den Max jeder*$_{nom}$ *zu kennen bedauert*
            because ART Max everyone   to know   regrets

(7)   a.   *weil   Max niemanden zu kennen glaubt*
            because Max no one   to know   believes
      b.   *weil   Max niemanden zu kennen bedauert*
            because Max no one   to know   regrets

The observed contrast in (6) can be readily explained by the hypothesis that the two verbs (and consequently their respective arguments) are clause mates in (6-a) but not in (6-b). According to the terminology introduced by Bech (1955) the first construction is "coherent," and can be analysed as (8-a), whereas the second construction is "incoherent," and is represented as (8-b):

(8)   a.   *weil* [$_{IP}$ *den Max*$_i$ [$_{IP}$ *jeder* [$_{VP}$ t$_i$ [$_V$ *zu kennen glaubt*]]]]
      b.   **weil* [$_{IP}$ *den Max*$_i$ [$_{IP}$ *jeder* [$_{CP}$ PRO [$_{VP}$ t$_i$ *zu kennen*]
            bedauert]]]]

Returning to the examples in (7), a clear contrast can be observed with repect to the scope of the negation contained in "no one." Whereas (7-a) can be paraphrased as "Max doesn't believe himself to know anyone," an analogous paraphrase with wide scope negation is impossible in (7-b); the

only available reading is synonymous with Max's regretting that he doesn't
know anyone (cf. also Lerner/Sternefeld 1984).

These examples illustrate that coherence is triggered by a lexical property of the matrix verb involved, a fact that seems to have gone unnoticed
in G. Bech's classical description of coherence in German (see v.Stechow
(1984), Grewendorf (1987)). Furthermore, the analysis of (7) presupposes
that *Scrambling* can be described as an adjunction to IP. Analyses of
"coherence" along these lines will be justified or disputed in most papers of
the present volume (cf. den Besten, Evers, Fanselow, v.Stechow, Sternefeld, and Webelhuth).

The following data may motivate the view that other categories than IP
are available as target positions for *Scrambling*:

(9)   a.   *weil*   *Max* [$_{VP}$ [$_{VP}$ *da$_i$*   [$_{VP}$ *nichts*   [$_{PP}$ t$_i$ *mit*]
           because Max   there/it   nothing   with
           anfangen]] *konnte*]
           do   could

      b.   [$_{NP}$ *der* [$_{AP}$ *seiner Studien$_i$* [$_{AP}$ [$_{NP}$ *im höchsten Maße*]
           the   of-his studies   in highest degree
           [$_{A'}$ t$_i$ *überdrüssige*]]] *Student*]
           tired   student

In (9-a) the demonstrative pronominal-like element *da* has been scrambled
away from its postposition, in (9-b) the object of an adjective has been
scrambled in front of the specifier of AP. These observations are expressed
in the

2nd Generalization:
Scrambling is adjunction to IP, VP, or AP.

The second generalization excludes adjunctions to NP, PP, and CP, which
are highly ungrammatical, as attested in (10):

(10) a.   **weil* *er* [$_{PP}$ *Maria* [$_{PP}$ *mit* t]] *gesprochen hat*
           bec. he   Mary   with   talked   has
      b.   *[$_{NP}$ *meines Vaters* [$_{NP}$ *das Auto* t]]
           my   father's   the car
      c.   *[$_{CP}$ *meinem Vater* [$_{CP}$ *ich verdanke viel* t]].
           to-my   father   I   owe   much

d.*(%)[$_{CP}$ *meinem* <u>*Vater*</u> [$_{CP}$ *daß ich viel* t *verdanke*]] *weiß ich.*
to-my   father   that I   much owe   know I

Perhaps some comments are in order. In (a) and (b) we have adjoined scrambled phrases to the maximal projections immediately dominating them. Therefore, movement could not have been "too far away"; rather *Scrambling* seems to have chosen the wrong landing site. Similarly in (c) and (d): as has been pointed out in Chomsky (1986) and argued for in terms of theta theory, adjunction is possible only to a maximal projection that is a non-argument (hence, not to NP or CP). Note that this restriction provides us with the correct result with respect to adjunction to IP and VP. Adjunction to AP, however, is not without problems given the hypothesis that APs can, at least in principle, function as arguments. The surface string (d) is grammatical in some southern dialects of German (which is indicated by %). In these cases, however, the fronted NP arguably moved into the specifier position of CP and the sentence would not have the "*Scrambling* structure" depicted in (d). This is confirmed by the fact that the kind of extraction illustrated in (d) is possible in southern variants of German only if the *that*-clause itself occupies the specifier position of CP, cf.

(10)   e. **weil*   *ich* [*meinem Vater daß ich viel   verdanke*] *weiß*
            because I   to-my   father that I   much owe   know

        f. **weil*   *ich weiß* [*meinem Vater daß ich viel   verdanke*]
            because I   know to-my   father that I   much owe

It can be shown (see Grewendorf (1988)) that the relevant restriction concerns the occupation of the CP-Spec position by a lexical element rather than adjunction to CP.

Even if it were correct that *Scrambling* can be reduced to adjunction only to IP, as will be demonstrated by Fanselow in this volume, restrictions on landing sites still leave us with a mass of ungrammatical applications of *Scrambling*. As Webelhuth (1987) has pointed out, a number of these cases could be treated by analogy with *wh*-movement: by and large it seems that all conditions that restrict *wh*-movement also restrict *Scrambling*. Observe in particular that (11-a), a variant of (9-a), is as ungrammatical as the corresponding *wh*-extractions in (11-b) and (11-c):

(11)   a. **weil*   *Max* <u>*dieser*</u> <u>*Frage*</u>   *nichts*   [*mit* t] *anfangen*
            because Max this   question nothing   with   do
            konnte
            could

b. *Welcher Frage   konnte Max nichts   mit anfangen?
    which   question could Max nothing with do

c. *die Frau,   deren Frage   Max nichts   mit anfangen
    the woman whose question Max nothing with do
    konnte
    could

The difference between (11), (10-a) and (10-b) on the one side, and (9-a)
on the other may be attributed to a directionality constraint formulated in
Koster (1987) (see also Grewendorf (1988)); note that the only (and, as surface strings, grammatical) underlying sources of (9-a) and (11-a) are the following:

(12) a. *weil Max nichts [damit] anfangen konnte*
      b. *weil Max nichts [mit dieser Frage] anfangen konnte*

The scrambled element is "canonically governed" in (12-a) but not in (12-
b), where canonical government is defined as a subcase of government that
holds if the direction of government is the same as with the verb, i.e., to the
right in SVO languages and to the left in SOV languages. Since German is
SOV (underlyingly), (11) can be ruled out by Kosters condition of "global
harmony." As another application of Koster's theory *vide* Bayer (this volume) who is *inter alia* concerned with the interaction of *Scrambling* with the
relative scope of quantified NPs and quantifying particles.

Having turned from the target position of *Scrambling* to its source, it is
natural to ask for the categorial status of the scrambled elements.
Webelhuth (1987) assumes that *Scrambling* of VP, AP and Adv is ungrammatical in most cases:

(13) a. *weil* [$_{PP}$ *ohne   Liebe*] *niemand* t *glücklich wird*
          bec.   without love no one happy   gets

      b. *weil* [$_{VP}$ *die Suppe essen*] *Kasper nicht* t *wollte*
          bec.   the soup eat   Kasper not   wanted

      c. *weil* [$_{AP}$ *krank*] *Hans* t *ist*
          bec.   sick   John is

      d. *weil* [$_{Adv}$ *gut*] *Hans* t *tanzt*
          bec.   good John dances

In a discussion of his theory, v.Stechow/Sternefeld (1988) have, however,
observed that it is very well possible — presupposing an appropriate intonation — that *Scrambling* involves adverbials and APs:

(14) a. weil *freiwillig*$_{Adv}$ *das* [$_{IP}$ *niemand tun würde*]
         bec. willingly   this   no one do would

     b. weil *das freiwillig*$_{Adv}$ [$_{IP}$ *niemand tun würde*]
         bec. this willingly   no one do would

     c. weil [*betrunken*]$_{AP}$ [$_{IP}$ *niemand hineinkommt*]
         bec. drunk   no one gets-in

On the other hand, it seems beyond doubt that VPs and IPs resist *Scrambling* in German. Compare, for instance, the following cases of pied piping in German which, according to the analyses of Grewendorf (1986) and Haider (1986), involve *Scrambling* of VP in (15-a) and of CP in (15-b):

(15) a. * *die Ratten* [$_{CP}$ *welche*$_i$ [$_{IP}$ [$_{VP}$ t$_i$ *fangen*] [$_{IP}$ *Hubert* t *wollte*]]
         the rats   which   catch   Hubert wanted

     b.   *die Ratten* [$_{CP}$ *welche*$_i$ [$_{IP}$ [$_{CP}$ PRO t$_i$ *zu fangen*]
         the rats   which   to catch
         [$_{IP}$ *Hubert* t *versuchte*]]
         Hubert tried

The contrast between (a) and (b) might readily be explained by the third generalization and a condition concerning the difference between coherent and incoherent constructions:

3rd Generalization:
   All maximal projections can be scrambled, except IP and VP.

(16) a. All control verbs that select an infinitive with *zu* can be constructed "incoherently."
     b. All control verbs that select an infinitive without *zu* must be constructed "coherently."

Condition (16) is a descriptive generalization which should fall out as a theorem of a theory of coherence, cf. Part III of this volume. Let us explicitly assume that this difference between coherence and incoherence is formally captured by the existence of a CP in incoherent constructions whereas, on the relevant level of syntactic representation, no such CP can be found in incoherent constructions:

(17)   A verb is the matrix verb of an "incoherent" construction if and only if it embeds a CP.

Given the third generalization about *Scrambling* and the two assumptions (16) and (17) concerning the coherence/incoherence distinction, the contrast observed in (15) can now be derived as follows: In (15-a) the matrix verb is a control verb that embeds an infinite without *zu*, hence it must be an element of a coherent construction. As a consequence of (17), this verb cannot embed a CP; the only choice is between IP and VP. But by the third generalization neither of these can be scrambled, hence the ungrammaticality of (15-a). In contrast, the infinitive in (15-b) can be construed as incoherent, i.e., as a CP, which has been scrambled in accordance with the third generalization.

Let us briefly mention some further generalizations about *Scrambling*.

4ᵗʰ Generalization:
Scrambling cannot apply to *wh*-phrases.

This generalization has already been illustrated by multiple questions like the following:

(18) a. *Wem   hat der Student welche Frage   beantwortet?*
          who(m) has the student which question answered
      b. *? *Wem   hat welche Frage   der Student beantwortet?*
          who(m) has which question the student answered

(19) a. *Warum hat jeder   welches Buch gekauft?*
          why   has everyone which book bought
      b. *? *Warum hat welches Buch jeder   gekauft?*
          why   has which book everyone bought

It should be noticed that examples like

(20)   *Warum ist welchen Studenten ein Fehler   unterlaufen?*
          why   is which   students a   mistake happened

do not provide evidence against the fourth generalization, provided that the ergative hypothesis proves to be correct with respect to German (see den Besten (1982) and Grewendorf (1989)).

But given Chomsky's assumption that adjunction to IP is not permitted, the fourth generalization could be advanced as an argument against an analysis of *Scrambling* as *wh*-movement. Appealing to Chomsky's analysis of focus (see chapter 4 in Chomsky 1977), a similar point could be made by pointing out that focussed phrases cannot be scrambled either, as has already been illustrated in (2) above.

5th *Generalization*:
  Scrambling cannot apply to focussed phrases.

Examples like the following

(21) a. *daß die *Bücher* er der *Studentin* gegeben *hat*
             that the books he the student given has
      b. *daß ihr *er* die *Bücher* gegeben *hat*
             that her he the books given has

suggest a further generalization according to which *Scrambling* is not allowed to cross a pronominal subject:

6th *Generalization*:
  Scrambling is not allowed to cross over a pronominal subject.

In this generalization, "crossing" is simply intended to mean "to be put in front of." As for the following generalization, however,

7th *Generalization*:
  Scrambling is not allowed to leave the domain of the subject.

a more technical account is required, as the grammaticality of examples like (5-a), repeated here for convenience, has shown:

(22)   *weil* den *Max jeder* —— *kennt*

We would like to assume that the scrambled object in (22) is within the domain of the subject because it is adjoined to the maximal projection that immediately dominates the subject. So we can make the seventh generalization more precise using the *Barriers* terminology:

7th *Generalization (revised)*:
  Scrambling is not allowed to leave the domain of the subject in the sense that the maximal projection immediately dominating the subject may not exclude the scrambled element.

This generalization can be illustrated by the following examples of ECM-constructions. Although it is possible to scramble an object clitic *es* within the infinitive, thereby adjoining it to IP, cf.

(23) a.   *weil der Lehrer den Schüler es machen läßt*
           bec. the teacher the pupil   it do   lets
      b.   *weil der Lehrer* [$_{IP}$ *es* [$_{IP}$ *den Schüler machen läßt*]]
           bec. the teacher   it   the pupil   do   lets

Scrambling this object clitic in front of the matrix subject leads in many cases to an ungrammatical result:

(24) a.   *weil   die Mutter den Vater es (das Baby) wickeln läßt*
           because the mother the father it (the baby) swaddle lets
      b.   **weil   es die Mutter den Vater wickeln läßt*
           because it the mother the father swaddle lets

The present volume unites a series of articles which focus on *Scrambling* and the various issues related to this topic. Part II is concerned with the controversy mentioned above between advocates of a movement approach and advocates of a base structure approach to *Scrambling*. The crucial topic in this controversy is the relationship between *Scrambling* and configurationality, since the justification of a VP-node is a prerequisite for a movement analysis of *Scrambling*. Part III contains articles which address the question of how the possibility of *Scrambling* correlates with a certain structure of infinitives. Discussing the issue of the "coherence" and "incoherence" of infinitives, these articles also refer to the traditional problem of "tree pruning." The contributions in Part IV deal with (ordering) properties of surface subjects which have also been analyzed in terms of *Scrambling*. In this volume, however, these properties are shown to result from the ergative nature of a certain class of verbs or adjectives respectively, i.e., they are accounted for in terms of Burzio's (1986) ergative hypothesis. Part V is concerned with the relevance of Chomsky's *Barriers* (1986) for an explanatory analysis of *Scrambling* phenomena; in more general terms, the articles in this part deal with the question of what constitutes a domain for *Scrambling* and other local processes.

Most of the contributions in this volume have been prepared for the section "Explanative Analysen in der Syntax des Deutschen" of the annual meeting of the *Deutsche Gesellschaft für Sprachwissenschaft* in Augsburg in 1987. Many of these articles present analyses that refer to the most recent developments in generative grammar, i.e., to the so-called *Barriers*-framework developed in Chomsky (1986).

Let us now briefly survey in more detail what these articles are about.

Part II, *Scrambling and Configurationality*, includes the contributions of Webelhuth, den Besten/Webelhuth, Haider, and Fanselow.

In his *Diagnostics for Structure*, **Webelhuth** lays down the foundations for a theory of *Scrambling*. He collects the most convincing evidence for both a VP-node and a *Scrambling* rule in German, evidence emerging from subject-object-asymmetries w.r.t. categorial selection, word-order, extractions from arguments and adjuncts, topicalization of argument-verb-complexes, the focus projection problem and many other domains.

Categorial selection (= strict subcategorization or c-selection) is a relation between a lexical head and an argument of a head. In German, this relation is *internal* with respect to the maximal projection of the head, this fact being a consequence of Webelhuth's *C-selection Universal*:

(25)   "For any nominative-accusative language the following holds: if the language has a VP, then the main verb does not impose c-selectional restrictions on its external argument."

The external argument of the VP (in the sense of Williams (1981)) is its subject, as shown in (26):

(26)

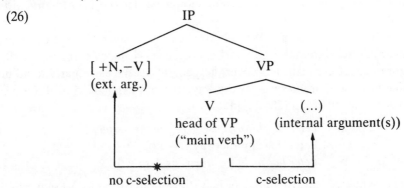

According to Webelhuth, the external position always has nominal features, usually it is an NP. Following Kayne, Holmberg, and others, he assumes that the head of CP (usually *daß* 'that') is also nominal; as a consequence, only CPs and NPs can appear in the subject position, the choice between these categories being a matter of semantic or so-called s-selection.

Assuming that German does in fact have a VP, (25) has a number of interesting consequences, the most remarkable being illustrated in the following pairs of active/passive sentences:

(27) a. *Daß Reagan wiedergewählt wurde, bekam eine große*
     that Reagan reelected   was, got   a   great
     Bedeutung zugemessen.
     significance attributed

   b. **Wir messen eine große Bedeutung zu, daß*
     we attribute a   great significance (part.), that
     Reagan wiedergewählt wurde.
     Reagan reelected   was

As a consequence of restrictions on categorial selection within VP, the indirect object of the verb *zumessen* 'attribute' must be a dative NP, it must not be a CP. Therefore (27-b) is ungrammatical. On the other hand, the corresponding passivized sentence (27-a) is claimed to be grammatical: the verb *bekommen* 'get' promotes the indirect object to a subject, therefore no categorial restriction can operate on the argument as a subject; since the s-selection of *zumessen* admits for a clausal argument, (27-a) is grammatical. The c-selection universal and the hypothesis that German has a VP provide for a natural explanation of these data, whereas it is not clear how the observed asymmetries in c-selection should be derived in a theory without VP.

In the same spirit, Webelhuth shows that some distinction between external and internal arguments is crucial in virtually every aspect of the grammar of German; moreover, he generalizes the asymmetry to adjuncts like *nicht* 'not' or *übrigens* 'by the way,' thereby explaining the difference in word order between (28-a) and (28-b):

(28) a. *Peter hat übrigens* [$_{VP}$ *nicht gespielt*].
     Peter has by-the-way   not   played

   b. **Peter hat nicht* [$_{VP}$ *übrigens gespielt*].

The sentence adverb *übrigens* is VP-external, whereas VP-adverbs like *nicht* or *sorgfältig* 'carefully' are VP-internal. Again, this difference is shown to have various consequences for the process of topicalization in German. Given that some such distinction between external vs. internal "Satzglieder" has to be recognized by any descriptively adequate theory, Webelhuth has collected significant evidence that the traditional theory, which captures the distinction by way of postulating a VP, is the most elegant and simple one that could be imagined.

The paper by **den Besten and Webelhuth** deals with a particular aspect of "remnant topicalization" that has been left unexplained in the author's

earlier article den Besten/Webelhuth (1987). The problem they try to solve
is the following. In the earlier paper they assumed, following Chomsky
(1986), that only maximal projections can be topicalized, and that apparent
counterexamples like

(29)   *Gelesen hat Hans das Buch nicht.*
          read   has John the book not

can be accounted for by a movement theory of *Scrambling* according to
which a VP can be "emptied" (in the SOV-languages) by adjoining parts of
it to VP or IP. (29) is then analyzed as a topicalization of the resulting VP-
remnant, with the traces in the VP being bound by some reconstruction
device that was shown to be necessary on independent grounds.

A crucial problem for this account of VP-topicalization resulted from
the fact that a VP-remnant cannot contain a stranded preposition, even
though the proposed reconstruction mechanism should ensure proper binding of the preposition-governed trace in the topicalized VP. The grammatical *Scrambling* structure in (30-a) cannot be converted into a grammatical
topicalization structure, as (30-b) shows.

(30) a.   *weil   Hans da$_i$ nicht* [$_{VP}$ [t$_i$ *mit*] *gerechnet*] *hat*
           because John there not   with counted   has

      b.   *[$_{VPi}$ [t$_j$ *mit*] *gerechnet*]$_i$ *hat Hans da$_j$ nicht* t$_i$
           with counted   has John there not

In order to explain the ungrammaticality of (30-b), the authors assume that
R-pronouns in postpositional structures are base-generated after the preposition and then moved into the specifier position of the PP:

(31)   [$_{PP}$ [$_{AdvP}$ *da$_i$*] [$_{P'}$ [$_P$ *mit*] [$_{AdvP}$ t$_i$]]]

Consequently, in (30-b) the R-pronoun extracted from the PP before VP-
topicalization has left behind a trace in the specifier position of the PP.

Comparing the stranding case with cases of extraction out of DPs and
NPs for which likewise a trace in the respective specifier positions has to be
assumed, den Besten/Webelhuth arrive at the hypothesis that traces in
specifier position are not reconstructable. This hypothesis provides an
explanation for the ungrammaticality of (30-b) — as opposed to the grammaticality of (29) — in terms of the binding theory: an unbound trace is
present in the specifier position of the PP within the topicalized VP. To rule
out a derivation of (30-b) according to which the extraction of the R-pronoun has taken place through adjunction to VP, the authors modify their

hypothesis to the effect that only argument traces can be reconstructed.

Finally, the authors draw attention to an unsolved problem concerning the observation that even though *Scrambling* of a PP out of its D-Structure position seems to make this PP an island, cf.

(32)   *Da_j hatten wir   [t_j mit]$_i$ nicht t_i gerechnet.
         there$_j$ had   we   [t_j with]$_i$ not t_i counted

extraction from a scrambled PP is possible in conjunction with VP-remnant topicalization:

(33)   [$_{VP}$ t_k gerechnet] hatte Hans da$_i$ nicht [t_i mit]$_k$
         [$_{VP}$ t_k counted]   had   Hans there$_i$ not   [t_i with]$_k$
         'Peter had not expected that to happen'

An alternative to a *Scrambling* analysis of VP-topicalization is proposed by **Haider**. He presents arguments that are supposed to show that topicalized verbal projections are *base generated* in the Spec-C position. These arguments are based on the following consideration.

As has already been demonstrated in the last sections, there are topicalizations of V-projections that appear to be smaller than maximal projections. In order to maintain the idea that a VP has been topicalized in these cases, an analysis in terms of movement has to assume that the VP has been emptied before topicalization by means of *Scrambling*, i.e., adjunction to S or VP.

However, Haider points out that there are several constructions for which the topicalized V-projection displays properties that cannot be attributed to its putative source in the base position. He therefore criticizes an account of VP-topicalization in terms of *Scrambling* as too weak: there are topicalization structures that cannot be derived by means of *Scrambling* as movement.

Furthermore, he tries to show that *Scrambling*-by-adjunction is too strong a concept as well: it permits overgeneration in the sense that VP-topicalizations that can be shown to have a source derivable by *Scrambling* turn out to be ungrammatical.

Presenting evidence that there are base-generated V-projections in non-base positions, Haider proposes a representational account of topicalization according to which topicalized verbal projections are subject to the following two well-formedness conditions: they must be maximal projections, and they must provide a θ-role for the subject in the "middle field." He then tries to demonstrate that this account provides an adequate analysis for the data that have turned out to be problematic for the *Scrambling* approach.

Finally, Haider points out some consequences of a representational account with respect to Case- and θ-assignment. A particular consequence of this account is that German, as opposed to Dutch or English, has a V-projection containing the subject as well as its objects: in German there is no maximal V-projection intervening between subject and object.

Fanselow wants to demonstrate that free constituent order is the result of a rule of *Scrambling* which is an instance of the general scheme 'Move α' and whose behavior is completely predicted by the *Barriers*-theory. Being subject to the principles restricting movement processes in general, a rule of *Scrambling* is claimed to provide a better account of free-word-order phenomena than an analysis in terms of unordered base structures.

Fanselow distinguishes between three types of *Scrambling*, providing natural languages with different options of constituent order:

(34) a.   reordering by NP-movement as in German or Turkish.
      b.   reordering by *wh*-movement as in Hungarian, Japanese, or Makua.
      c.   "reordering" as binding of *pro* as in Warlpiri or German.

In German, *Scrambling* can be shown to adjoin objects and adverbials to IP. Since Chomsky (1986) has demonstrated that *wh*-phrases are not allowed to adjoin to IP, Fanselow's *Scrambling* approach predicts that *wh*-phrases *in situ* should not be able to undergo *Scrambling*, a prediction that is in fact borne out.

On the other hand, as shown by May (1985), quantified NPs can very well adjoin to IP (and VP). Based on Hornstein's (1984) and Aoun's (1985) analysis, according to which quantifier raising creates anaphoric traces, Fanselow assumes that *Scrambling* also leaves anaphoric gaps. This assumption gains support from the fact that scrambled structures do not license parasitic gaps, and that traces resulting from *Scrambling* are subject to principle (A) of the binding theory.

As *Scrambling* affects the grammaticality of *wh*-phrases *in situ*, Fanselow concludes that *Scrambling* applies between D-Structure and S-Structure rather than between S-Structure and PF, as assumed by Williams (1984).

If *Scrambling* is adjunction to IP with A-binding of the trace, we should expect the adjoined element to be able to move up in a cyclic manner, adjoining to VP and IP of the matrix clause. This, however, would lead to the undesirable prediction that *Scrambling* might indeed cross clausal boundaries in a general way. Fanselow solves this problem by taking adjunction to IP to be a "dead end street," stipulating that no category can be removed from the adjunction slot of IP. Given that *wh*-traces must be in the specifier position of CP at LF, this would account for Chomsky's (1986) restriction on *wh*-extraction, according to which *wh*-operators may not adjoin to IP in the course of cyclic extractions.

A crucial question concerns the difference between English and German with respect to *Scrambling*. Fanselow tries to demonstrate that reorderings in English create gaps which exhibit the behaviour of variables. Consequently, *Scrambling* in English is analyzed as *wh*-extraction (to a certain extent, it exhibits unbounded dependencies). In order to establish the hypothesis that *Scrambling* in English does not involve NP-movement, Fanselow relies on several crucial assumptions of the *Barriers*-theory and on differences between the Case marking systems of English and other languages.

Finally, Fanselow briefly discusses cases of NP-split, i.e., *Scrambling* of parts of NP. As a clue to an understanding of this phenomenon, he points out that it occurs only in languages that exhibit Case agreement within NP. Claiming that the abstract agreement features within NP permit the identification of an empty pronominal NP-head *pro*, he analyzes the split-NP construction in terms of A-bar-binding of *pro* by the lexical element split from the NP.

We then turn to Part III: *Scrambling and the Structure of Infinitives*.

In his study on coherent infinitives in German, **von Stechow** focusses on the role of so-called Status-government (which is Gunnar Bech's term for the government of "verbal Case") in the analysis of structures with infinitives and participles (the verbal Cases) in German. In twenty small sections he illuminates various problems of these non-finite constructions, including an analysis of all types of auxiliar constructions in German. In the course of his analysis he touches upon too many questions to be exhaustively discussed in this overview, amongst them and worth mentioning, the question, on which syntactic level this special relation of government is to be checked, the problem whether or not there are definiteness effects in German, the question of how "long-distance passives" might be made to fit into the framework of the Government and Binding Theory, how Burzio's Generalization can be accomodated to the existence of so-called "recipient passives" in German, the question whether Haider's (1984) theory of blocking and de-blocking of θ-roles by the auxiliaries *haben* 'have' and *sein* 'be' can be improved to be consistent with the facts, the question of how and why we have to distinguish between exactly five different empty elements in German, etc. etc.

To begin with the last topic mentioned, the number five is at odds with the usual classification of four empty elements (anaphor, variable, PRO and pro): A problem with this classification arises from the observation that it is inapt to capture another distinction needed on independent grounds: pro has to be a non-argument in German (as in impersonal passive constructions like (35-a)), whereas it must be allowed to be an argument in pro-drop languages like Italian, cf. (35-c).

(35) a. *daß* [pro] *gegessen wird*
    that   eaten   is
    "that there is eating"

  b. **daß* [pro] *ißt*
    that   eats

  c. [pro] *mangia*
        eats

This state of affairs is particularly unsatisfactory because the argument status of all other empty categories is assumed to be fixed: PROs and variables are arguments, but anaphors are not. Why don't we have non-argument PRO's and variables?

Given that we have to distinguish between five EC's, we face the problem of classifying an odd number, which is one too many to result from a classification using just two features ±α and ±β, and which is at the same time too small to be the result of a cross-classification that employs three independently given features. V.Stechow's solution is inspired by the idea that three features do constitute the intuitively correct number of items needed to make the appropriate distinctions, but that there might well be independent reasons why certain feature combinations do not exist. The details of this approach should be looked up in place; let us mention just one effect of the analysis: if we choose the correct features, the analysis gains support from the observation that some feature combinations could *in principle* arise in (ungrammatical) constructions like the following:

(36)   *Johann wünscht [$_{CP}$ [e] gelacht zu werden].
        John   wants   laughed to be
        "John wants there to be laughing"

It seems that the ungrammaticality of (36) (which involves a non-argument
PRO) is best explained by the assumption that certain combinations of features are ruled out by principles of UG. To assume the existence of such
elements as e in (36) above would be on a par with the hypothesis that variables are non-arguments, which also contradicts the UG-principles of GB.

Another important part of the analysis is v.stechow's GPSG-style use
of syntactic features for Case-, Status-, and θ-assignment. An interesting
novelty of his system is the introduction of "blocking features." Formally, a
blocking feature specifies (by notational convention) that it blocks the
assignment of another feature which is specified in the blocking feature
itself. Thus, the blocking feature * [α___] specifies, that the feature α cannot
be assigned, because the category which assigns the feature α to its left, and
therefore has the feature [α___], is neutralized with respect to its ability to
assign this feature, precisely because it has been assigned the blocking feature. For a concrete example, consider the lexical entry of the auxiliary werden, which serves as a passivizer in German and "absorbs" the ability to
assign accusative Case. This property of werden is expressed by the lexical
feature [*[accusative___]___], implying that the feature *[accusative___] will
be assigned (to a VP) to the left of werden. Feature percolation assures that
the blocking feature assigned to the VP ends up at the transitive verb,
which is the head of the embedded VP and which in itself bears the feature
[accusative___]. At this point, the following blocking convention applies:

(37)   If a category has both the feature [α___] and *[α___], it is
        neutralized with respect to α-government.

As a consequence of (37), the transitive verb is prevented from assigning
accusative Case to its direct object, but it may still assign dative or genitive
Case to indirect objects.

Having defined the formal apparatus of blocking, v.stechow carries
out the analysis of a number of different coherent constructions in terms of
blocking features and the blocking convention, discussing inter alia the middle construction, ergative constructions, and the distribution of auxiliaries,
showing that his analysis is superior to Haider's (1984) analysis in terms of
blocking and de-blocking.

Prinzhorn examines the infinitival complements of certain classes of

German verbs: (i) raising verbs like *scheinen* (*seem*), *drohen* (*threaten*); (ii) a special class of subject-control verbs ("restructuring verbs") like *versuchen* (*try*) (as opposed to *bedauern* (*regret*)); and (iii) ECM-verbs like the causative verb *lassen* (*let*) and some verbs of perception. He states the following generalizations about the sentential character of these complements and the formation of verb-complexes: verb-complex formation obligatorily takes place with raising verbs resulting in monosententiality; the second class of verbs has the option of forming a verb-complex showing monosentential word-order properties if this option is selected; the verbs of the third class take complements without the infinitival marker *zu* (*to*) and obligatorily form a verb-complex. However, they exhibit some opacity effects with respect to serialization. So it appears that verb-complex formation does not necessarily imply monosententiality.

Using Chomsky's theory of extended chains and Zubizarreta's notion of an adjunct theta role, Prinzhorn analyzes the respective relations between verb-complex formation, *Scrambling*, and monosententiality as a reflex of the formation of extended chains necessary for antecedent government. The formation of a verb-complex is thus not considered to take place in the lexicon but has to result from movement processes necessitated in the syntax.

Likewise, **Evers** assumes that all observable surface properties of infinitival constructions must be derivable from properties of universal grammar. In particular he subscribes to the stronger thesis that no reference should be made to those properties of categorial selection that are concerned with the choice of INFL- or COMP-elements. If no statements referring to verbal affixes and the like are allowed, the observed distribution of *to*-infinitives and "naked" infinitives must be explained (in part) on semantic grounds. Evers furthermore relies on the hypothesis — recently confirmed by Baker (1988) — that the INFL-element *to* can be theta-marked by the verb. He then goes on to discuss the theories of Baker, Haegeman and others, trying to establish that an analysis along the line of Evers (1975) could be defended against various theories of reanalysis, in that his theory provides for a better trigger for V-raising than a lexical ad-hoc feature like [+restructure].

One of the most elementary problems of *Scrambling* is addressed by **Sternefeld**, who tries to give an explanation of the data in (5) and (6) in terms of the theories developed by Chomsky (1986) and Baker (1988). Within the *Barriers* framework it is easy to derive the clause-boundedness of *Scrambling*, if it can be shown that CP is a minimality barrier in the sense of Baker. The main problem concerns the attempt to apply this movement rule successively, i.e., after *Scrambling* has first applied entirely within a CP but is then re-applied to get the scrambled element out of CP into the matrix clause. In order to show that CP is still a barrier for the second application of *Scrambling*, some refinements of Baker's theory are unavoidable: if we are allowed to adjoin to IP we have to make sure that this adjoined position cannot be used as an "escape hatch" to scramble out of CP to the matrix VP. Sternefeld shows how to modify Baker's theory in such a way that there is no difference as to being adjoined to a phrase or being included in a phrase. It can now be demonstrated that CP is a minimality barrier for scrambling "out of" IP.

Turning next to the analysis of coherent constructions, Sternefeld follows Baker in assuming that the "visible" part of the infinitive, namely the VP, is moved into the SpecC position of the infinitive. He finally demonstrates that this position behaves as an argument position of the matrix and that therefore scrambling out of a coherent infinitive is on a par with mono-clausal scrambling. This result shows that the analysis of coherence does not necessarily involve any of the deletion processes proposed earlier; from a wider perspective it seems to give support to a mono-representational theory of grammar (vide Sternefeld, in press).

Part IV deals with relations between *Scrambling and Ergativity*. It includes the papers by Cinque and Grewendorf.

Cinque argues that the ergative/unergative distinction motivated by Perlmutter (1978) and Burzio (1981, 1986) for intransitive verbs extends to adjectives as well. He claims that there is a certain class of adjectives whose S-Structural subject is a D-structural object. This claim contradicts both the conclusion drawn in Abraham (1983), Toman (1986) according to which adjectives are ergative in general, and that in Burzio (1986), Stowell (1987) according to which there are no ergative adjectives at all.

As a first theoretical consideration in support of his claim, Cinque points out that there are adjectives entering the same alternation that can be found with Burzio's (1981), (1986) transitive (AVB)/intransitive (BV) verb pairs, cf.

(38) a.   *Il   capitano   affondò   la   nave.*
            The   captain   sank   the   boat.

b.   *La   nave affondò.*
     The boat sank.

(39) a.   *Gianni è   certo/sicuro* [*che verró*].
           Gianni is certain/sure that I will come.
      b.   [*Che verró*]   *è   certo/sicuro.*
           That I will come is certain/sure.

The empirical evidence that Cinque adduces in support of his hypothesis is
exclusively taken from Italian. Using seven ergativity tests that include *ne*-
cliticization and *wh*-extraction from inverted subjects, anaphor binding into
the subject, long distance anaphor-binding by the subject, and complementizer selection, he demonstrates that properties typical of D-Structural
objects can, in a fairly coherent way, be found with S-Structural subjects of
adjectives like *noto* (well-known), *certo* (certain), *oscuro* (obscure), *chiaro*
(clear), *probabile* (likely). In his account of the subject/object asymmetries
relevant in this context, he relies on the Empty Category Principle (ECP) in
the *Barriers*-version of Chomsky (1986) and on a slightly modified version
of principle (A) of the binding theory, this modification being inspired by
Belletti/Rizzi's (1986) assumption that a sentence obeys this principle if it
satisfies it at some level of representation, either D- or S-Structure (or possibly LF).

Concluding that there exists a class of ergative adjectives in Italian,
Cinque notes, however, that, quite generally, these adjectives are not morphologically related to ergative verbs. Consequently, a problem arises for
the so-called "Lexicalist Hypothesis" according to which morphologically
related verbs, nouns, and adjectives are represented in the lexicon as
single, categorically unspecified entries with certain unique θ-marking and
selectional properties. This hypothesis thus gives rise to the expectation
that an adjective morphologically related to an ergative verb should, in
principle, exhibit the same θ-grid as the corresponding verb, i.e., should
have its subject generated in the internal object position.

Even though this expectation is not fulfilled, no problem for the
Lexicalist Hypothesis arises because, as Cinque shows, unlike the situation
with the noun/verb case, it has to be assumed for the verb/adjective case
that the adjectival form is derived from an already morphologically derived
verbal form rather than from an underived, category-neutral, stem. On the
assumption that a category-changing morphological derivation necessarily
affects the θ-grid of the input as well (see Levin/Rappaport (1986)), an

explanation that is in line with the Lexicalist Hypothesis can be given for the fact that nouns morphologically related to ergative verbs are also ergative while adjectives morphologically related to ergative verbs are not.

Grewendorf's paper deals with *Scrambling* phenomena which are related to ergative structures. Using tests like extraction from subject sentences and the combination of extraction and extraposition, Grewendorf shows that there exist ergative structures in German, and that the ergative hypothesis provides a prerequisite for explaining the possibility of postpositioning the subjects of a certain class of verbs in German. However, the fact that these subjects are base-generated in object position at D-Structure is not sufficient for explaining their particular behavior at S-Structure. Grewendorf therefore argues that there exists an empty expletive pronominal subject in German which can occupy the subject position at S-Structure if NP-movement does not take place. Furthermore, he demonstrates that the unmarked possibility of "postposing" the subject of verbs like *gefallen* (please), *helfen* (help), *schaden* (harm) cannot be analyzed in terms of the ergative hypothesis since, contrary to common assumptions, these verbs can be shown not to be ergative.

Part V, *Barriers and Domains*, includes the contributions of Staudacher, Bayer, and Toman.

Staudacher's article deals with the question of why long *wh*-extraction from embedded verb-second sentences is possible when the matrix sentence is a verb-second sentence but impossible when the matrix sentence is an embedded sentence with verb-final order, cf.

(40)   *Wen$_i$ behauptet Hans, t$_i$' habe   Maria t$_i$ getroffen?*
         Who claims   Hans,   had$_{Subj}$ Maria   met?

(41)   **Ich weiß nicht, wen$_i$ Hans behauptet, t$_i$' habe Maria t$_i$*
         I   know not   who Hans claims   had Maria
         getroffen?
         met

Staudacher tries to give an account of these facts within the *Barriers*-framework. Since the relation of the intermediate trace t$_i$' to the trace t$_i$ is the same in the two cases, the author assumes that the difference in grammaticality is due to the relation between the *wh*-phrase and the intermediate trace, this relation being possibly affected by the position of *behauptet*.

It appears that the strong deviance of (41) cannot be explained by the interrupting effect of a barrier between the intermediate trace and the *wh*-phrase, because the embedded verb-second sentence is L-marked by the matrix verb *behaupten*. Therefore, it must be a barrier by minimality that is responsible for the difference between (40) and (41). Assuming that there is no adjunction to VP available in the matrix sentence, Staudacher suggests that the ungrammaticality of (41) is due to a CP barrier created by the matrix verb *behaupten* as a minimality effect. The crucial question, then, is whether or not the verb-second movement in (40) can neutralize this effect. Staudacher gives a positive answer to this question and shows how verb-second creates an extended chain which results in antecedent government of the intermediate trace by the trace of the fronted verb.

Staudacher points out, however, that this analysis is not without problems because an ECP account of the ungrammaticality of (41) cannot be sustained for the following reason. According to Lasnik/Saito's approach, which has been fully integrated into the *Barriers*-theory, the intermediate trace does not have any LF function because the trace in the originating position is θ-governed. The intermediate trace can thus be deleted and so is no longer subject to the ECP.

In addition to the wrong prediction that (41) should be unexceptionable, the ECP-account makes a further prediction that does not accord with the facts: that there should be a sharp contrast between (41) and the adjunct extraction in (42):

(42)   *Ich weiß nicht, wie$_i$ er meint t$_i$' habe Maria t$_i$ das
        I   know not   how he thinks   had   Maria the
        Problem gelöst.
        problem solved

Staudacher discusses two alternative solutions of these problems which are suggested by the strong deviance of both sentences. The first one appeals to the view (see chapter (11.) of *Barriers*) that antecedent government is necessary for proper government even in those cases where θ-government is present. Provided again that adjunction to VP is not available in German (extractions out of VP being accounted for by a modified version of minimality), this solution amounts to stipulating that, due to a special property of the German "prefield," traces in CP-specifier position have to be treated on a par with traces in A-positions and are thus subject to the ECP already at S-Structure.

According to the second solution, the adjunct case (42) is still ruled out
as an ECP-violation whereas the deviance of the argument case (41) is
explained in terms of subjacency. In order for the latter account to work,
one has to make the following assumption. Since barriers by minimality are
not relevant to subjacency, the CP-barrier protecting the intermediate trace
in the verb-second complement of (41) has to be created by a blocking category or by inheritance. Assuming that L-marking is not sufficient for ruling out a blocking category, Staudacher defines the concept of *head-marking*, according to which a maximal projection fails to be a blocking category
if(f) its head is selected by or coindexed with a non-empty zero-level sister
of this maximal projection. Assuming that it is a marked property of verbs
licensing verb-second complements that they do not select the heads of
their complements (otherwise verb-second would not be possible),
Staudacher concludes that these complements are barriers qua blocking
categories. This yields an explanation for the ungrammaticality of (41) in
terms of subjacency. In order to explain the grammaticality of (40),
Staudacher assumes that verb-second in the matrix sentence leads to coindexing of *behauptet* with *wen* because of specifier-head agreement. The
resulting index-unification creates an extended chain which ensures antecedent government of the offending trace t_i'.

In his work on "Interpretative Islands," **Bayer** is concerned with the
syntax of scope-bearing particles like *nur* 'only' or *sogar* 'even.' The scopal
relations are shown to be constrained by largely the same principles that
also constrain overt syntactic movement. One of the highlights of this article is Bayer's explanation of the grammaticality contrast in (43):

(43) a. *weil   das ein Normalbegabter   mit   nur*
         because this a   normally-gifted-person with only
         Studieren nie   schafft
         studying   never achieves
      b. * *weil das ein Normalbegabter nie mit nur Studieren schafft*

Assuming that both *nie* and *nur Studieren* have to gain clausal scope in LF,
Bayer shows that the paths created by movement are connected in (43-a),
but disconnected in (43-b). To see how his explanation works, let us take a
look at the structure of (43-b), depicted in (44), irrelevant details being
omitted:

(44)

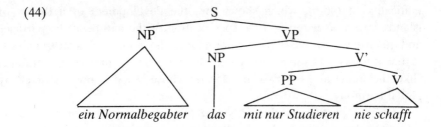

According to Kayne's theory of g-projections, it is clear that the path of *nie* can be projected along the V-projection up to the clause S. Turning next to *nur Studieren*, Bayer assumes that the path of this quantified NP goes up from the NP-node to the PP, but any further percolation is blocked because the head of P, which is the governor of NP, does not govern in accord with Koster's condition of global harmony; i.e., it does not govern in the canonical direction, which is to the left of a head in German. In other words, if we reach a projection of a head that does not govern canonically, any path will stop at this point. Since PP is a node of the path of *nur Studieren*, and the projection of V that immediately dominates this PP is a node of the path of *nie*, the nodes of both paths form a subtree of (44), in accord with Kayne's connectedness condition. Therefore connectedness saves the construction (43-a).

As the reader may easily verify for himself, the above assumptions readily explain the deviance of (44-b): the PP cannot be connected with the path of *nie*, which does not constitute a path spanning the offending quantifier phrase.

The above reasoning comprises parts of the answer to a more general question: if it is assumed that particles can be adjoined to all maximal projections, how can we explain the restrictions that govern adjunctions like the following?

(45) a. *Er schafft es nur mit Studieren.*
      he achieves it only with studying

    b. **Er schafft es mit nur Studieren.*
      he achieves it with only studying

    c. *Er schafft es mit nur zwei Schlägen.*
      he achieves it with only two blows

We have alreday mentioned the explanation of (45-b), which was formulated in terms of global harmony. But now we have to account for the grammaticality of (45-c), which shows that the development of a theory of islands for scope requires some specification of the nature of the particles and quantifiers involved. We cannot go into the details of Bayer's analysis; suffice it to say that some particles can be parasitic on "primary quantifiers" (like the numeral *zwei* 'two' in (45-c)), whose scope is not restricted by global harmony.

Besides particles within PPs and NPs, Bayer investigates contrasts related to the syntax of APs like those in (46)

(46) a. *weil   er (nur) auf die Sportschau gespannt war*
         because he only for the sportsnews curious was
     b. *weil er gespannt (*nur) auf die Sportschau war* and in many

other types of construction, showing that they confirm his explanation in terms of global harmony and connectedness.

The preceding discussion relates to the immediate predecessors of the Barriers theory and can therefore serve as a testing-ground for the claim that this framework has completely incorporated earlier explanations of island phenomena in terms of conditions on extraction domains (*cf.* the work of Kayne, Pesetsky or Huang). The second half of his paper (beginning with section 3.5.2.) relates more closely to other topics of the present monograph.

In this part of his essay, Bayer is concerned with various problems of free word order. He sketches a base-generated, non-transformational theory of scrambled constituents, grounded on a theory of "fused categories," i.e., complex categories that are at the same time projections of different lexical heads, for instance of V^0 and $INFL^0$. The following structure exemplifies that a single node may represent more than one level of projection for each category present:

(47)

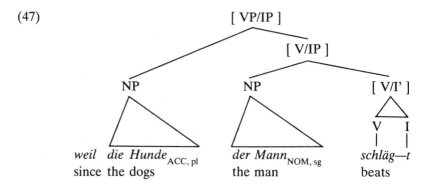

The theory of "double categorization" is not fully worked out in this paper, but it might turn out to provide an elegant way to both have the cake and eat it.

The theory of verb-projection raising (VPR) developed by Haegemann & Riemsdijk (1986) interacts with the scopal theory of particles in an interesting way, because VPR changes the direction of government and thereby changes the relevant configuration for the application of global harmony. Bayer concludes that these data provide additional evidence in favour of the global harmony hypothesis, although some interesting empirical problems remain.

Recent progress in morphological theory has led to the incorporation of syntactic principles into the grammar of word formation, among them the mechanisms of feature projection that had been developed in the context of X-bar-syntax. As a particular (re-)formulation of such a mechanism, consider the following conditions:

(48)   *Feature Inheritance*: a mother node receives/duplicates/has feature specifications of the daughter node.

(49)   *Head-Projection-Line Priority*: if more than one daughter is a candidate for (48), the one of the head-lines has priority.

Toman's paper on inheritance in word formation centers around the question of whether we really need the priority condition (49), which has been adopted by Selkirk, Lieber, Williams and others. He draws attention to the fact that reported cases of inheritance from non-heads are so rare that they might be neglected altogether. A relevant case in point are prefixes of V as in *be-schreiben* 'describe' which are sometimes analyzed as exceptions to the general rule that the head is on a right branch in German. The solution envisaged by Toman involves a distinction between "morphological" and "semantic" heads: as a causative prefix, *be-* is a head, which operates on the θ-structure of its argument, but as a syntactic component of the verb it is a non-head which gives way to the inheritance of morphological features (like strong inflection) of the head *schreiben*.

In his careful study, Toman compares morphological inheritance with similar problematic types of projections from non-heads like syntactic pied piping in [*How deep*] *is this well*, suggesting that the problematic "projection" of the *wh*-feature is best described in the grammar of scope rather than in the grammar of feature projection. Similarly the phenomenon of θ-inheritance from non-heads contradicts the generalization (50),

(50)   Only morphological features can be inherited.

and therefore should not fall into the domain of inheritance proper. Since θ-inheritance is functionally different from morphological inheritance in that it extends the *scope* of a θ-assigner, we may conclude that θ-inheritance is again subject to a theory of scope rather than to a theory of morphological inheritance.

The paper concludes with a discussion of inflection affixes, which constitute well-known candidates for heads that require the projection of all of the features of the non-head. A solution to this problem is sought in a treatment of inflectional suffixes as phrasal affixes,- an analysis first proposed for the [NP [INFL-VP]] analysis of the clause, then adopted and extended in Chomsky's *Barriers*. The INFL node is merged with a lexical head in phonology rather than in syntax, therefore inflectional affixes cannot cause problems in the syntax of words.

REFERENCES

Abraham, Werner (ed.). 1982. *Satzglieder im Deutschen. Vorschläge zur syntaktischen, semantischen und pragmatischen Fundierung*. Tübingen: Narr.
―――. 1983. "Adjektivrektion im Deutschen." Ms University of Groningen.
―――. (ed.). 1985. *Erklärende Syntax des Deutschen*. Tübingen: Narr.
―――. 1986. "Word Order in the Middle Field of the German Sentence." In: Abraham and De Meij (eds).
―――. and Sjaak de Meij (eds) 1986. *Topic, Focus, and Configurationality*. Amsterdam: Benjamins.
Aoun, Joseph. 1985. *A Grammar of Anaphora*. Cambridge, Mass.: MIT Press.
Asbach-Schnitker, Brigitte; & Johannes Roggenhofer (eds.). 1987. *Neuere Forschungen zur Wortbildung und Historiographie der Linguistik*. Tübingen: Narr.
Baker, Mark. 1988. *Incorporation. A Theory of Grammatical Function Changing*. Chicago: Chicago Univerity Press.
Bech, Gunnar. 1955. *Studien über das deutsche verbum infinitum, Band 1*, Kopenhagen. 2nd. ed. 1983. Tübingen: Niemeyer.

Belletti, Adriana; and Luigi Rizzi. 1986. "Psych-verbs and Th-Theory." *MIT Lexicon Project Working Paper, 13.*

den Besten, Hans. 1982. "Some Remarks on the Ergative Hypothesis." *Groninger Arbeiten zur germanistischen Linguistik 21*, 62-82; (also in Toman (ed), and in Abraham ed. (1985))

————. and Gert Webelhuth. 1987. "Remnant Topicalization and the Constituent Structure of VP in the Germanic SOV Languages." Paper presented at the GLOW-Colloquium, Venice, March 30-April 1, 1986.

Bierwisch, Manfred. 1963. *Grammatik des deutschen Verbs.* Berlin: Akademie Verlag.

Burzio, Luigi. 1981. "Intransitive Verbs and Italian Auxiliaries." Massachushetts Institute of Technology.

————. 1986. *Italian Syntax.* Dordrecht.

Chomsky, Noam. 1977. *Essays on Form and Interpretation.* Amsterdam: North-Holland.

————. 1986. *Barriers.* Cambridge, Mass.: MIT Press.

Engel, Ulrich. 1972. "Regeln zur 'Satzgliedfolge.' Zur Stellung der Elemente im einfachen Verbalsatz." *Linguistische Studien I (=Sprache der Gegenwart 19)*, 17-75.

Etzensberger, J. 1979. *Die Wortstellung der deutschen Gegenwartssprache als Forschungsobjekt.* Berlin/New York: De Gruyter.

Evers, Arnold. 1975. "The Transformational Cycle in Dutch and German." Diss., University of Utrecht.

Fanselow, Gisbert. 1986. "On the Sentential Nature of Prenominal Adjectives in German." *Folia Linguistica XX*, 341-38O.

————. 1987. *Konfigurationalität. Untersuchungen zur Universalgrammatik am Beispiel des Deutschen.* Tübingen: Narr.

Grewendorf, Günther. 1986. "Relativsätze im Deutschen: Die Rattenfänger-Konstruktion." *Linguistische Berichte 105.* 409-434.

————. 1987. "Kohärenz und Restrukturierung. Zu verbalen Komplexen im Deutschen." In: Asbach-Schnitker & Roggenhofer (eds).

————. 1988. *Aspekte der deutschen Syntax. Eine Rektions-Bindungs-Analyse.* Tübingen: Narr.

————. 1989. *Ergativity in German.* Dordrecht: Foris.

Haegeman, Liliane; and Henk van Riemsdijk. 1986. "Verb Projection Raising, Scope and the Typology of Rules Affecting Verbs." *Linguistic Inquiry 17*, 417-466.

Haider, Hubert. 1984. "Was zu haben ist und was zu sein hat." *Papiere zur Linguistik 30*, 23-36.

————. 1986. "Der Rattenfängerei muß ein Ende gemacht werden." Ms., University of Vienna.

Hoberg, Ursula. 1981. *Die Wortstellung in der geschriebenen deutschen Gegenwartssprache.* München: Hueber.

Höhle, Tilman N. 1982. "Explikation für 'normale Betonung' und 'normale Wortstellung'." In: Abraham ed., (1982).

Hornstein, Norbert. 1984. *Logic as Grammar.* Cambridge, Mass.: MIT Press.

Kayne, Richard. "Connectedness." *Linguistic Inquiry 14*, 223-249.

Koster, Jan. 1986. "The Relation between pro-drop, Scrambling, and Verb Movement." *Groningen Papers in Theoretical and Applied Linguistics, TTT Nr. 1*, University of Groningen.

————. 1987. *Domains and Dynasties: The Radical Autonomy of Syntax.* Dordrecht: Foris.

Lenerz, Jürgen. 1977. *Zur Abfolge nominaler Satzglieder im Deutschen.* Tübingen: Narr.

————. 1981. "Zum gegenwärtigen Stand der Wortstellungsforschung." *Beiträge zur Geschichte der Deutschen Sprache und Literatur 103*, 6-30.

Lerner, Jean-Yves; and Wolfgang Sternefeld. 1984. "Zum Skopus der Negation im komplexen Satz des Deutschen." *Zeitschrift für Sprachwissenschaft 3.*, 159-202.

Levin, B. and M. Rappaport. 1986. "The Formation of Adjectival Passives." *Linguistic Inquiry 17*, 623-661.

Lötscher, Andreas. 1981. "Abfolgergeln für Ergänzungen im Mittelfeld." *Deutsche Sprache 29.*, 44-60.

May, Robert. 1985. *Logical Form its Structure and Derivation.* Cambridge, Mass.: MIT Press.

Perlmutter, David. 1978. "Impersonal Passives and the Unaccusative Hypothesis." *Proceedings of the Annual Meeting of the Berkeley Linguistic Society 4*, 157-189.

Postal, Paul. 1971. *Cross-over Phenomena.* New York: Holt, Rinehart & Winston.

Reibel, D. A.; and Schane (eds.). 1969. *Modern Studies in English.* Englewood Cliffs, New Jersey: Prentice Hall.

Reis, Marga. 1986. "Die Stellung der Verbargumente im Deutschen. Stilübungen zum Grammatik-Pragmatik-Verhältnis." Paper presented at the 5th Lund Sumposium "Sprache und Pragmatik," May 12-16, 1986.

Riemsdijk, Henk van. 1985. "Against Adjunction to the Head." Ms. University of Tilburg.
Rizzi, Luigi. 1982. *Issues in Italian Syntax*. Dordrecht: Foris.
Ross, John Robert. 1967. "Constraints on Variables in Syntax." Diss., Massachusetts Institute of Technoloy. (Published as *Infinite Syntax!*, 1986 Norwood, New Jersey: Ablex).
———. 1969. "A Proposed Rule of Tree-Pruning." In Reibel and Schane (eds).
Stechow, Arnim von; and Wolfgang Sternefeld. 1988. *Bausteine syntaktischen Wissens*. Opladen: Westdeutscher Verlag.
———. 1984. "Gunnar Bech's Government and Binding Theory." *Linguistics 22*, 225-241.
Sternefeld, Wolfgang. (in press). "Derivation and Representation. A Theoretical Synopsis." In H. Haider & K. Netter (eds.). *Derivation and Representation*. Dordrecht: Foris
Stowell, Tim. 1987. "As *So*, Not So *As*." Ms., University of California Los Angeles.
Thiersch, Craig L. 1982. "A Note on 'Scrambling' and the Existence of VP." *Wiener Linguistische Gazette 27-28*, 83-95.
Toman, Jindrich. (ed.) 1985. *Studies on German Syntax*. Dordrecht.
———. 1986. "A (Word-)Syntax for Participles." *Linguistische Berichte 105*, 367-408.
Webelhuth, Gert. 1984/85. "German is Configurational." *The Linguistic Review 4*, 203-246.
———. 1987. "Eine universale Scrambling-Theorie." Paper presented at the annual meeting of the "Deutsche Gesellschaft für Sprachwissenschaft," Augsburg.
Williams, Edwin. 1981. "Argument Structure and Morphology." *The Linguistic Review 1.1*, 81-114.
———. 1984. "Grammatical Relations." *Linguistic Inquiry 15*, 639-673.

II. Scrambling and Configurationality

Diagnostics for Structure[1]

Gert Webelhuth
University of Massachusetts at Amherst

> *Especially the postulation of higher constituents needs special arguments. Linguistic expressions prima facie only have extension in one dimension, they are linear. The postulation of hierarchical organization, of a "hidden" extension in the second dimension is everything but immediately evident. Eisenberg (1985)*

0. Introduction

For several years a heated debate has been going on in the grammatical literature over the difference between configurational and nonconfigurational languages. Hale (1982), (1983), Jelinek (1984) and many other works have appeared on this subject. Saito and Hoji (1983) and Saito (1985) among others have discussed whether Japanese has a VP-node. Haider (1981, 1982, 1985), Tappe (1981, 1986), den Besten (1985), Thiersch (1982), Kratzer (1984), Webelhuth (1984/85), Scherpenisse (1985) and Fanselow (1987) discuss the same issue with respect to German. Until about two years ago the majority position probably was that "it is neither necessary nor advantageous to assume the existence of a VP-constituent" (Haider 1982). Webelhuth (1984/85) puts the arguments against a VP-constituent to the test and concludes that "the description of German in ... non-configurational terms is unmotivated." This position seems to be adopted almost universally now in the literature and no work has appeared in the meantime questioning this conclusion. Because the goal of the paper just mentioned was to show that the "configurational" theory was not really touched by the arguments given against it, it did not provide much positive evidence for a VP-constituent. The present paper is thus a sequel to Webelhuth (1984/85) in that it tries to collect the evidence for a VP-constituent and a scrambling rule which I find most convincing. It contains a number of original arguments, but that is not its main objective: rather, the paper is a summary of my own research and that of the by now lively community of formal linguists working on German. I consider it a worthy goal to sum up the results of the last two years of research, especially since the relevant arguments are scattered in a number of published and unpublished papers; it is not rare that scientific progress is not fully appreciated by a wider audience because the relevant evidence is never presented in its entirety. I will therefore draw freely from my works and those of colleagues to document the advance the field has made over the past years, so that the results about new areas of the syntax of German that are currently being achieved can be added to the firmly established fragmentary picture, thus enlarging this picture cumulatively.

I will begin with a terminological innovation which is supposed to avoid the notion "configurational" and its derivatives, because it is hard to tell at this time what an individual author means by these terms: I will refer to a theory which assumes a VP-node and hence a necessary structural subject-object asymmetry as an *asymmetric* theory, while I call all other theories *symmetric* theories.

The symmetric theories thus differ from the asymmetric theory in that they do not require that an external argument in the sense of Williams (1980, 1981) be outside the predicate formed by the main verb and the set of its internal arguments.[2]

## 1.	C-selection

### 1.1	*Categorial Realization of θ-roles*

The first argument I want to discuss presupposes the theory of syntactic selection of Grimshaw (1979). Grimshaw argues that semantic selection and syntactic selection are two independent phenomena, i.e., neither of them is recoverable from the other. In particular she argues that verbs can semantically select a propositional, interrogative or exclamatory complement. This complement will be realized either as a sentence or as a noun phrase, depending on the syntactic selection of the verb. The verb *wonder*, for example, which selects an interrogative complement, can only realize it as a sentence, since it is not subcategorized for an NP. The verb *ask* can realize a question both as a sentence and as an NP, since it is sub-categorized for both these categories. Note the following sentences:

(1)   John wondered [$_{CP}$ what time it was]
(2)   *John wondered [$_{NP}$ the time]
(3)   John asked [$_{CP}$ what time it was]
(4)   John asked [$_{NP}$ the time]

From (1)—(4) we can thus conclude that individual verbs can determine the syntactic category of their objects, i.e., they can c-select their complements.

This is of course also true for German verbs, i.e., there are verbs which c-select both an NP and a sentence and verbs which c-select only a sentence but not a noun phrase object:[3]

(5)   *Er bedauert* [$_{NP}$ *die Zerstörung der Stadt*]
        he regrets   the destruction the city
(6)   *Er bedauert* [$_{CP}$ *daß die Stadt zerstört wurde*]
        he regrets   that the city destroyed was
(7)   *Er drohte*   [$_{NP}$ *die Ermordung der Geisel*]
        he threatened   the murder   the hostage
(8)   *Er drohte*   [$_{CP}$ *die Geisel zu ermorden*]
        he threatened   the hostage to kill

As Grimshaw observed, there are no verbs in English that c-select a noun phrase object while disallowing a sentence.[4]

The same seems to be true for German, but there exists a much more interesting asymmetry between noun phrase selection and sentence selection, namely categorial selection of subjects. Classical generative grammar has assumed that verbs cannot c-select their subjects

> Verbs are not strictly subcategorized in terms of the types of Subject NP's ... (Chomsky 1965: 96)

since these elements are outside the strict subcategorization domain of the verb.

With Grimshaw's theory as a background we can formulate the following very interesting generalization of natural language:

The C-selection Universal
For any nominative-accusative language the following holds: if the language has a VP, then the main verb does not impose c-selectional restrictions on its external argument.

The generalization follows from the fact that the main verb does not govern its subject and will hence be unable to impose categorial restrictions on it. All the verb can do is assign a thematic role to the subject which presumably incorporates semantic selection in the sense of Grimshaw, but not c-selection.[5]

For a language with a VP Grimshaw's theory thus predicts the absence of a verb WONDER which is like *wonder* differing only in that it allows a sentence to realize its external argument while disallowing this realization by an NP. The reason for this is that the noun phrase outside the VP can get assigned the normal Case of subjects and will thus not violate the Case Filter of Chomsky (1981). But there is no other module in the grammar which can block the realization of the theta-role assigned under predication by a verb as an NP. The verb itself does not govern out of the VP and will also be unable to restrict the realization of the external θ-role.

English, a language with a VP, does in fact not have a verb like WONDER. We thus have a VP-test which in principle is applicable to any natural language, since it doesn't depend on word order or constituency tests: for German the test gives clear and convincing results: no verb taking an external argument exists which could be substituted for the blanks in the following sentences:[6]

(9)   *Daß Hans angekommen ist* [$_V$ _____]
         that Hans arrived   has

(10)   ** Hansens Ankunft* [$_V$ _____]
         Hans'   arrival

The absence of a verb like WONDER in German can only be explained on principled grounds by the asymmetric theory as defined above, because it derives the c-selection universal as a theorem which makes claims both about English and German.[7] The symmetric theories, however, which allow all verbs to govern their external as well as their internal arguments are unable to give a non-accidental account of this subject-object asymmetry of c-selection, because according to them the generalization noted is an accidental fact about all the lexical entries of verbs in German, whereas in English the same fact finds a structural explanation.

To conclude this section we look at one final paradigm. The paradigm includes verbs with indirect objects. As the contrast between the (a) and the (b)-sentences in (11) and (12) shows, neither of the verbs allows its indirect object to be realized by a sentence, only noun phrases are possible (as is generally the case with indirect objects):

(11) a. *Wir messen* [$_{NP}$ *der Wiederwahl Reagans*] *große*
we measure   the reelection   Reagan   great
Bedeutung bei
meaning   to
'We attribute great significance to Reagan's reelection'

(11) b. **Wir messen große Bedeutung bei* [$_{CP}$ *daß Reagan*
we   measure great   meaning   to   that Reagan
wiedergewählt wird]
reelected   is
'We attribute great significance to *(the fact) that Reagan is reelected'

(12) a. *Wir weisen* [$_{NP}$ *dem Zerfall des Protons*] *eine geringe*
we   attribute   the   decay   the   proton   a   small
Wahrscheinlichkeit zu
probability   to
'We attribute small probability to the decay of the proton'

(12) b. **Wir weisen   eine geringe Wahrscheinlichkeit zu*
we   attribute a   small   probability   to
[$_{CP}$ *daß das Proton zerfällt*]
that the   proton decays
'We attribute small probability to *(the fact) that the proton decays'

Note now that our asymmetric theory predicts that if there were a way for the verbs above to ungergo a lexical rule which externalizes the indirect object, then the ban against the realization of the formerly internal θ-role should be lifted, since the verb cannot categorially influence the external argument. German has a lexical passive which makes the indirect object of the base verb into the subject of the derived verb as can be shown with the two NP-examples analogous to (11a) and (12a):

(13)   [$_{NP}$ *Die Wiederwahl Reagans*] *bekam große Bedeutung*
the reelection   Reagan   got   great   significance
beigemessen
attributed
'Reagan's reelection got attributed a lot of significance'

(14)   [_NP *Der Zerfall des Protons*] *bekam eine geringe*
         the   decay   the proton   got   a   small
         Wahrscheinlichkeit zugewiesen
         probability   attributed
         'The decay of the proton got attributed a small probability'

And, most significantly, the externalized analogues of (11b) and (12b)
are grammatical as well, as predicted by the asymmetric hypothesis:

(15)   [_CP *Daß Reagan wiedergewählt wurde*] *bekam eine*
         that Reagan reelected   was   got   a
         große Bedeutung beigemessen
         great significance attributed
         'That Reagan got reelected got attributed great signifi-
         cance'

(16)   [_CP *Daß das Proton zerfällt*] *bekam eine geringe*
         that the proton decays   got   a   small
         Wahrscheinlichkeit zugewiesen
         probability   attributed
         'That the proton decays got attributed a small probability'

These selectional asymmetries due to the morphological operation of
externalization in the sense of Williams (1981) thus lend further strong support to the asymmetric hypothesis.[8]

1.2 Selection of Clause-Types

There are other interesting internal — external asymmetries with
respect to government by the verb. As is well-known (for example from den
Besten 1985), German subordinate clauses come in two types, where one
type is introduced by a lexical complementizer (or a WH-word) and the
verb remains in the sentence-final position (cf. (17)) and the other has main
clause order, i.e., there is no complementizer and the verb is in second
position (cf. (18)):

(17)   *Er sagte* [*daß er Hans kennt*]
         he said   that he Hans knows
(18)   *Er sagte* [*er kenne Hans*]
         he said   he know Hans

It is now interesting to note that not all verbs which are subcategorized for a complement clause allow both types of subordinate clauses: the main clause variant is much more restricted than the complementizer variant. Note, for example, the difference between *sagen* (to say) which allows both complement types and *beobachten* (to observe) which disallows the main clause type:

(19)   *Er sagte Hans werde verreisen*
         he said Hans would leave
(20)   *Er sagte daß Hans verreisen werde*
         he said that Hans leave   would
(21)   * *Er beobachtete Hans wolle   verreisen*
         he observed   Hans wanted leave
(22)   *Er beobachtete daß Hans verreisen wollte*
         he observed   that Hans leave   wanted

It is in fact unpredictable which verbs will allow the main clause types and which ones won't, and for many verbs native speakers disagree on whether the main clause type is allowed. Each individual verb will thus have to be subcategorized for some feature from which it will follow that only one clause type is allowed. A further generalization about the two clause types is that every verb which allows the verb-second subordinate clause also allows a complementizer-introduced clause but not vice versa. The analysis we give should express this fact.

The most striking difference between verb-second and complementizer-introduced subordinate clauses is that although both can be used as complements, only the latter can be the external argument of a head, as the following example sentences document:

(23)   *daß Hans verreisen wird stimmt   nicht*
         that Hans leave   will correct-is not
(24)   * *Hans werde verreisen stimmt   nicht*
         Hans would leave   correct-is not

A theory of German sentence structure should thus be able to account principally for the following generalizations:

(25)   −complement sentences can either be verb-second or complementizer-introduced
         −every head allowing a verb-second complement also allows a complementizer-introduced complement
         −external argument sentences can only be of the complementizer-introduced variety.

The asymmetric theory allows us to derive the preceding generalizations in a satisfactory manner, since it provides an inventory of grammatical relations which cuts argument clauses in just the right way between complements and external arguments, if we strengthen the theory slightly in the following way. In the following table I have juxtaposed those categories which can appear in subject position and those which can perform the complement function:

(26)

	Ext. Argument	Int. Argument
NP	+	+
PP	−	+
AP	−	+
VP	−	+
IP·	−	+
AdvP	−	+

Adjective phrases and verb phrases can be complements in Small Clause constructions (e.g. "I consider [John sick]" and "I saw [John leave]") and IP appears as the complement of raising and ECM-verbs. Adverbial phrases can also be heads of Small Clause complements (for example after *live* or *send*). But none of these categories can act as the external argument of a head and this is also true for prepositional phrases which can easily be internal arguments.

Since in the absence of cross-linguistic variation the facts in table (26) have to be captured in a principled manner, the following universal hypothesis is adequate:

(27)   External arguments are $[+N, -V]$

(27) will prevent individual verbs in individual grammars from c-selecting any non-nominal external arguments. This is then the second strong universal which the asymmetric theory allows us to formulate. This stands in stark contrast to the symmetric theories which have never led to any interesting cross-linguistic predictions, having solely survived on the descriptive failures of admittedly naive asymmetric proposals.

The law in (27) will restrict the category set of external arguments to {NP, CP} and only those CPs can function as external arguments which have a nominal head. This will automatically exclude the verb-second sentences from carrying the external argument role, since they have a verb in the head-position of CP with X'-theory making CP a non-nominal projection. Complementizer-introduced clauses can occur in external argument position, however, since we assume that the complementizer is a nominal category, at least in German where it is derived diachronically from a demonstrative pro*noun*.

The incorporation of (27) into Universal Grammar thus derives the third generalization in (25). The absence of a similar restriction on the complementation relation derives the first generalization, since then verbal CPs are not barred from the complement position of a head.

What remains to be derived, then, is the second generalization which expresses the fact that all heads allowing a verbal complement clause also allow a nominal one, but not vice versa. I do not want to pursue this question here, since it does not seem to be related to the VP-question. A universal default rule fixing the categorial representation of propositional arguments would allow us to make the correct prediction.

The asymmetric model thus captures the generalizations about argument subordinate clauses in German on a principled basis. None of the distributional and selectional properties of German have been attacked by the symmetric theories and this is certainly no accident, since these theories lack the crucial theoretical inventory which is indispensible for a solution to the problems: the difference between VP-external and VP-internal arguments of the verb.

1.3 *Selection of Tense*

Since the reader by now will be familiar with the structure of the first argument, let me just describe in a few words a third external — internal asymmetry with respect to selection. Verbs can impose finiteness restrictions on their argument subordinate clauses. *ankündigen* (to announce), for example, allows both non-finite and finite complement clauses, but *beobachten* (to observe) only allows finite clauses. The same is true for *herausfinden* (to find out). Our theory predicts that no such verb-particular selection should be possible for adjunct sentences and for subject sentences. This is in fact correct: although certain adjuncts can only be finite, others only non-finite, this is not verb-dependent, but rather depends on the conjunction introducing the adjunct. The same is true for subject sentences: if a certain subject sentence is restricted to tensed or non-tensed, then this is due to semantic factors (namely that tensed subject sentences denote propositions whereas non-tensed ones denote actions/states but not propositions; that is *To go to Paris is true* is akward, because propositions but not actions can be true etc.). The semantic facts do not explain the object sentence facts, though, since for example both *He observed that he was right* and **He observed to be right* are semantically plausible, since one can observe both facts and actions.[9]

We can now sum up the discussion of the different subsections of section 1: the following c-selectional subject-object asymmetries in German are easily taken to be consequences of the universally given distinction between verb phrase-external and verb phrase-internal arguments of the verb:

(28)   –propositional subjects can always be expressed by a noun phrase, while propositional objects sometimes can only be expressed by other categories
       –subjects have to be nominal, whereas objects can be non-nominal
       –heads cannot impose finiteness restrictions on their external arguments, but can impose them on their objects.

2.   External Topicalization

2.1   *External vs. Internal Arguments*

The second argument I want to discuss is the elaboration of an argument originally developed by Thiersch (1982). Thiersch noted an interesting subject — object asymmetry with respect to topicalization to the preverbal main clause topic position in German.

Note first the fact — often stressed by the adherents of the symmetric theory — that within German sentences the external argument and the internal arguments can appear in both linear orders:

(29)   *Gestern   hat niemand   [dem   Großvater   geholfen]*
        yesterday has nobody:NOM the:DAT grandfather helped
        'Yesterday nobody helped grandfather'

(30)   *Gestern   hat dem   Großvater   [niemand   geholfen]*
        yesterday has the:DAT grandfather nobody:NOM helped
        'Yesterday nobody helped grandfather'

One might therefore expect that the preverbal main clause topic position which hosts *gestern* in both (29) and (30) and which can host the bracketed expression in (29) consisting of the non-finite main verb and an internal argument can also host the bracketed expression in (30) consisting of the same main verb and its external argument. This expectation is not borne out, however, as the following sentences show:

(31) [dem Großvater   geholfen] hat gestern   niemand
       the   grandfather:DAT helped   has yesterday nobody:NOM

(32) *[niemand   geholfen] hat gestern   dem   Großvater
       nobody:NOM helped   has yesterday the:DAT grandfather

The fronting of the external argument together with its non-finite verb is ungrammatical if an internal argument is stranded in the sentence as in (32). This is unexpected in a theory which base-generates both (29) and (30) without a structural asymmetry between the external argument and the internal ones.

However, the solution to this problem in the configurational theory is also not obvious, since for example the theory of Webelhuth (1984/85) was refuted in Thiersch (1985) and later by research reported in Webelhuth/den Besten (1987). In my article I argued that the crucial difference between (31) and (32) is that in the first case the VP is topicalized, while in the second case it has to be IP, since the external argument moves along with the verb phrase. The verb phrase of the latter sentence would have to contain an unbound trace in indirect object position. The sentence with the unbound trace in topic-position could then be ruled out by the Binding Theory, requiring that every variable be bound, i.e., be coindexed with a c-commanding constituent.

While Craig Thiersch was the first one to notice that the difference between sentences like (31) and (32) might argue for a structural subject-object asymmetry, he also was the first one to notice that an explanation of the difference in terms of an unbound trace ruled out by the Binding Theory cannot be maintained. He noted that certain seemingly unbound traces in topic positions have to be tolerated by the Binding Theory, for otherwise English sentences like (33) should be ungrammatical:

(33) John was afraid that he might get killed and
       [$_{VP}$ killed t] he was vp

In this sentence a passive VP is topicalized which according to the analysis of passive in standard GB-theory has to contain a trace. Webelhuth/den Besten (1987) pursue Thiersch's observation and give a long list of arguments for such unbound traces in TOP. They end up claiming that an unbound trace in TOP should be treated like a bound trace by the binding theory if the trace was bound before topicalization.

With this result the earlier explanation that I gave of the difference between (31) and (32) within the asymmetric framework has to be given up.

We therefore have to reconsider these data. The approach that I will present here is proposed by Grewendorf (1989). Grewendorf's first important observation concerns a difference among the following sentence types:

(34)   *weil das Buch PETER gelesen hat*
        bec. the book Peter   read   has
(35)   *weil das Buch PETER gefallen hat*
        bec. the book Peter   pleased has
(36)   *weil dem Jungen eine GESCHICHTE eingefallen   ist*
        bec. the boy   a   story   occurred-to has

The first sentence contains a transitive verb with an agentive subject, the second one an external theme-subject and the third one contains an ergative verb with an internal theme/patient subject. In the first two sentences the focus on the subject is maximal, i.e., the subject cannot project its focus to the whole sentence. Consequently, this leads to a contrastive interpretation of the subject. In the sentence with the ergative subject, however, the whole sentence can be the focus, so that the sentence could be an answer to the question:

(37)   *Warum hat man den kleinen Hans nicht bestraft?*
        why   has one the small   Hans not   punished?
        'Why didn't they punish small Hans'

(34), however, could not be a felicitous answer to the following question:

(38)   *Warum liegt denn hier eine Bibel?*
        why   lies then here a   bible
        'Why is a bible lying here'

The same effect we find with an external theme:

(39)   *Warum habt ihr denn eine Bibel gekauft?*
        why   have you then a   bible bought
        'Why did you buy a bible'

(35) is not a good answer to this question.

Passive subjects behave like ergative subjects and direct objects with respect to their focus possibilities:

(40) *weil Hans ein AUTO gestohlen hat*
 bec. Hans a car stolen has
(41) *weil ein AUTO gestohlen wurde*
 bec. a car stolen was

Both of these sentences can be answers to the following question:

(42) *Warum werden die Meiers von der Polizei verhört?*
 why are the Meiers by the police questioned
 'Why are the Meiers questioned by police'

This shows that the constituent carrying the theme/patient role of *stehlen* can project its focus to the whole sentence no matter whether it is the direct object of the verb or the subject of its passive. In both cases *ein AUTO* behaves like an internal argument.

On the basis of these paradigms we can conclude with Grewendorf (who attributes the observation to others, cf. his work) that the generalizations can be captured with the following formulation: internal arguments can project their focus to constituents containing them; external arguments cannot do that.

With this we return to Thiersch's topicalization cases. We find that a verb can only take elements to the front which are capable of projecting a focus (cf. (34) and (40)):

(43) *[PETER gelesen] hat das Buch noch nie*
 Peter read has the book never
(44) *[ein AUTO gestohlen] hat Hans noch nie*
 a car stolen has Hans never

We can explain these facts if we assume that a topicalized constituent containing a verb has to be focussed. Why this should be the case is less clear, but the facts seem to call for this characterization. (43) would then be ungrammatical, since an external argument does not project a focus to the constituent containing it and the verb, since external arguments never project foci, as we saw. In the second sentence we have a normal VP topicalized which can inherit the focus feature from its direct object. That this is the correct solution is also suggested by the fact that (43) is at the extreme end of a grammaticality hierarchy. Thus, this sentence already becomes better, if the external argument is made heavy and indefinite:

(45) *[ein alter Mann gelesen] hätte das Buch niemals*
 an old man read had the book never

And, as I already noticed in Webelhuth (1984/85: sentence (122)), these topicalizations become more or less fully grammatical, if the external argument and an intransitive verb are fronted:

(46)   [*Leute getanzt*] *haben hier noch nie*
           people danced   have   here   never

In retrospect, this observation is interesting, because the external argument can also project its focus to the whole sentence when it is not topicalized:

(47)   *weil plötzlich Leute getanzt haben*
           bec. suddenly people danced have

(47) can answer the question:

(48)   *Warum war denn dann so   ein Lärm?*
           why   was then   then such a   noise
           'Why was it so noisy then'

These additional examples thus fully corroborate Grewendorf's idea that the focus projection possibilities of a constituent in the middle field determine its topicalizability together with the verb.

What is important for the topic of this paper is that the relevant generalizations *can* be formulated in terms of the concepts: (a) external vs. internal argument; (b) definite/indefinite and (c) focus projection. To my knowledge no successful account of the facts discussed here has been given which does not involve these three concepts. Thiersch's original observation is thus still in support of the external-internal argument distinction, although in a slightly different fashion than suggested in his original paper and in my follow-up.

2.2 *Internal vs. External Adjuncts*

If the explanation for the topicalization contrast discussed in the previous subsection is correct, then one would expect other topicalization asymmetries between elements generated external and internal to a putative VP-constituent. The different adverb classes are a good test ground in this respect.

On semantic grounds we can distinguish sentence adverbs like the speaker-oriented item *übrigens* (by the way) and VP-adverbs like *sorgfältig* (carefully). This difference shows a number of syntactic reflexes: only the VP-adverbs can follow the negation, the sentence adverbs have to stay to the left of it:

(49)   *Peter hat übrigens   nicht gespielt*
        Peter has by-the-way not   played
(50)   * *Peter hat nicht übrigens   gespielt*
        Peter has not   by-the-way played
(51)   *Peter hat nicht sorgfältig gespielt*
        Peter has not   carefully   played

If the negation demarcates the left bracket of the VP, this means that the speaker-oriented adverbs occur outside of the VP while the VP-adverbs are inside. This predicts that in sentences with adverbs of both kinds the sentence adverbs have to precede the VP-adverbs, which is correct:

(52)   *Peter hat übrigens   sorgfältig gespielt*
        Peter has by-the-way carefully   played
(53)   * *Peter hat sorgfältig übrigens   gespielt*
        Peter has carefully   by-the-way played

If *sorgfältig* is forced but *übrigens* is disallowed to modify a VP (or something smaller) then we predict that the former adverb should be topicalizable with a verb while the latter shouldn't be; the sharp contrast between the following two sentences makes the picture complete and consistent:

(54)   *[sorgfältig gespielt] hat Peter nicht*
        carefully   played   has Peter not
(55)   * *[übrigens   gespielt] hat Peter nicht*
        by-the-way played   has Peter not

Other ungrammatical examples of the kind (55) are the following:

(56)   * *[ja   gespielt] hat Peter nicht*
        by-the-way played   has Peter not
(57)   * *[vermutlich gekommen] ist   Peter nicht*
        probably   come   has Peter not
(58)   * *[doch   gelesen] hat Peter das Buch*
        indeed read   has Peter the book
(59)   * *[etwa   gelesen] hat Peter das Buch?*
        indeed read   has Peter the book

We can conclude that the asymmetric theory can handle these facts concerning different adverb classes, since it has at its disposal the structural difference between elements within and outside of the verb phrase constituent. And as predicted, those elements which independently motivated tests qualify as external adjuncts behave like external arguments with respect to topicalization together with the verb. And internal adjuncts pattern with internal arguments. There is no logical necessity that the facts should fall out this way, but they do, so that we ought to account for them as naturally as possible. Since the selectional differences in the last section provided evidence for a structural difference between elements closely related to the verb and those which are not the most natural account seems to be to make the topicalization asymmetries also follow from this structural difference, rather than admitting new devices into the grammar whose coverage does not exceed the one phenomenon at hand.

3.   Parallelism of WH-movement and Scrambling

3.1 *Extraction from Maximal Projections*

The third diagnostic for structure in the German sentence that I want to present is an empirical argument in support of the fronting rule postulated within the asymmetric theory presented in section 2.1. I thus follow Saito (1985: 34F) in his judgement:

> The proposed arguments against the extreme non-configurationality hypothesis can be divided into two groups: those for a VP and those for an analysis of the free word order phenomenon in terms of a movement rule. If there is good reason to assume a scrambling rule of some form in Japanese, the motivation for the non-configurational analysis of the free word order phenomenon is weakened considerably.

The argument I am going to present shows that unless one accepts the existence of such a fronting rule one is committed to the view that German not only lacks a VP-node but in addition lacks NPs, APs and PPs, constituents whose existence in German has not even been doubted by the defenders of the claim that German is not asymmetric. In German, the three nodes just mentioned behave just like in English and there are clear constituency tests showing their reality.

In what follows I will give triples of sentences the first of which contains one of the maximal projections mentioned in the main clause topic position thus establishing that the fronted element is a constituent. The second sentence shows that an element from the maximal projection can be extracted by WH-movement. The last sentence then shows that the same element can also undergo internal topicalization to the pre-subject position like the object noun phrase in (30). The latter sentences thus show that either one accepts their derivation by the internal topicalization rule discussed, or one also accepts a symmetric treatment of these seeming discontinuities, i.e., one not only claims the non-existence of a VP in German, but by analogy of all other lexical maximal projections in the language:

Adjective Phrases

(60) [*stolz   auf seine Kinder*] *war Hans noch nie*
     proud of his   kids   was Hans never

(61) [*auf wen*]$_k$ *war Hans noch nie* [t$_k$ *stolz*]
     of   whom was Hans never   proud

(62) *Deshalb war* [*auf seine Kinder*]$_k$ *auch Hans* [t$_k$ *sehr stolz*]
     thus   was of   his   children also Hans   very proud

Prepositional Phrases[10]

(63) [*dafür*]   *haben die Leute   lange gekämpft*
     there-for have   the people long   fought
     'the people have fought for that for a long time'

(64) [*wo*]$_k$ *haben die Leute   lange* [t$_k$ *für*] *gekämpft*
     what have   the people long   for fought
     'what did the people fight for for a long time'

(65) *weil* [*da*]$_k$ *die Leute   lange* [t$_k$ *für*] *gekämpft haben*
     bec. there the people long   for fought   have
     'because the people have fought for that for a long time'

Noun Phrases

(66) [*einen Film   über   England*] *hat sich niemand angeschaut*
     a   movie about England has refl nobody watched
     'nobody watched a movie about England'

(67) [*über wen*]$_k$ *hat sich niemand* [*einen Film* t$_k$] *angeschaut*
     about what   has refl nobody a   movie   watched
     'what did nobody watch a movie about'

(68) *weil sich* [*über England*]$_k$ *niemand* [*einen Film* t$_k$]
     bec. refl about England   nobody a   movie
     angeschaut hat
     watched   has
     'because nobody watch a movie about England'

(60)–(68) show in a rather dramatic way that the attempt to explain the permutability of verbal arguments in German by just denying the existence of a VP-node is too hurried a solution, for the problem posed by seemingly discontinous VPs is mirrored by virtually every other major maximal projection of the language. Still, the existence of such maximal projections in the language is beyond doubt. The symmetric theories are thus missing an important generalization by just barring VP-nodes from German (finite) sentences.

3.2 *Island-Sensitivity of Free Word Order Structures*

The last section showed that the attempt to account for word order freedom in German by postulating the non-existence of a VP-node in this language fails, because it is not general enough: there also exist discontinous NPs, APs and PPs on the surface. It was shown that the existence of a scrambling rule closely mirroring the properties of WH-movement could account for the parallelism of WH-movement and free word order phenomena. In this section we will provide further evidence for the existence of such a scrambling rule by showing that the phenomenon of free word order displays properties which are usually only found in movement structures: in other words we will see that scrambling obeys several of Ross' (1967) island constraints on movement transformations. It is obvious that if this claim is correct, this comes as a total surprise under the symmetric theories, since there the inverted object - subject sequences are base-generated and hence it would be a strange accident if inverted base-generated sequences were sensitive to movement constraints. Under our asymmetric theory, however, the sensitivity of scrambling to movement constraints is expected, since scrambling, like WH-movement and NP-movement, is just an instance of 'Move alpha'; since there are no construction-specific stipulations within our framework and the constraints affect all instances of 'Move alpha' alike, within our theory there is no way of making scrambling insensitive to the island constraints.

We conclude that if indeed it can be shown that the inverted sequences show island effects, then this is a very strong argument in favor of the articulated asymmetric structure we are hypothesizing for German.

3.2.1 *The Specificity-Condition on Extraction from NP*

We start out with another look at sentences like (67):

(69)   [*über   was*]$_k$ *hat sich niemand* [*einen Film* t$_k$] *angeschaut*
            about what has refl nobody a   movie   watched
            'what did nobody watch a movie about'

In this sentence a prepositional phrase has been extracted by WH-movement out of a noun phrase.[11] It has been noted frequently that this kind of extraction out of noun phrases is subject to a specificity-constraint. Chomsky (1986b), for example, gives the following sentences from English (his (184), (185)):

(70)   *Who did you see John's picture of
(71)   Who did you see 3 pictures of

In German we find the same specificity constraint, since (73) with a specific noun phrase is markedly worse than (72) which is comparable to (69):

(72)   *Von wem   hast du [ein Bild* t] *gesehen*
            of   whom have you a   picture seen
(73)   **Von wem   hast du [Peters Bild* t] *gesehen*
            of   whom have you Peter's picture seen

We do not find a specific/non-specific contrast in the following pair, where the extracted prepositional phrase is an object of the verb, although the string of words is almost identical:

(74)   *Von wem   hast du [ein Bild]*   t *bekommen*
            from whom have you a   picture   received
            'Who did you get a picture from'

(75)   *Von wem   hast du [Peters Bild]* t *bekommen*
            from whom have you Peter's picture received
            'Who did you get Peter's picture from'

In section 3.1 we had argued for the existence of a scrambling rule on the basis of the fact that the WH-movement example in (67) is paralleled by the scrambling example in (68): the theories that try to account for the free word order phenomenon in terms of doing away with a VP-projection cannot generate (68), since here the fronted prepositional phrase is not an object of the verb. We can now strengthen our argument for the existence of a scrambling rule by observing that the specificity condition on extraction displayed in the WH-movement examples (72)–(73) also governs the free word order phenomena not involving WH-movement: the contrast between (72) and (73) reappears in (76) vs. (77):

(76)   *Ich wünschte daß* [*von Brigitte Bardot*] [*weniger Bilder* t]
        I   wished   that of   Brigitte Bardot   less   pictures
        veröffentlicht werden
        published   are
        'I wished that less pictures of Brigitte Bardot are published'

(77)   *Ich wünschte daß* [*von Brigitte Bardot*] [*Peters Bilder*]
        I   wished   that of   Brigitte Bardot   Peter's   pictures
        veröffentlicht werden
        published   are
        'I wished that Peter's pictures of Brigitte Bardot are pub-
        lished'

However, we do not find a specificity condition on the reordering of prepositional objects of verbs and the subject, like we did not find such a specificity condition on WH-movement in (74), (75):

(78)   *weil* [*von mir*] *niemand* [*Peters Bilder*] t *bekommen hätte*
        bec. from me   nobody   Peter's pictures   received   had
        'because nobody would have received Peter's pictures from
        me'

We conclude that the analogy between the asymmetries between (72), (73) on the one hand and (76) , (77) on the other hand are strong evidence for the movement character of free word order sentences. Unter the asymmetric theory the output structures must have been derived by movement and given the non-construction-specific conditions on "Move alpha" are expected to be sensitive to the island conditions, much like WH-movement. The symmetric theories remain silent on the parallelism just noted, since in these theories the free word order structures are base-generated and no scrambling rule exists. These structures thus constitute important empirical evidence against these theories.

3.2.2 *The Left-Branch Condition*

We now turn to another well-known island condition. This is the left-branch condition, accounting, for example, for the difference between (79) and (80):

(79)   *Whose did you see brother

(80)   Who did you see a brother of

In (79) the WH-word has been extracted from a left branch within the noun phrase, in (80) from a right branch. Since the first sentence is ungrammatical, movement of certain elements on left branches is impossible in English. (81) supports this claim:

(81)   *How is John [t proud of his children]

The degree specifier of the adjective phrase is on a left branch and cannot be extracted.

Left-branch condition (LBC) effects can be found in some contexts in German Wh-movement, too:

(82)   *Wessen wurde [t Auto] gestohlen
          whose was   car   stolen
          'whose car was stolen'

(83)   *Wie ist Hans [t stolz   auf seine Kinder]
          how is Hans   proud of his children
          'how proud is Hans of his children'

In contrast with (82, 83), WH-movement can extract from right branches in NPs and APs, as we saw in (67) and (61), repeated here:

(84)   Über was   hat sich niemand [einen Film t] angeschaut
          about what has refl nobody a   movie watched
          'what did nobody watch a movie about'

(85)   Auf wen   war Hans noch nie [stolz t]
          on whom was Hans never   proud
          'who was Hans never proud of'

If the free word order phenomenon, as the asymmetric theory argues, is a movement phenomenon, then the grammaticality pattern found in (82, 83) vs. (84, 85) should reappear in free word order constructions. This is the case, as the following sentences show:

(86)   *weil [meines Bruders] gestern [t   Auto] gestohlen wurde
          bec. my   brother's yesterday car   stolen   was
          'because my brother's car was stolen yesterday'

(87)   *weil [sehr] Hans [t stolz   auf seine Kinder] ist
          bec. very Hans   proud of his children is
          'because Hans is very proud of his children'

(88)   *weil sich [über England] niemand [einen Film* t]
        bec. refl about England nobody a   movie
        angeschaut hat
        watched   has
        'because nobody watched a movie about England'

(89)   *weil [auf seine Kinder] jeder   [sehr stolz* t] *ist*
        bec. of his   children everybody very proud is
        'because everybody is very proud of his children'

We believe that the close parallelism between the WH-movement sentences above and (86)–(89) argue strongly in favor of the movement
analysis of free word order, and hence for the asymmetric theory.

3.2.3 Extraction of R-pronouns

Further parallels between WH-movement and free word order can be
found in prepositional phrases. (65) above shows that R-pronouns can be
extracted from prepositional phrases in German. Contrast this with the
non-extractability of non-R-elements:

(90)   *[wessen Freiheit] haben die Leute lange [t für] gekämpft*
        whose freedom have the people long   for fought
        'whose freedom did the people fight for for a long time'

The same contrast between R-pronouns and other noun-phrases reappears
in sentences not involving WH-movement: compare (65) with the ungrammatical (91) which mirrors (90):

(91)   *weil [ihre Freiheit] die Leute lange [t für] gekämpft*
        bec. their freedom the people long   for fougth
        haben
        have
        'because the people have fought for their freedom for a
        long time'

Moreover, we find conditions under which even R-pronouns cannot be
extracted by WH-movement. In exactly these cases the free word order
structures are impossible, too. I give two examples:

(a)   The R-pronoun can be extracted from the PP, if the PP follows the
        negation, but not if it precedes it:

(92)   *Wo   hat   Peter [t mit] nicht gerechnet
        where has Peter   with not   counted
        'what did Peter not expect to happen'

(93)   *weil da   Peter [t mit] nicht gerechnet hat
        bec. there Peter   with not   counted has
        'because Peter did not expect this to happen'

(b)   WH-movement out of a PP which is itself embedded within a PP is
       impossible, as (95), based on (94) shows:

(94)   Er ist [bis [da   hin]] gefahren
        he is to   there up   driven
        'he drove all the way up there'

(95)   *Wo   ist er [bis [t hin]] gefahren
        where is he to   up   driven
        'where did he drive to'

The free word order structure (96), like WH-extraction in (95), is impossible:

(96)   *weil da   jemand   [bis [t hin]] gefahren ist
        bec. there somebody to   up   driven   is
        'because somebody drove all the way up there'

To sum up: under the movement analysis of the free word order phenomenon that the asymmetric theory is committed to, the close parallelism between restrictions on WH-movement and restrictions on the free word order structures is expected. In contrast, under the symmetric theories, which argue for a base-generation of the free word order structures, this parallelism comes as a surprise, so that the asymmetric model is at a clear explanatory advantage.

4.   Further Asymmetries

I will now present a number of other asymmetries which suggest that the distinction between elements generated internal and external to the VP plays a role in German grammar. Space limitations prevent me from going into as much detail as I would like to.

4.1 *Verb Raising*

German has a phenomenon which is referred to as "Verb Raising" in the literature (cf. Evers 1975, Bech 1957 and Kvam 1979) for detailed studies). In sentences containing this construction the verb of a complement leaves its constituent and "raises" up to the verb governing the complement. The result of this process is a verb cluster. Here is an example: the S-structure in (98) is derived from the D-structure (97) by verb raising:

(97)   *Peter [das Buch zu lesen] versucht*
        Peter the book to read tries
(98)   *Peter [das Buch v] [zu lesen versucht]*
        Peter the book to read tries

One consequence of verb raising having applied is that the whole verb cluster can appear to the right of the negation although only the highest verb is negated:

(99)   *Peter das Buch nicht [zu lesen versucht]*
        Peter the book not to read tries

Verb raising seems to be at least in part lexically driven, since the class of verbs that trigger it is somewhat idiosyncratic. Thus, although no object control verb allows this process, some subject control verbs do while others don't. Assuming that Evers' arguments for a verb cluster really hold up, then the best solution to this process is to describe it through a Chomsky-adjunction of the lower verb to the higher one. Chomsky (1986b) claims that traces of moved verbs are also subject to the ECP. If this is correct, then our asymmetric theory can achieve the following result consistent with Chomsky's version of the ECP:

(100)   External argument sentences never allow the verb to raise
        out of them

The reason for this is obvious: a verb that moves out of an object to Chomsky-adjoin onto the governing verb will move up the tree, ending up in a position which c-commands its trace, so that the ECP can be satisfied. However, a verb coming out of an external argument clause would have to move down into the VP to adjoin to the main verb; this would disrupt the c-command relation between it and its trace so that an ECP-violation is inescapable. The following sentence modelling such a state of affairs is indeed so ungrammatical as to be virtually incomprehensible:

(101)   *weil [das Buch v] dem Hans nicht [zu lesen gefiel]
          bec. the book   the Hans not   to read pleased
          'because it did not please Hans to read the book'

The difference between external and internal arguments lying at the heart of the asymmetric theory is thus a good candidate to distinguish the existing cases of verb raising from the non-existing ones.

One more aspect of verb raising should be mentioned, though. As I said above, adjunct clauses also do not allow verb raising. In the previous section I argued that some adjuncts can be generated within the VP. We thus have to set up the theory in such a way that VP-internal adjuncts do not qualify for verb raising. There are a number of options here: we could make the assumption that these VP-adjuncts hang high enough in the VP that their verb would also have to move down to adjoin to the head of the VP. Then these structures would induce ECP-violations, like the extractions from external argument clauses. Another possibility would be to link the absence of verb raising with adjuncts to the fact that even certain subject control verbs do not allow verb raising, although their complements should be in the right constellation phrase-structurally. Those verbs allowing raising would then have to be slightly different subcategorizationally from those disallowing it. If the syntactic process of verb raising is triggered by a lexical feature of some kind to distinguish the two verb classes, then it is easy to derive the fact that adjuncts do not participate in this process: adjuncts are not represented in the lexical entries of particular verbs and hence cannot be marked for verb raising. The same is true for external arguments which are not c-selected as we saw in section 1 above. Either way the asymmetric theory has a good chance to capture the verb raising generalizations, using its primitive notions, because the facts divide the constituent types playing a role in this construction into two natural groups: complements of the verb and everything else; that is the kind of phenomenon that our theory would lead us to expect. For the symmetric theories this recurring pattern is rather unsettling.

4.2 Extraction Asymmetries

And the asymmetric pattern is more pervasive. There are a number of extraction rules which are sensitive to the difference between complements of the verb and adjuncts/external arguments. Den Besten (1985) was the first to notice these contrasts. German, like Dutch and the Scandinavian languages, have a process which splits up noun phrases by WH-moving the question pronoun *was* (what) out of the NP leaving behind a prepositional phrase:

(102)   *Was   hat   Peter   [$_{NP}$ t *für   Bücher*] *gelesen*
          what   hat   Peter   for   books   read
          'What kind of books did Peter read?'

This extraction is impossible out of external arguments, although to my ears the contrast is not very sharp:

(103)   ??*Was   haben   Peter   [$_{NP}$ t *für   Bücher*] *gefallen*
          what   have   Peter   for   books   pleased
          'What kind of books pleased Peter?'

However, the contrast seems to be real. I found another nice piece of evidence for the relevant contrast. The reader will remember that we analyzed the negation as demarcating the left bracket of the VP. This means that if we add a negation to (102) after the split noun phrase, this means that the noun phrase must have undergone scrambling; consequently the noun phrase should be in an adjoined modifier position from which extraction is impossible. The resulting sentence should thus be much worse than (102). This is indeed the case: the following sentence is markedly worse than its counterpart without the negation:

(104)   ??*Was   hat   Peter   [$_{NP}$ t *für   Bücher*] *nicht   t   gelesen*
          what   has   Peter   for   books   not   read

It does not come as a surprise that adjuncts pattern with the phrases from which extraction is blocked:

(105)   **Was   hat   Peter   [$_{NP}$ t *für   Wochen*] *im   Bett   gelegen*
          what   has   Petert   for   weeks   in   bed   lain

However, this sentence is much worse than the extractions from the arguments, suggesting that some additional factor is at play here.

     In section 3 we saw that the by now familiar external vs. internal pattern also shows up when we try to extract the complement of a noun. I will not repeat these cases here. Rather, I want to take another look at the extraction from external and internal argument clauses. This issue was already discussed in Webelhuth (1984/85) so that I will keep the discussion short. Extraction from complement sentences is possible:[12]

(106)   *Welches Buch glaubst du [daß Hans* t *gelesen hat]*
        which   book   believe you   that   Hans   read   has

Extraction from external argument sentences and from adjuncts, whatever the absolute judgement may be, leads to a sharply degraded result compared to the sentence type just given:

(107)   ?* *Welches Buch hat es dich enttäuscht,   [daß Hans* t
         which   book   has   it   you   disappointed that   Hans
         gelesen hat]
         read   has

(108)   * *Welches Buch ist Hans [ohne* t *zu lesen] eingeschlafen*
         which   book   is   Hans   without to read   asleep-fallen
         'Which book did Hans fall asleep without reading it?'

Again, the extraction from the adjunct is worse than that from the external argument, suggesting that some additional factor is at play. But the contrast between the external and internal argument clauses is rather reliable.

Fanselow (1987) presents some data from extractions out of WH-islands which might show that it makes a difference whether an external or an internal argument is extracted:

(109)   *Bücher weiß ich nicht [wer* t *liest]*
         books   know I   not   who   reads

(110)   * *Kinder weiß ich nicht [was* t *lesen]*
         Children know I   not   what   read

In Southern German the first sentence reportedly is fully grammatical while the second one is ungrammatical. In standard German there is also a difference, but it is one between one and two stars to my ears. Non-linguistic informants that I have consulted invariably feel this contrast even if they say that the first sentence is already "non-German." These data, once they have been more carefully researched, might thus also lead to a treatment in terms of the asymmetries introduced by our general approach.

A similar contrast is reportedly found in the following paradigm concerning subject and object extraction from a subjunctive clause. This claim was brought to my attention by David Pesetsky (personal communication) who checked it with German informants and found a contrast:

(111)   *Welches Mädchen wünschtest du   [daß Peter* t *heirate]*
         which   girl   wished   you   that   Peter   marry:SUBJ

(112)   *Welcher Junge wünschtest du   [daß t Maria heirate]
         which   boy   wished   you that Maria   marry:SUBJ

I will leave it to the reader to decide whether these judgements are correct. To sum up: there are a number of reasonably sharp contrasts between extractions from complements and extractions from non-complements: den Besten's *was für* — split, extraction from complements to nouns and extraction from complements vs. external arguments show that where extraction is worse then it is typically in the case of a non-complement. The results are fully consistent with the results obtained earlier: external arguments are c-selectionally independent of the verb, they are more resistant to topicalization together with the verb and they are extraction islands. That much seems to be firmly established. Fanselow's and Pesetsky's data might show that external arguments also behave differently from complements when *they* are extracted, but the data in this domain are rather muddy and one would probably not want to build an argument on them alone. It goes in the right direction, however, given the more thoroughly supported conclusions.

5. Conclusion

The goal of this paper was to draw together the most convincing evidence for both a VP-node and a scrambling rule in German. I do not consider it that crucial that there is so much evidence for these two theoretical constructs, but rather that the evidence comes from very diverse sources:[13] the c-selectional arguments show that the difference between external and internal arguments plays a role in the German lexicon; the topicalization cases display that the percolation of the focus feature is sensitive to an asymmetric constituent structure and the movement arguments presented in sections 3 and 4 show that the theory of transformations is sensitive to a VP-induced difference between external and internal arguments and adjuncts. These are the most convincing constituent tests that we know of today: subcategorization and transformational analyzability; that both of these modules consistently favor an asymmetric construal of German is a very important result. Other considerations strengthen this conclusion: Hoberg (1981: 44) presents a statistical study of different word orders in the German middle field with the result that the subject — object order occurs 96% of the time with only 4% left for the opposite order. By themselves, statistical studies have to be interpreted very cautiously, especially since Hoberg's study is about written German. However, in the case at hand, her results can be interpreted as corroborating our picture of German sentence structure: the purely syntactic modules of subcategorization and transformational analyzability unambiguously point to German as an asymmetric language with external arguments farther removed from verbs than internal arguments. Hoberg's result exactly fits into this picture: only 4 percent of the sentences that she investigated have a word order differing from the order the asymmetric theory claims to be basic and all of the "exceptional" sentences have precisely the structure which can be derived by wellformed chain formation, i.e., by movement of an object to a position higher up in the tree, c-commanding its starting site. These structures have rather special communicative usages, as Lenerz (1977) has shown (cf. his "Agensbedingung"), so that their relatively rare occurrence can be accounted for straightforwardly. Hoberg's work can thus be seen as a nice and independent piece in the mosaic of evidence for the asymmetric theory.

With the now overtly visible overwhelming success of the asymmetric framework it is tempting to go back to the original selection of arguments against this framework in Webelhuth (1984/85) to see where it was open for attack at the time. It turns out — as the article showed — that practically all counterarguments concerned differences between *English* and *German* in the treatment of their respective subject positions. But all of these differences could be shown to be irrelevant to the VP-debate in the wider context of the Germanic languages: the existence of subjectless sentences in German could be shown to extend to VP-containing languages like Dutch and Icelandic and the absence of a *that*-trace effect in both of these languages and also in some Swedish and Norwegian dialects showed that the difference between English and German is related to other parameters which group German with (some of) the VP-containing Scandinavian languages against the VP-containing language English. Thus, the modular approach to grammatical phenomena espoused in recent years has helped us to sort out the various problems in German syntax in fruitful ways, showing that a stronger consideration of data from other (Germanic) languages might help us to avoid the pitfalls of the VP-debate.

All in all, the VP-debate — though at times harsh and polemical from both sides — has revived work on German syntax and has helped to establish a lively research community which will hopefully turn its attention to other problems now in order to complement the basic fragment of German grammar that we have arrived at so far.

Notes

1. I would like to thank Emmon Bach, Hans den Besten, Noam Chomsky, Richard Kayne, Joyce McDonough, Scott Meyers, David Pesetsky, Martin Prinzhorn, Luigi Rizzi, Gautam Sengupta, Thilo Tappe and the participants of the U Mass Roundtable on Configurationality for helpful comments on first drafts of this paper. Any remaining errors and mistakes are of course my own.

2. Chomsky (1986a: 61) writes about the VP:

   The conclusion that the VP-configuration with the asymmetry of subject-object relations it induces holds cross-linguistically, is plausible, if it is found in some languages.

3. Other verbs behaving like *bedauern* and *drohen* are *abraten* (to advice against), *sich ärgern* (to be annoyed by), *auffordern* (to urge), *aufpassen* (to pay attention), *sich beeilen* (to hurry), *sich beklagen* (to complain), *sich bemühen* (to be eager), *bitten* (to ask for), *drängen* (to urge), *einladen* (to invite), *einwilligen* (to agree to), *sich entscheiden* (to decide), *sich entschließen* (to decide), *sich erinnern* (to remember), *sich erkundigen* (to inquire), *ermahnen* (to admonish), *ersuchen* (to fear), *sich freuen* (to be happy about), *sich fürchten* (to fear), *gratulieren* (to congratulate), *helfen* (to help), *hindern* (to hinder), *informieren* (to inform), *nötigen* (to press), *sich scheuen* (to avoid), *überreden* (to convince), *sich überzeugen* (to convince oneself), *warnen* (to warn), *sich wundern* (to wonder).

4. cf. the interesting discussion in Pesetsky (1982). Of course the implicational statement "If NP, then S" only makes sense with arguments that are semantically propositional.

5. For a discussion of idiomatic expressions like "ihm ist ein Stein vom Herz gefallen" (he is relieved) and "mir ist ein Licht aufgegangen" (something occurred to me) cf. the treatment of (58)–(63) in Webelhuth (1984/85).

   The restrictions on the subjects of weather-verbs and the verb *geben* (exist) in German as in English have to be governed by θ-theory, as it follows from Burzio's Generalization that the seemingly expletive elements in these sentences must have a θ-role, given that the verbs assign accusative case, as shown in (i) and (ii):

   (i) *Es regnete Blumen*
        it rained flowers:ACC
   (ii) *Es gibt Einhörner*
        it exists unicorns:ACC

6. It might seem as if *stimmen* (to be true) is a counterexample to this generalization, for we find (i) but not (ii):

   (i) *Daß Hans angekommen ist, stimmt*
        that Hans arrived   has is-true
   (ii) **Hansens Ankunft stimmt*
        Hans' arrival is-true

   My informants tell me that the same contrast exists in English. To see why (ii) is worse than (i) note the following contrast:

   (iii) *To go to Paris is false
   (iv) To go to Paris is wrong

Non-finite sentences often denote actions and actions can be morally right or wrong, but they cannot be true of false. Only propositions can be true or false. Hence, (iii) is ungrammatical, since *false* assigns a propositional external θ-role, but the non-finite sentence does not denote a proposition. This is also what rules out (ii). *Hans' arrival* does not denote a proposition, it denotes an event and events cannot be true or false. To see that *stimmen* is not a counterexample to the c-selection universal, we have to find a noun phrase which is enough proposition-like to satisfy the s-selection of the verb. Thus contrast (ii) with (v) which has the deictic pronoun *das* (that) in subject position:

(v) *Das stimmt*
     that is-true

As in English, this sentence is grammatical, because the deictic noun *das* is sufficiently propositional semantically.

Other evidence that *stimmen* — as our theory predicts — does allow an NP-subject comes from extraposition. If the subject sentence in (i) is extraposed, then *stimmen* allows the noun phrase *es* (it) in subject position:

(vi) *daß es stimmt, daß Hans angekommen ist*
      that it is-true   that Hans arrived   has

Note that the two tests, i.e., (a) acceptance of a demonstrative pronoun and (b) extraposition with *es*-insertion distinguish *stimmen* from the verbs we have argued not to accept a noun phrase object, e.g. *drohen* (threaten). (vii) shows that *drohen* does not accept the demonstrative and (viii) that it does not allow an expletive pronoun linked to an extraposed sentence:

(vii) * *Die Entführer   haben das gedroht*
        the kidnappers have   that threatened
(viii) * *Die Entführer   haben es gedroht   [die Geiseln zu ermorden]*
         the kidnappers have   it threatened the hostages to kill

As far as I know, there are then no counterexamples to the c-selection universal.

7.   One might imagine an attempt to derive the absence of a verb like WONDER from Case-theory. Even without a VP, an external θ-role (to the extent that this notion makes sense in a theory without a VP) could always be expressed by an NP, because nominative case is not dependent on the verb. That external θ-roles can always be expressed by NP would thus follow from the fact that there is a Case-assigner independent of the verb. Internal arguments, however, are Case-dependent on the verbs and verbs without Case-features will not be able to licence an internal θ-role as an NP (this is the theory of Pesetsky 1982).

      This approach fails on empirical grounds, because it predicts that the subjects of all passive verbs will be expressible by both CP and NP, even if as an object the θ-role could only be expressed by CP. This is because in passive sentences nominative case is no longer assigned to the external argument of the verb, since there is no external argument for passive verbs. The prediction is wrong, since even if *drohen* (from (7) in the main text) is passivized, the theme θ-role may only be expressed by a CP; an NP is still disallowed:

(i)   *Es wurde gedroht*   [$_{CP}$ *die Geiseln zu ermorden*]
      It was threatened   the hostages to kill
(ii) * *Es wurde* [$_{NP}$ *die Ermordung der Geiseln*] *gedroht*
      It was   the murder   the hostages threatened

Case theory is thus of no help to the symmetric theories.

8. The point made in (11)–(16) can also be made with the following sharp contrast in catego-
    rial realization of the same θ-role involving the two versions of the word *überraschen* (sur-
    prise/d). The version which selects an internal propositional theme does not allow it to be
    realized as an NP:

    (i)   *Ich war überrascht* [*wie sehr   er sich verändert hatte*]
          I   was surprised   how much he refl changed had
    (ii) **Ich war seine Veränderung sehr überrascht*
          I   was his   change   very surprised

    However, the propositional theme may be realized by NP, as we deal with the verb which
    externalizes this θ-role:

    (iii) *weil mich überraschte* [*wie sehr   er sich verändert hatte*]
          bec. me surprised   how much he refl changed had
    (iv) *weil seine Veränderung mich überraschte*
          bec. his   change   me   surprised

    Other verbs showing this effect are *ärgern* (to be annoyed by), *einladen* (to invite), *sich
    entscheiden* (to decide), *ermahnen* (to admonish), *freuen* (to be happy about/ to make sb.
    happy), *helfen* (to help), *hindern* (to hinder), *informieren* (to inform), *nachdenken/
    nachdenklich machen* (to reflect on/ to make reflecting), *nötigen* (to press), *überzeugen*
    (to convince), *warnen* (to warn), *wundern* (to wonder), *zwingen* (to force).

9. There are a number of counterexamples to my claim that the finiteness of external argu-
    ment sentences is not restricted by the main verb: *sich zutragen* (to happen), *sich ereignen*
    (to happen) do not allow non-finite subject sentences. It seems that this extends to the
    whole semantic class of happen-verbs: *passieren* (happen), *geschehen* (happen) (both
    maybe ergative). I hope that a semantic explanation can be found for why all these verbs
    pattern together in not accepting non-finite subject sentences.

10. The extraction of R-pronouns is only allowed in some dialects of German. Our theory
    predicts, however, that if a dialect allows extraction by WH-movement, then it should
    also allow extraction by scrambling. If this is correct, then it supports our theory, because
    the symmetric theories do not make this prediction, since the free word order phenome-
    non in these theories is not analyzed in terms of movement, while WH-constructions are.

11. There is a debate as to whether extraction from noun phrases is really possible. Grewen-
    dorf (1989), for example, argues that extraction is impossible, and that what seems to be
    extracted has been reanalyzed out of the NP. In my talk at the annual meeting of the Ger-
    man Linguistic Society in Augsburg in March 1987 I presented a number of strong argu-
    ments against this view. Thilo Tappe (personal communication) argues in unpublished
    work that the position taken here is correct, i.e., that extraction from NP *is* possible. Fan-
    selow (1986) takes the best of both worlds: on page 68 he takes the fact that extraction
    from NP is *ungrammatical* to be evidence for the fact that nouns are not proper gover-
    nors; on page 229 he needs an argument that scrambling traces are anaphors — there the
    fact that extraction from NP is *grammatical* is taken to show this (this is only one of the
    many inconsistencies in this work: on page 232 a number of sentences are starred because
    German allegedly does not allow a quantified NP to scramble. On the next page other
    examples are given which show that such scrambling *is* possible, if the subject itself is
    quantified; but among the earlier four starred example sentences three also have quan-
    tified subjects. I have not been able to find a lot of consistent argumentation in this work
    and I therefore mostly ignore it; cf. also the final footnote).

12. In Southern German these sentences seem to be fully grammatical; in the standard dialect we get a mild subjacency violation. In the case of extraction from subject sentences the violation is much stronger, however.

13. With Fanselow (1986) the literature also contains a language acquisition argument for a VP in German. But the argument is based on such a careless treatment of the data and the inference is so obviously invalid that I did not give it any space in the main text. If I understand it correctly, the structure of the argument is as follows:
    1. Fanselow has found n arguments for a VP in German
    2. Therefore, German has a VP
    3. The linguistic behavior of children shows that they *know* that German has a VP
    4. All the evidence in 1. for a VP requires that the child have information that certain sentences are ungrammatical
    5. Children don't hear ungrammatical sentences
    6. Because of 4. and 5. children have no overt evidence for a VP in German and can therefore not learn that the language has a VP
    7. German children *know* that German has a VP (see 3. above); if one knows something, then one has either learned it or the knowledge is innate
    8. Since German children know that German has a VP (3.) but could not have learned it (6.), the fact that German has a VP has to be innate

Note the following exactly parallel argument:
    1. Fanselow has found n arguments that English is not pro-drop
    2. Therefore, English is not pro-drop
    3. The linguistic behavior of children shows that they *know* that English is not pro-drop
    4. All the evidence in 1. for English not being pro-drop requires that the child have information that certain sentences are ungrammatical (*"e rained")
    5. Children don't hear ungrammatical sentences
    6. Because of 4. and 5. children have no overt evidence for English not being pro-drop and can therefore not learn that English is not pro-drop
    7. English children *know* that English is not pro-drop (see 3. above); if one knows something then one has either learned it or the knowledge is innate
    8. Since English children know that English is not pro-drop (3.) but could not have learned it (6.) the fact that English is pro-drop has to be innate.

The conclusion in 8. is obviously untenable: if at all, then the drop value of the pro-drop parameter is unmarked, so that English children, not hearing any evidence against this value, since all the relevant sentences would be ungrammatical in English, should never give up this unmarked value. The argument has many other consequences, mostly absurd ones: an Indonesian child should know innately that the English modifier of AP *enough* only governs to the left, for otherwise the English child could not learn this. The fact that the German preposition *ohne* (without), unlike many other prepositions (e.g. *mit* (with)), does not allow an R-pronoun to the left of it (cf. *da-mit* (therewith) vs. **da-ohne* (therewithout)), has to be known innately to a Bengali child, for otherwise a German child could not know it.

The reader will find the false premises and the invalid inferences in the argument by him/herself. All I wanted to point out is that arguments of this quality are of no help to us in building a grammar of German and that such an unsubstantiated usage of concepts like innateness and learning discredits the program of Generative Grammar rather than doing it any good.

Bibliography

Abraham, Werner (ed). 1983. *On the Formal Syntax of the Westgermania.* Amsterdam: Benjamins.

Bech, Gunnar. 1957. *Studien zum deutschen Verbum infinitum.* 2nd. ed. 1983 Tübingen: Niemeyer.

den Besten, Hans. 1985. "The Ergative Hypothesis and Free Word Order in Dutch and German." In: Toman (ed).

————. 1983. "On the Interaction of Root Transformations and Lexical Deletive Rules." In Abraham (ed).

Chomsky, Noam. 1965. *Aspects of the Theory of Syntax.* Cambridge, Mass.: MIT Press.

————. 1981. *Lectures on Government and Binding.* Dordrecht: Foris.

————. 1986a. *Knowledge of Language: Its Nature, Origin and Use.* New York: Praeger.

————. 1986b. *Barriers.* Cambridge, Mass.: MIT Press.

Eisenberg, Peter. 1985. *Grundriß der Deutschen Grammatik.* München: Hueber.

Evers, Arnold. 1975. "The Transformational Cycle of Dutch and German." Diss., University of Utrecht.

Fanselow, Gisbert. 1986. "Konfigurationalität." Diss., University of Passau.

Grewendorf, Günther. 1989. *Ergativity in German.* Dordrecht: Foris.

Grimshaw, Jane. 1979. "Complement Selection and the Lexicon." *Linguistic Inquiry* 10.

Haider, Hubert. 1981. "Empty Categories and Some Differences between English and German." *Wiener Linguistische Gazette* 25.

————. 1982. "Dependenzen und Konfigurationen." *Groninger Arbeiten zur Germanistischen Linguistik* 21.

————. 1985. "A Unified Account of Case and θ-marking: The Case of German." *Papiere zur Linguistik.*

Hale, Ken. 1982. "Preliminary Remarks on Configuratinality." In: *Proceedings of the New England Linguistic Society 12.*

————. 1983. "Warlpiri and the Grammar of Non-configurational Languages." *Natural Language and Linguistic Theory* 1.1.

Hoberg, Ursula. 1981. *Die Wortstellung der geschriebenen deutschen Gegenwartssprache.* München: Hueber.

Jelinek, Eloise. 1984. "Empty Categories, Case and Configurationality." *Natural Language and Linguistic Theory* 2.1.

Kratzer, Angelika. 1984 "On Deriving Syntactic Differences between German and English." Ms., Technische Universität Berlin.

Kvam, Sigmund. 1979. "Diskontinuierliche Anordnung von eingebetteten Infinitivphrasen im Deutschen. Eine Diskussion der topologischen Einheiten Kohärenz und Inkohärenz." *Deutsche Sprache* 7.

Pesetsky, David. 1982. "Paths and Categories." Diss., Massachusetts Institute of Technology.

Ross, John. 1967. "Constraints on Variables in Syntax." Diss., Massachusetts Institute of Technology.

Saito, Mamoru. 1985. "Some Asymmetries in Japanese and Their Theoretical Implications." Diss., Massachusetts Institute of Technology.

Saito, Mamuro; and Hoji, Hajime. 1983. "Weak Crossover and Move α in Japanese." *Natural Language and Linguistic Theory* 1.2.

Scherpenisse, Wim. 1985. *The Connection between Base Structure and Linearization Restrictions in German and Dutch*. Frankfurt: P.Lang.

Tappe, Thilo. 1981. "VP and Coherent Infinitives in German." Ms., University of Göttingen.

———. 1986. "Struktur und Restrukturierung: Eine Untersuchung zur Strukturkonzeption der Generativen Grammatik." Diss., University of Göttingen.

Thiersch, Craig. 1982. "A Note on Scrambling and the Existence of VP." *Wiener Linguistische Gazette* 27/28.

———. 1985. "VP and Scrambling in the German Mittelfeld." Ms., University of Cologne.

Toman, Jindrich. (eds). 1985. *Studies in German Grammar*. Dordrecht: Foris.

Webelhuth, Gert. 1984/85. "German is Configurational." *The Linguistic Review* 4.

———. and H. den Besten. 1987. "Adjunction and Remnant Topicalization in the Germanic SOV-languages." Paper given at the GLOW Conference in Venice, March 30 - April 2, 1987.

Williams, Edwin. 1980. "Predication." *Linguistic Inquiry* 11.

———. 1981. "Argument Structure and Morphology." *The Linguistic Review* 1.

Stranding

Hans den Besten   &   Gerth Webelhuth
University of Amsterdam   *University of Massachusetts at Amherst*

This paper is a sequel to Webelhuth/Den Besten (1989) which deals with the phenomenon of remnant topicalization in the Germanic SOV-languages, an example of which is given below:

(1)   [*Gelesen*] *hat Hans das Buch nicht*
     read   has Hans the book not

What is interesting about (1) is that impressionistically it contains a non-maximal projection in the specifier position of COMP which is prohibited by the universal theory of movement outlined in Chomsky (1986). According to this otherwise well-motivated theory only maximal projections are allowed to move to specifier positions of COMP and INFL. Thus, if the topicalized constituent in (1) really belonged to the categories V_0 or V_1 then this theory of movement would have to be given up. Given that — as just noticed — this theory is otherwise empirically successful and is obviously more restricted than an alternative theory allowing all X-bar projections to move, we set out in the paper mentioned above to show that the topicalized constituent in (1) really belongs to the maximal projection "verb phrase" rather than to any of the non-maximal verbal projections. In fact, it could be shown that the "Universal Theory," as we termed our framework, was both empirically and conceptually far more satisfactory than the "Language-particular Theory" which allows individual grammars to select the bar-level of the movable constituents of a language. Among the crucial advantages of our theory over its alternative could be found that it correlates the fact that German and Dutch as the only Germanic scrambling languages are also the only languages allowing remnant topicalization: since

the scrambling operation can remove parts of the VP within the middle
field in the SOV-languages it became understandable why only these two
languages allowed VP-remnants to topicalize. The alternative theory has no
insight to offer concerning this correlation; both properties of the SOV-languages have to be stipulated independently.

Our reason for writing the current paper stems from the fact that we
had to leave one aspect of remnant topicalization unexplained in the earlier
article. The problem was the following: we argued that the sentence in (1)
has the structure in (2) and according to the theory this sentence was possible, because the scrambling rule could produce the sentence in (3):

(2) $[_{VP}$ t *gelesen*] *hat Hans* $[_{I'}$ *das Buch* $[_{I'}$ *nicht* vp]]
       read   has Hans   the book   not

(3)   *weil   Hans* $[_{I'}$ *das Buch* $[_{I'}$ *nicht* $[_{VP}$ t *gelesen*] *hat*]]
       because Hans   the book   not   read   has

The VP-remnant of (3) would be the topicalized part of (2) with the trace in
the topic position of (2) being bound by some reconstruction device that
was shown to be independently necessary.

However, although our theory makes the correct prediction for (2) and
(3) it fails to predict that the grammatical scrambling structure in (5) cannot
be converted into a grammatical topicalization structure, since (4) is
ungrammatical:

(4)   *$[_{VP}$ [t *mit*] *gerechnet*] *hat Hans* $[_{I'}$ *da* $[_{I'}$ *nicht* vp]]
       with counted   has Hans   there not
       'Hans did not expect that to happen'

(5)   *weil Hans* $[_{I'}$ *da* $[_{I'}$ *nicht* $[_{VP}$ [t *mit*] *gerechnet*] *hat*]]
       bec. Hans   there not   with counted   has
       'because Hans had not expected that to happen'

(5) contains an example of the limited type of preposition/postposition
stranding that is possible in German: as is wellknown, only members of the
restricted class of R-pronouns can strand prepositions. The word *da* in (5)
belongs to this class. However, as (4) shows, the remnant-PP cannot be
topicalized together with the rest of the VP over the R-pronoun and our
theory was unable to explain this fact, since the proposed reconstruction
mechanism could not distinguish between the verb-governed trace in TOP
in sentences like (2) and the preposition-governed trace in TOP in sentences like (4).

Here, we would like to address this problem through both a careful examination of the relevant example sentences and a broadening of the domain of investigation. Besides preposition stranding we will consider three other constructions that show a similar behavior. Two of these we introduce now, leaving the third one till later in the paper.

Consider the following sentence which is an example of what is known as *was-für*-split in the literature:

(6)   *Was   hat Hans* [t *für Leute*] *getroffen?*
        what has Hans   for people met
        'What kind of people did Hans meet?

These structures, analyzed for the first time for German in Den Besten (1985), are described most succesfully as being derived by a movement rule moving the question word *was* (what) out of an object noun phrase to the sentence-initial operator position, referred to as the "O-position" from now on in accordance with Webelhuth (to appear).

The second additional construction that will concern us involves extraction from NP:

(7)   *Bücher hat Hans* [*keine* t] *gelesen*
        books   has Hans   none   read
        'Hans has not read any books'

In this case, according to the standard X'-theoretic analysis of noun phrases, the head of the noun phrase is extracted to the O-position, leaving the determiner of the noun phrase behind. Obviously, for us to adopt this analysis would be self-defeating, since we are claiming that non-maximal projections cannot move to O. We are thus forced to assume that the topicalized constituent in (7) is a maximal projection, in this case an NP. We thus accept the DP-analysis of nominals proposed independently in Abney (1987). According to this theory, the structure of (7) will be (8):

(8)   [$_{NP}$ *Bücher*] *hat Hans* [$_{DP}$ *keine* np] *gelesen*
        books   has Hans   none   read

We will refer to structures like (8) as "DP-split."[1]

Before we turn to an examination of the properties of the three constructions considered here we want to introduce the structures that we hypothesize for each. Let us begin with the preposition stranding phenomenon. As the following sentences show, R-pronouns obligatorily precede strandable prepositions/postpositions, unlike full DPs which must follow the preposition:

(9)   a.   [da-mit]   b.   *[mit-da]
           there-with   with-there
(10) a.   *[dem Unglück mit]   b.   [mit dem Unglück]
           the   accident with   with the   accident

We will assume that the wellformed R-pronoun structure in (9a) is derived
from the structure in (9b), i.e, that the R-pronoun is base-generated after
the preposition and undergoes a movement rule into the specifier position
of the prepositional phrase. (9a) thus has the following structure:[2]

(11)

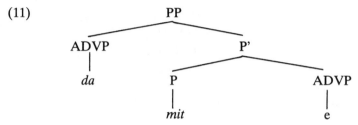

So much for the preposition stranding cases. For DP-split we subscribe to a
very similar hierarchical structure:

(12)

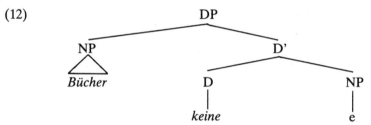

(12) is the structure of the DP before the NP gets extracted to the O-position. This means that we follow Chomsky (1986) in claiming that extraction
from DP is only possible through the specifier position. What the extracted
phrases in (11) and (12) have in common is that they have left their containing constituent through its specifier position.

From this analysis of preposition standing and DP-split it is not far to
the following pre-extraction analysis of was-für-split structures:

(13)

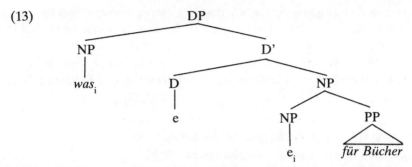

According to (13) *was-für*-constituents are DPs with an empty head, much like indefinite plurals like [e Bücher] (books). The extracted phrase *was* (what) is taken to be an NP modified by a prepositional phrase. To be consistent with what was said about extraction from DP in connection with DP-split we have to assume that the WH-word leaves the DP through its specifier position also in *was-für*-constructions.

In the following discussion we will represent the internal structure of the phrases that are extracted from in a slightly simplified manner. According to our theory, the traces in the respective positions are crucial to an understanding of the behavior of the whole phrase. We will hence omit all other traces.

We will now present examples of phrases with the structures (11)–(13) in eight different constructions of German. The descriptive generalizations gained from this survey will then be compared to a generalization concerning topicalization of clauses in German and it will be hypothesized that these sets of generalizations are consequences of a single, arguably universal, property of the reconstruction mechanism provided by Universal Grammar.

The first construction that we look at involves simple topicalization:

(14)   *Da   hatten wir nicht* [t *mit*] *gerechnet*
         there had   we   not   with   counted
(15)   *Bücher hat er* [t *keine*] *gelesen*
         books has he none   read
(16)   *Was hat er* [t *für Bücher*] *gelesen?*
         what has he   for books   read

Let us introduce some terminology to distinguish between the preposed phrases and the bracketed phrases in (14)–(16). We will call the former "the operator" and the latter "the remnant". In the light of the three sentences just given we can say that in all three constructions the operator can be moved to the operator position leaving the remnant behind in the middle field.

The next sentences show that the inverse is not possible, i.e., the remnant cannot be topicalized with the operator staying in the middle field:

(17)   *[t *mit*] *hat er da*   *nicht gerechnet*
        with has he there not   counted

(18)   *[t *keine*] *hat er Bücher gelesen*
        none has he books   read

(19)   *[t *für Bücher*] *hat er was gelesen*
        for books   has he what read

It is also impossible to scramble the remnant over the operator in the middle field:

(20)   *weil er* [t *mit*] *da*   *nicht gerechnet hat*
        bec. he   with there not   counted   has

(21)   *weil er* [t *keine*] *wohl Bücher gelesen hat*
        bec. he   none well books   read   has

(22)   *weil er* [t *für Bücher*] *was gelesen hat*
        bec. he   for books   what read   has

Likewise, it is ungrammatical to topicalize the remnant together with the remainder of the VP, leaving the operator in the middle field. This was the problem which we could not solve in our earlier paper:

(23)   *[[t *mit*] *gerechnet*] *hat er da*   *nicht*
        with counted   has he there not

(24)   *[[t *keine*] *gelesen*] *hat er Bücher*
        none read   has he books

(25)   *[[t *für Bücher*] *gelesen*] *hat er was*
        for books   read   has he what

And, finally, it is also not allowed to topicalize the operator together with the rest of the VP, leaving the remnant behind in the middle field:[3]

(26)   *[Da   gerechnet*] *hat er nicht* [t *mit*]
        there counted   has he not   with

(27)   *[Bücher gelesen*] *hat er* [t *keine*]
        books read   has he   none

(28)   *[Was gelesen*] *hat er* [t *für Bücher*]?
        what read   has he   for books

(29) states the generalization that we arrive at on the basis of the examples in (14)–(28):

    (29)   In the following constructions an extracted operator has to c-command the remnant at S-structure:
                (a) Preposition stranding
                (b) *was-für*-split
                (c) DP-split

The three constructions listed in (29) thus differ systematically from VP-remnants like (2) which do not have to be c-commanded by the extracted phrase at S-structure. We should therefore be eager to determine whether there is some crucial difference between each of the first three constructions and the VP-remnant configuration which we can make our reconstruction mechanism sensitive to. Our preliminary hypothesis will be the following:

    (30)   Traces in specifier positions are not reconstructable

If (30) can be derived as a theorem from Universal Grammar, then our theory can distinguish between the three constructions in which remnant topicalization is impossible and the one construction where it is possible, under the assumption that the postulated structures (11)–(13) are correct at least in so far as the extracted phrase has left the containing constituent through the specifier position. The Binding Theory will block all of the sentences in (17)–(28) for the same reason: since at S-structure all traces have to be bound — either directly or through reconstruction — these sentences contain an unbound trace in specifier position: the reason is that there is no direct c-command relation between the trace and its antecedent at S-structure, but the specifier trace also does not qualify for reconstruction. The VP-remnant construction in (2), however, can be derived, since the trace although not directly c-commanded by its antecedent — can be bound by reconstruction, this process not being blocked here.

As a corroborating piece of evidence for our claim that the crucial difference between the good and the bad remnant topicalization cases lies in the occurrence of a specifier trace take the following sentence:

    (31)   *[Gesagt [t$_i$ *daß er lesen will*]]$_k$ *weiß ich nicht*
             said   that he read wants know I   not
             was$_i$ er vp$_k$ *hat*
             what he   has

This sentence has the following characteristics: it contains two sentential embeddings; the intermediate verb phrase has been topicalized together with its object clause. Before topicalization, however, an argument from the object clause has been extracted to the intermediate COMP. (31) is thus a clause with long VP-topicalization with the VP having a trace in specifier position of one of its arguments.

As the reader can see this type of structure is completely ungrammatical, in contrast to a sentence with a topicalized VP with an argument trace in it. The fact that the sentence is ungrammatical is not very surprising as such, since it contains a WH-island violation: the topicalized VP has been moved over the filled intermediate COMP. What is crucial to our argument is the degree of ungrammaticality of (31). It is practically unintelligible, whereas other violations of the WH-island condition lead to comparatively mild violations:

(32)   ?* Gelesen weiß ich nicht was er   hat
        read   know I   not what he   has
        'I don't know what he has read'

In fact, sentences like (32) are reportedly grammatical in Southern German where the WH-island condition is only weakly operative, at least under extraction of non-subjects. However, even in these dialects (31) is judged completely ungrammatical. Similarly, the Dutch equivalent of (32), i.e., *Gelezen weet ik niet wat hij heeft*, does not sound that bad and may deserve only one or two question marks, whereas the Dutch equivalent of (31), i.e., *Gezegd dat hij wil lezen weet ik niet wat hij heeft*, deserves a full star. The (near-)grammaticality of sentences like (32) in Dutch and Southern German may also be related to the fact that the latter varieties of Continental West Germanic allow extractions out of finite CPs much more freely than Northern German does. In Northern German such extractions are usually considered to be ungrammatical or at least questionable. Despite these differences all three varieties of SOV Germanic reject sentences like (31), which we would like to claim is due to the trace in the intermediate specifier position inside the topicalized VP.

This also holds for the following sentence which has the same structure as (31) just that this time the lowest sentence is non-finite. Non-finite CPs usually allow extraction more easily than finite clauses, as is wellknown. Nevertheless, the following sentence is strongly ungrammatical:

(33) *[*Versuchen* [t *mir zu geben*]] *weiß ich nicht*
      try   me to give   know I   not
      was er vp *wollte*
      what he   wanted

We conclude that the relevant difference between (31) + (33) and (32) is the existence of a trace in specifier position in the former sentences and the absence of such a trace in the latter. If this difference between these sentences is to be captured in the grammar, then the reconstruction mechanism will have to be made sensitive to the different positions of the traces. It follows right away that the generalization in (29) can be automatically derived as well, once (31)–(33) have been taken care of.

By way of a curiosity, note that by the same token sentences like (34) and (35), which combine features of (23)/(25) and (38), may be expected to be ungrammatical, as they are:

(34) *[[t_i *mit*] *gerechnet*]$_k$ *weiß ich nicht wo$_i$* *er* vp$_k$ *hat*
      with counted   know I   not where he   has

(35) *[[t_i *für Bücher*] *gelesen*]$_k$ *weiß ich nicht was$_i$ er* vp$_k$ *hat*
      for books   read   know I   not what he   has

(34) and (35) are just two more ungrammatical sentences exemplifying the generalization in (29) which we are certain can be derived, once (31)–(33) have been accounted for.

With these prospects in mind let us return to (30), repeated here for convenience:

(36) Traces in specifier position are not reconstructable

We had said above that this is a preliminary version of the principle that will solve the preposition stranding problem. But is it too weak in one sense, because it will still not rule out one permissible derivation of the following ungrammatical string:

(37) *[*Mit gerechnet*] *hatte Peter da*   *nicht*
      with counted   had Peter there not
      'Peter had not expected that to happen'

It *will* rule out the following structure of (37):

(38) *[[t_k *mit*] *gerechnet*] *hatte Peter da$_k$* *nicht*
      with counted   had Peter there not

The trace in the specifier position of the prepositional phrase is not bound, since it cannot be reconstructed. But the following derivation does not run into this problem, since reconstruction of the trace in specifier position is not necessary, since it is c-commanded at S-structure:

(39)   *$[t_k [t_k$ *mit] gerechnet] hatte Peter da$_k$* *nicht*
         with   counted   had   Peter there   not

(39) contains a derivation in which the operator after leaving the prepositional phrase has first adjoined to the VP and then to I'. It is likely that this double adjunction is possible, since the positioning of the adverbial phrase on the surface is rather free. But, if this double adjunction is possible, then there is no reason why the trace adjoined to the VP could not move along with the VP under remnant topicalization, as in (39). The specifier trace is bound by the adjoined trace in TOP, so that (36) loses its force.

To rule out the structure in (39) on a par with that in (38) we have to strengthen our principle (36) to the following one:

(40)   Only argument traces can be reconstructed

(40) will now block reconstruction of both the non-argument traces in the topicalized constituents of (38) and (39), thus barring all unwanted derivations of this string, so that the grammar predicts it to be ungrammatical — as desired. We will cling to (40) as the principle operative in distinguishing between the good cases of remnant topicalization and the bad ones. It allows us to capture the major generalizations about VP-remnants as opposed to NP, CP and PP-remnants and also enables us to maintain the conclusions that we arrived at in our earlier article: the stricter version of the theory of movement, which restricts movement to specifier position to maximal projections does not have to be given up and the correlation between the availability of remnant topicalization and the existence of scrambling in a language can be derived in a principled manner from Universal Grammar.

One problem still remains unsolved, however, even if we invoke (40) as a universal principle. Contrast the following examples with (14)–(16):

(41)   *Da   hatten wir [t mit]   nicht gerechnet*
         there had   we   with not   counted
(42)   *Bücher hatte er [t einige] nicht gelesen*
         books had   he some   not   read
(43)   *Was   hat er [t für Bücher] nicht gelesen*
         what has he for books   not   read

These sentences show that the operator cannot be extracted if the containing phrase has been scrambled out of its D-structure position before the extraction takes place. Assuming that the negation delimits the left bracket of the VP, all the bracketed expressions in (41)–(43) have to occupy adjoined positions, since they occur to the left of the negation. To capture the ungrammaticality of these examples the simplest statement to make is that extraction out of adjoined positions is impossible. Assuming this statement or a similar one to be correct, our theory of remnant topicalization predicts that the following sentence is ungrammatical:

(44) $[_{VP}\, t_k$ *gerechnet*$]$ *hatte Peter da*$_i$ *nicht* $[t_i$ *mit*$]_k$
          counted   had Peter there not   with
          'Peter had not expected that to happen'

The reason we predict this sentence to be ungrammatical is the following: the prepositional phrase at the end of the sentence is an argument of the verb heading the topicalized VP. Since the prepositional phrase is missing from the topicalized phrase, it must have been scrambled out before topicalization of the VP. But then it should occur in a derived position in (44) and should thus be an extraction island as much as in (41). This is not the case as the grammaticality judgement shows: (44) is perfectly grammatical. We do not have a convincing solution to this problem. Obviously, if our overall theory of remnant topicalization is to be maintained, we have to find an alternative to the simplest solution mentioned above that distinguishes (41) and (44): we cannot maintain the claim that *every* adjoined phrase is an extraction island.

Maybe it is possible to claim that a phrase adjoined in the government domain of a higher verb allows extraction, since it is governed by a lexical head, whereas a phrase adjoined to an Infl-projection does not have this option. This would distinguish between (41) and (44), since the latter could be given a structure in which the prepositional phrase is adjoined to the verbal projection headed by the verb *hatten*, while in (41) the PP would have to adjoin to I'.

However, another hypothesis suggests itself as soon as we take some other facts about preposition stranding into consideration. First of all, note that surprisingly, it is possible to strand a preposition heading an adjunct-PP, as the following examples shows:

(45)   *Da   hat   Peter   es* [t *mit*]   *geöffnet*
        there has   Peter   it   with   opened
        'Peter opened it with that'

(46)   *Da   haben   wir   Geld* [t *für*]   *gesammelt*
        there have   we   money   for   collected
        'We have collected money for that'

The instrumental phrase in (45) and the benificiary in (46) are not extraction islands, although these phrases are probably not subcategorized by the verb, especially the latter one. If this is true, then the grammaticality of (45)–(46) further suggests that occurring in a non-argument position is not a sufficient condition for islandhood. We will leave these structures for further research, but we can use them to demonstrate another fact about preposition stranding.

Recall that in sentences without topicalized VPs a stranded preposition heading an argument PP must immediately precede the verb, as can be derived from examples (14) and (41), which we repeat here as (47) and (48):

(47)   *Da   hatten   wir   nicht* [t *mit*]   *gerechnet*
        there had   we   not   with   counted

(48)   *Da   hatten   wir   [t mit]   nicht   gerechnet*
        there had   we   with   not   counted

Although this observation seems to warrant the conclusion that a stranded preposition may only head an argument PP, a weaker conclusion cannot be excluded, and is even required given the grammaticality of (45) and (46). As a first approximation of the condition we have in mind, let us state that a stranded preposition must immediately precede the verb. This condition, which we have couched in observational terms, predicts that also stranded prepositions heading adjunct-PPs must immediately precede the verb. This is the case indeed, witness the following examples:

(49)   a.   *Peter   hat   es   damit   nicht geöffnet*
              Peter   has   it   therewith   not   opened

        b.   *Da   hat   Peter   es* [t *mit*]   *nicht geöffnet*
              there has   Peter   it   with   not   opened

(50)   a.   *Wir   haben   dafür   Geld   gesammelt*
              we   have   therefor   money   collected

b. *Da   haben wir [t für] Geld   gesammelt
there have we   for   money collected

(49) and (50) are to be compared with (45) and (46). The a-examples of (49)–(50) show that the pertinent PPs do not have to be adjacent to the main verb. Yet, there is only one position for a remnant of a PP of the relevant type: a position immediately to the left of the main verb.

Before we try to come to grips with (44) in terms of this condition on preposition stranding, we would like to make some remarks about it. First of all, we repeat that our formulation of the condition is nothing but an approximation couched in observational terms and so is far from being explanatory. Furthermore, even this approximation is not fully correct because it is known that Small Clause predicates, among which directional phrases, preferably occur between a stranded preposition and the verb, although things become more complicated if PP complements of adjectives are considered.[4] Even so, we prefer to stick to our first approximation of the condition, since Small Clause predicates will not play a role in the following discussion.

Now, if we stick to the original (and not fully correct) approximation of the condition to the effect that stranded prepositions must immediately precede the verb, it is possible to give an alternative explanation for the grammaticality of (44), which we repeat here in a slightly more explicit version:

(51)   [t_k gerechnet]$_j$ hatte Peter da$_i$ nicht [t_i mit]$_k$ vp$_j$
          counted   had Peter there not   with

In (51)/(44) mit, the stranded preposition, immediately precedes the trace of the topicalized VP-remnant. The VP-remnant contains a trace and a lexical verb. Therefore, under reconstruction mit will precede t_k gerechnet. Suppose now that adjunction traces do not count for phonological visibility. It will then follow that under reconstruction mit in (51)/(44) will immediately precede the main verb gerechnet, which may explain the grammaticality of (51)/(44).

To sum up the preceding discussion: we have suggested two alternative solutions for the problem posed by the grammaticality of (51)/(44).

(52) a.   Government by a higher verb obviates the restrictions upon extraction out of an adjoined position.
      b.   The requirement to the effect that a stranded preposition be adjacent to the verb also holds under reconstruction —

modulo certain provisos — so that the restrictions upon extraction out of an adjoined position are obviated.

One may wonder whether a choice can be made between the two proposals. In fact we do have evidence favoring (52)b.

Consider the following sentence:

(53)   *Er hat noch nicht [das Vorwort davon   gelesen]*
         he has yet   not the preface thereof read

The PP *davon* can adjoin to higher positions in the sentence:

(54) a.   *Er hat noch nicht [davon$_i$ das Vorwort t$_i$ gelesen]*
      b.   *Er hat davon$_i$ noch nicht [das Vorwort t$_i$ gelesen]*

Both sentences are grammatical although (54)b. is definitely preferred over (54)a. Stranding in the pertinent adjunction positions is ungrammatical:

(55) a.   **Da$_j$ hat er noch nicht [[t$_j$ von]$_i$ das Vorwort t$_i$ gelesen]*
            there has he not yet   of   the preface   read
      b.   **Da$_j$ hat er [t$_j$ von]$_i$ noch nicht [das Vorwort t$_i$ gelesen]*

The crucial example here is (55)a. Its ungrammaticality is not predicted by (52)a. but follows from the adjacency constraint on preposition stranding. The latter constraint predicts that stranded *von* must be adjacent to *gelesen* if we want to get a grammatical result — whether the direct object has been taken out of its VP or not. This prediction is correct:

(56) a.   *Er hat da$_i$ noch nicht das Vorwort [t$_i$ von] gelesen*
            he has there yet not   the preface of read
      b.   *Er hat da$_i$ das Vorwort noch nicht [t$_i$ von] gelesen*

(Similarly for topicalization of *da*.)

Now, note that the adjacency requirement as implemented by (52)b. makes a strong claim for complex structures such as those in (53)–(56). It is predicted that VP-remnant topicalization cum preposition stranding will be possible only if the VP has been emptied of all non-verbal material. In so far as we can see, the facts confirm this predication:

(57)   *[t$_i$ t$_j$ gelesen]$_m$ hat er da$_k$ das Vorwort$_i$ noch nicht*
          read   has he there the preface yet   not
        [t$_k$ von]$_j$ vp$_m$
          of

(58)   **[Das Vorwort t$_i$ gelesen]$_k$ hat er da$_j$ noch nicht [t$_j$ von]$_i$ vp$_k$*
(59)   *[Das Vorwort t$_i$ gelesen]$_j$ hat er davon$_i$ noch nicht vp$_j$*

Although (57)–(59) are harder to judge than simple cases like (51), because of the complex dependencies that play a role here, intuitions about differences in grammaticality among (57)–(59) are clear: (58) is out: (57) — despite its complexity — is in; and (59) is a simple case of VP-remnant topicalization. The difference between (57) and (58) is predicted by (52)b.: if adjunction traces do not count for the adjacency requirement, *von* will be adjacent to the main verb in (57) after reconstruction. This is not the case in (58). The pair of (58)–(59) shows that preposition stranding is the offending element in (58).

This having been said, we hasten to add that (52)b. can only be the beginning of a solution for the problem posed by sentences such as (51)/(44) or (57). First of all, the adjacency requirement alluded to by (52)b. seems to have the properties of an ordinary government requirement. However, this might imply that a PP headed by a stranded preposition must be adjoined to its own VP, after which the original VP is topicalized. At this moment we do not find this consequence very appealing. Furthermore, the exact properties of the adjacency requirement are not clear to us yet, as we mentioned above. And finally, there is the nagging question of why PPs and NPs demonstrate differential behavior under adjunction. Therefore, we have to leave the preposition stranding structures for further research.

To sum up: we started out with the presentation of an empirical problem with our theory of VP-remnant topicalization in Webelhuth/Den Besten (1989): this theory could not explain why a VP-remnant cannot contain a stranded preposition/postposition. In the current paper we investigated the conditions under which preposition stranding is possible in the larger setting of three additional constructions: *was-für*-split, DP-split and the topicalization of clauses with a gap in them. We found that a trace which does not occur in an argument position has to be directly bound at S-structure, whereas argument traces can be bound under reconstruction. Thus, the proper formulation of the reconstruction mechanism solves the problem that we set out to attack. Since the crucial difference seems to be the arguments vs. everything else it is tempting to relate reconstruction to the θ-criterion in some fashion, e.g. by making the θ-criterion the trigger of reconstruction. Since a number of other considerations enter into a proper theory of reconstruction — among which a new type of problem concerning VP-remnant topicalization cum preposition stranding which we can hardly say we have fully solved — , we have not attempted to give a formal characterization of this process here.

Notes

1. We have not been able to evaluate Van Riemsdijk (1989) for the purpose of the present paper anymore.

2. Our argument will in the end actually not be dependent on whether the pronoun was moved to the specifier position or not, as long as it *does* occupy the specifier position at some point of the derivation. Our theory is compatible with a base-generation analysis, although we are not convinced by the arguments in Bennis (1986) that this analysis *has* to be right.

3. There is some uncertainty about the ungrammaticality of (27). This sentence is certainly better that (26) and (28). However, the absolute grammaticality judgement is unclear. We treat it as ungrammatical here, believing that its relatively good status is due to an analogical interpretation with gerundive nominals like *das Bücherlesen* (the reading of books).

4. Compare the pertinent remarks in Koster (1987).

References

Abney, S. 1987. "The English Noun Phrase in its Sentential Aspect." Diss., Massachusetts Institute of Technology.

Benincà, P., (ed.) 1989. "Proceedings of the workshop on Dialectology and Linguistic Theory, GLOW Conference, Venice, March 1987,"

Bennis, H. 1986. *Gaps and Dummies*. Dordrecht: Foris.

Den Besten, H. 1985. "The Ergative Hypothesis and Free Word Order in Dutch and German." In: Toman (ed.)

Chomsky, N. 1986. *Barriers*. Cambridge, Mass.: MIT Press.

Koster, J. 1987. *Domains and Dynasties. The Radical Autonomy of Syntax*. Dordrecht: Foris.

Van Riemsdijk, H. 1989. "Movement and Regeneration." In: Benincà (ed.)

Toman, J. 1985. *Studies in German Grammar*. Dordrecht: Foris.

Webelhuth, G. (to app.). "A Universal Theory of Scrambling." In: *Proceedings of the Tenth Conference on Scandinavian Linguistics*.

———. and H. den Besten 1989. "Adjunction and Remnant Topicalization in the Germanic SOV-Languages." Paper presented at the GLOW-Conference, Venice, March 30-April 2, 1987.

Topicalization and other Puzzles of German Syntax[1]

Hubert Haider
University of Stuttgart

1. Introduction

The two main issues dealt with in this paper are i) arguments for a *representational* concept of syntactic representations instead of a derivational one, and ii) arguments in favor of an *inclusive* verbal projection for German, i.e., a VP that contains the subject. The data on which the arguments are based is a common construction of German, the topicalization of a verbal projection:

(1) $[_{CP}$ [*Einen   Blinden   geführt*]$_i$ $[_{C'}$ *hat*$_j$ $[_{X\text{-max}}$ *ein*
         a   blind one guided   has   a
         Einäugiger e_i e_j]]]
         one-eyed
         'A one-eyed has guided a blind one'

According to a standard derivational analysis (cf. den Besten 1987), (1) is the product of two instances of movement: the finite Verb moves to the C-position, and a phrase moves to the SPEC-C-position. SPEC-C can host *only one phrase*, and it must be a *maximal projection* (cf. Chomsky 1986). Under a representational analysis, the verbal projection would be generated in SPEC-C and coindexed with an empty category in the functional base position. It will turn out that the latter approach is empirically superior to the former.

As to the status of V^{max}, an SOV language like German or Dutch is in principle open for one of two types of verbal projections. Either the subject is external to VP, like in English (exclusive VP) or the subject is part of the VP (inclusive VP). There are independent arguments (cf. Haider 1988,

1989a) that the VP in Dutch is *exclusive* whereas it is *inclusive* in German. The analysis of topicalization will support this claim. Upon first sight, however, it seems to provide an argument for an exclusive VP:

(2)   *[*Ein Einäugiger geführt*] *hat dort einen Blinden*
         a   one-eyed   guided   has there a   blind one
         'a one-eyed has guided a blind one there'

It is tempting to try to account for the difference between (1) and (2) in terms of the constituent structure of VP. In (1) a VP seems to be topicalized, while in (2) the subject together with the verb appears in front, with the object left behind. Since the subject does not form a constituent with the verb that excludes the object, (2) is illformed, because fronting of the subject and the verb would encompass the object too.

This account is too simple, however, as the examples in (3) reveal.

(3)   a.   [*Ein Außenseiter gewonnen*] *hat hier noch nie*
       b.   [*Ein Außenseiter gewonnen*] *hat es hier noch nie* (es = z.B. das Derby)
       c.   [*Ein Außenseiter gewonnen*] *scheint hier noch nie zu haben*
       d.   [*Ein Außenseiter gewonnen zu haben*] *scheint hier noch nie*

In each sentence a non-ergative subject is part of the verbal projection. In (3b) we find in addition an object left behind, and in (3c,d) the subject is part of a verbal projection that contains even a raising verb. The most exotic kind of evidence comes from split NPs, as illustrated in (4).

(4)   a.   [*Briefe geschrieben*] *hat sie mir bis jetzt* <u>*nur*</u> <u>*drei*</u> <u>*traurige*</u>
       b.   [*Außenseiter gewonnen*] *hat es bis jetzt* <u>*nur*</u> <u>*ein*</u> <u>*einziger*</u>

What we find in the initial position is the verb together with the head of an NP, with the rest of the NP at the end of the sentence. It will turn out that there is no movement process that could strip an NP of its head and move it to the front, together with the verb. In the following section I will present evidence for the claim that in (4) the topicalized verbal projection is base generated in its topic position.

2. Some empirical issues

The observations discussed in this section are organized under a particular perspective. I choose constructions for which the topicalized V-projection displays properties which do not obtain to its base position. Since these properties would be conserved under movement, however, they should be found in the base position, too. This will be taken as evidence for an analysis which assumes the topicalized projection to be base-generated in SPEC-C (see section 4).

2.1 *Extraposition*

An extraposed clause is usually taken to be adjoined either to VP or S, depending on its argument status (cf. Reinhart, 1983). As shown in (5a,c) and (6a) an extraposed clause may be adjoined to the topicalized V-projection.

(5)   a.   [*Fragen, ob wir einverstanden sind*] *wird er wohl müssen*

     b.   ** daß er wohl fragen ob wir einverstanden sind müssen wird*

     c.   [*Schreiben, daß er nicht kommen darf*] *hat er nicht mehr können*

     d.   ** daß er nicht mehr hat schreiben, daß er nicht kommen darf können*

     e.   *daß er nicht mehr hat schreiben können, daß er nicht kommen darf*

(6)   a.   [*Hunde füttern, die Hunger haben*] *würde wohl jeder*

     b.   ** daß wohl jeder* [*Hunde füttern, die Hunger haben*] *würde*

     c.   *daß wohl jeder* [*Hunde, die Hunger haben*] *füttern würde*

     d.   *daß wohl jeder Hunde füttern würde, die Hunger haben*

Since the extraposed variant with extraposition cannot occur in the base position (cf. 5b,d; 6b), extraposition must take place in the topicalized position, i.e., after topicalization. In this case, however, it cannot be maintained anymore that there are different positions for extraposed relative clauses in contrast with extraposed argument clauses. Both are adjoined to the same V-projection (cf. 5a,c and 6a). There is still one more problematic consequence for a derivational analysis. In a finite clause, the V-projection to which the extraposed clause is adjoined contains the *finite* Verb (cf. 6d). Hence we would expect that a clause which is extraposed out of a topicalized V-projection is adjoined to the VP of the *matrix* clause. Thus we would get (7) instead of (5a).

(7)   *Fragen wird er wohl müssen, ob wir einverstanden sind*

(7) could be generated also if extraposition is applied before topicalization.

Since we do not want to have ordered rules, this is what we would like to find. Since (5a,c) and (6) exist nevertheless, they must be derivable. Of course, one could assume that the topicalized V-projection originally contained the finite verb, which afterwards moved to the C-position, leaving a trace behind:

(8)   *[gesungen e$_i$] hat$_i$ er*

Unfortunately, a derivation of the type (8) must not be permitted. If it were possible, we would get sentences like (9), which are ungrammatical.

(9)   a.   **[Ihr ein Buch e$_i$] gab$_i$ Hans*
       b.   **[Ein Buch auf e$_i$] schlug Hans*

Hence we end up with a construction for which there is no satisfactory account in terms of VP-movement, i.e., in derivation-by-movement terms.

2.2 *Definiteness effect*

It has been noted by Kratzer (1984) that V^n-topicalization is affected by the definiteness effect, if a subject, ergative or unergative, is part of the projection.

(10)   a.   *Ein Fehler unterlaufen ist ihr noch nie*
        b.   *?? Dieser Fehler unterlaufen ist ihr noch nie*
        c.   *daß ihr dieser Fehler noch nie unterlaufen ist*
        d.   *Ein Außenseiter gewonnen hat hier noch nie*
        e.   *?? Der Außenseiter gewonnen hat hier noch nie*
        f.   *daß hier noch nie der Außenseiter gewonnen hat*

(11)   a.   *There arrived a man from Rio*
        b.   *?? There arrived the man from Rio*
        c.   *Es kam Herbert von Karajan*
        d.   *Es gewann die Mannschaft aus Schweden*

(11c,d) exemplify that in German there is no definiteness comparable to the one in English or Dutch in existential or presentative clauses. Again, if it is just a VP that is moved to the front, it is unclear why this VP should gain new properties.

2.3. Subjects within the topicalized projection

Subjects may appear in the topicalized V-projection precisely under two conditions, which have to be captured by the derivational account. First, the subject must be non-referential (definiteness effect). Secondly, a nonergative subject may appear in the fronted V-projection provided that there is at most one argument left behind which occurs immediately after the finite verb (cf. 12b vs. 12c). It is this property alone, which discriminates ergative and unergative subjects (cf. 12b vs. 13a).

(12)   a.   *Ein Außenseiter gewonnen hat da noch nie*
         b.   **Ein Außenseiter gewonnen hat da noch nie das Derby*
         c.   *Ein Außenseiter gewonnen hat <u>das</u> da noch nie*

         d.   *Linguisten gespeist haben dort noch nie*
         e.   **Linguisten gespeist haben dort noch nie Langusten*
         f.   *Linguisten gespeist haben <u>das</u> dort noch nie*

         g.   *Kinder gespielt haben hier noch nie*
         h.   **Kinder gespielt haben hier noch nie Tempelhüpfen*
         i.   *Kinder gespielt haben <u>das</u> hier noch nie*

(13)   a.   *Ein Fehler unterlaufen ist auch schon mal diesem Professor*
         b.   *Ein Fehler unterlaufen ist <u>ihm</u> auch schon mal*

         c.   *Ein Tiger entwichen ist doch erst kürzlich diesem Wanderzirkus*
         d.   *Ein Tiger entwichen ist <u>ihm</u> doch erst kürzlich*

In (12) I chose three transitive verbs with an optional direct object. If the subject is part of the topicalized constituent, the object cannot appear in its base position after the adverbials (cf. 12b,e,h). Ergative subjects behave differently (cf. 13a,c). Ergative subjects pattern in this construction like passive subjects, as expected.

(14)   a.   *Ein Job angeboten wurde damals sofort jedem Tagträumer*
         b.   *Ein Job angeboten wurde ihm damals sofort*

It will be made clear in the following section that the differences noted above cannot be captured adequately under a derivational approach employing scrambling.

2.4 *Inconsistent structure requirements*

If one takes the premisses seriously that only maximal projections appear in the SPEC-C position and that only one projection can be moved to this position, topicalization structures reflect inconsistent structure assignment requirements.

(15) a. *daß er ihren Argumenten folgen können wird*
      b. *Ihren Argumenten folgen wird er doch wohl können*
      c. *folgen können wird er ihren Argumenten doch wohl*

According to (15b) we would like to project structure (16a) on (15a), but on the example (15c) we would like to choose (16b).

(16) a. [[*seinen Argumenten folgen*] *können*]
      b. [*seinen Argumenten* [*folgen können*]]

One might try to stick to (16a) and derive (15c) by stringvacuous Chomsky-adjunction of the object to its mother VP and move the emptied VP. This move would still leave it mysterious, however, how (17a) and (17b) could be tackled.

(17) a. [*Ein Außenseiter gewinnen*] *hätte hier wohl kaum können*
      b. [*gewinnen können*] *hätte ein Außenseiter hier wohl kaum*

(17a) requires a structure in which the modal takes an S-complement, which is fronted. In order to derive (17b), the subject must be Chomsky-adjoined again to its mother constituent, the S, such that the emptied constituent contains only the modal. This cannot be the case, however, since S would contain also the adverbials and the finite verb, too. It is shown above that this would give rise to a construction like (9) and therefore has to be abandoned. This leaves (17) without a derivational source.

2.5 *Topicalization of non-constituents*

As pointed out in section 1, split NPs pose a serious problem for a derivational analysis, if they appear within a verbal projection. For convenience, the examples (4) are repeated under (18).

(18) a. [*Briefe geschrieben*] *hat sie mir bis jetzt nur drei traurige*
      b. [*Außenseiter gewonnen*] *hat es bis jetzt nur ein einziger*

(18) is the VP-topicalization variant of (19).

(19) a. *Briefe hat sie mir bis jetzt nur drei traurige geschrieben*
 b. *Außenseiter hat es bis jetzt nur ein einziger gewonnen*

The characteristics of constructions of the type (19) are the following. The element in SPEC-C must be the head of the split NP (cf. 20a). The NP must be indefinite (cf. 20b). The NP contains a gap (cf. 20c). The relation between the two parts obeys movement constraints (cf. 21).[2]

(20) a. ** Nur drei traurige hat sie mir bis jetzt Briefe geschrieben*
 b. ** Briefe hat sie mir bis jetzt nur die drei traurigen geschrieben*
 c. ** Briefe hat sie mir bis jetzt nur drei traurige Episteln geschrieben*

(21) a. *Bücher sagte man mir, habe er nur politische geschrieben*
 b. ** Bücher sagte man mir, wer nur politische geschrieben habe*
 c. ** Bücher nannte sie mir einen Mann, der nur politische geschrieben hat*

The fact that (19) does not permit a split variant in the base position, bars a movement account for (18).

(22) a. ** daß sie nur drei traurige bis jetzt Briefe geschrieben hat*
 b. ** daß es nur ein einziger bis jetzt Außenseiter gewonnen hat*

There is no V-projection consisting of the head of an NP and the verb.

2.6 Scope asymmetries[3]

(23) shows, that scope properties are subject to reconstruction.

(23) a. *daß Max jemandem kein Buch verkaufen darf*
 b. *Max darf$_i$ [jemanden kein Buch verkaufen e$_i$]*

Both in (23a) and in (23b) the negation may have scope over the modal. This can be accounted for by reconstruction: Since the trace of the modal is in the scope of the negation this carries over to the antecedent. That the middle field, i.e., the constituent in brackets in (23b) constrains the scope domain can be seen from (24):

(24) a. *daß jedem Lehrer ein Schüler gefallen möchte* (narrow, wide)
 b. *daß ein Schüler jedem Lehrer gefallen möchte* (narrow, wide)
 c. *[Jedem Schüler gefallen] möchte ein Lehrer* (wide)

To account for (24), we have to assume both that the middle filed restricts the scope domain (as in 23), to keep the existential quantifier in a narrow scope and we have to assume that the topicalized constituent does not reconstruct. Otherwise we would expect the same scope properties as in (24a,b). If (24c) is derived by movement we expect reconstruction, however.

2.7 *Independent evidence for base generated V-projections*

Left-dislocation provides evidence that there are base-generated V-projections in non-base positions on the one hand, and that there are differences between left-dislocation and topicalization on the other hand that provide insight into the nature of the dependency between the left peripheral position, be it SPEC-C or the LD-position, and its functionally equivalent clause internal position. Since the dependency is different, it is unlikely that one can be derived from the other, as suggested e.g. by Koster (1978). The following sample of contexts is sufficient to dismiss the claim that topicalization is derived from left-dislocation simply by replacing the pronoun in the SPEC-C Position by an empty operator.

(25) a. anaphor
            sich (*den) mag er am liebsten
            [$_{AP}$ *stolz auf sich*] *(das) war er schon immer*

      b. quantifier
            Jeder (*der) weiß das

      c. indefinite pronoun
            Jemand (*der) hat sich geirrt

      d. sentential adverb
            Vermutlich (*das) weiß er es

      e. predicatives[4]
            Stumm (*das) lächelt Mona Lisa

      f. NP-subconstituents
            Linguisten (*die) kenne ich nur kluge

      g. Extraposition out of a topicalized V-projection
            Rosen gezüchtet, (*das) hat er die prämiert wurden

      h. V-projection with subcategorized elements
            Gewartet (*das) hat er auf sie nicht

    i.   `Split NPs in V-projections
              Briefe geschrieben (*das) hat sie drei traurige
    j.   V-Projections that contain a non-ergative subject
              Ein Außenseiter gewonnen (*das) hat hier noch nie

These differences call for an explanation in terms of the syntactic relation that holds between the non-base position and the functional base position. For topicalization this relation is an antecedent-empty category relation, for LD, however, it is a relation between a phrase and a pronominal element it is coindexed with. Whatever account is given for this difference, this does not concern the fact that in LD-constructions we find verbal projections generated in non-base positions:

(26) a.   *[Ihr Blumen geschenkt] (das) hat er noch nie*
      b.   *[Ein Buch lesen] (das) würde er nie*
      c.   *Gelogen (das) hat er noch nie*
      d.   *Geregnet (das) hat es schon lange nicht mehr*

3. Scrambling — an inadequate solution

There are some recent attempts (cf. den Besten/Webelhut 1987) to revive Ross's idea how to handle free word order, namely by employing the concept of scrambling. Scrambling is interpreted as the result of free adjunction to VP, a concept introduced by Chomsky (1986) in the framework of "Barriers." According to a scramblingbased approach the topicalized V-projection in (27) is V^{max} in all cases:

(27) a.   *[e_i e_j geöffnet]*   *hat sie ihm$_i$ die Augen$_j$*
      b.   *[e_i die Augen geöffnet]*   *hat sie ihm$_i$*
      c.   *[ihm die Augen geöffnet]*   *hat sie*

In order to derive (27), the objects must be moved out of the VP. Adjunction of the objects to VP should leave a preposable empty VP. The result is (28) as a base structure for (27a).

(28) $[_{CP}$ C $[sie$ $[_{VP}$ ihm_i $[_{VP}$ *die Augen$_j$* $[_{VP}$ e_i e_j *geöffnet* $]]]$ *hat*$]]]$

It is easy to demonstrate that scrambling-by-adjunction is both too strong and too weak a concept. It is too strong because it overgenerates and it is too weak because there are topicalization structures which cannot be derived by means of scrambling. Let us start with the case of overgeneration:

A scrambling approach neither captures the definiteness effect (cf. 2.2) nor the subject-object dependency discussed in section 2.3. (29) shows that objects may appear in front of a definite subject. This means that the object is adjoined to S, which turns the basic S into a candidate for topicalization:

(29) a. *daß den Mann die Kinder nicht gestört haben*
      b. **[Die Kinder gestört] haben den Mann nicht*

The fact, that a subject may appear in the topicalized projection only if the remaining object — in case there is one — appears in front of the middle field does not follow from the way how scrambling works. For convenience, I repeat an example illustrating the relevant contrast:

(30) a. *Ein Außenseiter gewonnen hat dieses Jahr noch nie*
      b. **Ein Außenseiter gewonnen hat dieses Jahr noch nie das Derby*
      c. *Ein Außenseiter gewonnen hat es dieses Jahr noch nie*

For (30b) there exists a perfectly well-formed scrambled basevariant as a source for topicalization:

(31) a. *daß ein Außenseiter dieses Jahr noch nie das Derby gewonnen hat*
      b. *daß das Derby ein Außenseiter dieses Jahr noch nie gewonnen hat*
      c. *daß dieses Jahr noch nie das Derby ein Außenseiter gewonnen hat*

First the object is adjoined to S, which yields (31b). Then the adverbials are adjoined, which yields (31c). Now the emptied S-constituent is topicalized, which yields the ungrammatical (30b).

Scrambling is to weak for the derivation of the split-NP cases. For (32) there is no source for topicalization because splitting an NP by scrambling is ungrammatical, cf. (19a), (18a) and (22a), repeated under (32a), (32b) and (32c) respectively.

(32) a. *Briefe hat sie mir bis jetzt nur drei traurige geschrieben*
      b. *[Briefe geschrieben] hat sie mir bis jetzt nur drei traurige*
      c. **daß sie nur drei traurige bis jetzt Briefe geschrieben hat*

(32c) shows that the NP cannot be split within the middle field. A sentence like (33) would require a base structure like (32c).

(33)   *[Briefe geschrieben] hat sie mir nur drei traurige bis jetzt*

Scrambling is too weak, moreover, because it is completely unclear under that hypothesis why the topicalized V-Projection is an extraposition site (cf. sect. 2.1). It is too weak also because it overgenerates, if V-projections are topicalized that contain the finite verb.[5]

(34)   *[*Ihr ein Buch* e$_i$] *schenkte$_i$ er*

The ungrammaticality of (34) cannot be attributed to the fact that the projection contains the trace of the *finite* verb, because exactly this trace occurs in the case of what would be an S-topicalization:

(35)   [*Ein Außenseiter gewonnen* e$_i$] *hat$_i$ hier noch nie*

Since the topicalized constituent contains the subject, it must be topicalization of S. S, however, is IP and hence contains the finite verb. Scrambling is too strong again, because it rules out perfectly well-formed structures in the case of coordination:

(36)   *weil es$_i$ entweder* [*niemand* e$_i$ *bemerkte*] *oder* [*Maria alle bestochen hat*]

Under a scrambling analysis (36) violates the Across-the-board constraint, which forbids to conjoin a phrase containing a gap with another phrase that does not contain a corresponding gap. Scrambling leaves a gap in the base position. Finally it should be noted that a scrambling approach towards topicalization frequently involves *vacuous movement*. In (37) the object is string-vacuously adjoined to VP in order to turn the topicalized element into a VP. Chomsky (1986) provided arguments against vacuous movement, which can be strenghtened (cf. Haider 1989b) to a complete ban.

(37)   [e$_i$ *geholfen*]$_j$ *hat* [*sie* [$_{VP}$ *ihr$_i$* [$_{VP}$ e]$_j$

In the following section I will try to show that all these problems do not arise if we give up the idea that topicalization is the result of a movement process.

4. Towards a representational account of topicalization

Let us suppose that the V-projection in the SPEC-C position is base-generated in this very position just like the V-projection is base-generated in LD-constructions. These two constructions differ with respect to the relation they enter with the functional base position. For topicalization it is an antecedent — gap relation, for LD it is an antecedent — pronominal relation. The pronominal in (26) acts as a predicate pronominal whose interpretation is determined by the predicate it is coindexed with. If there is no predicate, the pronominal is interpreted deictically (cf. 26 and 38).

(38) a. *Das hat er noch nie*
      b. *Das würde er nie*
      c. *Das hat er noch nie*
      d. *Das hat es schon lange nicht mehr*

Semantically, the verbal projection in an LD-construction is interpreted as an autonomous predicate, whose interpretation determines the interpretation of the pronominal it is coindexed with. The analogous analysis for topicalization entails that the topicalized V-projection is interpreted as an autonomous predicate, too, i.e., as a maximal projection of V. In LF this V-projection will receive a semantic interpretation in its SPEC-C position. Since the topicalized phrase enters into an antecedent — gap relation by virtue of its occupying the SPEC-C position, the predicate in SPEC-C position will be related to the matrix predicate as if the topicalized predicate were a single verb:

(39) V_i^n *hat*$_j$ *er nicht* $[_{VC}[\ e_i\ ]\ e_j\ ]]$

The only well-formedness requirements for the verbal projection in (39) are a syntactic one and a functional-semantic one. It must be a *maximal* projection and it must *provide a θ-role* for the subject in the middle field. Hence any of the following instances of V^n will give a grammatical sentence in the context of (39):

(40) a. *getanzt*
      b. *mir geholfen*
      c. *mich absichtlich geohrfeigt*
      d. *ihr heimlich einen Kuß gegeben*
      e. *ihr einen Kuß auf die Wange gedrückt, daß es schnalzte*

From a semantic point of view, these are intransitive predicates. Some are basically intransitive (40a), some are intransitive due to saturation of all argument slots except one. Hence they fulfill the functional requirement of the gap the predicate in (39) is coindexed with. It is the gap of an intransitive verb, a gap that would arise if we inserted a verb like (40a) and moved it to the SPEC-C position. We could not insert the other predicates, however, since it is the slot of a V^0-category in the verbal cluster. The verbal cluster does not contain phrases. Hence these phrases do not have a derivational source. Let us investigate now how this hypothesis allows to handle the recalcitrant problems discussed in section 2 and 3.

4.1 *Extraposition*

In German, and presumably in all other languages as well, V^{max} is the adjunction site for extraposition, both for clausal arguments and non-arguments. Claims that different binding properties require different adjunction sites (cf. Reinhart 1983) are ill-founded. It is not the adjunction position that matters but the argument status. Principle C violations do not arise, despite of a c-commanding, preceding, coindexed NP, if the noun is contained in a non-argument clause. This is easy to see in German, where adverbials and likewise adverbial clauses appear between an object and the verb, i.e., VP-internal:

(41) a. *Der Vorsitzende hat ihr$_i$ [obwohl Marie$_i$ heftig protestierte] das Wort entzogen*

    b. *daß er$_i$ [als man Hans$_i$ davon berichtete] kollabierte, wundert mich nicht*

    c. *Man hat ihm$_i$ mehr Geld, als Hans$_i$ sich erwartet hatte, angeboten*

    d. *Man hat ihr$_i$ das Haus, das Maria$_i$ bekanntlich geerbt hat, streitig gemacht*

Non-argument clauses are opaque for principle C. Viewed from this perspective, it is not surprising that relative clauses are adjoined to the same V-projection in the topicalized position as object clauses; they are adjoined to the same projection in the base position as well. The V-projection in SPEC-C position is a maximal V-projection and hence an adjunction site for extraposition.

4.2 *Definiteness Effect*

A definiteness is found whenever a subject does not appear in its canonical position. This is easy to check for English. In a there-construction, the thematic subject appears VP-internally, in a noncanonical subject-position. In German, the canonical subject position is in the middle field and not in a V-Projection in SPEC-C. Hence the topicalized V-projection displays a definiteness effect for the subject. The fact that there is no definiteness effect in the middle field simply shows that any position in the middle field qualifies as canonical position for a subject. This is to be expected if German has an inclusive VP.

4.3 *Subjects within the topicalized VP*

If the topicalized VP contains a subject, it must be nonreferential, i.e, indefinite and, if it is non-ergative, its co-argument must not occur inside the middle-field. This follows from a closure property induced by non-ergative subjects.

(42)   The verbal projection that contains the non-ergative subject is closed for the projection principle

What (42) amounts to is that a θ-role cannot be passed on to an argument outside a VP that contains a non-ergative subject. Hence in the example (43) the object remains θ-less and violates the θ-criterion.

(43)   * *Ein Außenseiter gewonnen hat da noch nie das Derby* (cf. 12b)

What is the difference between (43) and (44) that allows to maintain (42), although the object is not in the same V-projection?

(44)   *Ein Außenseiter gewonnen hat das da noch nie* (cf. 12c)

There is one possibility, how the object might receive a θ-role, namely by means of a chain:

(45)   [*Ein Außenseiter* e_i *gewonnen*] *hat das$_i$ da noch nie*

What we have to explain now is why a chain is possible in (45) but not in (43). The answer is simple. In (44) the pronoun occupies the so-called Wackernagel-position, a position that immediately follows C. This is an adjunction position of the middle field. It is easy to show, that the c-command requirement for the antecedent of the gap can only be met in that position and not in the base position, which will explain the difference between (43) and (44). All we have to do is to adapt the definition of dominance to adjunction structures. According to Chomsky (1986), adjunction produces *segments* of categories.

(46) $[_{XP} Y [_{XP} Z]]$ (adjunction of Y to XP)

In (46), XP consists of two segments. Given that a category C *includes* an element E, if every segment of C dominates E, Z is included by XP, but Y is not. Now it is easy to adjust dominance to adjunction:

(47) a. A category C *c-dominates* X, iff C includes X
      b. A c-commands B iff
          a. A does not c-dominate B
          and
          b. every maximal projection that c-dominates A c-dominates B

(47) is a conservative extension of the original definitions, since in non-adjunction structures inclusion coincides with domination.

The difference between (43) and (44) follows immediately from (47): It is only in the Wackernagel-position, not in the base position, that an object can c-command an empty category in SPEC-C, because for the element in that position CP is the only maximal projection that includes it and CP dominates the gap. The difference between this account and the scrambling account is clear. Under the latter hypothesis, both the adverbial and the object would be in adjoined position and hence the object should be able to c-command, which is obviously not the case, as (48) illustrates:[6]

(48)   *Ein Außenseiter gewonnen hat da noch nie das Derby* (cf. 12b)

4.4 Inconsistent structure assignments

The problem of inconsistent structure requirements arises only under the movement analysis. If a V-projection is base-generated in SPEC-C, it can be any V-projection, provided it meets the *functional* requirements imposed on it by the kind of arguments that appear in the middle field.

(49) a. *Ihren Argumenten folgen wird er doch wohl können* (cf. 15b)
      b. *Folgen können wird er ihren Argumenten doch wohl* (cf. 15c)

In (49a) the topicalized V-projection can be replaced by any intransitive predicate, i.e., anything that is functionally equivalent, e.g. by the intransitive variant of *folgen*, as in (50a). In (49b) the functional properties are not affected by the modal, hence its omission would lead to (50b).

(50) a. *Folgen wird er doch wohl können*
      b. *Folgen wird er ihren Argumenten doch wohl*

Since this account is not bound to the assumption that the topicalized V-projection must correspond to an isomorpic structure in the base position before movement, the structural paradox cannot arise.

4.5 Topicalization of non-constituents

The definiteness affect observed with this construction indicates that the head noun in the V-projection is interpreted as a predicate. Evidence to this end comes from (51).

(51) a. [*Briefe geschrieben*] *hat sie nie <u>welche</u>*
      b. **daß sie nie welche Briefe geschrieben hat*
      c. *daß sie nie welche geschrieben hat*

The indefinite pronoun *welche* represents an NP. Hence it will receive the θ-role from the verb. But then no θ-role is left for the noun *Briefe* in (51a), which cannot be part of the object-NP, as (51b) shows. If it does not receive a θ-role it cannot be an argument but only a predicate. This seems to match the interpretation of (51a). *Briefe* specifies the denotation of the pronoun just like in (52).

(52)   *Das sind Briefe*

It seems that the role of *Briefe* in (51a) is the same as in (53).

(53)   [*Briefe geschrieben*] *hat sie mir bis jetzt <u>nur drei traurige</u>*

The noun restricts the denotation of the element the θ-role is assigned to but it does not bear it. Thus it does not close the V-projection even if it is in relation with a non-ergative subject, as in (54). If the head of the subject NP in the V-projection would close it, the remnant of the NP could not get its θ-role.[7]

(54)   [*Außenseiter gewonnen*] *hat es bis jetzt <u>nur ein einziger</u>*

The fact that the noun serves as a predicate correlates with the fact that it cannot appear without a concomitant NP that it agrees with. It is licensed only under predication (cf. 55).

(55) a. *[*Außenseiter gewonnen*] *hat es bis jetzt nicht*[8]
      b. *[*Außenseiter gewonnen*] <u>*das*</u> *hat es bis jetzt nur ein einziger*

In (55a) there is no phrase the noun is coindexed with, and in (55b) the phrase it should be coindexed with is not accessible.

4.6 *Scope asymmetries*

If the topicalized VP is base-generated in SPEC-C the scope properties become transparent. We can explain why (56c) does not have the same scope properties as (56a,b).

(56) a. *daß Max jemandem kein Buch verkaufen darf* (NEG: narrow or wide)

   b. *Max darf jemandem kein Buch verkaufen* (NEG: narrow or wide)

   c. *Jemandem kein Buch verkaufen darf Max* (NEG: narrow)

Scope is constrained by the VP. In (56a) and (56b) the negation and the modal share the same VP. In (56c) the negation is contained in a VP different from the VP that contains the modal. Hence the negation does not have scope over the modal outside its V-projection.

4.7. *Crossing constraint*

The scrambling analysis suffers from an explanatory deficiency. It is unclear why there shows up a crossing effect in some cases (cf. 58) and not in others (cf. 57).

(57) a. $[e_i \ e_j \ geöffnet]_k$ *hat sie ihm$_i$ die Augen$_j$ e$_k$*

   b. *[Ein Außenseiter gewonnen e$_i$] hat$_i$ hier noch nie*

(58) a. **[Ihr ein Buch e$_i$] schenkte$_i$ er*

   b. **[e$_i$ mit] haben sie da$_i$ nicht gerechnet*

   c. *Da$_i$ haben sie nicht [e$_i$ mit] gerechnet*

Under the base generation hypothesis (58a,b) but not (57a,b) turn out to be violations of a crossing constraint:

(60) a. *[geöffnet]$_k$ hat$_i$ sie ihm die Augen* e$_k$ e$_i$ (cf. (57a)

   b. *[Ein Außenseiter gewonnen]$_j$ hat$_i$ hier noch nie* e$_j$ e$_i$ (cf.57b)

   c. *[Ihr ein Buch e$_i$]$_j$ schenkte$_i$ er* e$_i$ e$_j$

   d. *[e$_i$ mit]$_j$ haben sie da$_i$ e$_j$ nicht gerechnet*

In (60c,d), but not in (60a,b) we observe a particular type of crossing dependences, which are ruled out on independent grounds (cf. Pesetzky 1982). In (60a,b) the two dependencies are different in type, a head-movement dependency and a phrase movement dependency. Hence crossing is irrelevant. In (60c,d), however, we find crossing dependencies of the same type, which is ruled out.

5. Some requirements for and consequences of a representational account

The claim that V-Projections are base-generated in SPEC-C requires some clarifictions as to how case- and θ-assignment applies. The fact that there are VP internal nominatives under any analysis in a Government & Binding framework (cf. den Besten 1985) irrespective of the particular assumptions about the canonical position of the subject should suffice to indicate that VP-internal NPs are acessible for nominative assignment for reasons independent from our present concern. Therefore I will not elaborate on that matter.

What is unique for the present claim, however, is that a clause may have two independent V-projections and that the verb in one projection may assign θ-roles to arguments in the other projection. The crucial concept for handling this situation is the syntactic role of auxiliaries. In Haider/Rindler-Schjevre (1987) and in Haider (1988), I tried to demonstrate that the finite verb is the syntactic main verb of the clause. Auxiliaries can act syntactically as main verbs by virtue of the transfer of the argument structure from the verb they govern in the verbal complex to the auxiliary. This mechanism applies without further complications to the topicalized V-projection, since they are coindexed with a verbal empty category in the base position that is c-commanded by the auxiliary. Under this perspective there is no direct transfer of the θ-roles from the verb in the topicalized projection to the arguments in the middle field just like there is no direct assignment of θ-roles from the main verb to the arguments in the middle field. In both cases it is the auxiliary which mediates the θ-role assignment and case assignment.

One of the consequences of the representational account is that German has an inclusive VP, i.e., a V-projection that contains the subject. Since it is beyond dispute that Dutch does not have an inclusive VP, we predict specific differences for the topicalization structures. Topicalized V-projections that contain a non-ergative subjects cannot occur in Dutch since non-ergative subjects cannot occur in V-Projections in Dutch. The following examples confirm this claim:

(61) a. *Een buitenstaander gewonnen heeft daar nog nooit* (cf.12a)
     b. *Linguisten gegeten hebben daar nog nooit* (cf.12b)
     c. *Kinderen gespeeld hebben hier nog nooit* (cf. 12c)

This difference falls in line with a lot of other systematic differences between subjects in German and in Dutch (cf. Haider 1988, 1989a), that receive an explanation in terms of the different status of V^{max} in the respective languages.

6. Conclusion

The aim of this paper is twofold. From the empirical point of view, it presents an analysis that covers the properties of topicalized V-projections. Topicalized V-projections are base-generated in SPEC-C. From the theoretical point of view, it is argued that the analysis of this constructions provides arguments for i) a representational view instead of a derivational one, and ii) an inclusive VP in German, i.e., a V^{max} that contains the subject, unlike the English or Dutch VP. A scrambling analysis is dismissed on empirical grounds.

Notes

1.   I am grateful to Klaus Netter for comments and criticism. It was his observation that pronouns in the Wackernagel-position behave differently.

2.   Henk van Riemsdijk discussed these constraints in his talk given at the Workshop on Dialectology in Venice, April 1, 1987. In V-projection structures of the type (18) the remnant of the NP tends to be clause final, i.e., immediately adjacent to the gap the V-projection in SPEC-C is coindexed with. This observation I owe to Gosse Bouma, personal communication.

3.   These data I owe to T. Höhle, who discussed them in a talk given at the GGS-workshop Konstanz, November 1986.

4.   Marga Reis, personal communication.

5.   This was noted by Jindrich Toman, in the discussion period.

6.   Günther Grewendorf, p.c., noted that (48) can be improved if the object precedes the adverbial and carries focus stress:

    (i) Ein Außenseiter gewonnen hat das DERBY hier noch nie

  The difference between i) and (48) follows immediately if it is recognized that the focus position for non-pronominal NPs coincides with the Wackernagel-position. Then the analysis given for (45) carries over to i) as well.

7. That the V-projection is not closed at all, neither for the θ-role of the subject nor for that of an object is illustrated by i).

(i) [*Außenseiter gewonnen*] *haben bis jetzt ein Derby nur wenige*

8. It is relevant here, that the NP is singular in number. So we know that *Außenseiter* is a noun and not an NP, since the NP requires an article. This is different for the plural. In i) *Außenseiter* is an NP without article, hence i) is wellformed.

(i) *Außenseiter gewonnen haben bis jetz noch nie*

Bibliography

den Besten, H. 1985. "Some remarks on the ergative hypothesis." In: W. Abraham (ed.) *Erklärende Syntax des Deutschen*. Tübingen: Narr.

———. 1987 "VP-Syntax." Paper presented at the annual meeting of the DGFS, Augsburg, March 1987.

———. & G. Webelhuth. 1987. "Remnant topicalization and the constituent structure of the VP in the Germanic SOV Languages." Paper given at the GLOW conference,Venice, March 30-April 2, 1987.

Chomsky, N. 1986. *Barriers*. Cambridge, Mass.: MIT-Press.

Haider, H. 1987. "Matching projections." Paper given at the GLOW conference, Venice, March 30-April 2, 1987.

———. 1989a. *Deutsche Syntax, generativ*. Tübingen: Narr.

———. 1989b. "θ-tracking systems — evidence from German." In: Muysken & Maracz (eds.).

———. & R. Rindler-Schjerve. 1987. "The parameter of auxiliary Selection: Italian-German Controls." *Linguistics* 25:1029-1055.

Koster, J. 1978. *Locality Principles in Syntax*. Dordrecht: Foris.

———. 1987. *Domains and Dynasties. The Radical Autonomy of Syntax*. Dordrecht: Foris.

Kratzer, A. 1984. "On deriving differences between German and English." Ms., Technische Universität Berlin.

Marácz, László K. and Pieter Muysken (eds.). 1989. *Configurationality. The Typology of Asymmetries*. Dordrecht: Foris.

Pesetzky, D. 1982. "Paths and Categories." Diss., Massachusetts Institute of Technology.

Reinhart, T. 1983. *Anaphora and Semantic Interpretation*. London: Croom Helm.

Scrambling as NP-Movement*

Gisbert Fanselow
University of Passau

0. Introduction and Survey

Within generative grammar, there are two main traditions concerning the status of free word and constituent order phenomena. On the one hand, it has been proposed that even free word order languages have a strictly ordered base structure, plus a rule of "scrambling" permuting the elements of a clause.[1] The other mainstream assumes that free order is a phenomenon already present at base structures. In the last decade, the issue has gained some theoretical interest. Theories such as Lexical Functional Grammar or Relational Grammar claim that the existence of free word order languages proves the impossibility of defining grammatical relations in terms of constituent structure and have developed approaches to natural language syntax quite different from traditional generative grammar. Within the Government and Binding model, several kinds of parameters have been proposed for handling free word order (cf., e.g. Hale 1983), which also bear far-reaching consequences on the nature of central principles of Universal Grammar like X-bar-Theory, the projection principle etc.

In this article, I shall concentrate on free constituent order phenomena, adding just a few remarks on free word order in section 4. I shall try to demonstrate that the scrambling approach to free constituent order is the correct one. Furthermore, scrambling will turn out to be an instance of the rule Move α whose behaviour is completely predicted by the *Barriers*-framework. The approach will yield a three-fold-parametrization of constituent order options in natural languages:

a)   Type 1: reordering by NP-movement (German, Turkish)
b)   Type 2: reordering by *wh*-movement (Hungarian, Japanese, Makua)
c)   Type 3: 'reordering' as binding of *pro* (Warlpiri, German)

1. The NP-movement type of scrambling

1.1 *A first subject-object asymmetry*

In a sense, the term "free word (constituent) order language" is mis-
leading since there are no languages in which word order is really arbitrary.[2] The central difference between "configurational" languages like
English or French and "non-configurational" ones like German, Japanese
or Warlpiri lies rather in the fact that, apparently, different principles govern the rules of serialization. Whereas word order is more or less exclusively determined by *grammatical* notions in English, serialization processes
seem to depend on pragmatic factors in non-configurational languages,
among them being distinctions concerning definiteness, theme-rheme,
topic-focus, etc. Let me illustrate this claim briefly. Consider first West
Greenlandic (1).[3]

(1)   a.   *piniartu-p puisi pisar-aa*
           hunter   seal   catch
      b.   *puisi piniartu-p pisar-aa*

West Greenlandic does not possess a system of determiners like the one we
are familiar with from standard European languages. In (1a), *puisi* (i.e., the
object) may be interpreted as being either definite or indefinite, but the
indefinite reading is not available for (1b). Word order thus appears to be
determined by pragmatic factors: a NP-object that is assigned an indefinite
interpretation may not precede the rest of the clause. More generally, one
might claim that definite NPs tend to precede indefinites in non-configurational languages.

Similar facts hold in Turkish, as can be seen from the contrast between
(2) and (3).[4]

(2)   a.   *Murat bir kitap ok-uyor*
           Murat a   book reads
      b.   *Murat kitab-ı   okuyor*
           Murat book-the reads

(3) a. *_bir kitap Murat okuyor_
     b.   _kitab-ı Murat okuyor_

Definite objects, but not indefinite ones, may be in first position in Turkish clauses, in accordance with the pragmatic regularity just mentioned.

In a broader sense, German syntax shows similar facts with respect to definiteness (cf. Lenerz 1977), but it also illustrates another interesting constraint on word order. Lenerz (1977) has observed that both objects and adverbials may not bear main stress if they are in first position, cf. the contrast in (4) where underline represents main stress.[5]

(4) a. _weil   im   Hilton der Präsident wohnt_
         because in-the Hilton the president resides
     b. *_weil im Hilton der Präsident wohnt_
     c. _weil   dem   Minister der   Präsident einen Brief_
         because the:DAT minister the:NOM president a:ACC letter
         gab
         gave
         'because the president gave a letter to the minister'
     d. *_weil dem Minister der Präsident einen Brief gab_

Following Abraham (1985a), we may equate bearing main stress with being in focus. Thus it can be observed that focus-NPs may not precede topic-NPs in German clauses. One might be tempted to conclude, then, that constituent order is free in languages such as German or Turkish from a grammatical point of view, the various serialization restrictions being determined by factors like definiteness or the topic-focus-distinction.

A major problem for this assumption, however, arises from the fact that a specific class of NPs may violate the pragmatic regularities just illustrated in free constituent order languages: subjects. In the West Greenlandic example (1a), e.g., _piniartu-p_, the subject, can be interpreted both with a definite and an indefinite reading, i.e., even if it occupies the first position in the clause. Likewise, in Turkish, the first NP of the sentence may be indefinite if it is a subject, cf. (5):

(5)   _bir adam sokağ-ın orta-sın-da taşı   oğlan-a at-tı_
         a   man road:GEN middle:LOC stone:ACC boy:DAT threw
         'a boy threw a stone at the boy from the middle of the road'

Furthermore, German subjects may be in focus irrespective of linearization:

(6)   a.   *weil <u>der Präsident</u> im Hilton wohnt*
      b.   *weil <u>der Präsident</u> dem Minister einen Brief gab*

Obviously there is no simple explanation for this exceptional status of subjects in theories which claim that base order is not influenced by grammatical facts. E.g., if there were no VP at base structure, there should be no reason for a special position subjects should have to occupy. Uszkoreit (1984) has proposed that both grammatical and pragmatic principles govern (German) word order. Obviously this is descriptively correct, but the grammatical factor must be stipulated in a completely ad hoc fashion contrary to the spirit of free base orders.

On the other hand, a configurational approach seems to work much better. West Greenlandic, Turkish and German are verb-final languages. A configurational framework will predict SOV-base-ordering and implies that *objects* but not *subjects* have undergone scrambling when in first position. If the application of scrambling is bound to factors like definiteness or being a topic, pragmatic factors are expected to hold for objects in first position but not for subjects, in accordance with the data.

1.2 *Scrambling as adjunction to IP*

Let us now investigate the properties of scrambling a bit closer. According to the *Government-and-Binding-* and the *Barriers*-framework (cf. Chomsky 1981, 1986a, respectively), there is only one movement rule, Move α, which may either transfer some category to the head or specifier position of another projection, or adjoin it to another category. The application of Move α is governed by various principles in a modular fashion. Obviously the two approaches to free word order make different predictions in this respect as well. If scrambling is "real," it will be governed by the principles restricting movement processes in general, i.e., the theory will predict that certain applications of scrambling will be ruled out by certain principles of Universal Grammar. On the other hand, if free word order is a base structure phenomenon, there will be no connection to movement processes. This would predict that restrictions on scrambling either should not exist or should be of a nature quite different from constraints on movements. Thus, there is another testing ground for scrambling.

Consider German (4d), e.g. The scrambled phrase *dem Minister* precedes the subject and follows the complementizer. As the specifier of CP

(SpecComp) precedes COMP in German, we have to conclude that *dem Minister* must have been adjoined to IP, yielding a structure like (7).

(7)

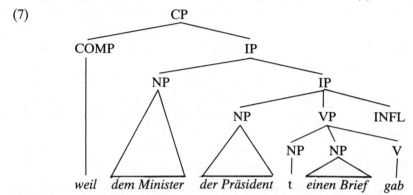

In his discussion of *wh*-extractions Chomsky (1986a) has demonstrated that *wh*-phrases are not allowed to adjoin to IP in the course of cyclic extractions. Otherwise the ungrammaticality of (8) could not be explained, since on the one hand the trace t' adjoined to IP would properly antecedent-govern the root trace t, and on the other hand t'' would do the same for t', as the intervening CP-node is L-marked and therefore no barrier.[6]

(8)   *how do you [t'' wonder what$_1$ [t' [PRO to fix t$_1$ t]]]

If scrambling adjoins objects and adverbials to IP, a prediction for multiple questions can be derived. *wh*-phrases in situ should not be able to undergo scrambling, since this process involves adjunction to IP, an option inaccessible for *wh*-phrases in general. The German examples given in (9) clearly demonstrate that this prediction is borne out.

(9) a.   *wie   hat wer gestern   das Auto repariert ?*
           how has who yesterday the car   fixed ?
           'who fixed the car yesterday how'

     b.   *wie hat das Auto gestern wer repariert ?*

     c.   *wie   hat der Mann gestern   was repariert ?*
           how has the man   yesterday what fixed ?
           'how did the man fix what yesterday'

     d.   **wie hat was der Mann gestern repariert ?*

(9a) illustrates the fact that there is no general restriction against *wh*-words immediately following COMP (here being filled by the moved verb) in German. (9b) illustrates that scrambling is applicable in multiple questions, but the contrast between (9c) and (9d) on the one hand, and between (9a) and (9d) on the other, clearly demonstrates that *wh*-phrases itself may not be scrambled, a fact completely predictable if scrambling adjoins phrases to IP. Furthermore, if we assume focus-NPs to pattern with *wh*-phrases in this respect, the contrast in (4) is a consequence of the barriers-framework as well.

Whereas *wh*-phrases and presumably focus-NPs may not adjoin to IP, quantified NPs may very well: May (1985) has argued convincingly that IP and VP are the primary adjunction sites of quantifier raising (QR). According to Hornstein (1984) and Aoun (1985), QR furthermore creates anaphoric traces and not variables: quantifiers α may have scope over phrases β only if β could bind an anaphor in the position of α.

(10) a.   somebody expects every Republican to be elected
      b.   somebody expects Bill to vote for every Republican
      c.   somebody expects that every Republican will be elected
      d.   somebody expects that Bill will vote for every Republican
(11) a.   the men expect each other to be elected
      b.   *the men expect Bill to vote for each other
      c.   *the men expect that each other will be elected
      d.   *the men expect that Bill votes for each other

Every Republican may have scope over *somebody* in (10a) only, i.e., only the LF (12a) is well-formed, but not (12b). Evidently the pattern is identical with the one presented in (11) for overt anaphora, hence it is quite likely that QR leaves anaphoric gaps.

(12) a. $[_{IP}$ every Republican$_i$ $[_{IP}$ somebody$_j$ $[_{IP}$ t$_j$ expects t$_i$ to be elected]]]
      b.   *$[_{IP}$ every Republican$_i$ $[_{IP}$ somebody$_j$ $[_{IP}$ t$_j$ expects Bill to vote for t$_i$]]]

A number of predictions follows from the assumption that scrambling — adjoining phrases to IP — leaves anaphoric gaps too. First, parasitic gap constructions are licensed for variables only but not for NP-traces. There should be no parasitic gaps with scrambling then. Consider now the contrast in (13) clearly demonstrating that those contexts allowing for parasitic gaps in German *wh*-constructions do not tolerate multiple gaps in scrambling contexts.[7]

(13) a.   *eine Zeitschrift, die*$_i$ *man anstatt* PRO t$_i$ *zu kopieren*
           a   journal   that one   instead of   to copy
           abonnieren sollte
           subscribe   should
           'a journal that one should subscribe to instead of copying'

      b. **weil   Linguistic Review Karl anstatt zu kopieren*
           because L.R.   K.   instead to copy
           abonnieren sollte
           subscribe   should
           'because Karl should subscribe to Linguistic Review instead
           of copying it'

Furthermore, NP-traces are subject to the theory of binding, hence we
should expect scrambling to relate those positions α, β only, where binding
of β by α satisfies principle A of the theory of binding and neither the ECP
nor Subjacency block movement. Broadly speaking, the main prediction is
that scrambling should be a clause-bound process, a fact that indeed seems
to hold in many if not most non-configurational languages.

Obviously, clauseboundedness would be predicted with a flat structure
of IP lacking a separate VP node as well, and it also can be stated in quite
a simple fashion with reference to f-structure units in LFG. While the
scrambling theory developed so far will allow for permutations of constituents within a clause as well, it will predict more permutations to be
grammatical than a simple clausemate condition would: *ceteris paribus*, any
position in an embedded clause which allows for anaphoric binding from a
matrix position should be affected by scrambling as well unless principles
different from condition A of the theory of binding (e.g. subjacency or the
ECP) would block empty categories in general.

The main array of data that allows for testing the different predictions
of the two hypotheses is ECM-constructions. The rules of anaphoric binding are quite complex here in German, as can be read off the data given in
(14)–(17).

(14) a.   *daß die Männer*$_i$ *[sich*$_i$ *die Bücher lesen] ließen*
           that the men   themselves   the books   read   let
           'that the men have themselves read the books'

    b.   *daß der Mann$_i$ [sich$_i$ (im   Spiegel) das Buch lesen]*
        that the man   himself in-the mirror   the book read
        sah
        saw
        'that the man saw himself reading the book in the mirror'

(15) a. *daß der Mann$_i$ [mich sich$_i$ helfen] ließ*
        that the man   me himself help let
        'that the man made me help him'

    b. *daß der Mann$_i$ [mich sich$_i$ helfen] sah*
        that the man   me himself help saw
        'that the man saw me helping him'

    c. *daß der Mann$_i$ [sich$_i$ mich helfen] ließ/sah*
        that the man   himself me   help let/saw
        (=15a/b with scrambling within the non-finite clause)

(16) a. *daß der Mann$_i$ [sich$_i$ das Unglück zustoßen] ließ*
        that the man   himself the accident happen   let
        'that the man made the accident happen to him'

    b. *daß der Mann$_i$ [sich$_i$ das Unglück zustoßen] sah*
        that the man   himself the accident happen   saw
        'that the man saw the accident happening to him'

    c. *daß der Mann$_i$ [das Unglück sich$_i$ zustoßen] sah*

(17) a. *daß der Mann$_i$ [mich für sich$_i$ arbeiten] ließ*
        that the man   me for himself work   let
        'that the man made me work for him'

    b. *daß der Mann$_i$ [mich für sich$_i$ arbeiten] sah*
        that the man   me for himself work   saw
        'that the man saw me working for him'

Subjects of ECM-constructions are öpen to anaphoric binding from the matrix clause like in English, cf. (14). Irrespective of serialization, object anaphora cannot be bound if a subject is present, as predicted by the theory of binding. However, as was first noticed by Reis (1976), this is true for "D-structure subjects" only, with *zustoßen* 'happen' being ergative. Following den Besten's (1985) proposal that nominative (and ECM-accusative) NPs in ergative and passive clauses are direct objects in German at S-structure as well, Grewendorf (1983) suggests that the exceptional behavior of anaphora in (16) is due to the absence of an S-structure subject in these clauses, with *das Unglück* 'the accident' being an object. We also regularily find binding of anaphoric elements in adjuncts from the matrix clause in (17), a fact I will return to below.

For the moment, however, it is sufficient to note that scrambling affects exactly those positions in ECM-contexts which allow for anaphoric binding.

(18)   *weil   mich niemand die Bücher lesen ließ/sah*
        because me   nobody the books   read lets/saw
        'because nobody made me read the books/saw me reading the books'

(19)   **weil   mir niemand Karl helfen ließ*
        because me   nobody K.   help lets
        'because nodody made Karl help me'

(20)   *weil   mir niemand ein Unglück zustoßen ließ*
        because me   nobody an accident happen let
        'because nobody caused an accident happen to me'

(21)   *weil   für Hans niemand mich arbeiten sah*
        because for H.   nobody me   work   saw
        'because nobody saw me working for Hans'

The examples (18)–(21) clearly demonstrate that scrambling is not a clause-bound process. While there is some evidence for clausal reanalysis in examples like (18), Grewendorf (1983) and Haider (1985) have demonstrated that clausal reanalysis does not apply in (21). Hence, this sentence exemplifies that scrambling can also affect elements from embedded clauses. Note that even if one were to follow LFG in assuming that the accusative NP in ECM-contexts isn't a clausal subject but an object of *lassen* 'let/make' or *sehen* 'see,' there is no way to consider *für Hans* 'for Hans' and similar adjuncts in (17) and (21) as constituents of the main clause. Locality conditions on scrambling cannot be stated in terms of the notion clause, rather, anaphoric binding is what seems to be relevant. This, however, can be expressed only if there is an anaphor that may be bound, i.e., if there is a trace. We shall reconsider the issue, however, in terms of the barriers framework in section 2.

While the situation found in West Greenlandic and similar languages (e.g. Russian) appears to be the same as in German, Turkish seems at a first glance to contradict our approach. Indeed, as (22) indicates, it is possible to extract elements via *scrambling* from nominalized clauses.

(22) a. *Ankara-dan   Erol [Ali-nin dön-düğ-ün]-ü bil-mi-yor*
     Ankara-from E.   A.:GEN return:NOM   know-infl-not
     'Erol doesn't know that Ali returned from Ankara'

    b. *okulu   ben [Ali-nin bu kadar çok sev-me-sin]-e*
      school:ACC I   A.:GEN so much very likes
      şaşir   dım
      surprised be
      'I am surprised that Ali likes school that much'

It does not appear to be possible, however, to scramble NPs that are more deeply embedded into the main clause, cf. (23), and Ergunvanli (1984).

(23) **Ankara-dan* [Erol-nin [Ali-nin t dön-düğ-ün] bil-me-di-*
    A.-from   E:GEN   A:GEN   return:NOM know-not-
    ğin]-i- sanıyor-du-m
    NOM ACC think:PROG-PAST-1P.SING
    'I thought Erol didn't know that Ali returned from Ankara'

A closer look at Turkish reveals, however, that nothing unexpected happens here. As has been noted by Faltz (1977), Turkish anaphora itself are exceptional insofar as anaphors contained in nominalized clauses may be bound from matrix positions even if a subject is present in the former, cf. (24).[8]

(24) *Orhan$_i$ [Mehmed-in$_j$ kendisin-e$_{i/j}$ palto al-masina]*
    Orhan M.:GEN   himself:DAT coat buy
    sevin-di
    pleased is
    'Orhan is pleased that Mehmed bought himself/him a coat'

Hence, while the behavior of anaphora in Turkish examples like (22) clearly presents a problem for binding theory, (21) does not do so for the theory of scrambling, since it merely exemplifies the claim that scrambling is not a clause-bound process but governed by the anaphoric nature of its trace. (23), on the other hand, seems to be blocked by subjacency, since as we shall see below, scrambling cannot be applied in a cyclic fashion.

1.3   *QR und scrambling*

1.1 and 1.2 have presented some evidence for the assumption of a scrambling rule, and it is quite obvious that it applies between D-structure and S-structure and not between S-structure and PF (as proposed by Williams (1984) and many other linguists): it affects the grammaticality of *wh*-phrases *in situ*, which it could not if it were to apply after S-structure, as PF-processes do not affect LF-representations in the standard model of the organization of grammar. Similar conclusions can be drawn from certain weak crossover effects of scrambling noted in the literature, cf. Saito & Hoji (1983), Webelhut (1985), but also Haider (1989).

We have also seen that the inapplicability of scrambling to *wh*-phrases and (presumably) focus-NPs reduces to properties of the adjunction slot. A problem, however, might be seen in the fact that scrambling appears to be sensitive to a definite-indefinite distinction as well (cf. (1) and (2)) which appears to be unpredictable: IP is the relevant adjunction slot for QR, and it is indefinite and quantified NPs that undergo this rule. Why, then, does scrambling of indefinite NPs have a status different from QR at LF ?

One major stumbling block in the search for a principled solution appears to lie in the fact that there are syntactic reorderings of quantified NPs in certain languages. E.g., Hawaiian Creole has a basic SVO-ordering, but quantified and indefinite NPs have to be preposed syntactically, cf. Bickerton (1981) and (25).

(25)   *eni kain lanwij   ai no can spik   gud*
         any kind language   I not ´can speak well
         'any kind of language, I do not know well'

Another feature often reported to hold in non-configurational languages is the apparent non-existence of QR at LF, i.e., semantic scope of quantifiers is identical with its syntactic scope at S-structure. Let us elaborate this point a bit more with examples from German.

(26) a. *daß eine Frau jeden   liebt*
          that some woman everybody loves
          'that some woman loves everybody'

      b. *daß jeder   eine Frau liebt*
          that everybody some woman loves
          'that everybody loves some woman'

(27) a. *daß   ein   Mann jeden   kommen sah*
         that some man   everybody come   saw
         'that some man saw everybody coming'

    b. *daß   jeder   einen Mann kommen sah*
         that everybody some man   come   saw
         'that everybody saw some man coming'

(28) a. **daß ein   Bewohner jeder   Stadt$_i$ sie$_i$ haßt*
         that some inhabitant every:GEN city   she hates
         (=28b)

    b. some inhabitant of every city despises it

(29) a. *eine   Frau   liebt jeder*
         some woman:ACC loves everybody:NOM
         'everybody loves some woman'

    b. *einen Mann sah   jeder   kommen*
         a:ACC man   saw   everybody:NOM come
         'everybody saw some man coming'

The examples in (26) and (27) appear to be unambiguous in German (cf. e.g. Jacobs (1982) for a discussion), i.e., *ein* 'a' must have scope over *jeder* 'every' in the a-examples and *vice versa* in the b-examples. (28a) is ungrammatical in German with the intended reading, showing that *jeder Stadt* '(of) every city' cannot have clausal scope as its English counterpart in (28b) does. LF-QR seems to be absent then in German, and similar facts have been reported for Hungarian, e.g., cf. Haider (1989) for further examples and discussion.

One major exception lies in examples like (29), which may be read with both scope assignments logically possible. (29) differs from (27) insofar as the first elements in (29) occupy the SpecComp-position (cf. Thiersch 1978) i.e., have been moved there via *wh*-movement, and several authors have reported similar facts in other languages: scope relations may be unaffected by *wh*-movement.

It is quite unconceivable, however, that languages lack UG-processes like QR or *wh*-movement completely. Chinese and Japanese appear superficially to lack *wh*-movement, but Huang (1982) has shown that the two languages nevertheless have *wh*-movement at LF. Following Chomsky (1986b), we may rather assume that languages differ with respect to a parameter regulating if a specific process applies at LF or at S-structure. If there is no LF-QR in German, then we should expect it to work at S-structure. Indeed, the data given in (30) are quite promising:[9]

(30) a. *weil   jeden   eine   Frau   liebt*
         because everybody:ACC a:NOM woman loves

     b. *weil   jeden   mindestens einer   zur   Party*
         because everyone:ACC   at least   one:NOM to-the party
         kommen sah
         come   saw
         'because at least one person saw everybody coming to the party'

The examples in (30) show that QR may apply syntactically in German: they are unambiguous with *jeden* 'every' having scope over *ein* 'a'. There is no analogue to (28b) in German for obvious reasons: subjacency is an S-structure constraint and will block syntactic extractions of the quantified object but not LF-extractions. Consider now, however, (31):

(31) a. **weil   ein Kind der   Mann sah*
         because a   child the:NOM man   saw
         'because the man saw a child'

     b. **weil   jedes Kind der   Mann sah*
         because every child the:NOM man   saw
         'because the man saw every child'

Obviously, quantified NPs cannot be adjoined to IP in German if the subject (or another phrase) is not quantified as well. The data presented in (1) and (2) have a similar status, and in Turkish scrambling of two quantified NPs is possible all the same, cf. Ergunvanli (1984).

Quantifiers must have clausal scope at LF. May (1985) has demonstrated, however, that adjunction to VP will have this effect as well. Since a category adjoined to α is not dominated by α (cf. Chomsky 1986a) and since scope of some category β is determined by the smallest category dominating β, β will have clausal scope in (32):

(32) $[_{IP}.....[_{VP} \beta [_{VP}...]]]$

The grammatical versions of (31), i.e., (33), however, are very well compatible with an S-structure analysis like (34):

(33) a. *weil   der Mann ein Kind sah*
         because the man   a   child saw
         (=31a)

b. *weil   der Mann jedes Kind sah*
    because the man   every child saw
    (=31b)

(34) $[_{IP}$ *der Mann* $[_{VP}$ *ein/jedes Kind*$_i$ $[_{VP}$ t_i *sah*]]]

The crucial difference between examples (30) and (32) lies in the fact that adjunction to IP will have a semantic effect (i.e., giving the object quantifier scope over the subject quantifier) in (30), but it will be semantically empty in (33). There is no scope-bearing element in the subject position. One might assume, then, that QR may not apply in a vacuous fashion in order to account for the contrast between (30) and (32). Note, furthermore, that non-vacuity is not only determined by interaction with other scope bearing elements, it is also affected by pronominal binding, cf. the contrast given in (35).

(35) a. *weil   jeden*$_i$ *seine*$_i$ *Eltern   lieben*
         because everybody:ACC his   parents love
         'everyone is such that his parents love him'

   b. ?* *weil   jeden   Peters Eltern   lieben*
         because everybody:ACC Peter's parents love
         'because Peter's parents love everybody'

1.4 *The defective nature of IP*

While the approach developed so far nicely predicts scrambling data in the languages we considered, there are still two problems we have to deal with. Consider first the structure given in (36):

(36) $[_{IP}$ α $[_{IP}$··· $[_{VP}$ β $[_{VP}$··· $[_{CP}$··$[_{IP}$ τ $[_{IP}$···δ···]]]]]]]

We are assuming, adopting some version of a generalized theory of binding, that it is possible to A-bind δ by the category τ in order to account for the locality of scrambling processes. Let us consider now, however, the position τ itself. We might assume that some category first adjoins to IP in the course of scrambling and is then adjoined to either position of β or α in a cyclic fashion. This would predict that scrambling might indeed cross clausal boundaries in a general fashion, an indesirable result for obvious reasons.

Clearly, τ is not dominated by the lower IP-node, and if we stick to the definition of locality domains for anaphoric binding given in Chomsky

(1981), (1986b), IP will not be the Minimal Governing Category for τ since it does not contain that category.

Furthermore, there will be no barriers between τ and β according to the definitions given in (37).

(37) a.   α is a blocking category for β iff
           a) α contains β
           b) α is a maximal projection
           c) α is not L-marked.

     b.   α is a barrier for β iff
           a) α dominates τ, τ a blocking category for β
           b) α is a blocking category for β, for α ≠ IP.

     c.   α is L-marked by β if α and β are sisters, β assigns a θ-role
           to α and β is a lexical category.

CP is L-marked in the normal case, hence it will be no blocking category. Furthermore, although IP will be a blocking category in case CP is present, IP does not dominate τ implying that CP cannot inherit barrierhood either. Moving any category from the position of τ to ß will not violate Subjacency and the ECP then. This incorrectly predicts that (38) should be okay and *every student* should have scope over *some professor* in (39).

(38)   *weil   ich die Maria dem   Hans versprach daß
        because I   the Mary the:DAT H.   promised   that
        Peter sieht
        Peter sees
        'because I promised Hans that Peter would see Mary'

(39)   he told some student that every professor would let him
        pass the tests

There is a way out of this dilemma, however. As mentioned above, Chomsky (1986a) has argued that *wh*-operators may not adjoin to IP in the course of cyclic extractions. If we make the natural assumptions that *wh*-phrases must be in SpecComp at LF, this would follow from the stronger assumption that adjunction to IP leads to a dead end: no category α can be removed from the adjunction slot of IP. This will not only imply Chomsky's restriction on *wh*-extractions but also the ungrammaticality of cyclic scrambling and QR.

IP would be predicted to be a defective category in still another sense. Perhaps the restriction just proposed derives from the fact that *traces* adjoined to IP are invisible for one or the other reason.

2. NP- vs. *wh*-type of extractions

Let us ask now what could account for the difference between English and German with respect to scrambling processes. Evidently it is not true that there is *no* reordering in English, since sentences like (40) are very well grammatical:

(40) a.   I introduced to him my famous father-in-law from Cambridge, Mass.

   b.   I think that John, she really likes

These processes differ, however, from German scrambling not only in pragmatic constraints on use but also, and more importantly, in grammatical properties. There is much evidence that these constructions involve variable gaps and not NP-traces as in German. First, heavy NP-shift in (40a) licenses parasitic gaps, in contradistinction to German reordering.

(41)   he insulted t by not recognizing immediately t his famous father-in-law from Cambridge, Mass.

To a certain extent, unbounded dependencies occur:[10]

(42) a.   I think that John, he might wish to invite

   b.   I think that John, he would never dare to invite

Both constructions block *wh*-movement:

(43) a.   *who did you give to t a book ?

   b.   *which book do you think that John, I gave to ?

The latter fact must be seen in connection with the ungrammaticality of (44) discussed in Chomsky (1986a):

(44)   *who did you wonder what to give to

(45)   ?what did you wonder how to fix ?

(44) certainly is much worse than (45), a fact Chomsky reduces to the assumption that at most one category of a certain type may adjoin to the same projection, i.e., multiple adjunction of NPs to VP is forbidden in the course of *wh*-extractions. If, in contradistinction to German, reordering blocks *wh*-extractions in English, we have to conclude that reordering involves *wh*-extraction itself. This is also suggested by (40) and (41).

"Scrambling" involves *wh*-movement in English and NP-movement in German and many similar languages then. Let us try to see first why NP-movement cannot be involved in English "scrambling."

According to the definitions given in (37), VP is an inherent barrier for government and movement. Furthermore, Chomsky (1986a) suggests that θ-government may be completely irrelevant for the determination of proper government in the sense of the ECP, being replaced by antecedent-government.

This will cause no problems in *wh*-extractions like (46), since positions adjoined to VP are neither excluded nor included by that category, hence there are no barriers between *what* and t^1 on the one hand, and t^2 and t^1 on the other.

(46)   what did he [t^1 [say [t^2 that Mary has [t [bought t]]]]]

As adjunction to VP, however, creates *wh*-gaps, this solution will not work in the case of NP-movement, cf. (47).

(47)   she$_i$ was kissed t$_i$

Here there is a barrier -VP- between t$_i$ and she$_i$, implying that (47) is a weak subjacency violation. Furthermore, since a barrier intervenes, *she* cannot antecedent-govern t$_i$, implying that there should be an overriding ECP-violation. Obviously, however, (47) is perfectly grammatical.

Chomsky notes, however, that *she* will be coindexed with INFL of the matrix clause, and V and INFL share indices either by movement of V to INFL or by agreement and feature government. Therefore, (47) should be structured as indicated in (48).

(48)   she$_i$ was$_i$ kissed$_i$ t$_i$

(48) is predicted to be grammatical if the ECP and subjacency are sensitive to the notion of binding in *extended chains* as defined in (49). (48) will violate no principles as t$_i$ can now be assumed to have *kissed*$_i$ as its proper antecedent.

(49)   Extended chain
        If $\Gamma = <\alpha_1,...,\alpha_j,\alpha_{j+1},...\alpha_n>$ is a chain or an extended chain with the index i, and if β is a category bearing the index i such that β c-commands α_k, k>j, then $<\alpha_1,...,\alpha_j,\beta,\alpha_{j+1},...,\alpha_n>$ is an extended chain with the index i.[11]

(50) a.   he was believed t to have kissed Mary
     b.   he seems t to have kissed Mary
     c.   *he seems that t$_i$ likes Mary

    d. *he is obvious that it seems t to like Mary

    e. *he was preferred for Bill to invite t

In (50a) and (50b) *he* is coindexed with the INFL node of the matrix clause and with the verb in question. Therefore, the embedding verb is also coindexed with the trace, and *<he,was,believed,t>* forms an extended chain in (50a). Furthermore, *believe* and t are separated by IP only, which is a blocking category but not a barrier on its own right. Both (50a) and (50b) are correctly predicted to be grammatical. Consider, on the other hand, (50c). Although *seems* and t form an extended chain, *seem* cannot antecedent-govern t for two reasons. First, although the CP-node of the embedded clause is L-marked and therefore constitutes no blocking category, CP will inherit barrierhood from IP. There is a barrier, then, between *seem* and t blocking antecedent-government. Furthermore, *that* governs t, implying that government by *seem* will be blocked by the minimality principle.

In cases of superraising like (50d) *obvious* but not *seems* is coindexed via agreement with *he* and t. The VP in the intermediate clause inherits barrierhood from IP, and so will CP. Therefore (50d) is correctly ruled out as an ECP-violation. As for long NP-extraction of objects, it suffices to say that only the matrix verb but not the complement verb is coindexed with the trace. Therefore the VP of the embedded clause and by inheritance, IP and CP constitute barriers.

Of course, it is tempting to reduce even binding theory's principle A completely to the concept of barriers, cf. Fanselow (to appear) for some suggestions. Let us return, however, to NP-movement dependencies that do not terminate in A-positions but in adjunction slots. Consider, first (51) which is ungrammatical in English with a normal intonation pattern.

(51)   *that nobody he [$_{VP}$ likes t$_i$]

(51) violates the ECP with a VP-barrier intervening between t$_i$ and its antecedent if we assume, following chapter 11 of Chomsky (1986a), that there is no θ-government.

Consider now quantifier raising, as exemplified in (52).

(52)   a.   Bill [every girl$_i$ [likes t$_i$]]

        b.   every girl$_i$ [Bill [likes t$_i$]]

        c.   every girl$_i$, some man$_j$, [t$_j$ [kissed t$_i$]]

Following May (1985), we may assume that QR may adjoin phrases to VP or to IP. If the quantifier is adjoined to VP, it will have clausal scope, since the first category dominating it is IP (the quantifier not being included by the VP). Therefore, although structures like (52b) would violate the ECP, there is no need for adjoining quantifiers to IP in object position in general, since VP-adjunction will do the same job, viz. giving clausal scope to the quantifier. In (52a), however, *every girl* is not excluded from the VP and can therefore antecedent-govern t_i. The LF-structure (52c) appears to be more problematic, since if the object is to be given scope over a subject quantifier, it must be adjoined to IP. In (52c) VP is a barrier for the relation between *everyone* and its trace. Therefore, (52c) should be out. Note, however, that Higginbotham & May (1981) have proposed that multiple quantifiers might be merged at LF, yielding (52d). A similar process has been proposed by Kayne (1983) in his discussion of multiple questions.

(52) d. [every girl some man] t_j [kissed t_i]

Crucially now, the merged quantifiers share the index of the subject, hence INFL and V enter into an extended chain with that index. But the object trace is as well bound by the merged quantifiers, hence coindexed with V and therefore properly governed. If we turn to languages like German, it must be observed in the first place that scrambling languages of the German type typically show a rich system of case. This is obvious for Turkish and West Greenlandic, the languages we have considered above.[12] Insights may be gained from the analysis of two further free constituent order languages, Hungarian and Makua.

Hungarian word order has been analysed in Kiss (1981). According to her, Hungarian clauses have a structure like (53), i.e., scrambling may either move NPs to theme or focus slots.

(53) [thematic elements [focus/*wh*-position [proper clause]]]

Crucially now, movement both to the theme and the focus position is unbounded, cf. (54) and Kenesei (1984).

(54) *ennek a lármának szeretném tudni, hogy mikor lesz*
      to this noise   I'd like   know   that   when   will-be
      vége
      end
      'I would like to know when this noise will be ended'

The absence of NP-type scrambling in Hungarian is no surprise, however, as Kiss (1985) has demonstrated that Hungarian is exceptional insofar as there are *no* NP-type dependencies at all (i.e., no raising and no passives), presumably due to some peculiarities in the Hungarian case system as Kiss suggests, but see Fanselow (1987, 1988a).

Reordering is of the *wh-* type in Makua as well, cf. the data given in (55) by Stucky (1985).

(55)   *lúwán- élẃ Aráarima ahéewa wiira Hin sepété áhó-théka-ú
         ni-nthhále*
         'that fence, A. heard that that Sepete built with bamboo'

This is quite expected since Makua lacks an overt system of case, grammatical functions being identified by verbal inflection. We may conclude, then, that scrambling shows NP-movement-type-dependencies if the language in question has a rich system of case, provided that there is NP-movement at all in these languages. The fact that structures such as (56) do not violate the ECP in these languages must be attributed to properties of the case system then.

(56) $[_{IP}\ \alpha\ [_{IP}\ NP\ [_{VP}\ t_i\ V]]]$

Recall the account for the grammaticality of (57), however.

(57) he_i may be invited t_i

According to Chomsky (1986a), the process of feature assignment to the verb by the modal enters into the composition of extended chains. English case assignment is a structural process, whereas case assignment in German and similar languages refers to lexical properties. Therefore we may assume that V assigns case to NP in German in a stricter and more direct fashion. Sticking to the logic of Chomsky's argument, there will be proper (antecedent) goverment of a trace by the verb in ˙German in non-passive clauses as well, predicting the acceptability of (56), and NP-type scrambling then.

3. Scrambling and *wh*-extractions

Obviously, the latter result predicts adjunction to VP to be unnecessary for proper government in the context of *wh*-extractions in free constituent order languages like German. It is natural to assume that there is a corresponding parametrization between languages: adjunction to VP leads to A-bar-binding in English but to A-binding in German. Consider now, however, (58).

(58) $wh_i...[_{VP} ..V^1.. [_{CP} t_i^1...[_{VP} V^2 t_i^2]]]$

If adjunction to VP is restricted to A-binding in scrambling languages, (58) is predicted to violate subjacency. t^1 is bound by wh_i with two barriers intervening: although CP is not L-marked, the matrix-VP will be, and IP inherits barrierhood from that category as well. Since V^1 does not assign features to t^2, V^1 cannot be entered into the extended chain of the *wh*-expression as in the case of small extractions. In sum, we predict scrambling languages to have considerable problems with long-distance *wh*-movement whereas fixed word order languages should not, due to the A-bar-properties of VP-adjunction.

Among the fixed word order languages, there figure prominently the Scandinavian ones, all notorious for their extraordinary liberality with respect to *wh*-movement. There is free *wh*-extraction in the Romance languages as well, in English, of course, but Chinese appears to be an exception in this context.

On the other hand, quite a number of scrambling languages do not allow for a syntactic *wh*-movement, e.g., Turkish and Japanese. Other languages, like certain dialects of Russian (cf. Comrie 1973), Latin and of German just allow for small *wh*-extractions, a fact also noted by Hawkins (1986) in his discussion of German-English contrast.[13] A very nice example of this quite typical situation is the array of data in Polish as discussed by Lasnik & Saito (1984). *Syntactic wh*-movement may extract phrases to the nearest SpecComp only, even if the *wh*-phrases has matrix scope at LF, cf. (59). This is completely predicted since LF-movement is not subject to subjacency.

(59a)   *Maria mysli ze   co   Janek kupił*
         Mary thinks that what J.   buys
         'what does Mary think John is buying ?'
    b.   **co Maria mysli ze Janel kupił*

The constraint against long *wh*-movement holds for indicative clauses only, however. Subjunctive complements are no islands for syntactic *wh*-extractions.

(60)   *co   Maria chce   zeby Janek kupił*
        what Mary wants that J.   buys
        'what does Mary want that Janek buy?'

There is a straightforward account for these facts, however. It is quite natural to assume that choice of the subjunctive is influenced by the matrix verb, thus, the matrix verb can be taken to assign feature to the embedded INFL and therefore to the verb. This feature sharing mechanism entering into extended chain composition, long distance *wh*-movement won't violate subjacency anymore. A similar account might be invoked to account for long-distance extractions in the southern dialects of German.[14]

4.   Some further data

We have tried to account for a number of distinctions in the realm of scrambling within the barriers-framework: different locality constraints on reordering, differences in case marking systems, differences with respect to the scope of *wh*-movement. Let me just sketch possible analyses for the free *word* order phenomena[15].

Quite a number of languages — e.g. Spanish or Italian — license reordering with clitic pronouns:

(61)   *a Maria Juan la   besó pro*
          to Mary Juan her kissed
          'Mary, John kissed'

The crucial factor either might be seen to lie in A-bar-binding of the clitic pronoun or of the *pro* category licensed by *la*. Data from Warlpiri or similar languages suggest that the latter approach should be the correct one, since Jelinek (1984) has demonstrated that Warlpiri has a rich system of object agreement which might be taken to identify *pro* generally. Jelinek herself goes on to assume that full NPs are in adjunct position generally in this language, thus accounting for free word order phenomena such as the ones illustrated in (62).

(62) a.   *kurdu-ngku wita-ngku ka   maliki wajilipi yalumpu-rlu*
          child-erg   small-erg AUX dog   chase   this-erg
          'this little child is chasing the dog'
     b.   *wawirri   ka   panti-rni ngarrka-ngku yalumpu*
          kangaroo AUX spear-NP man   erg   this
          'the man is spearing this kangaroo'

The spirit of the approach will work for free *word* order as well, since all languages allowing for scrambling of parts of NPs share an important property: case agreement within NP, this is true for the free word order languages Warlpiri (cf. Hale 1983), Dyirbal (cf. Dixon 1972), Yidiñ (Dixon

1979), West Greenlandic (cf. Fortescue 1979), Latin and German. Compare now German (63) with English (64).

(63) a. *ich habe ein rotes*
          (=64a)
      b. *ich möchte dieses*
          I   want   this

(64) a. *I have a red
      b.   I have a red one
      c.   I want this one

Olsen (1986) has demonstrated that this contrast reduces to case agreement, as the abstract agreement feature on the adjective suffices to identify *pro* as the nominal head of NPs, in contradistinction to English where a phonetic pronominal, *one*, has to be inserted. The split-NP-construction in (65) thus can be analyzed in terms of A-bar-binding of *pro* by the element in SpecComp. The situation appears to be basically the same in the other free word order languages, Fanselow (1988b) for some discussion.

(65) $Geld_i$ *habe ich keines* pro_i
          money have I   no
          'I don't have any money'

5. Conclusions

Considering the data discussed in this article, I think one cannot escape the conclusion that scrambling is a grammatical phenomenon in its strictest sense: the options for reordering elements are determined by principles independently motivated by other constructions: the theory of binding, subjacency, the ECP, the determination of *pro*, the special status of IP etc. Furthermore, scrambling interacts with other processes of grammar: it may block *wh*-items *in situ*, it may act as the S-structure counterpart of quantifier raising, and it affects to a certain degree the possibility of long-distance *wh*-movement. To this, we have to add the well-known observation of weak-crossover effects on scrambling mentioned above. Obviously, free word order cannot be explained by assuming that base order is free, it results from the application of Move α and the identification of *pro* in a completely predictable fashion.

Notes

*   This article is a revised version of papers I presented at the 11th GGS-meeting, Regensburg, October 1986, and at the DGfS annual meeting, Augsburg, March 1987. I would like to thank Sascha Felix and Peter Staudacher for many helpful suggestions, Roberta Ebeling for checking my English, and Luise Haller and Gabi Neszt for preparing the text file for publication.

1.   Cf., e.g., Ross (1967), and Williams (1984) for a more recent approach.

2.   This seems to hold even for languages with extensive means of reordering like Dyirbal or Warlpiri, cf. Dixon (1972) for the former language and Nash (1980) and the reference cited therein for the latter.

3.   West Greenlandic data are taken from Fortescue (1984).

4.   Turkish data are taken from Ergunvanli (1984).

5.   We have to restrict our attention on subordinate clauses here: in main clauses, the first and second positions are the specifier of CP and COMP^0, respectively and are governed by different principles, cf., e.g. Thiersch (1978), Fanselow (1987), among others.

6.   Cf. (37) below for a definition of the relevant notions.

7.   Cf. Felix (1985) for a general discussion of German parasitic gap constructions, and below for some comments on parasitic gaps created by adjunction to VP.

8.   There are two different anaphoric forms, *kendi* and *kendisin*, in Turkish. Faltz reports that dialects may differ with respect to the question which one of these allows for long distance binding.

9.   Some apparent exceptions to this claim are dealt with in Fanselow (1988 a)).

10.   For some speakers of German, especially in the dialect described in Felix (1985), parasitic gaps are possible with scrambling adjoining some phrase to VP (but not in the case of adjunction to IP, see above), cf. (i):

(i)   *er hat Maria ohne* t   *anzuschauen* t *geküßt*
        he has Mary without   looking at   kissed
        'he has kissed Mary without looking at her'

As predicted by the approach proposed in this paper, long-distance scrambling is possible for VP-adjunction in these dialects, cf. (ii):

(ii)   *weil   er   dem   Mädchen sicher   Hans ein   Buch geben   sah*
        because he the:DAT girl   certainly Hans a:ACC book give   saw
        'because he certainly saw Hans giving a book to the girl'

The data have been brought to my attention by Eleonore Brandner and Karin Donhauser. See Fanselow (1989 a)) for an elaborate treatment of these facts in a rather different framework.

11.   In order to avoid further complications, I have cited the notion of extended chains developed in Fanselow & Felix (1987) rather than the original version of Chomsky (1986a).

12. Dutch also allows for reordering to a certain degree, lacking an overt system of case,
     however, cf. den Besten (1987). Since den Besten observes that Dutch scrambling trig-
     gers parasitic gap phenomena, Dutch scrambling is of the Hungarian rather that the Ger-
     man type of reordering. Den Besten also suggests, in the theory he developed together
     with Gert Webelhut, that the crucial factor for scrambling would be the SOV- vs. SVO-
     distinction. This cannot be correct, however, since SVO-languages like Russian or Mod-
     ern Greek allow for scrambling as well. According to Hankamer (1971) the major differ-
     ence between the two types of languages seems to be that SVO-scrambling also may
     affect the verb (cf. Russian or Modern Greek), which it does not in SOV-languages
     (examples would be Japanese, German or Turkish), but there might be some problems
     with Latin since this language is usually assumed to be of the SOV-type while the verb
     undergoes scrambling as well. To the extent that Hankamer's generalization is empirically
     correct, it appears to be plausible to reduce it to facts about focus structure in the way
     suggested by Hankamer himself.

13. One might wonder why crossing the VP-barrier in small *wh*-extractions does not cause
     problems with subjacency in these languages. Note, however, that a weak violation of
     subjacency is also predicted for structures like (i) in the *Barriers*-framework:

     (i)   John may [be invited t_i]

     While chain-coindexing ensures proper government of t_i by *invited*, *may* does not L-mark
     the VP which is a barrier, then. Consequently, *John* and t_i or *may* and *be* are separated
     by one barrier, predicting a weak violation of subjacency. Some mechanism must be
     invoked, then, in any case to account for the absence of such effects in the course of small
     NP-movements.

14. If there is a correlation between the facts noted in (10) and long- distance extraction of
     wh-words in the relevant dialects, no problem would arise in any case.

15. For reasons discussed in Fanselow (1988b)), the term *free word* order is a gross overstate-
     ment. No language seems to allow for a free reordering of words.

Bibliography

Abraham, W. 1985a. "Word Order in the Middle Field of the German Sen-
     tence." Ms., Groningen.

———. (ed.) 1985b. *Erklärende Syntax des Deutschen*. Tübingen: Narr.

Aoun, J. 1985. *A grammar of anaphora*. Cambridge, Mass.: MIT Press.

den Besten, H. 1985. "Some remarks on the ergative Hypothesis." In:
     Abraham (ed.).

———. 1987. "VP-Syntax." Paper presented at the annual meeting of the
     DGfS, Augsburg, March 1987.

Bickerton, D. 1981. *Roots of Language*. Ann Arbor: Karoma.

Bhatt, C., E. Löbel & C. Schmidt. (eds.). 1989. *Syntactic Phrase Structure
     Phenomena in Noun Phrases and Sentences*. Amsterdam: Benjamins.

Chomsky, N. 1981. *Lectures on Government and Binding*. Dordrecht: Foris.

———. 1986a. *Barriers*. Cambridge, Mass: MIT-Press.

———. 1986b. *Knowledge of Language*. London: Praeger.

Comrie, B. 1973. "Clause Structure and Movement Constraints in Russian." Diss., University of Cambridge.

Dixon, R.M. 1972. *The Dyirbal language of North Queensland*. Cambridge: Cambridge University Press.

———. 1979. *A Grammar of Yidiñ*. Cambridge: Cambridge University Press.

Ergunvanli, E.E. 1984. *The Function of Word Order in Turkish Grammar*. Berkeley: University of California Press.

Faltz, L. 1977. "Reflexivization. A Study in Universal Grammar." Diss., University of California, Los Angeles.

Fanselow, G. 1987. *Konfigurationalität*. Tübingen: Narr.

———. 1988a. "German Word Order and Universal Grammar." In: Reyle & Rohrer (eds.).

———. 1988b. "Aufspaltung von NPn und das Problem der 'freien' Wortstellung." *Linguistische Berichte* 114, 91-113.

———. 1989. "Coherent Infinitives in German." In: Bhatt et. al. (eds.).

———. (to appear). "Barriers and the Theory of Binding." In: Haider & Netter (eds.)

———. & S. Felix. 1987. *Sprachtheorie II*. Tübingen: Francke.

Felix, S. 1985. "Parasitic gaps in German." In: Abraham (ed.)

Fortescue, M. 1984. *West Greenlandic*. London: Croom Helm.

Grewendorf, G. 1983. "Reflexivierung in deutschen AcI-Konstruktionen - Kein transformationsgram matisches Dilemma mehr." *Groninger Arbeiten zur germanistischen Linguistik* 22, 120-196.

Haider, H. 1985. "Argumentreduktionsphänomene im Deutschen." *Linguistische Berichte* 101, 3-33.

———. 1989. *Parameter der deutschen Syntax*. Tübingen: Narr.

Haider, H. & K. Netter. (eds.). (to appear). *Derivational and Representtional Approaches to Generative Syntax*. Dordrecht: Reidel.

Hale, K. 1983. "Warlpiri and the grammar of non-configurational languages." *Natural Language and Linguistic Theory* 1, 5-48.

Hankamer, J. 1971. "Constraints on Deletion in Syntax." Diss., Yale University.

Hawkins, J. 1986. *A comparative typology of English and German*. London: Croom Helm.

Higginbotham, J. & May, R. 1981. "Questions, Quantifiers and Crossing." *The Linguistic Review* 1, 41-80.

Hornstein, N. 1984. *Logic as grammar*. Cambridge, Mass: MIT Press.

Huang, J. T. 1982. "Move WH in a Language without WH-movement." *The Linguistic Review* 1, 531-574.

Jacobs, J. 1982. *Syntax und Semantik der Negation im Deutschen*. München: Fink.

Jelinek, E. 1984. "Empty Categories, Case and Configurationality." *Natural Language and Linguistic Theory* 2, 39-76.

Kayne, R. 1983. "Connectedness." *Linguistic Inquiry* 14, 223-250.

Kenesei, I. 1984. "Word Order in Hungarian Complex Sentences." *Linguistic Inquiry* 15, 328-341.

Kiss, K. 1981. "Structural relations in Hungarian. A 'free' word order language." *Linguistic Inquiry* 12, 185-213.

———. 1985. "Is the VP universal?" Ms., Massachusetts Institute of Technology.

Lasnik, H. & Saito, M. 1984. "On the Nature of Proper Government." *Linguistic Inquiry* 15, 235- 289.

Lenerz, J. 1977. *Zur Abfolge nominaler Satzglieder im Deutschen*. Tübingen: Narr.

May, R. 1985. *Logical Form*. Cambridge, Mass.: MIT Press.

Olsen, S. 1986. "Die sogenannten substantivierten Adjektive im Deutschen. Deutsch als *pro*-drop-Sprache." Paper, presented at the GGS-meeting Regensburg, October 1986.

Nash, D. 1980. *Topics in Warlpiri Grammar*. New York: Garland.

Reis, M. 1976. "Reflexivierung in deutschen AcI-Konstruktionen. Ein transformationsgrammatisches Dilemma." *Papiere zur Linguistik* 9, 5-82.

Reyle, U. & C. Rohrer. (eds.). 1988. *Natural Language Parsing and Linguistic Theories*. Dordrecht: Reidel.

Ross, J.R. 1967. "Constraints on Variables in Syntax." Diss., Massachusetts Institute of Technology.

Saito, M. & Hoji, H. 1983. "Weak Crossover and Move α in Japanese." *Natural Language and Linguistic Theory* 1, 245-259.

Stucky, S. 1985. *Word Order in Makua Syntax*. New York: Garland.

Thiersch, C. 1978. "Topics in German syntax." Diss., Massachusetts Institute of Technology.

Uszkoreit, H. 1984. "Word order and constituent structure in German." Diss., University of Texas at Austin.

Webelhut, G. 1985. "German is configurational." *The Linguistic Review* 4, 203-246.

Williams, E. 1984. "Grammatical relations." *Linguistic Inquiry* 15, 639-673.

III. Scrambling and the Structure of Infinitives

Status Government and Coherence in German

Arnim von Stechow
University of Constance

1. Introduction

Since Gunnar Bech's classical *Studien über das deutsche verbum infinitum* (=VI) we distinguish between two kinds of government, *case government* and *status government*. The former notion has got to the top in generative grammar since Chomsky's *Lectures on Government and Binding* (=GB) whereas the latter notion seems to be largely unknown among generative grammarians. For Bech, however, status government is *the* central notion around which his syntax of the German verb is organized.

In this article, I will mainly be concerned with the question how status government interacts with other grammatical principles. My aim is to show that *status government entails coherence*. A 'coherent construction' is a construction that doesn't embed a sentence. This claim is not compatible with Bech's original theory, according to which the status of incoherent infinitivals is also governed. I will show that my deviation from Bech in this respect is well motivated.

It will follow that coherent verbs like *wollen* 'to wish' or *lassen* 'to let' can't embed a sentence at the level where status is checked. At this point, the question arises at which level of grammatical representation status is checked. There are three possibilities:

A. Status is checked at D-structure
B. Status is checked at S-structure
C. Status is checked after S-structure

Quite surprisingly, a choice between the different alternatives is not an easy matter. It will depend on a number of non-trivial assumptions.

Option A assumes that status government is a sort of subcategorization ('verb selection'). Option B puts status government on a par with government of structural case. Option C assumes that status government triggers reanalysis. Option B is not very plausible for principled reasons: S-structure is the level where syntactic properties are checked, and status government certainly is a lexical property. In section 20, I will discuss some arguments that indicate that option C is the correct alternative.

En passant, the article tries to overcome some descriptive problems of German grammar by refining the GB-notion of government. The idea is this. In GB, a head X governs a phrase YP iff YP is immediately dominated by a projection of X. X may assign a feature α (e.g. a case, a status or a theta role) to YP, and we then say that X assigns α to YP under government. Let us call this kind of feature assignment α-government. I will argue that there are certain processes which can easily be defined by means of α-government but which can't be defined in terms of purely structural government. One process is the so-called recipient passive, discussed in section 17. The recipient or dative passive shows dative-nominative alternation. This alternation is triggered by the superordinate auxiliary (e.g. *kriegen* 'to get'), which 'absorbs' *dative*-government but not *accusative*-government.

A part of the article is not directly concerned with government: It is a somewhat lengthy reflection on the theory of empty elements. In addition to the four empty elements which ar assumed in GB-theory, *PRO, pro, NP*-trace and *Wh*-trace, we need a further empty element called *E*, which is an empty expletive. In the Italian literature, this element is called expletive *pro*. Safir (1985) calls it *EXE*. The necessity of assuming *E* in German was first argued for in Sternefeld (1982). In the literature about Italian, expletive *pro* is defined by stipulating that, in addition to the features [+pronominal, −anaphor], it has the feature [−argument], whereas referential *pro* has the features [+pronominal, −anaphor, +argument]. It seems to be more convenient, however, to assume that expletive *pro* and referential *pro* are different empty elements with independent syntactic properties: In German, we have the former but not the latter, a fact that would remain quite mysterious if the two elements were basically the same. Furthermore, if the distinction between expletive *pro* and referential *pro* had to be made only by means of the features [±argument], then the question would arise why the same subdivision should not be possible for *PRO*. In other words, there should exist an expletive *PRO*, i.e., a *PRO* with the feature [−argument]. But there is no such element. For these reasons, I don't call the expletive empty element *pro*, but *E*. It would seem then that we need exactly five empty elements, *viz., PRO, pro, E, NP*-trace and *Wh*-trace. Thus, the question arises how we derive the existence of exactly these five. A structural definition in the style of GB-theory is not possible or, at least, not in sight. A definition on the basis of feature combinations doesn't seem to be able to generate the odd number of five empty elements: A combination of two two-valued features in the GB style produces four elements and if we add one two-valued feature, we obtain eight elements. How can we get to the magic number five, then? An answer is given in section 7.

The existence of E leads to the question why there are no impersonal passives in Italian, where we have to assume empty expletives for subject-predicate inversions. In the case of impersonal passives, E has to be the subject of the sentence. In this paper, I assume that E is the subject of *all* German passives. As a consequence, no NP-movement has to be assumed for these constructions. I believe that this is a desirable result in view of the fact that there is no evidence for NP-movement in German passives, as has often been noted in the literature. Perhaps this analysis exaggerates the importance of E. In particular, it is not compatible with the view that case inheritance via E should go hand in hand with the definiteness effect. *Vide* section 18 for a discussion. This part of the analysis can easily be respelled as a conventional movement analysis. But even those who prefer a movement (plus scrambling) analysis for German passives have to assume the E-expletive for impersonal passives and some other impersonal constructions. Thus, the theory of empty elements developed in this article is justified on independent grounds.

With respect to GB-theory, the article contains only some small deviations. In particular, the non-lexical dative is treated as a structural case. This move will make it possible to treat the dative-nominative alternation which we find in the so called recipient passive. Furthermore, the notion 'case absorption,' which is assumed in the Chomskyan passive theory, is not described by stipulating a categorial difference between the morphology of the active and the passive verb: rather, case absorption is governed by superordinate passivizers like *werden* and is described by 'neutralization features.' I find this description revealing and suggestive, but anyone who prefers a case theory in strictly configurational terms is welcome to retranslate whatever I say into the exact terminology of GB-theory. In any case, the recipient passive requires a revision of Burzio's generalization, which is given in section 17.

Unfortunately, space limitation prevents me from adequately discussing the relevant literature on German syntax. It will be obvious that I am indebted to authors like Bech, den Besten, Bierwisch, Evers, Fanselow, Grewendorf, Haider, Höhle, Kratzer, Lenerz, Haegeman and Riemsdijk, Reis and Sternefeld, to mention a few. For some relevant references, see the bibliography. I am particularly indebted to discussions with Josef Bayer, Catherine Fabricius-Hansen, Giuliana Giusti, Hubert Haider, Angelika Kratzer, Wolfgang Sternefeld and Dieter Wunderlich. I wish to thank Stephen Berman for checking my English.

2. Status Government

Status is a morphological property of the non-finite verb (=*supinum*). According to Bech, we have to distinguish between the following three statuses of the supinum:

(1)   first status: *schenken* 'give'
          second status: zu *schenken* 'to give'
          third status: *geschenkt* 'given'

Thus, the first status is the bare infinitive, the second status is the 'prepositional' infinitive, and the third status is the past participle. The status of a supinum is governed by the superordinate verb:

(2)   *weil Ede niemanden zu belästigen versucht haben will*
                  no one   to molest   tried   have wants
                         st.2 ⟵——⟶ st. 3 ⟵——⟶ st.1 ⟵——⟶

In this example, *will* 'wants' governs first status (= st.1). *Haben* 'have' is of first status but governs third status, *versucht* 'tried' (optionally) governs second status (st.2).

Status government is perhaps an irreducible lexical property. A 'functional' explanation for its existence would be that status government serves the purpose of distinguishing between different meanings of the same (governing) verb. The following list illustrates this claim:

(3) | verb | status governed | meaning |
          |------|-----------------|---------|
          | *haben* | status 2 | necessity/possibility |
          | *haben* | status 3 | past |
          | *sein* | status 2 | necessity/possibility |
          | *sein* | status 3 | past |
          | *werden* | status 1 | future |
          | *werden* | status 3 | passive |

From this list, one would guess that status government is confined to auxiliaries only. This, however, is not the case. Also certain 'control verbs' govern status, for instance, *wollen* 'to want' governs first status and *wünschen* 'to wish' optionally governs second status. Furthermore, certain 'raising verbs' like *scheinen* 'to seem' and *plegen* 'to be used to,' which traditionally are not regarded as auxiliaries, govern status, in this case the second one.

3. Coherence

In German syntax, a subordinating construction is called *coherent* if it doesn't embed a sentence. In VI, Bech gives, among others, the following criteria for coherence. First: The negative element of a 'cohesion' may have wide scope with respect to a superordinate verb which is connected via status government to the verb the cohesion depends on. The following examples illustrate the phenomenon (Cf. VI, § 80).

(4)   a.   *weil   sie   nichts   sagen wollte*
             because she nothing say   wanted
        b.   because she didn't want to say anything
        c.   because she wanted to say nothing

(4a) means the same as (4b). It *could* mean (4c), if such a reading were a reasonable one. On the other hand, the English sentence (4c) can't mean the same as (4b). A plausible explanation is that, at the relevant level of grammmatical representation, *wollen* doesn't embed a sentence whereas *to want* does. In (4a), the cohesion in question is *nichts* = *nicht+etwas* (not+something). I won't go into the question of what the appropriate analysis of cohesion is. The only thing that matters here is that the scope of the negative element of a cohesion is limited to the sentence where it occurs. In order to show this, we have to consider an incoherent verb like *bedauern* 'to regret,' which embeds a sentence.

(5)   a.   *weil sie bedauerte, nichts zu wissen*
        b.   because she regretted to know nothing
        c.   because she didn't regret to know anything

(5a) unambiguously means (5b) and never (5c). To summarize the criterion: If the negative element of a cohesion negates a 'higher' verb, then there is no sentence barrier between the cohesion and the negated verb.

Another criterion for coherence is the non-existence of extraposition in a coherent construction (Cf. VI, § 73 ff.).

(6)   a.   *weil   sie   nicht wagt, ihn zu stören*
             because she not   dares him to disturb
       b.   **weil   sie   nicht darf ihn stören*
             because she not   may him disturb

Wagen 'to dare' may be constructed incoherently, whereas *dürfen* 'may' is obligatorily coherent. Therefore no extraposition is possible in (6b). The explanation is straightforward: If extraposition is a rule that applies to sentences, then it can't apply to *ihn stören*, given that this sequence isn't a sentence. If it were a sentence, *dürfen* would be an incoherent verb.

A third criterion, which illustrates the same point as the second criterion, is this: In coherent constructions there is no 'relative clause pied-piping' (This is not Bech's terminology, of course.) (Cf. VI, § 81).

(7)   a.   *ein Umstand,   den   zu berücksichtigen   er immer*
             a   circumstance, which to take into account he always
             vergißt
             forgets
       b.   **ein Umstand,   den   berücksichtigen   er immer*
             a   circumstance, which take into account he always
             muß
             must

Vergessen 'to forget' is an incoherent verb, i.e., it embeds a sentence. On the other hand, *müssen* 'must' is a coherent verb, it doesn't embed a sentence. The only thing we have to assume to explain the contrast of the two examples is that 'relative clause pied-piping' involves movement of an embedded sentence at some stage, say [*PRO den zu berücksichtigen*]. Clearly, the relevant rule can't apply in the case of (7b), given that *müssen qua* coherent verb doesn't embed a sentence. For details concerning 'relative clause pied-piping,' see van Riemsdijk (1985) and Haider (1985).

A fourth criterion to distinguish between coherent and incoherent constructions is the following: In a coherent construction we can get rid of an 'impossible empty subject.' I will illustrate the observation by means of examples.

(8)   a.   *die Wahrscheinlichkeit, [daß hier gelogen wurde],*
             the probability   that here lied   was[=passive]

       ist unerfreulich
       is unpleasant
  b. **die Wahrscheinlichkeit, [hier gelogen worden zu sein],*
       the probability   here lied   been   to be
       ist unerfreulich
       is unpleasant
  c. *weil   [hier gelogen worden zu sein] scheint*
       because here lied   been   to be   seems

In all these cases, we embed an impersonal passive. A look at examples (a) and (b) convinces us that the ungrammaticality of the (b)-sentence is not due to semantic reasons: we know what the (b)-sentence would mean, *viz.*, by and large, the same as the (a)-sentence. Thus, the reason for the ungrammaticality is likely to be a syntactic one. The explanation is not that a noun like *Wahrscheinlichkeit* doesn't embed infinitivals: It is easy to find examples with infinitival complements. The reason rather is that the infinitival [*hier gelogen worden zu sein*] is ungrammatical as such because it requires a completely featureless empty subject, which is impossible. Call this impossible subject e^*. Whatever features we choose for a classification of empty elements (±theta-role, ±case, ±argument, ±anaphor, ±pronoun), e^* has none of these. We return to a general theory of empty elements in section 7.

Now, (8c) embeds exactly the same string as (8b), but (8c) is perfectly grammatical. The explanation is again straightforward if we make the usual GB-assumption that every sentence has a subject ('extended projection principle'). Then we obtain a structural difference between (8b) and (8c): (8b) embeds a sentence, which, according to the subject principle, must have a subject. This subject can only be the impossible empty element e^*, hence the ungrammaticality of (8b). On the other hand, the coherent verb *scheinen* doesn't embed a sentence. Therefore we need not assume the impossible element e^* in the case of (8c).

The next examples illustrate the same point with another impersonal infinitival:

  (9) a. *weil   die Möglichkeit, daß ihr kalt wird,   besteht*
         because the possibility   that her cold becomes exists
      b. **weil   die Möglichkeit [e^* ihr kalt zu werden] besteht*
         because the possibility   her cold to become exists
      c. *weil   ihr kalt werden kann*
         because [her cold become] can

These sentences mean more or less the same. As before, we have to assume that *Möglichkeit* embeds a sentence with the impossible empty subject e^*. On the other hand, the coherent verb *können* 'can' doesn't embed a sentence at all. Hence the contrast in grammaticality.

A fifth criterion is reflexivization: The antecedent of a reflexive must be within the same sentence. Consider the following contrast:

(10) a. *weil   der König$_i$ den Bauern für sich$_i$ arbeiten ließ*
     because the king$_i$ the peasant for himself$_i$ work   let

   b. **weil   der König$_i$ den Bauern veranlaßte, für sich$_i$*
     because the king$_i$ the peasant motivated, for himself$_i$
     zu arbeiten
     to work

A reflexive embedded in a PP may refer to a subject (not necessarily 'the nearest'), provided the latter is within the same sentence. This shows that the infinitival *den Bauern für sich arbeiten* in (a) can't be a sentence in the relevant sense, whereas the infinitival *für sich zu arbeiten* in (b) must be a sentence.

4. Status Government Implies Coherence

Gunnar Bech has observed that verbs governing the first or the third status are always coherently constructed. He calls this generalization the *rule of coherence* (Cf. VI, § 65). Verbs governing the second status may be either coherent or incoherent. I propose to generalize this rule in the following way:

(11)   *The generalized rule of coherence*
     If a verb actually governs a status, then it is coherently constructed.

It follows that an incoherent verb like *bedauern* 'to regret' doesn't govern a status at all, a deviation from Bech, who assumed that it governs the second status. In section 6, I will argue that the second status of non-finite clauses is not governed 'from outside' but rather by the (empty) complementizer. This does not imply that the second status is never governed by a superordinate verb. For instance, a verb like *wünschen* 'to wish' optionally governs the second status: If it does, it doesn't embed a clause at the level where status is checked, if it doesn't, it embeds a clause. The adverb 'actually' in (11) refers to verbs that optionally govern a status.

Bech didn't try to derive the rule of coherence from general principles, but I think that such a derivation is possible. The rule follows from the notion of government, provided we define it in an appropriate way. Let me show this.

Consider first a 'control verb' like *wollen* 'to want,' which governs the first status. Suppose that *wollen* embeds a sentence in D-structure, i.e., (12a) has the D-structure (12b). This assumption is reasonable, because *wollen* may embed finite clauses.

(12) a.   *weil   sie schlafen will*
           because she sleep   wants
     b.   *weil sie [$_{CP}$ø[$_{IP}$PRO schlafen]] will*

Since the first status of *schlafen* is governed by *will*, the intervening CP-node must be deleted (or made transparent for government, an option I shall neglect, because it amounts to much the same thing), because government across CP is not possible, given the usual GB-assumptions. Now, in GB-theory, IP is not a barrier for government. Therefore, the verb *will* can perhaps govern the status of the embedded VP *schlafen*. But then the empty subject PRO is structurally governed by the verb *will*, which is not possible. The following picture illustrates the situation after CP-deletion:

(13)   *sie* [$_{IP}$ PRO [$_{I'}$ [$_{VP}$ *schlafen*] INFL]] *will*
                        1.status ←————————⏌
              ←——————————————————⏌
                    structural government

Since this structure is illformed, we must 'delete' PRO. This, however, entails that we also 'delete' the empty node INFL, because the extended projection principle requires that every IP has a subject. (We are assuming that every 'sentence' is at least an IP and possibly a CP. It would be rather implausible to apply the principle to CP only but not to IP, because the subject position is in IP and not in CP.) Suppose now we didn't delete INFL together with PRO. Then we would have an IP as well, since INFL has a maximal projection. But then we could not have 'dropped' PRO. But we have dropped PRO. Therefore, INFL must be deleted and the relevant surface structure of (12a) can't be (13). It must be something like (14).

(14)   *sie* [$_{VP}$ *schlafen*] *will*
                st.1 ←————⏌

I don't want to commit myself to an answer to the question whether (14) is actually base generated or not. What I am claiming is that, at the level where status is checked, the structure of (12a) must be (14) or something equivalent. It can't be (12b).

Let us consider now a control verb (optionally) governing the 2. status, for instance *wünschen* 'to wish.' The D-structure of (15a) is (15b):

(15) a. *weil   sie zu tanzen wünscht*
          because she to dance   wishes
     b. *weil sie* $[_{CP}$ ø $[_{IP}$ *PRO* $[_{I'}$ $[_{VP}$ *tanzen*$]$ $[_{I}$ *zu*$]]]$ *wünscht*

We are assuming that the 2. status morpheme *zu* is in INFL in D-structure. *Zu* is incorporated into the adjacent verb by a later rule (or, perhaps, the verb moves to INFL). After CP-deletion, IP is governed and the 2.status 'percolates' to the INFL-position. But, again, the subject PRO is structurally governed, which is not possible. We illustrate the situation:

(16)   *weil sie* $[_{IP}$ *PRO* $[_{I'}$ $[_{VP}$ *tanzen*$]$ $[_{I}$ *zu*$]]$ *wünscht*

                    structural government

         st.2 ←——————————————————————

                    status government

Since this configuration is not possible, we have to delete IP as before. If we make the standard assumption that the governed element is maximal, it follows that the second status morpheme *zu* must already be incorporated into the verb, when status government is checked. In other words, the S-structure of (15a) can't be (16), it has to be (17):

(17)   *weil sie* $[_{VP}$ *zu tanzen*$]$ *wünscht*
                    2.st. ←——————————

Note incidentally that (17) is not compatible with the view that the governed verb moves to INFL: If it did, we would basically have the structure (16), which we excluded. We return to the question whether the verb moves to INFL or whether INFL is incorporated into the verb in section 6.

If we compare (17) with (14), we observe the following: In the case of *wollen* 'to want' it was not clear whether we actually had to assume a sentential complement in D-structure. But this time, it is pretty clear that *wünschen* embeds a sentential complement in D-structure, because it can be constructed incoherently:

(18)   *sie hat gewünscht, lange   zu schlafen*
          she has wished,   longtime to sleep

It would seem then that the 'PRO-drop' which we have to assume for a
coherent construction is not compatible with the extended projection principle, which entails that a D-subject position is projected to every syntactic
level. Furthermore, it is not clear how the theta-criterion is satisfied at the
level where status government is checked, because, in (17), the subject *sie*
seems to have two thematic roles, *viz.* the subject roles of 'to wish' and 'to
dance.' A slight revision of the two mentioned principles will solve this
apparent inconsistency. I don't want to discuss this revision but refer the
reader to von Stechow & Sternefeld (1988: chapter 12). Basically, a particular NP may be the subject of different verbs. So the pair of nodes $[NP,V_1]$
will be the subject relative to the verb V_1, and $[NP,V_2]$ will be the subject
relative to the verb V_2. So one NP in a tree may be a component of two different grammatical functions, and the projection principle and the theta-
criterion refer to this notion of grammatical function.

We have seen that government of the first and the second status
implies coherence. For verbs governing the third status, i.e., past participles, this claim is not controversal, because virtually nobody assumes that
these verbs embed sentences at some level of grammatical representation. It
would, however, be in the spirit of G. Bech to say that also these verbs
embed sentences at D-structure, because he assumes a logical subject for
each verb. Let me briefly discuss what such an assumption amounts to. It is
tempting to say that a temporal auxiliary like *haben* 'to have' is a raising
verb (cf. Postal 1974 for a similar claim). So the S-structure of (19a) would
be (19b).

(19) a. *weil   sie gelacht hat*
         because she laughed has
     b. *weil sie$_i$ [$_{IP}$ t$_i$ [$_{VP}$ gelacht] INFL] hat*
                      st.3 ←————————————┘

The completely empty INFL is, however, an artefact and should perhaps
not be admitted at S-structure. An analysis more in the spirit of the former
discussion would be to delete it. Then we can't have a subject trace, i.e.,
the S-structure must be (20).

(20)   *weil sie [$_{VP}$ gelacht] hat*
                   st.3 ←————————┘

This discussion suggests that the easiest way to analyze (19a) is to base-generate the surface (20).

Let me summarize this section. Whatever the right D-structures of the sentences discussed are, the usual principles governing government lead us to the conclusion that status government implies coherence. This is a rather satisfying result, because it reduces the phenomenon of coherence to a single source. We have to learn status government anyway as a lexical idiosyncrasy. Coherence follows from the notion of government. Earlier generative approaches like Evers (1974) stipulated a lexically governed rule of *clause union*, in the same way as S'-deletion is a lexical stipulation in GB-theory. A more revealing way to explain the phenomenon of coherence is to say that status government imposes certain restrictions on grammatical representations. There is no particular rule of clause union. Clause union rather is a consequence of certain wellformedness conditions.

5.   Formal Notions: X'-Scheme, Government, Feature Inheritance

In this section I introduce the principles that entail the predictions made in the last section.

I am going to assume an X'-scheme in the style of Muysken (1982).

(21)   The X'-Scheme
Any branching satisfies the condition

$$[X,\alpha\text{-proj},\beta\text{-max}] \to \ldots [X,\alpha'\text{-proj},\beta'\text{-max}] \ldots$$

where (i) α,α',β and β' are variables for + or −, (ii) the transition from − to + is not permitted (in the sense of the direction of the arrow) and (iii) the dots . . . stand for an arbitrary sequence of [+max]-categories.

Let me comment on the different feature combinations [±m(ax)] and [±p(rojection)].

(22) a. $[X,+m,+p]$ is a maximal projection of X, i.e., an XP.
      b. $[X,-m,+p]$ is a non-maximal but non-lexical category, which is abbreviated as X'.
      c. $[X,+m,-p]$ is a maximal lexical category, e.g. an article. Abbreviation: X^m.
      d. $[X,-m,-p]$ is a non-maximal lexical category. Abbreviation: X.

I will assume that the X'-scheme holds at least at D- and S-Structure.

I will now introduce Aoun and Sportiche's notion of structural government (cf. Aoun & Sportiche 1981) and then extend the notion in order to cover the traditional relations of case- and status-government.

(23)   *X structurally governs Y* iff X and Y are dominated by the same maximal projections.

We assume that X contains the feature $[-p]$ and Y contains the feature $[+m]$. In other words, the governor is lexical and the governee is maximal, usually phrasal. In order to be consistent with the discussion in the previous section, we have to add the qualification that IP doesn't count as a barrier for government. In other words, Y may be dominated in addition by IP.

The following definition generalizes the notion to feature government.

(24)   The projection X *α-governs* the projection Y iff X has the feature __α (or α__), Y has the feature α and X structurally governs Y.

The notation '__α' or 'α__' means that α is required 'at the right side' or 'at the left side' respectively. The 'direction of government' is indicated for convenience only. In what follows, this information is never needed. Hence we could have chosen a 'direction-free' notation.

According to definition (24) we can distinguish between *case government, status government, theta government* or whatever, depending on whether α is a case, a status or a thematic role. The definition captures a very general notion of feature assignment under government. Further restrictions like adjacency are possible but require further specifications. In German, case government does not require adjacency, as we would expect in a language with morphologically visible case. Consider the following examples:

(25) a.   *weil   Ede* [$_{VP}$:ACC [$_{NP}$ *das Geld*:ACC][$_{V'}$[$_{PP}$ *in   die*
            because Ede   the money   into the
            Tasche] steckt:ACC__]]
            pocket   put

      b.   *weil   wir*[$_{VP}$[$_{NP}$ *den Direktor*:ACC][$_{V'}$[$_{NP}$ *dem*
            because we   the director   to the
            Präsidenten] vorstellten:ACC__DAT__]]]
            president   introduced

c. *weil*   *er*[_{VP}[_{NP} *seiner Freundin*:DAT][_{V'}[_{NP} *seinen*
    because he   to his girl friend   his
    Hut:ACC] *schenkte*:ACC_DAT_]]]
    hat   gave

These sentences show the unmarked word order. In (a), the accusative governed by the verb is separated from it by a directional phrase. In (b) it is separated by a dative NP, only in (c) it is adjacent. According to our definition of case government it is no problem to base generate these word orders.

Let us next say a few words about feature inheritance. For the time being we need only the following principle, which is generally accepted in the literature:

(26)   *The head principle*
        Features are inherited/projected along the head-line in the
        sense of the X'-scheme.

The reader may check for himself that these definitions entail the generalized rule of coherence. Let me illustrate only one relevant example:

(27) a. *weil   sie nichts sagen wollte*
         because she nothing say   wanted
     b. *weil sie* [_{CP} ø [_{IP} PRO [_{I'} [_{VP} *nichts sagen*][_Iø]]]] *wollte*
                                                                              st.1__

(b) is the D-structure of (27a). *Wollen* 'to want' governs the first status, which can't be assigned to the embedded verb, because status government is not possible across the CP-barrier. After CP-deletion we must delete IP with PRO and the empty INFL as well for the reasons discussed in the last section. Then the first status can be assigned to the embedded VP, where it percolates to the head *sagen*. The following picture gives the relevant part of the surface structure.

(28)   *weil sie nichts sagen wollte*

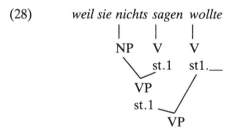

It follows from the formal definition of feature government that CP is a parameter relevant for incoherence, because status government across CP is not possible. Nothing commits us to consider IP as well a relevant barrier. Thus, it is not ruled out that a coherent verb like *lassen* 'to let' embeds IP (cf. section 13), it is only ruled out that *lassen* embeds CP at the level where status government is checked. Thus, the informal notion *sentence*, which has been used in section 3, is reconstructed as CP.

A final remark concerns the question at what level of grammatical representation status government is checked. The only thing we will assume in the following discussion is that status government is not necessarily checked at D-structure. We don't differentiate yet between the level of S-structure proper, i.e., the level where the rules for structural case and the binding principles apply, and the level where status is governed. We will refer to both kinds of structures as S-structures. In section 20 will we argue that status government has to apply after S-structure.

6. Feature Government by INFL and COMP

In this section I want to defend the following claims. First: The dependencies between COMP and INFL on the one hand and between INFL and VP on the other hand are best spelled out in terms of feature government: COMP and INFL are connected by [±tense]-government, and INFL and VP are connected by AGR-government. Second: In the case of non-finite IPs, a complication arises: *zu* is in INFL and must be incorporated into VP after reanalysis. Third: There is no movement of the finite verb to INFL.

We assumed that INFL contains the preposition *zu* in the case of infinitives, an assumption widely made in the current literature. *Zu* is incorporated only into supina in first status, as the following pattern shows:

(29) a. *zu schenken*
    b. **zu zu schenken*
    c. **zu geschenkt*

In (b), *zu* incorrectly combines with a verb in the second status and in (c) it incorrectly combines with a verb in the third status. These observations quite naturally lead to the following hypothesis:

(30) $[_I zu]$ governs the first status.

It is now tempting to say that there is no second status at all: The second status could be regarded as a merely descriptive category that describes a

verb in the 1.status with *zu* incorporated. It is, however, practical to have
the second status in the morphology already, because such a move enables
us to make a distinction between sentential and non sentential prepositional
infinitivals: If the infinitival contains *zu* in the syntactic INFL-position, then
it is sentential. Otherwise it is not sentential. The following two S-structures
illustrate the relevant contrast:

(31)   *weil   sie gewünscht hat* ∅ PRO *in Frieden sterben zu*
         because she wished   has | | in peace   die   to

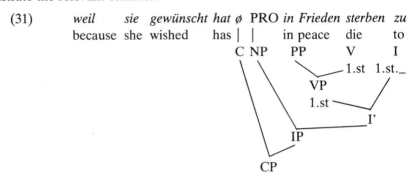

Here, we have *zu* in the syntactic INFL-position. It governs first status,
which is assigned to the embedded VP, whence it percolates to the head
verb. After *zu*-incorporation, we obtain the correct surface. This is the sentential infinitival.

Let us consider the coherent construction next. At the level where
status government is checked, we have to assume the following structure:

(32)   *weil sie* [$_{VP}$ [*in Frieden*] [$_V$ *zu sterben*]] *gewünscht hat*
             st.2 ←   ⌐

Remember that *wünschen* 'to wish' optionally governs second status. This
feature can't be assigned to the embedded IP across the CP barrier. Hence,
CP-deletion is necessary. For the reasons discussed in the last section, we
have to delete PRO and the INFL-node. We can do the latter only if we
incorporate the *zu* under INFL into the left-adjacent verb. The result will
be the structure (32). Here, the feature [+zu] is assigned to the embedded
VP, whence it percolates to the head. It follows that status government has
to be checked after clause union and *zu*-incorporation. In section 20, we
will discuss the question what this ordering of the rules implies for the
organization of the grammar of German.

One might further object that the stipulation of a rule of *zu*-incorpora-
tion (which is a version of 'Affix-hopping') is *ad hoc*. The following observation, however, which is due to Marga Reis, makes the existence of a rule

of *zu*-incorporation quite plausible, as has been argued in von Stechow & Sternefeld (1988: chapter 11):

(33) a. *ohne   es zu wissen*
         without it to know

   b. *ohne   es gewußt zu haben*
                    st.3 ←————⏌
         without it known to have

   c. *ohne   es wissen zu können*
                    st.1 ←————⏌
         without it known to can

   d. ?*ohne   es wissen können zu haben*
                    st.1 ←——⏌ st.1^e ←————⏌
         without it known can   to have

   e. **ohne es zu haben wissen können*

   f. *ohne es haben wissen zu können*
                st.1 ←————⏌
                ⏌————————————→ st.1^e

As the pictures show, *haben* governs third status and, under certain conditions, the so called 'Ersatzinfinitiv,' here denoted by st.1^e. *Können* governs first status. All these infinitivals are sentential, hence the most superordinate verb should be in the second status. Consider now (d) to (f). (d) shows the status we would expect. But for certain reasons, this construction is not very acceptable. We form a 'complex verb' and move *haben* to the beginning of it, the so called 'Oberfeld.' Since *haben* is the most superordinate verb of the infinitival, it should be in the second status. (e), however, is ungrammatical. The 'Oberfeld' doesn't admit verbs in the second status. As (f) shows, *zu* is found at the final verb *können*, though this verb should have the status of the 'Ersatzinfinitiv' st.1^e. The situation is explained, if we assume that the rule of *zu*-incorporation operates after the formation of the complex verb. In other words, before *zu*-inversion, the relevant S-structure of (33f) is something like this:

(34)   *ohne* [$_{IP}$PRO [$_{I'}$ [$_{VP}$ *es* [$_V$ *haben* [$_V$ [$_V$ *wissen*] *können*]]] *zu*]

After *zu*-incorporation we obtain the surface (33f). Let us therefore assume the following rule.

(35)   *zu*-incorporation
         [$_I$*zu*] is incorporated into the left-adjacent (noncomplex) verb.

The rule operates after the checking of status government and after the formation of the complex verb.

Let me next turn to INFL in the finite (subordinate) clause. The standard GB-assumption is that INFL contains the agreement features AGR, in German, person and number, and the feature [+tense]. The nominative rule is this:

(36)   NP is nominative if governed by $[_I +AGR]$.

In the formalism defined in the previous section, we would say that $[_I+AGR]$ has the feature [nominative__]. Hence, the relevant configuration for nominative government is the following:

(37)

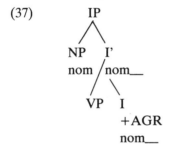

Now, agreement is a special relation different from government. In GB this relation holds between the head of a category and its specifier and is indicated by cosuperscripting. Thus, the relevant structure for subject-predicate agreement is this:

(38)

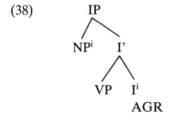

Cosuperscripted categories share those features which can be shared (tense as a verbal feature can't be shared by the subject-NP, of course). The question is how the main verb in VP can have the features in INFL. We could either stipulate the agreement relation between VP and INFL, or we could move the main verb to the INFL-position. The first option has an *ad hoc* flavour. Furthermore, it doesn't seem to be advocated by anyone and should be justified by some more principled considerations. The second option, on the other hand, is widely accepted among generative grammarians. According to this view, the relevant S-structure is the following:

(39)

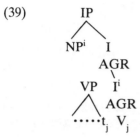

This structure raises the question how we should interpret the category INFL. If categories are projections of features, the finite verb moved to INFL should be an INFL itself. This view, however, is not compatible with the structure (39). If the finite verb were an INFL, then there couldn't be a VP: No V, no VP. A position along these lines is taken in Kratzer (1984). It may be the correct position but I will not discuss it here, because it deviates from the common practice and would need a careful justification, which I can't give here. The common practice seems to entail that INFL is an abstract category which may contain quite heterogeneous material like AGR, [± tense], the preposition *zu*. Since the features of the finite verb must be checked, one way of doing this is to move the verb to that position, as indicated in (39). This analysis would entail that INFL is a positional category.

The V-movement analysis is problematic for another reason: If we consider an example which is like (33f) with the exception that the most superordinate verb is finite, then we find that the finite morphology is realized at the beginning of the complex verb. Consider the following examples:

(40) a.   *weil   er das nicht wissen können **hat***
      because he that not   know   can   has
   b.   *weil   er das nicht **hat** wissen können*
      because he that not   has know   can

(a) is the structure before the formation of the complex verb. After reanalysis, the finite verb is at the beginning of the complex verb, as (b) shows. These facts are hard to explain, if we assume that the finite verb has to move to INFL. The formation of complex verbs with inversions is entirely independent of the finite/non-finite distinction. Only the class of the verbs involved matters (for details, *vide* Haegeman & Riemsdijk 1984).

Thus the derivation of the two complex verbs discussed here is presumably something like this:

(41) 1.   ...*wissen* $_{VP}$] *können* $_{VP}$] *hat* $_{VP}$] [AGR$_1$]$_{I'}$], S-structure,
                           AGR ⟵⎯⎯⏌   Checking of AGR

     2.   ...[*hat* [*wissen können* $_V$] $_V$] $_{VP}$] [AGR$_1$] $_{I'}$], Formation of the
                                                          complex verb by
                                                          reanalysis

If we want to check AGR after reanalysis, we must make sure that the initial *hat* is the head of the complex V. This is not possible without a special stipulation, in view of the general fact that the head of a complex V is the rightmost V. In other words, AGR-checking presumably has to apply before reanalysis. On the other hand, *zu*-incorporation must apply after the formation of the complex V, as should be clear from the previous discussion. For convenience, we repeat the relevant derivation:

(41') 1.   ...*wissen* $_{VP}$] *können* $_{VP}$] *haben* $_{VP}$] [*zu*$_1$]$_{I'}$], S-structure

      2.   ... [*haben* [*wissen können* $_V$] $_V$] $_{VP}$][*zu*$_{I'}$ $_{I'}$], Formation of the
                                                           complex verb by
                                                           reanalysis

      3.   ...[*haben* [*wissen* [*zu können*] $_V$]$_V$]$_{VP}$][$_I$]$_{I'}$], *zu*-incorporation

It seems to me that this is the simplest way to analyze the data mentioned. Therefore, I will assume that something along these lines is correct.

We still have to say what the mechanism of AGR-checking which is presupposed in (41) actually is. I see no reason why this relation should not be AGR-government. Let us tentatively assume that INFL and COMP govern their own features:

(42)   [X,+α] governs α, where X is INFL or COMP, and α is any
           (morphological or inflectional) feature of X.

Given this principle, the structure accounting for the agreement relation would be (6-16):

(43)   [$_{IP}$ NP^i [$_{I'}$ VP   [$_I$ AGR]^i]]
                       AGR ⟵⎯⎯⏌

In other words, rule (41) assigns the agreement features of the INFL-node to the governed VP, whereas the subject obtains the agreement features by means of cosuperscripting — the usual device, which is entirely independent of principle (42).

This analysis avoids at least one difficulty of the movement analysis: If the latter would apply to English, then an irregular verb should be able to move to COMP via INFL, since the material in INFL can move to COMP (Subject-auxiliary-inversion). This, however, is not possible, as the following contrast shows:

(44) a. $[_{CP}$ has$_i$ $[_{IP}$ Max $[_{I'}$t$_i$$[_{VP}$left]]]]
      b. $*[_{CP}$ left$_i$ $[_{IP}$ Max $[_{I'}$ t$_i$, $[_{VP}$ t$_i$]]]]

If there is no movement from V to INFL, then (44b) can't be generated. If there is such a movement, then we have to account for the illformedness of (44b), but it is not clear how this should be done without additional stipulations. If we assume principle (42), then there is no reason why V should move to INFL.

Principle (42) enables us to analyze the relation between COMP and INFL, because it yields the following government structures for CPs, where α is [+tense] or [−tense]:

(45)

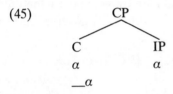

The only thing we have to assume is that *zu* is the morphological realization of $[_I$-tense]. As a consequence we can derive the following two statements for German:

(46) a. COMP with [−tense] governs *zu*.
      b. COMP with [+tense] governs [INFL, +tense].

Both generalizations are empirically correct. Thus, the 'path' between COMP and INFL, whose existence has been argued for on independent grounds in Pesetsky (1982), is reconstructed in this approach as [±tense]-government by COMP.

Let me add a remark why the AGR-relation between INFL and SpecI should not be considered as an instance of government, though SpecI is structurally governed by INFL. The reason is that two occurrences of the same feature can't be governed by the same head. Formally, this can be spelled out the following way: When a feature α and a government feature __α or α__ 'meet' in a tree, i.e., when the features are directly dominated by the same node, then they cancel:

(47)

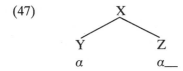

In categorial notation, this cancellation mechanism could be written as α $\alpha\backslash\Lambda \Rightarrow \Lambda$, where Λ stands for an empty category. For more details, *vide* Sternefeld (1982). A consequence of this convention is that INFL can't AGR-govern both the VP and SpecI. Since we have assumed that INFL AGR-governs VP, the AGR-relation between INFL and SpecI must be spelled out by means of a different device, *viz.* something like cosuperscripting.

To conclude the discussion of this section: The 'abstract' categories INFL and COMP seem to have the property of governing the features which they contain. If this generalization is true, we can describe the COMP-INFL-agreement in Bavarian (cf. Bayer 1984) by that method: A COMP with AGR would govern AGR and thereby assign these features to IP where they percolate to INFL. An INFL with AGR governs AGR and assigns AGR correctly to the embedded VP:

(48)   *Vater,   erzähl* [$_{CP}$ *wie-st* [$_{IP}$? [$_{I'}$[*im Krieg gewesen*
                              AGR
                              $\longmapsto$ AGR
          Father, tell   how-2.sing. in the war been
          bi-st $_{VP}$][$_{I}$AGR]]]]
                   AGR$\longleftarrow$
          be-2.sing.

The question remains how the AGR-features can get to COMP in this construction and why we have no subject. But these problems won't concern me in this article.

7.   The Place of *E* in the System of Empty Elements

The GB-classification of empty categories, which assumes the four empty NPs *PRO, pro, NP*-trace and *variable*, is not adequate for German. In this section l want to give a classification that yields five empty elements, namely the four mentioned plus the empty expletive *E*.

The classification starts from an insight which has first been expressed in Sternefeld (1982). In order to analyze impersonal passives in German, we need an empty subject *E*, which can neither be *PRO* nor *pro*, because

PRO has the features [+argument,−case], *pro* has the features [+argument,+case], whereas *E* has the features [−argument,+case]. Given that the latter feature combination characterizes expletives like *there* or *it*, it is convenient to call *E* the *empty expletive*.

(49)   [$_{CP}$ *weil* [$_{IP}$ *E*   *jetzt getanzt wird*]]
                              −argument
                              +case
                        because   now danced is

In von Stechow & Sternefeld (1988), we have argued that also in Italian inversions we must have an *E*-subject:

(50) E^i *ha   telefonato   Gianni*^{i}
                  has called   Gianni

If the empty subject were (referential) *pro* in this construction, the theta-criterion would be violated, because *pro* is an argument and a chain can't have two arguments. If, on the other hand, *E* is a non-argument, then the chain is wellformed. *E* is presumably in a theta-position. But this is no problem, because the theta-role is not assigned to the element occupying that position, but to the chain. The situation is analogous to passivized infinitivals, where an argument may occupy a non-theta-position (compare, e.g., *PRO to be arrested t*). Note that *Gianni* inherits nominative from the subject *E* via agreement, as indicated by cosuperscripting. In what follows we will make the usual GB-assumptions on chains formed by means of cosuperscripting. In particular, these chains can never cross a CP-barrier. If we classify empty non-traces of CPs by means of the features [±argument] and [±case], we arrive at the following system:

(51)   *Empty non-traces*

	PRO	pro	e	e*
case	−	+	+	−
argument	+	+	−	−

*e** is what we have called the impossible subject in section 3. Let me repeat a relevant example:

(52)   *weil die Möglichkeit*[$_{CP}$[$_{IP}$*e**   *ihr kalt zu werden*]
                                        −argument
                                        −case

            the possibility   her cold to become
            besteht
            exists

The ungrammaticality of (52) follows from the following assumption:

(53)   An empty CP-subject with features $[-\text{argument}, -\text{case}]$ doesn't exist.

This assumption is quite natural, if we assume that empty elements must be visible. Since e^* has no features at all, we can't identify it.

Let me now turn to empty non-subjects, i.e., traces. In GB-theory, traces in case-position count as arguments. This, however, would make the features $[\pm\text{argument}]$ redundant. The motivation for our classification is this: In (50), the case of an inverted subject, E is in a θ-position but, as we have seen, it can't be an argument. Therefore, the property $[+\text{argument}]$ can't be structurally defined but has to be stipulated. Hence, there is no reason to say that a trace in case-position should be an argument and one without case should not be an argument. The following move seems to be more natural to me: *traces are never arguments in the sense of our terminology*. This assumption is reasonable enough if we conceive of traces as traces of a moved argument expression. Given this assumption, we obtain the following two traces:

(54)   *Traces*

	NP-trace	Wh-trace
argument	−	−
case	−	+

To be sure, this classification makes sense only if we have in mind a more general concept of chains than A-chains. We have to include non-A-chains (*vide* Aoun 1981 or Koster 1981/82). Given this more general concept of chain, in (55), *who* would be the argument of the chain, whereas t_i and $t_{i'}$ would be $[-\text{argument}]$:

(55) who_i [t_i' was arrested t_i]
            $+\text{arg}$ $-\text{arg}$ $-\text{arg}$

This classification seems to be a rather big deviation from GB-theory. But this isn't the case. Recall first that E is identical to what is called *expletive pro* in the literature about Romance. Most people don't dispute the existence of this element (an exeption being Haider 1987), but I know of no principled definition of it. Recall further that, in GB-theory, 'argument' refers to a certain type of expression. That a subject-trace with case can be called argument is nothing but a reflection of the fact that the trace is locally bound by an operator in non-argument position. It makes no difference if we call the subject-trace a non-argument and the operator binding it an argument in such cases, because there is a one-to-one correspondence between the two locutions with respect to this situation: If there is a variable in the sense of GB-theory, then there will always be an operator locally binding it. Thus, the variable will be the head of an A-chain and will be an argument in the GB-terminology. If we generalize the notion of chain, the head of the chain will be the operator locally binding the variable. If a chain can have only one argument, it is convenient to call the operator an argument and to call the variable a non-argument. The theta-criterion has to be formulated with respect to this kind of chain, of course. The binding theory can be formulated as in GB. The only thing we have to assume is that *Wh*-traces are not anaphors, while *NP*-traces are. Subjects have to be distinguished from traces by the features [±trace], which simply means '±bound.'

We see now why the feature combinations [+trace,+argument,±case] don't exist: Since [+trace] means 'trace of an argument expression,' the existence of one of the two combinations would entail that there is a chain with two arguments, a violation of the θ-criterion.

To conclude this discussion: We have to assume the following five empty elements:

(56)		pro	PRO	E	e*	Wh-t	NP-t	*	*
	trace	−	−	−	−	+	+	+	+
	argument	+	+	−	−	−	−	+	+
	case	+	−	+	−	+	−	+	−

The feature combinations with asterisk don't exist for the reasons given. Notice that this account is, despite some small changes in terminology, entirely standard. The classification can explain why we have this odd number of five empty elements, a number which can't be explained by a mere combination of features. A drawback of this taxonomy is that it doesn't show the parallelism between empty elements and their lexical counterparts, for instance, that between *NP*-traces and reflexive pronouns.

8. The Relation between Case- and Theta-marking

In section 5, I have expressed the view that the order of complements is not configurationally determined in German. Therefore, I have to say how the relation between grammatical functions, theta-marking and case-government is spelled out. In English, grammatical functions are configurationally defined, they are certain positions in a tree. Both case and theta-roles are assigned to particular grammatical functions. (This complete coincidence of particular cases with particular positions in a structure may be the structural reason for the morphological invisibility of case in English. Functionally, case is redundant in English.) In German, the situation is more complicated. In the finite clause, the grammatical functions of the verb are defined by case-government. The subject of a verb is the NP governed by INFL, the direct object is the accusative NP governed by the verb and the indirect object is the dative NP governed by the verb. At least for the objects, case is not redundant: it makes visible grammatical functions, which then may be theta-marked by the verb.

A slight complication arises from the following circumstance: case-government serves the purpose of defining grammatical functions and the latter are the bearers of particular theta-roles. On the other hand, the particular government properties of a verb are defined by its theta-grid. The idea is roughly that a verb with two thematic roles governs accusative, whereas a verb with three thematic roles governs accusative and dative. Since there is a general rule for this kind of dative government we may consider this dative as a structural case. These are the rules for structural cases, of course. Lexical case has to be stipulated by means of particular lexical entries.

I am assuming the following argument structure for verbs: A verb may govern up to three 'structural' thematic roles (θ-roles) which are ordered in the following sense: There may exist one external θ-role, which is denoted by θ_1, and there may exist up to two internal structural θ-roles, which are denoted as θ_2 and θ_3. The order is ultimately derived from a thematic hierarchy (Cf., e.g., Foley-van Valin 1984). Impersonal verbs and ergative verbs have no external role. Let me illustrate how I conceive of the relevant entries:

(57)	a.	*sehen*	$\theta_1\ \theta_2$	'to see'
	b.	*schlafen*	θ_1	'to sleep'
	c.	*fallen*	θ_2	'to fall' (ergative)
	d.	*scheinen*	θ_2	'to seem' (impersonal)
	e.	*schenken*	$\theta_1\ \theta_2\ \theta_3$	'to give'
	f.	*schmecken*	$\theta_2\ \theta_3$	'to taste' (ergative)
	g.	*versuchen*	$\theta_1\ \theta_2$	'to try'
	h.	*helfen*	$\theta_1\ \theta_2$ (dat)	'to help'

Several remarks are in order. Firstly, this characterization is not complete. We have to distinguish between different logical types of roles. For instance, there are 'individual roles' as in (a) to (c). In (d), θ_2 is a 'proposition role,' whereas in (g), θ_2 is a 'property role,' because 'to try' never embeds a proposition (*I *try that John will sleep* vs. *I try to sleep*). A proper notation, for instance logical types, should bring out these differences. For the following discussion, I will assume that the relevant distinctions can be drawn. Secondly, it is seen that the order of the roles is crucial. Usually, only the distinction between external and internal θ-role is made in the literature following Williams (1981). I am assuming an ordering of the internal roles because the rule for structural dative will require that. Given this generalization, we can replace the talk about *the external role* by *the first role*, *the first internal role* by *the second role* and *the second internal role* by *the third role*. Note thirdly that, according to this terminology, impersonal and ergative verbs do not govern a first θ-role. (h) is the entry of a verb that governs lexical dative.

Let me now formulate the rules for structural accusative and structural dative:

(58) a.   A verb with θ_2 governs accusative.
     b.   A verb with θ_3 governs dative.

The only difference with respect to GB-theory is that a bitransitive verb governs two structural cases. Thus, dative is normally associated with the third theta-role. An exception is lexical dative (cf. (57h)). In this case, dative is associated with the second theta-role. θ-marking may be defined as follows:

(59) a. θ_1 is assigned to the 'next' NP c-commanding VP.
     b. θ_2 is assigned to the accusative position governed by the verb.
     c. θ_3 is assigned to the dative position governed by the verb.

Theta-marking is like government with the exception of the special proviso for the subject. (If the subject were base generated inside the VP and moved to SpecI for reasons of case assignment, then it would be theta-governed, too.) As a consequence we have it that grammatical functions play no theoretical role in the theory, since they are definable (*vide* Williams 1984, Reis 1982 or Sternefeld 1985 for a similar position). Thus, we could define the NP to which θ_2 is assigned as direct object and the NP to which θ_3 is assigned as indirect object.

For the above examples, case government is derived from the thematic properties of a verb. In this sense it is a structural relation. No such generalization holds for status government. Status government is an irreducible lexical property.

Note that this way of defining the rules for the two object cases is only a slight deviation from standard practice. A more conventional alternative would have been to define the grammatical functions direct object and indirect object configurationally and to assign accusative and dative to these under government. The only reason why I have not chosen this kind of definition is that I am not sure whether the German objects occupy a fixed position in D-structure.

The theory proposed here has to meet several difficulties. First, the case rules have to apply at D-structure already, because theta-marking is a D-structure process. Second, the rule of case-neutralization, which is needed for the analysis of the passive construction and which we will discuss in the next section, has to be checked at S-structure only. At S-structure, the rules for structural case have to apply again. These consequences are not very appealing and suggest that a strictly configurational analysis in the standard way of GB-theory might be correct, even for a partially 'non-configurational' language like German. Since I have come to that view — which is expressed in von Stechow & Sternefeld (1988) — only by exploring this particular variant of the theory, it is worth having presented it here, to my mind.

9. Neutralization of Case-government

The Chomskyan passive theory assumes that the passivized form of a verb is neutralized with respect to the features $[\pm N]$. In particular, a passive verb doesn't have the feature $[-N]$. Since objective case is governed by $[-N]$'s, the direct object is not case-marked and therefore has to be moved to a case position (*vide, e.g.,* Chomsky 1981).

In the present account, accusative is not determined by the verbal category alone but is derived from the thematic roles of the verb. Only passive auxiliaries embed neutralized categories, which can't govern the accusative case. I see, however, no indication that this is really so. Compare the following examples:

(60) a.   *weil   Karl Ulrike   ein grünes Sommerkleid*
           because Karl Ulrike:DAT a   green   summerdress:ACC

> *geschenkt hat*
> given has

b. *weil Ulrike ein grünes Sommerkleid*
because Ulrike:DAT a green summer dress:NOM
geschenkt wurde
given was

There is not the slightest morphological evidence that *geschenkt* belongs to different categories in the two sentences. Furthermore, there is no evidence for movement, as has been observed by many authors (for instance, den Besten). Finally, this kind of neutralization theory can't account for the 'dative passive,' which is discussed in section 17. As the name suggests, the dative passive may informally be described as the 'absorption' of dative government by certain auxiliaries (e.g. *kriegen* 'to get').

A straightforward move is to assume that the different government properties of the participles are determined by the superordinate verbs, i.e., *haben* and *werden*. The latter is a passivizer and blocks accusative government. Here is a blocking mechanism which accounts for the facts:

(61) a. A government feature of the form *[α__]__(or *[__α]__,__
[α__] or __[__α]) is to be read as 'Blocking of α -government.'
b. If a category has both the feature [α__] and *[α__] it is neutralized with respect to α-government.
c. The feature *[α__], where α is a case, is a verbal feature.

The relevant lexical entries for temporal *haben* and passive *werden* are the following ones:

(62) a. *haben* third status__
b. *werden* third status __ *[accusative__]__

(62) contains the information that the subordinate verb is neutralized with respect to accusative government. According to this lexical stipulation, (60b) can be analyzed in the following way:

(63) $weil[_{IP}E^i[_{I'}[_{VP}[_{VP}Ulrike[_{V'}ein\ Kleid^i\ [_{V}geschenkt]]\ wurde]INFL]$
dat ⟵――――――――――┘ +tense
*[acc__] ⟵――――――――――┘
nom ⟵――――――――――――――┘
because Ulrike a dress given was

By its lexical properties, *geschenkt* governs accusative and dative. *Werden* assigns the blocking feature *[accusative__] to the embedded VP where it percolates to the head *geschenkt*. Therefore, accusative government is neutralized. Note that this passive analysis is entirely configurational but doesn't require movement, because the 'surface subject' *ein Kleid* 'a dress' inherits nominative from the empty *E*-subject by the mechanism of case inheritance, which was motivated for the subject-VP inversions mentioned at the occasion of the Italian example (50). Thus, even at S-structure, the nominative-NP occupies an object position. Note that case can never be inherited across a CP-barrier, because cosuperscripted elements of a chain can't cross a CP-barrier. Thus, apart from the linear order of the constituents, (63) is equivalent to a structure that assumes NP- movement.

This account is in the spirit of the Chomskyan passive analysis. The only difference is that the blocking mechanism is not spelled out in categorial terms. The lexical stipulation, which every passive theory has to assume, is located at another place, *viz.* in the entry of the passivizer. It is not even clear that the lexical entries of passivizers have to contain the blocking feature. In section 16, I will show that the neutralization of accusative government follows from the semantics of passivizers, provided we accept Burzio's generalization.

That we do not need movement in (63), is not an outcome of neutralization of case government, it rather is a consequence of the existence of the empty expletive *E* in German, which makes possible the assignment of nominative into the VP. I owe the insight that the German passive should be analyzed along these lines to a discussion with W. Sternefeld.

A. Kratzer has pointed out to me that the passivization of certain idioms gives a particularly clear indication that there is no movement in German passives. Consider the following examples:

(64) a.   *weil   man dem   Direktor das Fell gerbte*
          because one to the director the skin tanned
     b.   *weil dem Direktor*:DAT *das Fell*:NOM *gegerbt wurde*
     c. ?? *weil das Fell*:NOM *dem Direktor*:DAT *gegerbt wurde*

Jemandem das Fell gerben, literally 'to tan the skin to someone,' is an idiom meaning 'to give a person a good hiding.' The unmarked word order of the passivized construction is exactly as at D-structure. When the D-object is brought to the clause-initial position, the sentence looses its idiomatic character, as (c) illustrates. If movement were required on structural grounds, we wouldn't expect this contrast.

We could perhaps say that there is scrambling in the style of G. Webelhuth or H. den Besten after movement: First we bring the D-object to a nominative position, and then we scramble the dative-object before the subject, as indicated by the following picture:

(65) $[_{IP}$*dem Direktor*$_j$ $[_{IP}$ *das Fell*$_i$:NOM$[_{I'}[_{VP}[_{VP}$ t_j:DAT t_i *gegerbt*] *wurde*] I]]]

Such a move would, however, seriously undermine the motivation for D-structure. Idiomaticity is a lexical property and should be checked at D-structure only. The example suggests that this lexical property should also be checked after scrambling (and it is not even clear exactly how it should be checked). The passive analysis proposed here avoids all such complications.

Josef Bayer has objected that this neutralization theory has the consequence that the subject of a passive sentence obtains no theta-role. Consider, e.g., (63), here repeated as (66):

(66)   *weil*$[_{IP}$ $e^i[_{I'}[_{VP}[_{VP}$ *Ulrike*$[_{V'}$ *ein Kleid*$^i[_{V}$*geschenkt*]]*wurde*]INFL]
              dat ⟵   ⟶   +tense
       *[acc__] ⟵

The verb *geschenkt* should assign the role θ_2 to the NP *ein Kleid*. By (59b), however, θ_2 is assigned to the accusative position governed by the verb but, at S-structure, *ein Kleid* is not an accusative position.

As has been mentioned in the last section, the conflict is solved, if we make the following assumptions:

(67) a. The case-rules apply both at D-structure and at S-structure.
      b. Case-neutralization applies at S-structure, but not at D-structure.

These assumptions insure that, at D-structure, the NP *ein Kleid* of sentence (66) can be an accusative-position and therefore receive the role θ_2 by the verb *geschenkt*. At S-structure, accusative government is neutralized and *ein Kleid* may inherit nominative from the empty subject E. This analysis is very near to Gunnar Bechs way of talking. He would say that *ein Kleid* is the 'logical accusative' of *geschenkt*, whereas it is the nominative of *werden*. 'Logical accusative' is thus reconstructed as 'structural accusative at D-structure.'

10. Impersonal Passives

The analysis of impersonal passives is straightforward:

(68) a.   *weil E   getanzt wurde*
            *[acc.__]⟵┘
           because danced was

      b.   *weil E   ihr geholfen wird*
            dat.⟵┘   ┐
                 *[acc.__]⟵┘
           because her helped   is

In (68a), the intransitive *getanzt* doesn't govern accusative. Therefore, the blocking feature *[acc.__] has no impact on the government properties of the verb. The theta-role of the subject is 'absorbed' on semantic grounds. In order to give an idea why this is so, let us assume the following tentative meaning rule for passive *werden*.

(69)   V(*werden*)(P) is true iff P≠ø, where P is a property and V stands for the semantic interpretation.

According to this rule we have it that '*getanzt wurde*' is true if the property of dancing is instantiated, i.e., if the set of dancers is non-empty. It is clear that this semantic analysis excludes a matrix subject, i.e., a subject of *werden*. This conforms with the standard assumptions made for passives in GB-theory. This is so, because the statement that P is not empty is equivalent to saying that there is something that has P. In other words, the subject role of P is bound by a syntactically invisible existential quantification. The analysis is compatible with the fact that the subject of a passivized verb can be made explicit inside the VP by means of a prepositional phrase, in German by *von*+NP or *durch*+NP. The only thing we have to assume is that these prepositions determine the logical subject of VP. So the relevant meaning rule for a 'by-phrase' is this:

(70)   The adverb meaning V(*von*)(NP) applied to VP is the proposition which is true iff VP is true of NP.

As an example, consider the following sentence:

(71)   *weil E[$_{VP}$ ihr[$_{PP}$ von Ede] geholfen] wird*
                   her   by Ede helped   is

According to (70), the embedded VP expresses the proposition which is true if the property of helping her is true of Ede. The passive operator redundantly says that this property is not empty. (I consider propositions as zero-place properties. A true proposition is certainly not an empty property.) If the VP did contain a subject position, this passivization would be equivalent to a vacuous quantification over the subject position. But since there is no subject position in the VP, we should not speak of vacuous quantification. So the treatment is compatible with Chomsky's claim that there is no vacuous quantification in natural language.

Returning to (68b), we obtain an impersonal passive by neutralization of accusative government. The possibility of dative government is not affected by *werden*.

Let me now briefly speculate about the question why we do not have impersonal passives in English or Italian. Consider the following examples.

(72) a. *There was coughed
      b. *E è stato tossito
           is been coughed

Haider (1987) concludes from the Italian example that there are no empty expletives: If empty expletives did exist, (a) should be grammatical. It seems to me that this explanation can't be correct, because we have to explain why there isn't an impersonal passive with *there* as subject in English. So the existence of impersonal passive doesn't depend on whether a language has an empty expletive or not.

I think the explanation has to be sought in a subtle parametric variation of the theta criterion. The criterion stipulates a 1-1-correspondence between the θ-role and the argument of a chain. It doesn't exclude however the possibility of having chains without θ-role and argument. Exactly this is the case for the construction (72)(a) and (b), where we have to assume the chains (*there*) and (*e*) respectively, which consist of a single non-argument but have no thematic role. For German, chains of this kind are admissible, the constructions that correspond to (72) are grammatical. Presumably this is the marked option of the theta criterion. English and Italian only have chains with both a theta-role and an argument, probably the unmarked option.

Consider again an Italian inversion:

(73) E^i ha telefonato Giuliana^i

Here we have to assume the unmarked chain (E^i, *Giuliana*^{i}) containing exactly one argument and one θ-role. The theta-role is assigned to the empty subject position, the argument is *Giuliana*.

11. Middle

It is tempting to treat the middle operator *sich* in the same way as passive *werden*. It blocks accusative government. Observe first that 'medial' *sich* occurs in an adverbial position and not in an argument position, as the following example shows:

(74)   *weil   es sich   hier angenehm lebt*
        because it itself here pleasantly lives

Leben 'to live' is an intransitive verb, whose subject is the expletive *es*. Hence *sich* isn't an argument of the verb. Let us therefore tentatively assume that medial *sich* is a passivizer that governs the blocking feature __*[accusative]. (75a) is therefore analyzed as (75b):

(75) a. *weil   sich   das Buch leicht liest*
          because itself the book easily reads

      b. *weil* [$_{IP}$ E^i[$_{I'}$[$_{VP}$ *sich das Buch*^{i} *leicht* [$_V$ *liest*]] INFL]]
          └────────────────→ *[acc.__]

Medial *sich* assigns the blocking feature *[accusative__] to the V *liest*, neutralizing its accusative government. The direct object *das Buch* obtains its case by cosuperscripting with the empty expletive.

In a number of papers, Hubert Haider has argued that, in contrast to the passive, a verb in the middle assigns an external theta-role. His argument is that we can't activate the agent, as the ungrammaticality of the following example shows (cf. Haider 1986: 214).

(76)   **Das sagt sich   von Hubert leicht*
        That says itself by   Hubert easily

According to Haider the ungrammaticality is explained, if we assume that the subject role of *sagen* 'to say' is not absorbed but assigned to the subject and made visible by *sich*.

A completely different, in fact complementary, way of looking at these data is to say that the middle operator serves to express an entirely agentless construction. In a passive construction, the agent is implicit. The only pecularity is that its role isn't assigned to the subject position. In the middle, however, there is no agent at all. Haspelmath (1987) provides cross-linguistic evidence for this view. The middle is, in fact, a special case of the so-called *anticausative constructions*. It is typical of these constructions that they express spontaneous events:

(77)   *Das Buch verkauft sich*   *von allein*
          The book sells   itself(=MIDDLE) by itself.

It is difficult to express the idea of complete agentlessness in usual semantic terms, because the notion of semantic subject is implicit in the notion of predicate or relation. The following rule gives a rough idea of how we may conceive of complete agentlessness:

(78)   V(MIDDLE)(P) is true iff P is not empty but there is no x of which it is known that it is P.

This semantics accounts for the oddness of (76), because according to this meaning rule, (76) would mean something like 'Some people say that, still, of no one of them it is known that he says that, but Hubert says that.' (A more adequate semantics would perhaps adopt a Davidsonian view, according to which verbs express events which may or may not have agents.)

This analysis of the middle looks quite attractive. Let us look whether it carries over to Italian. In the preceding section, I have said that there are no chains without theta-roles and arguments in Italian and English.

(79)   *Si   è ballato*
          Itself is danced

If *si* were analyzed as a passivizer, then we would have to assume the *E*-subject without connection to an argument and a theta-role. Since this option is not available for Italian, the construction must have the following structure:

(80) E_i si_i *è ballato*

Here, the external theta-role of *ballare* 'to dance' is assigned to the empty expletive *e*. *Si* behaves like a reflexive pronoun in so far as it is bound by *E*. The relevant chain is this:

(81)   (E,   si)
          $+\theta$ $-\theta$
          $-arg$ $+arg$

Thus, I quite agree with Haider on the fact that, in (80), the subject is θ-marked. It follows from our assumptions that this must be so. The analysis doesn't imply, however, that this construction is somehow passivized. The *si* in (80) is the impersonal *si* meaning 'someone.' This is seen from the fact that accusative government is not neutralized in this construction:

(82)   *Si   mangia   le   mele:*ACC
          one eats   the apples

Note that we have no agreement between *mangia* and *le mele*, which shows that the latter is both a D- and an S-object. It follows that we shouldn't confuse these constructions with medial constructions, which are in some sense 'passives.' In medial constructions we have agreement between the verb and the D-object. Consider the following examples:

(83) a.   *Le mele   si   mangiano*
          the apples itself eat:PL
     b.   *Si mangiano le mele*
     c.   **Le   mele   si   mangia*
          The apples itself eat:SG

(b) is derived from (a) by an inversion chain. The ungrammaticality of (c) shows that this construction must be very different from (82). The straightforward conclusion is that (83)(a) and (b) must be analyzed like the German middle. Thus the S-structures of (83)(a) and (b) are likely to be something like (84)(a) and (b) respectively:

(84) a.   *Le mele$_i$ si mangiano t$_i$*
     b.   *E^k si mangiano le mele^k*

The relevant chains for the two cases are (85)(a) and (b) respectively:

(85) a. $(le\ mele_i,\ t_i)$
          $-\theta$ $+\theta$
          $+arg$ $-arg$
     b. $(E^k,\ le\ mele^k)$
          $-\theta$ $+\theta$
          $-arg$ $+arg$

Note that medial *si* doesn't play any role for chain formation. If we want to include it into chains (as is usually done in the Romance literature) then we would have to say that medial *si* is a non-argument. In any case we have to distinguish between impersonal *si* and medial *si*. The two elements can't have the same theoretical status. Furthermore, impersonal *si* can't be exactly the same as the ordinary reflexive, because the latter requires an antecedent that is an argument. Perhaps it is a parameter of Italian that reflexives may refer to non-arguments. If this were so, then impersonal *si* could be regarded as an ordinary reflexive. Details aside, the analysis of the Italian middle which is discussed here is in agreement with common practice in Romance syntax. I therefore believe that Haider's arguments against the existence of empty expletives are not convincing.

12. Ergativity

Ergative verbs can't govern the accusative, hence they have the feature *[accusative__] by lexical stipulation. As before, no movement is necessary in order to account for the unmarked word order:

(86) a. *weil   Max   der Pudding   schmeckt*
          because Max:DAT the pudding:NOM tastes well

     b. *weil* $[_{IP}E^i[_{I'}[_{VP}$ *Max* $[_{V'}$ *der Pudding^i*$[_V$ *schmeckt*$]]]$INFL$]]$
          dative ⟵——————————————⟶
                                           *[acc__]

The direct object inherits nominative from the subject by cosuperscripting.

13. *Lassen*

Among the various problems which arise for generative accounts of the syntax of *lassen* 'to let,' Reis (1976) has pointed out the following ones:

(87) a. **weil   Ede$_i$ Caroline   sich$_i$ rasieren läßt*
          because Ede Caroline:ACC himself:ACC shave   lets

     b. *weil   Max$_i$ sich$_i$ den Pudding*
          because Max:NOM himself:DAT the pudding:ACC
          schmecken läßt
          taste   lets

     c. *weil   Caroline   den Tisch   von Ede abräumen*
          because Caroline:NOM the table:ACC by Ede clear
          läßt
          lets

Lassen is an *accusativus cum infinitivo* verb (A.c.I.-verb). The problems to solve are these: the A.c.I.-subject blocks long reflexivization if it is a D-subject, as is shown by (a). An ergative A.c.I.-subject, however, doesn't block long reflexivization, as (b) illustrates. (c) shows that we can have an embedded infinitive with passive properties: The agent of the infinitival is expressed by a PP, viz., *von Ede* 'by Ede.'

These data are entailed by and large if we assume the following lexical properties for *lassen*:

(88) a.   *lassen* governs 1.status.
      b.   *lassen* embeds a proposition.
      c.   *lassen* governs accusative.
      d.   *lassen* optionally neutralizes accusative government.

The crucial stipulations are (c) and (d). Let us discuss first (c). Although the semantic object of *lassen* is a proposition and *lassen* is not transitive, it nevertheless governs accusative. This behaviour is exceptional and must therefore be stipulated. We assume that lexical case must obligatorily be assigned. Therefore the surface structure of (87a) must either be (89a) or (89b).

(89) a.   *weil Ede* [$_{IP}$ *Caroline* [$_{VP}$ *sich rasieren*]] *läßt*
                                st.1 ←—————————⌐ |
                       acc ←————————————————————————⌐

      a.   *weil Ede* [$_{VP}$ *Caroline* [$_{V'}$[$_{VP}$ *sich rasieren*] *läßt*]]]
                                      1.st ←—————————⌐ |
                          acc ←————————————————————————⌐

Since *lassen* can never embed a sentence with an overt complementizer, we may assume that these structures are base generated. The latter alternative requires generalizing the notion of subject as indicated in Emonds (1985):

(90)   The subject of VP is the 'nearest' NP c-commanding VP.

Because of the extended projection principle, there will always be such an NP in IP. To be sure, the choice of the second alternative requires some other refinements. For instance, we don't want to say that the subject of embedded VP is subcategorized by *lassen*. But we need these refinements for the treatment of small clauses anyway. For details, vide von Stechow & Sternefeld (1988: chapter 12).

To be sure, (89a) would not be a correct structure if IP counted as a sentence in the sense of the coherence criteria discussed in section 3. And it would not be a correct S-structure if we did forbid empty heads on S-structure. For the rest, the two analyses are entirely equivalent. The only thing I want to assert with certainty is that *lassen* can't embed a CP because, in that case, neither the accusative of the subordinated subject nor the second status of the embedded verb could be governed by *lassen*. On the other hand, both (89a) and (89b) have the right properties for checking case or status.

Consider next the structure of (87b). It must be (91a) or (91b).

(91) a.   *Max$_i$ [$_{IP}$ E^j [$_{I'}$[$_{VP}$ sich$_i$ [$_{V'}$ die Suppe^j schmecken]] INFL]] läßt*
acc ◄───┘

b.   *Max [$_{VP}$ E^j [$_{V'}$[$_{VP}$ sich [$_{V'}$ die Suppe^j schmecken]] läßt]*
acc ◄──┘

In both analyses, the ergative subject *die Suppe* inherits accusative *via* cosuperscripting, as always in such constructions. (The binding category for *sich* is the opacity domain of the subject of the verb that case governs *sich*. *Vide* von Stechow & Sternefeld 1988: p. 94.) This analysis is compatible with recent analyses proposed by Fanselow (1986) and Grewendorf (1986).

Let us finally turn to example (87c). This time we need the lexical stipulation (88d), i.e., that *lassen* may absorb accusative government of the subordinate verb. Exactly as in the previous cases, we have two possible analyses, *viz.* (92a) and (92b):

(92) a.   *Caroline[$_{IP}$E^i[$_{I'}$[$_{VP}$ den Tisch^i[$_{V'}$von Ede abräumen]]INFL]]läßt*
acc ◄───┘

b.   *Caroline[$_{VP}$E^i[$_{V'}$[$_{VP}$ den Tisch^i[$_{V'}$von Ede abräumen]] läßt]*
acc ◄──┘

The two alternative analyses raise the following questions:

1. Why does the verb *abräumen* 'to clear the table' not theta-mark its subject?

2. Why does the verb *abräumen* not accusative-govern its object?

Suppose *abräumen* did theta-mark the subject of IP. Then the subject would be *pro*, because it receives accusative by *läßt*, and an empty element that is both theta- and case-marked must be *pro*. But there is no *pro* in German. It follows that *abräumen* can't theta-mark its subject. Thus, the first question is answered.

As to the second question, let us suppose that *abräumen* assigns structural accusative to its object. Then we would have a verb that assigns structural case to its direct object but doesn't theta-mark its subject, a contradiction to Burzio's generalization, which we will discuss in section 16 and 17. Since we assume that Burzio's generalization is a valid principle, *abräumen* can't case-govern its object. This answers the second question.

14. Gerundivum

The analysis of gerundiva is straightforward: *ist* governs the 2.status
and blocks accusative government.

(93)   *weil E^i [*$_{VP}$ *das Buch^i kaum zu verstehen]   ist*
             *[acc.__] ←——————————————
            because   the book hardly to understand is

Thus, the modal *ist* blocks the accusative government of the subordinate
supinum *zu verstehen*. Hence the direct object *das Buch* is not case governed by *zu verstehen*. It inherits nominative from the empty expletive *E* via
cosuperscripting. Note that this is another case where the embedded verb
doesn't assign its subject-role. Haider (1984) has argued that the preposition *zu* always 'absorbs' the subject-role. It has to be 'reactivated' by *haben*:

(94)   *weil   er das Buch zu lesen hat*
            because he the book to read has

According to Haider, the VP *das Buch zu lesen* doesn't assign a subject-
role, but *das Buch zu lesen hat* assigns one. It seems to me that this analysis
is unnecessarily complicated, if only for the fact that we need an additional
mechanism for reactivating the theta-role in the case of infinitive clauses
with a PRO-subject. As to its 'passive' properties, the gerundive construction (93) is parallel to the 'passivized' infinitive (87c), which we have discussed in the last section. In that case we did not have a preposition *zu* which
could be made to function as a passivizer. Therefore, the solution must be
as in the last section: either the subject role isn't assigned because no structural position is available, or *ist* is analyzed as a modalized passivizer. In
other words, in (93), *ist* means the same as 'werden kann' (passive+*can*).

Let me again illustrate the first option. Suppose, the embedded verb
did theta-mark the subject. Then the·subject must be *pro*, an option not
available in German. Furthermore, *das Buch* could not inherit nominative
by cosuperscripting, because the chain (*pro^i, das Buch^i*) contains two arguments and two theta-roles, a violation of the theta criterion. The following
picture illustrates the impossibility:

(95)   *pro^i [*$_{VP}$ *das Buch^i kaum zu verstehen] ist*
            θ_1 θ_2 ←——————————————
            ←——————————————————————

Let me return to the option that modal *ist* is a modalized passivizer. Let us assume that *ist* governs the blocking feature *[accusative__]. If this is correct, then modal *sein* 'to be' will have the following lexical properties:

(96) Modal *sein*
    a.   governs 2.status.
    b.   blocks accusative government, i.e., has the feature *[acc.__]__.

These lexical properties account for the analysis (93).

15. Choice of Auxiliaries: Checking of θ_1-marking

Haider (1984a) claims that *sein* 'to be' — no matter whether it has a temporal or a modal meaning — generally blocks assignment of the external theta-role. The question is what blocking of theta-marking could mean. A VP theta-marks its subject in virtue of the semantics of its head-verb. A passive-operator like *werden* 'absorbs' a subject role on semantic grounds. Since the auxiliary *sein* only carries temporal information, it can't change the theta-marking properties of the subordinated verb. The only sense I can make of the locution 'blocking a theta-role' is that *sein* requires a subordinated verb that doesn't theta-mark its subject. We can express this property in the following way:

(97)   *sein* governs the feature $[-[\theta_1\_]]\_$.

Haider (1984b) claims that *haben* deblocks a blocked theta-role. 'Deblocking' makes even less sense than blocking. We can express Haider's way of talking by saying that *haben* requires a subordinate verb that theta-marks it subject. The relevant lexical property is the following:

(98)   *haben* governs the feature $[\theta_1\_]\_$.

We further assume the following general convention.

(99)   If a verb doesn't theta-mark its subject, then it has the feature $-[\theta_1\_]$.

Our assumptions entail the distribution of the auxiliaries *sein* und *haben*. Consider the following examples.

(100) a.   *weil   Wladimir [$_{VP}$ seinen Hut verloren] hat*
                          $\theta_1\!-$
                     $[\theta_1\_]\leftarrow$_____|
       because Wladimir   his   hat   lost   has

b.   *weil   *Wladimir* [$_{VP}$ *seinen Hut verloren*] *ist*

$$\theta_1 \text{---}$$
$$-[\theta_1\text{---}] \longleftarrow \rule{3cm}{0pt} \bigg|$$

because Wladimir   his   hat   lost   is

(100b) is ungrammatical, because *verloren* 'lost' theta-marks its subject, although *sein* requires a verb not theta-marking its subject. In (100a), however, the VP theta-marks its subject, as *haben* requires.

In the case of ergative verbs, we obtain the complementary pattern, as the following examples show:

(101) a.   *e[$_{VP}$ *Ulrike gekommen*] *hat*
                Ulrike come   has

$$-[\theta_1\text{---}]$$
$$+[\theta_1\text{---}] \longleftarrow \rule{3cm}{0pt} \big|$$

b. E^i [$_{VP}$ *Ulrike^i gekommen*] *ist*
$$-[\theta_1\text{---}]$$
$$-[\theta_1\text{---}] \longleftarrow \rule{3cm}{0pt} \big|$$
         Ulrike come   is

Note that feature incompatibility, i.e., the combination $\{+\alpha, -\alpha\}$ is not the same thing as feature neutralization, i.e., the combination $\{\alpha, *\alpha\}$. The latter means that neither α nor $-\alpha$ is present, whereas the former means that α is both present and not present, an impossibility.

Requiring the checking feature $[\theta_1\text{---}]\text{---}$ for *haben* in general is not compatible with our analysis of the middle, which has been discussed in section 11. Since medialized verbs do not theta-mark their subject, the superordinate auxiliary should be *sein*, not *haben*, contrary to the facts:

(102) a.   *weil E^i* [$_{VP}$ *sich das Buch^i gut verkauft*] *ist*
$$\underline{} \longrightarrow *[acc.\text{---}] \bigg|$$
$$-[\theta_1\text{---}]$$
$$-[\theta_1\text{---}] \longleftarrow \rule{3cm}{0pt} \bigg|$$
     because   itself the book well sold   is

b.   *weil E^i* [$_{VP}$ *sich das Buch^i gut verkauft*] *hat*
$$-[\theta_1\text{---}]$$
$$+[\theta_1\text{---}] \longleftarrow \rule{3cm}{0pt} \bigg|$$
     because   itself the book well sold   has

According to Haiders generalizations concerning auxiliary choice, (a) should be grammatical and (b) should be ungrammatical (given our analysis of the middle). But it is the other way round. I conclude that Haider's generalizations (98) and (99) are too strong. Reflexivization of a verb doesn't affect the choice of auxiliaries in German: We can only have *haben*, no matter whether it is 'ordinary' reflexivization or medialization. In Italian, the opposite is true: Reflexivized verbs always select *essere* 'to be,' no matter what the argument structure of the verb is. In other words, *essere* combines with reflexive *si*, with medial *si* and with impersonal *si*. I don't know whether it is possible to derive these different distributions from deeper principles. It seems to me, however, that an explanation in terms of argument structure of the kind proposed by Haider is not possible.

16. Burzio's Generalization and Neutralization of Accusative-government

If we reflect on the examples of the last section, we discover that the neutralization of accusative government is a *concomitans* of the feature $-[\theta_1\_\_]\_\_$, i.e., of the fact that the subject isn't theta-marked. This is hardly a coincidence, but follows from an appropriate version of *Burzio's generalization* (See Burzio 1981). The generalization is this:

(103)   A verb assigns structural case to its (direct) object if and only if it theta-marks its subject.

As it stands, the generalization is not yet general enough because it is not compatible with the recipient passive, as we will see in the next section. We will revise the condition in the next section. Burzio's generalization might provide a justification for the stipulation that the 'passivized' infinitive under *lassen*, which has been discussed in section 13, doesn't govern accusative. If it did, we would seem to have a counterexample to Burzio's generalization. In other words, (92) — here repeated as (104) — appears to be the right analysis of the construction discussed:

(104)   *Caroline E^i [$_{VP}$ den Tisch^i [$_{V'}$ von Ede abräumen]] läßt*
          *[acc__] ⟵⟶
          *[θ$_1$]__ ⟵⟶

Consequently, *lassen* seems to be a potential passivizer. In other words, we assume that it has the following property:

(105)   *lassen* optionally governs the feature *[acc__].

Burzio's generalization would then imply that the embedded verb doesn't theta-mark a subject. This analysis is supported by the fact that it is not possible to embed 'open' passives under *lassen*:

(106) a. *Caroline den Tisch von Ede abräumen ließ*
       Caroline the table by Ede clear   let
    b. **Caroline den Tisch von Ede abgeräumt werden ließ*
       Caroline the table by Ede cleared   be   let

We can never iterate passives. The contrast seems to suggest that we can't embed a passive under a potential passivizer either. The question remains, why *lassen* should be able to govern the feature *[acc__]. Let us assume that *lassen* optionally means *passive+cause*. The subject role of the subordinated verb would then be absorbed by the passive component of the complex meaning.

Note that we could have described the same facts by assuming that *lassen* optionally governs the feature $-[\theta_1$__]. Burzio's generalization would then imply that the embedded verb can't govern the accusative. Thus, the result obtained for *sein* 'to be' generalizes to any verb that 'blocks' theta-marking of the subject. In other words, that passive *werden* has the neutralization feature *[accusative__]__, can be deduced from the fact that it governs the feature $-[\theta_1$__]. The latter property is a reflex of the semantics of passive *werden*. (Our meaning rule (69) has made sure that *werden* makes a proposition out of a predicate. In fact, it is the existential quantifier. Therefore, no theta-role is left that could be 'assigned' to the subject of *werden*, which also is the subject of the verb embedded under *werden*.) Hence, these lexical properties of passive *werden* follow from its semantics on rather general grounds. Thus, it might even be a misnomer to call these properties lexical. If the lexicon doesn't contain redundancies, then passive *werden* contains only its meaning rule and the information that it governs third status.

The same consideration holds for gerundiva, which have been discussed in section 14: Modal *sein* blocks θ_1-marking of its subordinated verb in virtue of its semantics. Recall that it means 'passive+modal.' Therefore, the feature *[accusative__]__ can be deduced from the semantics also in this case. To conclude: the feature *[accusative__]__ seems to be largely redundant. It is inferrable from $-[\theta_1$__], provided, we can justify Burzio's generalization on independent grounds. Sometimes, however, the feature has to be stipulated, for instance, for 'medial' *sich*.

17. The Recipient Passive and Burzio's Generalization

The so called recipient passive is an apparent counterexample to Burzio's generalization. It is illustrated by the following examples:

(107) a. *weil   wir ihm   die Haare   schnitten*
          because we him:DAT the hair:ACC cut

     b. *weil   er   die Haare   geschnitten kriegte*
          because he:NOM the hair:ACC cut   got

(108) a. *weil   man   ihm   widersprach*
          because one:NOM him:DAT contradicted

     b. ?*weil   er   widersprochen bekam*
          because he:NOM contradicted   received

The analysis of this 'dative passive' is exactly parallel to the analysis of the 'accusative passive.' The only thing we have to assume is that *kriegen* 'to get' and *bekommen* 'to receive' neutralize dative government.

(109) *kriegen* and *bekommen*
    a.   govern the 3.status
    b.   neutralize dative government, i.e., have the feature
       *[dative__]__.

The S-structure of (107b) is the following:

(110)   *weil* $E^i[_{VP}$ *er*^{i} *die Haare geschnitten] kriegte*
         [dative__] ⟵————————————————⌐
    because   he the hair   cut   got

Dative government is absorbed and *er* 'he' inherits nominative from the empty subject *E*. Hence the dative/nominative alternation.

Let us now turn to (108b). Wegener (1985) assumes that this sentence is grammatical, but I tend to agree with Höhle's judgement that it is not grammatical. In any case, (108b) is much less acceptable than (107b). To my mind, the reason for the difference in grammaticality is due to the fact that the dative governed by *widersprechen* is not structural but lexical. Lexical dative is checked at D-structure. The fact that lexical dative can't be absorbed may be pertinent for the question where status is checked. I will return to this point in section 20.

The analysis of the recipient passive which is given here presupposes that dative may be structural case. This assumption is not compatible with Burzio's generalization, because in the case of dative neutralization, the subject-theta-role is absorbed and, nevertheless, the direct object is accusative-governed. Similarly, Burzio's generalization is violated, if we passivize a bitransitive verb by means of *werden*, i.e., if we neutralize accusative government. As a result, we must either give up Burzio's generalization, or we can't maintain the present analysis, or we have to revise Burzio's generalization. Obviously, we choose the last alternative.

(111)   *Burzio's Generalization generalized*
          A verb assigns structural case to its objects if and only if it theta-marks its subject.

If we compare this statement with the original (103), then the modification proves to be rather subtle: The only thing we did is to replace the singular 'object' by the plural 'objects.' This is to be read as 'all of its objects.' The new version is compatible with our treatment of the passive, because (111) is equivalent with the following statement:

(112)   A verb doesn't assign structural case to one of its objects if and only if it doesn't theta-mark its subject.

(17-6) correctly describes the state of affairs we encounter in the case of passivized ditransitive verbs, no matter, whether accusative or dative government is neutralized. Hence, our analysis does not violate general principles of grammar.

Remember at this point that Burzio's generalization, too, is only valid for structural case. Compare the following example:

(113)   *weil   E   ihr geholfen wurde*
                    dat⟵⎯⎯⎯⎯⎯⎯⎯┘
          because   her helped   was

Passives of verbs that govern lexical case are not covered by Burzio's generalization. We have to account for this fact by a stipulation restricting the range of application of case neutralization:

(114)   Government of lexical case can't be neutralized.

The necessity of adding this stipulation makes it even more doubtful — remember the doubts expressed in section 8 — that the strategy of defining the direct and indirect object via case government at D-structure is correct. In order to apply principle (114) at S-structure, we must assume that lexical D-case can be distinguished from structural D-case, say by means of the features [±lexical]. A theory which assigns lexical case at D-structure and

structural case at S-structure needs no stipulation of this kind. But it
requires strictly configurationally defined object positions.

The existence of the recipient passive has been disputed by Haider
(1984b). Yet, Haider offers no consistent theory that could account for the
phenomenon. His proposals have convincingly been criticized by Reis
(1985) and Wegner (1985). Hence, I assume that the present analysis,
which is in the spirit of Bech's VI and of Höhle (1978), is correct.

18. The Long-distance Passive

The long-distance passive, which has been introduced into the theoretical discussion by Höhle (1978), is at odds with all relevant grammatical
principles and can only be treated by means of lexical stipulation. This is
what I want to show here. The phenomenon is illustrated by the following
sentence.

(115)   *weil   gestern   der Wagen   zu reparieren versucht*
          because yesterday the car:NOM to repair   tried
          wurde
          was

If we did analyze this sentence by movement under the usual assumption,
then we would have to move too far, as the following picture shows:

(116)   *der Wagen$_i$ gestern*[$_{VP}$[$_{CP}$PRO[$_{VP}$ t$_i$ zu reparieren]]
          the car   yesterday   to repair
          versucht] wurde
          tried   was

Now, *versuchen* 'to try' may be coherently constructed, and German passives generally don't require movement. Hence, the S-structure is perhaps
(117):

(117)   *E^i gestern*[$_{VP}$[$_{VP}$ *der Wagen^i zu reparieren] versucht] wurde*
          yesterday   the car   to repair   tried   was

Werden is a passivizer and 'absorbs' the subject-role of *versucht*. But where
is the subject-role of *zu reparieren*? To be sure, *zu reparieren* can't theta-
mark its subject. If it did, we would have a counterexample to Burzio's
generalization. Thus, the situation is parallel to the case of *lassen* 'to let,'
where we had to assume that it could optionally be a passivizer (cf. section
16). Let us suppose then that *versuchen* has the following lexical property:

(118)   If *versucht* has the feature *[accusative__], then it governs
          the feature $-[\theta_1\_\_]$.

In other words, under *werden, versucht* would mean *passive+try*. Given this
stipulation, the subject-role of *zu reparieren* is correctly 'absorbed' in (117).
The problem with this analysis is, however, that it doesn't make sense. We
see this immediately, if we give an explicit paraphrase of the meaning (117)
should have according to this analysis:

(119)   Yesterday, it has been tried that the car be repaired.

Never mind that this is no English. The important point is that, in this paraphrase, a passivized clause is embedded under 'tried.' This is a proposition
meaning 'Someone repairs the car.' This embedding is not possible on
semantic grounds, because 'to try' embeds a property, not a proposition, as
is witnessed by the ungrammaticality of the following sentence:

(120)   *Ede tried that Caroline repaired the car.

Hence, the analysis sketched can't be correct. The only way to describe the
long-distance passive I can see at the moment is by stipulation. Let us
assume that the lexicon contains transitive complex verbs like *zu reparieren
versuchen* 'try to repair.' These behave like ordinary transitive verbs and
can therefore be passivized. Note that this stipulation is not equivalent to
the claim that status is governed at D-structure: The analysis compatible
with this assumption is (117), and (117) has been refuted.

To conclude, I have no syntactic explanation for the long-distance passive.

19. The Empty Expletive and the Definiteness Effect

According to the theory of Safir (1985), a chain of type (expletive[i],
NP[i]) shows the definiteness effect, where NP[i] inherits its case by
cosuperscripting. In other words, NP[i] should always be an indefinite NP.

The analysis given for passives are not compatible with this theory.
Consider a relevant example.

(121)   *weil* $E^i[_{VP}$ *ihr   das/ein Fahrrad^i gestohlen] wurde*
          because   e[i]   her   the/a   bicycle[i]   stolen   was

There is no definiteness effect in these examples, though the direct object
inherits nominative from the empty subject *E*.

A possible reaction is that the analysis (121) can't be correct. We could avoid the definiteness effect constellation by moving the D-object to the nominative position and by successively scrambling the dative in front of it. I have rejected this analysis in section 9, therefore, I don't want to come back to it. Another way of escaping from the definiteness effect constellation is the theory developed in Kratzer (1984). Kratzer claims that German finite verbs belong to the category INFL in syntax. Now, it is well-known that German allows for the formation of complex verbs, i.e., the two verbs *gestohlen + wurde* may form a single constituent at some level of grammatical representation (*vide* Bech VI, Evers 1975, Höhle 1978, Haegeman & Riemsdijk 1984, Sternefeld 1982). Suppose we have complex verbs at S-structure. According to the theory of Kratzer, nothing prevents us from having the S-structure (122) for our example:

(122)   *weil* [$_{IP}$ *ihr* [$_{I'}$ *das/ein Fahrrad* [$_{I'}$[$_V$ *gestohlen*] [$_I$ *wurde*]]]
                            nom. ⟵———————⸳ '
              dat. ⟵————————————⸳

If we assume that the complex finite verb [$_{I'}$ *gestohlen wurde*] inherits the case government properties of its constituents, then the complex verb may directly nominative-govern the D-object of *gestohlen* and no definiteness effect has to be assumed, since there is no empty subject in this construction.

Now, sometimes we can't reanalyze the D-structure in this way but we have instead to assume case inheritance via *E*. According to Kratzer (1984), we always observe the definiteness effect in such cases. She gives examples of the following kind:

(123) a.   [$_{VP}$ *ein Fehler   unterlaufen*] *würde ihr   nie*
                      an error:NOM occur   would her:DAT never
        b. *[$_{VP}$ *dieser Fehler   unterlaufen*] *würde ihr   nie*
                       this   error:NOM occur   would her:DAT never

In these examples, the nominative NP *ein Fehler/dieser Fehler* is inside a topicalized non-finite VP. Hence the nominative must be inherited from an empty subject *E*, because non-finite verbs don't govern the nominative. According to Kratzer, (123b) therefore shows the definiteness effect, as indicated by the asterisk.

If this theory is correct, then my analyses of passive constructions have to be accommodated along these lines. On the other hand, I am not sure whether Kratzer's explanation is tenable.

Note first that, in a lot of cases, the definiteness effect is very weak.

(124) a. *Das/ein Fahrrad gestohlen wurde ihr*
          the/a   bicycle   stolen   was   her:DAT
      b. *Das/ein Waschbecken zugefroren ist uns   diesen Winter*
          the/a   handbasin   frozen   is   us:DAT this   winter
          erst einmal
          only once

There is no contrast in acceptability here, though the sentences get worse if
we choose the demonstrative pronoun *dieses* 'this.' The second sentence has
been taken from Bayer (1986: 171).

Note further that we find no definiteness effect in Italian inversions:

(125)   *E^i ha telefonato Giovanni^i*
          has called   John

Furthermore, we don't observe the definiteness effect in topicalized VPs
which contain an A.c.I.-subject:

(126)   [$_{VP}$ *einen/den/diesen Hammer fallen*] *hat Ede nicht lassen*
              a/the/this   hammer fall   has Ede not   let

Fallen 'to fall' is an ergative verb. Hence it doesn't accusative-govern its D-
object. It follows that the accusative is inherited by an expletive outside the
topicalized VP. Compare section 13 for the structure before topicalization.
According to the theory of Kratzer (1984), (126) should show the definiteness effect, but it doesn't.

I tentatively conclude from this discussion that case inheritance from
the empty expletive isn't a sufficient reason for the appearance of the definiteness effect.

20. Where is Status Checked?

In this last section I want to treat the question at what level of grammatical representation status is checked. The result of the investigation will
be that status is most likely checked after S-structure, *viz.* at the level of
reanalysis. The following arguments concerning coherent control verbs are
due to Wolfgang Sternefeld (*vide* von Stechow & Sternefeld 1988: chapter
12).

The first alternative is that status is checked at D-structure. What follows from such an assumption? Let us consider first a coherent control
verb.

(127)   *weil   sie* [$_{VP}$ *den Park besichtigen*] *will*
                          St.1 ←——————————⌐
             because she   the park visit   wants

For the reasons given in section 3, *wollen* 'to want' must embed a VP at D-structure in this case. We have to assume then that *wollen* theta-marks this VP. Since this verb also embeds a CP, we need two lexical entries. Some people might say that an approach of this kind misses a generalization, but this objection is not pertinent, because the information conveyed by the first entry is needed anyway in order to account for the control properties of the verb. It states that *wollen* is a 'subject control verb.' The relevant semantic rule expressing this property is the following:

(128)   V(*will*)(VP) is true of subject x iff x wants that
             VP is true of x.

Consider now the following ungrammatical sentences:

(129) a. **weil*   *den Park besichtigen   gewollt   wird*
          because the park visit   wanted   is
      b. **weil*   *sie   den Park besichtigen gewollt wird*
          because she the park visit   wanted   is

(129b) is correctly ruled out, because, under our assumptions, both *wollen* and passivizing *werden* embed a VP. Therefore, there is no position for the subject *sie* 'she.' But (129a) can't be ruled out, because the following structure is well-formed:

(130)   *weil E*[$_{VP}$[$_{VP}$ *den Park besichtigen*] *gewollt*] *wird*

Semantically, this structure makes sense, too. It means that someone wants to visit the park.

The traditional acount to block (129a) is to say that modal verbs can't be passivized in German. But this is only a description of the facts. For us, this description is not even a viable exit, because we assume that there is no morphological distinction between active and passive participles. The past participle of *wollen* certainly exists (*gewollt*), so there is no morphological reason why this participle should not be embeddable under passive *werden*. We therefore conclude that the lexical account can't explain the ungrammaticality of (129a).

Let us assume next that coherent control verbs embed CP at D-structure. Consider first whether it is possible to derive the ungrammatical sentences (129a):

(131) a.　　*weil E* [$_{VP}$[$_{CP}$ PRO *den Park besichtigen*] *gewollt*] *wird*
　　　　　　　　　　　　acc ←————⌐

　　　　　because　　　　　　the park visit　　　　　wanted is

　　　b.　*weil E* [$_{VP}$ [$_{VP}$ *den Park besichtigen*] *gewollt*] *wird*
　　　　　　　　　　st.1 ←——————————⌐

　　　　　　　　　　st.3 ←————————————————⌐

The representation where status is governed must be (131b). But this structure is not well-formed. Since *besichtigen* 'to visit' accusative-governs its
object, it theta-marks its subject by Burzio's generalization. But there is no
position that could receive the subject-role. If the role were assigned to *E*,
then this position would be converted into (referential) *pro*, an option not
available in German. So (131b) violates the theta-criterion. (In von
Stechow & Sternefeld (1988: chapter 12), it is argued that (131b) violates
the projection principle.) Thus, (129a) can't be derived, no matter whether
status is checked at S-structure or thereafter.

Consider next example (129b).

(132) a.　*weil E*[$_{VP}$[$_{CP}$ *sie*[$_{VP}$ *den Park besichtigen*]] *gewollt*] *wird*
　　　　　because　　she　　the park visit　　　　　wanted is

　　　b.　*weil E^i*[$_{VP}$[$_{IP}$ *sie^i*[$_{VP}$ *den Park besichtigen*]] *gewollt*] *wird*
　　　　　　　　　　　　　st.1 ←——————————⌐

　　　　　　　　　　st.3 ←————————————————⌐

　　　c. *weil sie^i*[$_{VP}$[$_{IP}$ t$_i$[$_{VP}$ *den Park besichtigen*]] *gewollt*] *wird*

The derivations (a,b) and (a,c) presuppose that status is checked together
with structural case, i.e., at S-structure. Hence, the S-structure of the D-
structure (132a) is either (132b) or (132c), the two structures being equivalent in all important respects. In (132b), the subject of IP inherits case *via*
cosuperscripting with *E*, in (132c), *sie* is raised to the nominative position.
Since the two structures are wellformed, (129b) should be grammatical,
contrary to the facts. Hence this account is unlikely to be correct.

　　Let us give up the assumption that status is checked at S-structure. Our
next and final assumption is the following:

(133)　　Status-government is checked after S-structure, i.e. after
　　　　　the binding principles and after the checking of structural
　　　　　case.

Under this assumption, the derivation of (129b) is not possible anymore.
Witness the following structures:

(134) a. *weil E^i[$_{VP}$[$_{CP}$ sie^i[$_{VP}$ den Park besichtigen]] gewollt] wird
     b. *weil sie_i[$_{VP}$[$_{CP}$ t_i[$_{VP}$ den Park besichtigen]] gewollt] wird

(134a) and (134b) are the S-structures which correspond to (132b) and (132c). Both structures are illformed, because neither case-inheritance nor NP-movement is possible across the CP-barrier. Recall that we have to assume the CP-barrier between E and sie at the one hand and between sie and t at the other hand, because CP is deleted only at the level where status government is checked, i.e., after S-structure.

If conclusion (133) is correct, then it is far from being trivial. Though status-government is a lexical property, it is checked at the latest level of grammatical representation, $viz.$ the level where reanalysis applies. Since status government implies coherence and coherence is important for the determination of the scope of operators, the reanalysis level must be the input for the LF-rules. This conclusion is compatible with the view expressed in Haegeman & Riemsdijk (1984), who also argue that the level of reanalysis must precede the level of logical form.

It follows that raising verbs which obligatorily govern second status embed IP or VP at D-structure. Consider the following two possible S-structures:

(135) a. weil E_j^i[$_{IP}$$t_j$[$_{VP}$ Dieter   das $Pfeifchen^i$ zu schmecken]]
     because   Dieter:DAT the pipe:NOM to taste well
     pflegt
     uses
     b. weil E^i [$_{VP}$ Dieter das $Pfeifchen^i$ zu schmecken] pflegt

Since schmecken 'to taste well' is ergative, the D-object inherits nominative via cosuperscripting. If pflegen 'to use' embeds IP at D-structure, we have to assume NP-movement for the empty expletive, as (a) shows. If pflegen embeds VP, no movement is necessary.

For A.c.I.-verbs like lassen 'to let,' NP-movement is not required for analogous constructions, no matter whether these verbs embed IP or NP+VP in D-structure. Compare the following two alternative S-structures:

(136) a. weil Dieter [$_{IP}$ E^i[$_{VP}$ sich sein $Pfeifchen^i$ schmecken]] läßt
             acc. ←_____|
     b. weil Dieter [$_{VP}$ E^i[$_{V'}$[$_{VP}$ sich sein $Pfeifchen^i$ schmecken] läßt]]

Concerning case-theory, the alternative analyses are equivalent. If we embed IP at D-structure, we have to stipulate that IP doesn't count as a sentence with respect to the criteria for coherence. Among other things, we have to stipulate that IP can't be moved, e.g., it can't be extraposed. A reason for not embedding IP in the case of A.c.I.-constructions might be that we don't want to allow empty heads at S-structure.

Let us summarize our findings concerning the organization of the German grammar.

1. At D-structure, theta-roles are assigned to GFs. In the variant explored here, the objects are defined via case government. A more conventional (and presumably preferable way) is to define all GFs configurationally.

2. At S-structure, the rules for structural case, case neutralization and the binding principles apply.

3. Only after S-structure, do the rules of reanalysis (CP-deletion, IP-deletion, V-raising, *zu*-incorporation, etc.) apply. Call the output of these rules *R-structure* ('reanalysis structure'). Status government is checked at R-structure.

4. R-structure is the input for the 'PF-rules' on the one hand and the 'LF-rules' on the other hand.

Bibliography

Abraham W. (ed.). 1982. *Satzglieder im Deutschen. Vorschläge zur syntaktischen, semantischen und pragmatischen Fundierung.* Tübingen: Narr.

Aoun, J. 1981. "The Formal Nature of Anaphoric Relations." Diss., Massachusetts Institute of Technology.

————., and D. Sportiche. 1981. *On the Formal Theory of Government.* Ms., Massachusetts Institute of Technology.

Asbach-Schnitker, B. and J. Roggenhofer. (eds.) 1987. *Neuere Forschungen zur Wortbildung und Historiographie der Linguistik.* Tübingen: Narr.

Bayer, J. 1984. "COMP in Bavarian Syntax." *The Linguistic Review* 3, 209-274.

————. 1986. "Review of Kenneth J. Safir: Syntactic Chains." *Studies in Language* 10, 167-186.

Bech, G. 1955. *Studien über das deutsche verbum infinitum.* 2nd ed. Tübingen: Niemeyer.

Chomsky, N. 1981. *Lectures on Government and Binding.*Dordrecht: Foris.

Emonds, J. 1985. *A Unified Theory of Syntactic Categories.* Dordrecht: Foris.

Evers, A. 1975. "The Transformational Cycle in Dutch and German." Diss. University of Utrecht.

Fanselow, G. 1986. *Konfigurationalität. Untersuchungen zur Universalgrammatik am Beispiel des Deutschen.* Tübingen: Narr.

Foley, A.W. and R.D. van Valin. 1984. *Functional Syntax and Universal Grammar.* Cambridge: Cambridge University Press.

Grewendorf, G. 1987. "Kohärenz und Restrukturierung. Zu verbalen Komplexen im Deutschen." In: Asbach-Schnitker and Roggenhofer (eds).

———. 1989. *Ergativity in German* Ms., University of Frankfurt. Dordrecht: Foris.

Haegeman, L. and H. van Riemsdijk. 1984. "Verb Projection Raising, Scope and the Typology of Verb Movement Rules." *Tilburg papers in language and literature* 64, University of Tilburg.

Haider, H. 1984a. "Was zu haben ist und zu sein hat." *Papiere zur Linguistik* 30, Heft 1, 23-36.

———. 1984b. "Mona Lisa lächelt stumm — Über das sogenannte deutsche 'Rezipientenpassiv'." *Linguistische Berichte* 89, 32-42.

———. 1985. "Der Rattenfängerei muß ein Ende gemacht werden." *Wiener linguistische Gazette, 35/36,* 27-50.

———. 1989. *Parameter der deutschen Syntax.* Tübingen: Narr.

———. 1987. "Expletives *pro* — Eine Phantomkategorie." Ms. University of Vienna.

———. and R. Rindler-Schjerve, 1987. "The Parameter of Auxiliary Selection: Italian German Contrasts." *Linguistics* 25, 1029-56.

Haspelmath, M. 1987. "Transitivity. Alternatives of the Anticausative Type." *Arbeitspapiere des Instituts für Sprachwissenschaft Nr. 5.* University of Cologne.

Höhle, T. 1978. *Lexikalistische Syntax: Die Aktiv-Passiv-Relation und andere Infinitkonstruktionen im Deutschen.* Tübingen: Niemeyer.

Koster, J. 1982/3. "Enthalten syntaktische Repräsentationen Variablen?" *Linguistische Berichte* 80, 70-100./83, 36-60.

Kratzer, A. 1984. *"On deriving Syntactic differences between German and English." Ms.*

Postal, P. 1974. *On Raising*. Cambridge, Mass.: MIT. Press.

Pesetsky, D. 1982. "Paths and Categories." Diss. Massachusetts Institute of Technology.

Muysken, P. 1982. "Parametrizing the notion 'head'." *Journal of Linguistic Research 2,* 57-75.

Reis, M. 1976. "Reflexivierung in deutschen A.c.I.-Konstruktionen. Ein transformationsgrammatisches Dilemma." *Papiere zur Linguistik* 8, 5-82.

———. 1982. "Zum Subjektbegriff im Deutschen." In: Abraham (ed).

———. 1985. "Mona Lisa kriegt zuviel — Vom sogenannten 'Rezipienten-passiv' im Deutschen." *Linguistische Berichte* 96, 140-155.

Riemsdijk, H. van. 1985. "On Pied-Piped Infinitives in German Relative Clauses." In: Toman (ed.).

Safir, K. 1985. *Syntactic Chains*. Cambridge: Cambridge University Press.

Stechow, A. von. and W. Sternefeld. 1988. *Bausteine syntaktischen Wissens. Ein Lehrbuch der modernen generativen Grammatik*. Opladen: Westdeutscher Verlag.

Sternefeld, W. 1982. "Konfigurationelle und nicht-konfigurationelle Aspekte einer modularen Syntax des Deutschen." *Arbeitspapiere des SFB 99,* 8. University of Constance.

———. 1985. "Deutsch ohne grammatische Funktionen: Ein Beitrag zur Rektions- und Bindungstheorie." *Linguistische Berichte* 99, 394-437.

Toman. J. (ed). 1985. *Studies in German Grammar*. Dordrecht: Foris.

Torris, T. 1984. *Configurations syntaxiques et dépendances disconuées en allemand contemporain*. Diss. University of Paris VII.

Wegener, H. 1985. "'Er bekommt widersprochen' — Argumente für die Existenz eines Dativpassivs im Deutschen." *Linguistische Berichte* 96, 127-139.

Williams, E. 1981. "Argument Structure and Morphology." *The Linguistic Review* 1, 81-114.

———. 1984. "Grammatical Relations." *Linguistic Inquiry* 15, 639-673.

Head Movement and Scrambling Domains

Martin Prinzhorn
University of Vienna

In this paper, I will discuss a wellknown construction of German, namely the infinitival complements, which in some descriptive work are called **coherent** (Bech 1955) or in generative grammar are analyzed by means of **reanalysis** in terms of **verb-raising** (Evers 1975) or **parallel structures** (Haegeman & van Riemsdijk 1985). Another approach to analyze this construction is the one by Haider (1989) who assumes a lexical amalgamation process of the two verbs in question which yields a single word in syntax.

Bech (1955) noticed that German infinitival complements differ w.r.t. their sentential character. Three classes of verbs take complements which show some special properties:

A.   The verbs which are semantically analogous to the English raising verbs **always** form a complex with the verb of their complement and the freedom in word order is identical with the simple sentence.

B.   A large class of subject control verbs **optionally** forms a verb complex and, in that case, shows monosentential word order properties.

C.   Causative verbs and verbs of perception take complements without the infinitival marker "zu," they **always** form a verb complex and they **optionally** assign exceptional case to the thematic subject of the complement. In the latter case some opacity effects w.r.t. serialization occur.

So from a theoretical point of view the following questions arise:Is the complex verb formation a lexical process and are the verb complexes base-generated in a simplex sentence structure? If so, what are the relevant conditions that allow such a process? Is the complex verb formation the result of a syntactically triggered operation and if so, is there a mapping from biclausal to monoclausal structures in syntax or is the monoclausal behavior simply a reflex of other grammatical conditions?

The last question has to do with the basic line one takes on the concept of reanalysis: Should it be a primitive notion of grammar or should it be defined by other principles?

The line I would like to take here is the following: Although the analysis should capture the lexical properties of the verbs involved, the most straightforward way of encoding these properties is compatible with a strictly syntactic movement analysis. The price one has to pay for avoiding a lexical rule or a reanalysis process in the syntax is the (lexically triggered) weakening of the strict version of the theta criterion. To do this I will use Zubizarreta's (1982) notion of "adjunct" theta role.

In the first part the data are discussed. Part two deals with Chomsky's (1986) idea of a close relationship between head movement and NP-movement, which is then used in part three for the analysis of the German infinitive constructions.

1. The data

1.1. *"Raising verbs" in German*

This class consists of the verbs "scheinen" (seem) and "pflegen" (to be in a habit of doing s.th.) and of the impersonal variants of control verbs like "versprechen" (promise) and "drohen" (threaten). They allow for the same finite/infinite alternations as their English counterparts:

(1) a. *weil   es schien,   daß Peter einschlafen würde*
         because it seemed,   that Peter fall asleep   would
     b. *weil   Peter einzuschlafen schien*
         because Peter to fall asleep seemed
     c. *weil   (es) drohte,   daß der Abend langweilig*
         because (it) threatened, that the evening boring
         werden würde
         become would
     d. *weil   der Abend   langweilig zu werden   drohte*
         because the evening boring   to become threatened

The obligatoriness of verb complex formation is seen in (2), where an intervening adverb yields ungrammaticality and (3), where the scope of the negation is ambiguous between the two verbs:

(2)   *weil   Peter einzuschlafen *immer* schien
            because Peter fall asleep   always seemed

(3)   weil   Peter *nicht* einzuschlafen schien
            because Peter not   fall asleep   seemed

Another test criterion for verb complexes is their possibility to be topicalized and show up in pre-finite position in main clauses. At best this holds up marginally for the verbs in question since these verbs hardly show up as participles:

(4) a. *weil   Peter einzuschlafen geschienen hat
          because Peter to fall asleep   seemed   has

    b. *Einzuschlafen* geschienen hat Peter noch nie
        to fall asleep   seemed   Peter never

    c. ?weil   der Abend   auszuarten   gedroht   hat
         because the evening to degenerate threatened has

    d. ?Auszuarten   gedroht   hat der Abend schon   sehr
        to degenerate threatened has the evening already very
        früh
        early

Infinitival complements in German can appear in extraposition, that is to the right of the finite verb. This is not possible with the class of raising verbs, as the contrast of (5)a. versus (5)b. and c. shows:

(5) a. weil   Peter versprach, der Maria   zu helfen
         because Peter promised,   Maria:DAT to help

    b. *weil   Peter schien, der Maria   zu helfen
        because Peter seemed,   Maria:DAT to help

    c. *weil   der Orkan   drohte,   die Häuser zu
        because the thunderstorm threatened the houses to
        zerstören
        destroy

All these criteria indicate a verb complex; the criteria for monosententiality are fronting of unstressed pronouns and passivisation of the whole construction. Unstressed pronouns tend to be in sentence-initial position in simplex sentences:

(6) a. ?weil   Peter *ihr* half
         because Peter her helped

    b. weil   *ihr* Peter half
        because her Peter helped

The objects of the infinitival complements of "raising verbs" can be fronted over the matrix subject:

(7) a. *weil*   *ihr* *Peter zu helfen schien*
         because her Peter to help seemed
     b. *weil*   *sie*   *der Orkan*   *zu zerstören drohte*
         because them the thunderstorm to destroy   threatened

Passivisation is at best marginally possible, since it also involves participle formation:

(8) a. **weil   der Maria (von Peter) zu helfen geschienen wurde*
         because Maria:DAT (by Peter) to help   seemed   was
     b. *?weil   die Häuser vom   Orkan   zu zerstören*
         because the houses by the thunderstorm to destroy
         gedroht   wurden
         threatened were

Like the topicalisation test for verb complexes, the fact that the examples in (8) are bad, seems to be reducible to the lack of participle forms of these verbs. All other criteria indicate that in "scheinen"-constructions verb complex formation always takes place and monosententiality is always given. But these constructions shed no light on the precise relation between verb complexes and monosententiality.

1.2. *Optional restructuring verbs*

The largest class of verbs which allow restructuring is subject control verbs and has the possibility of selecting a sentential complement only. Some examples are given in (9):

(9)   *versuchen* (try), *versprechen* (promise), *glauben* (believe), *behaupten* (claim), *verbieten* (forbid), *hoffen* (hope), *vergessen* (forget), *fürchten* (fear), *erwarten* (expect)

If we contrast such a verb like "versuchen" (try) with the verb "bedauern" (regret), which doesn't allow restructuring, both verbs have the possibility of an embedded infinitival complement, which can be extraposed:

(10) a. *weil*   *Peter [PRO ihn   zu verletzen] versucht*
         because Peter [PRO him to violate]   tries
     b. *weil*   *Peter [PRO ihn   zu verletzen] bedauert*
         because Peter [PRO him to violate]   regrets

    c.   *weil*   *Peter versucht* [PRO *ihn zu verletzen*]
        because Peter tries   [PRO him to violate]
    d.   *weil*   *Peter bedauert* [PRO *ihn zu verletzen]*
        because Peter regrets [PRO him to violate]

The two verbs differ w.r.t. pronoun fronting and passivisation, which are only possible with "versuchen":

(11) a.   *weil*   __*ihn*__ *Peter zu verletzen versucht*
          because him Peter to violate   tries
      b. *weil*   __*ihn*__ *Peter zu verletzen bedauert*
          because him Peter to violate regrets
      c.   *weil*   *Paul von Peter zu verletzen versucht wurde*
          because Paul by Peter to violate   tried   was
      d. *weil*   *Paul von Peter zu verletzen bedauert wurde*
          because Paul by Peter to violate   regretted was

Fronting and passivisation are not possible if the complement is extraposed:

(12) a. *weil*   *ihn der Peter versucht zu verletzen*
        because him   Peter tries   to violate
      b. *weil*   *der Paul von Peter versucht wurde zu verletzen*
        because   Paul by Peter tried   was   to violate

If fronting (and passivisation) takes place then the criteria of a verb complex formation are fulfilled, whereas with "bedauern" the verbs are separable (13)b. and the negation can not have matrix scope (14)b.

(13) a. *weil*   *ihn der Peter zu verletzen* __*niemals*__ *versucht*
        because him   Peter to violate   never   tries
      b. ?*weil*   *der Peter ihn zu verletzen* __*niemals*__ *bedauert*
        because   Peter him to violate never   regrets

(14) a.   *weil*   *ihn der Peter* __*nicht*__ *zu verletzen versucht*
          because him   Peter not   to violate   tries
      b.   *weil*   *der Peter ihn* __*nicht*__ *zu verletzen bedauert*
          because   Peter him not   to violate regrets

Topicalisation of the two verbs is only possible in the case of "versuchen":

(15) a. __*Zu*__ __*verletzen*__ __*versucht*__ *hat Peter den Paul niemals*
         to   violate   tried   has Peter Paul   never
      b. *__Zu__ verletzen bedauert hat Peter den Paul niemals*
         to   violate   regretted has Peter   Paul never

These verbs allow restructuring, whereby monosententiality always implies verb complex formation. One cannot easily find an answer to the connection of monosententiality and verb complex formation from an empirical point of view. If the complement is in nonextraposed position, the two verbs are adjacent and already seem to form a complex. Even without fronting or passivisation the separation of the Verb complex yields a marginal result, but it is clearly better than in the fronted case:

(16) a. ?*weil*   *Peter der Maria zu helfen ja schon oft*
          because Peter   Maria to help   already often
          versprochen hat
          promised   has

      b. *weil   *ihr Peter zu helfen ja schon oft*   *versprochen*
          because her Peter to help   already often promised
          hat
          has

For these matters the scope of the negation is also a quite delicate criterium. But the ambiguity seems to be clearer in the case of object fronting (17)b.:

(17) a. *weil*   *Peter der Maria nicht zu helfen versprach*
          because Peter   Maria not to help   promised

      b. *weil*   *ihr Peter nicht zu helfen versprach*
          because her Peter not   to help   promised

In case of fronting or passivisation verb complex formation has to take place, whereas in the non-extraposed case without any of these processes a biclausal structure seems to be possible.

1.3. *Causative verbs and verbs of perception*

Causative verbs like "lassen" (let) and verbs of perception like "hören" (hear) or "sehen" (see) take verbal complements without the infinitival marker "zu." Exceptional case is optionally assigned to the thematic subject of the complement verb. Examples are in (18)

(18) a. *weil*   *Peter den Paul   schlafen ließ*
          because Peter   Paul:ACC sleep   led

      b. *weil*   *Peter den Paul   schnarchen hörte*
          because Peter   Paul:ACC snore   heard

Pronoun fronting of the embedded thematic subject and passivisation are
always possible.

(19) a. *weil   ihn Peter   schlafen ließ*
         because Peter him sleep   led

     b. *weil   ihn Peter schnarchen hörte*
         because him Peter snore   heard

     c. *weil   der Paul (von Peter) schlafen gelassen wurde*
         because   Paul (by   Peter) sleep   led   was

     d. *weil   der Paul (von Peter) schnarchen gehört wurde*
         because   Paul (by   Peter) snore   heard was

A verb complex is always formed as the inseparability (20) and the possibility of matrix scope (21) shows:

(20) a. **weil   Peter den Paul   schlafen <u>ungern</u>   ließ*
         because Peter   Paul:ACC sleep   reluctantly led

     b. **weil   Peter den Paul   schnarchen <u>oft</u>   hörte*
         because Peter   Paul:ACC snore   often   heard

(21) a. *weil   der Peter den Paul   <u>kaum</u> schnarchen hörte*
         because   Peter   Paul:ACC hardly snore   heard

     b. *weil   der Peter den Paul   <u>ungern</u>   schlafen ließ*
         because   Peter   Paul:ACC reluctantly sleep   led

Also there is no option to extrapose the complement:

(22) a. **weil   Peter ließ, den Paul   schlafen*
         because Peter led,   Paul:ACC sleep

     b. **weil   Peter hörte, den Paul   schnarchen*
         because Peter heard,   Paul:ACC snore

The criteria for verb complex formation hold in any case. W.r.t. pronoun
fronting certain opacity effects occur if the embedded verb is transitive. The
thematic subject of the complement can still be fronted but the embedded
object cannot cross the matrix subject.

(23) a. *weil   Peter den Paul   die Maria   unterstützen ließ*
         because Peter   Paul:ACC   Maria:ACC support   led

     b. *weil   Peter sie   den Paul   unterstützen ließ*
         because Peter her:ACC   Paul:ACC support   led

     c. **weil   sie   Peter den Paul   unterstützen ließ*
         because her:ACC Peter   Paul:ACC support   led

The same opacity holds w.r.t. the binding domain of lexical anaphoras: If the thematic subject of the complement is lexicalized then it binds an anaphoric object, otherwise the matrix subject will be the antecedent (24).

(24) a. *weil   Peter den Paul$_i$ sich$_i$ waschen läßt*
        because Peter   Paul$_i$ himself$_i$ wash   lets

    b. *weil   Peter$_i$ sich$_i$ (von Paul) waschen läßt*
        because Peter$_i$ himself$_i$ (by Paul) wash   lets

Passivisation of the embedded subject is possible (25)a., the embedded object can not be passivized (25)b.:

(25) a. *weil   Paul (von Peter) die Maria   küssen gesehen*
        because Paul (by Peter)   Maria:ACC kiss   seen
        wird
        was

    b. **weil   die Maria Peter (von Paul) küssen gesehen wird*
        because   Maria Peter (by Paul) kiss   seen   was

This opacity effect does not hold if the embedded verb is ergative, then the embedded object pronoun can be fronted (26):

(26) a. *weil   ihm Peter einen Stein auf die Zehen fallen sieht*
        because him Peter a   stone on his toes   fall   sees

    b. **weil   ihm Peter einen Stein die Zehen zerquetschen sieht*
        because him Peter a   stone his toes crush   sees

With prepositional objects the opacity effect disappears, even if the embedded verb is transitive:

(27)   *weil   gegen   diesen Vorschlag Chomsky noch nie*
        because against this   proposal Chomsky never
        jemanden argumentieren hörte
        someone   argue   heard

Causative verbs and verbs of perception obligatorily form a verb complex but some opacity effects indicate that verb complex formation doesn't necessarily imply monosententiality.

2. NP-movement and Head-movement

One theoretical innovation in Chomsky's "Barriers" is the assumption of a close relation between NP-movement and Head-movement. Although one important instance of Head-movement is verb second in Germanic languages I will concentrate on passive and NP-raising.

To be transparent for Head-movement it is necessary for a constituent to be l-marked (28):

(28)   Where α is a lexical category, α **L-marks** β iff β agrees with the head of τ that is Θ-governed by α

(29) α Θ-**governs** β iff α is a zero-level category that Θ-marks β and α, β are sisters

Chomsky assumes that VP is theta-governed by I in order to make the movement from V to I possible. A X^0 category may only move to a head position which governs the maximal projection of the X^0 category. This makes head-movement strictly local. There is no option for the adjunction of heads and no direct interaction of Head-movement and A-bar-movement.

For a raising construction like (30)

(30)   *John seems* [t *to be angry*]

a structure like (31) is assumed

(31)   *John*$_i$ [$_{I'}$[*seem* + I]$_j$ [$_{VP}$ t$_j$ [$_{IP}$ t$_i$ *to be angry*]]]

[seem +I] is the antecedent of the trace t$_j$ and l-marks the VP in order not to be a barrier. The trace of "John" can not be licenced without further assumptions because adjunction to IP is not possible and antecedent government is excluded by the minimality condition. To make antecedent government possible Chomsky assumes a unification of the indices by Specifier-Head-Agreement. For (31) the extended chain (32) is relevant in order to facilitate antecedent government.

(32)   (NP, V$_I$, t$_V$, t$_{NP}$)

In "Barriers" this analysis also excludes the appearance of a raising verb with an auxiliary like in (32) because "seem" is not moved out of the VP, which is therefore not l-marked and a barrier.

(33)   [$_{IP}$ e [$_{I'}$[*will*] [$_{VP}$*seem* [$_{IP}$ NP *to* ...]]]]

This aspect of the analysis seems to be problematic for several reasons. In her thesis Zubizarreta (1982) notes cases of the marginal acceptability of raising verbs in the progressive and with modals.

(34) a.   *John is seeming to be a nice fellow*
      b.   **It is seeming that John is a nice fellow*
      c.   *John can appear to have left*

In these examples no Head-movement takes place and it is interesting that (34)a. where NP-movement is involved is better than (34)b. without NP-movement. Moreover as Chomsky notes English raising adjectives like "likely" would have to be lexically reanalyzed as "be likely" to make Head-Movement in the syntax possible.

Another problematic case in Chomskys analysis is passive. Since he wants to unify the conditions for NP-traces lexical government is not sufficient for passive and Head-movement has to licence antecedent government for the NP trace. If one uses adjunction structures for the base position of the auxiliary like in (35)b.

(35) a. *John was killed*
      b. *John*$_i$ [$_I$ *be* + I][$_{VP}$, t$_j$ [$_{VP}$ *killed* t$_i$]]

not only the conceptual point of the difference between A- and A-bar-movement regarding the possibility of adjunction is weakened but also for passive structures with auxiliaries like

(36)   *John will be killed*

this analysis doesn't work, since "be" cannot be raised to I and form a complex [will+be] or [be+will]. Raising to C would then allow forms like (37).

(37) a. **Will be John killed?*
      b. **Be will John killed?*

To solve this problem in a way which is compatible with all other cases of NP-movement Chomsky rejects the option for adjunction of auxiliaries and assumes coindexing between a trivial chain (be) and the subject position which makes head-head agreement between the I-position and aspectual verbs independent from raising. In other words, some predicates have to be lexically marked to allow NP-movement. Moreover the formation of a trivial chain is a way of encoding the possibility of a predicate to violate the strict version of the theta criterion. It has the advantage that there is no need for adjunction structures which split up categories to make them transparent for extraction.

I will now try to show that the analysis of NP-movement in connection and lexical encoding of modifying predicates yields some interesting consequences for German verb complexes.

3. An analysis of German verb complexes

If the analysis in "Barriers" shall be of any relevance for German, then NP-movement must exist in this language. This is a controversial question related to the discussion of the configurationality of German. Some authors, especially Haider (1989) do not assume a VP for German which excludes the external argument. I will not discuss the arguments of this debate but I will assume a difference of VP and IP in German. This necessitates two further assumptions. I will assume an unmarked word order in German, which is generated at D-structure. Any deviance from this word order will involve a rule of "scrambling," in the manner assumed by Thiersch (1984) and Webelhuth (1985, 1986). The conditions for licencing this rule of "scrambling" play a crucial role in the analysis of German verb complexes. I will also assume with Grewendorf (1989), Koster (1986) and Rizzi (1986) that German has the option of an empty category small pro in subject position, if this subject is non-referential. Passive has a structure like (38)

(38) a.   *weil*   [$_{IP}$ pro [$_{VP}$ *er unterstützt*] *wird*]
             because [pro [he supported]   was]

      b.   *weil*   [$_{IP}$ pro [$_{VP}$ *ihm   geholfen*] *wird*]
             because [pro [him:DAT helped]   was]

      c.   *weil*   [$_{IP}$ pro [$_{VP}$ *seiner   gedacht*] *wird*]
             because [pro [his:GEN thought]   was]

      d.   *weil*   [$_{IP}$ pro [$_{VP}$ *an dem Wagen gearbeitet*] *wird*]
             because [pro [on the car   worked]   was]

In (38)a. the nominative subject "er" can occur inside of the VP and then will be assigned it's case via pro.

3.1. *The "scheinen" class*

This solves an argument against raising by Ebert (1975). In the cases of (39)b. and c. I will assume raising of the empty category pro.

(39)   (Ebert 1975)
      a.   *Er scheint unterstützt zu werden*
             he seems supported to be

      b.   *Ihm   scheint geholfen zu werden*
             him:DAT seems helped   to be

c.   *Seiner   scheint nicht gedacht zu werden*
     his:GEN seems not   thought to be

d.   *An dem Wagen scheint noch gearbeitet zu werden*
     on   the car   seems still worked   to be

For a simple raising construction like (40)

(40)   *weil   Hans Maria   zu kennen scheint*
       because Hans Maria:ACC to know   seems

The D-structure looks like (41).

(41)

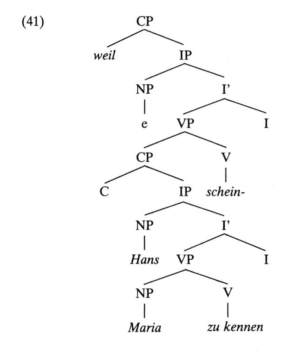

NP-movement is licenced by head movement of the verb from the embedded clause. Then the extended chain relation (42) makes antecedent government of the NP-trace possible.

(42) $K1 = (NP, t_{NP})$
          $K2 = (V+V+I, t_{V+V}, t_V)$
          $K3 = (NP, t_{NP}, V+V+I, t_{V+V}, t_V)$

NP-raising in this constructions is obligatory for the same reason as it is in English raising constructions. In German this forces the verb also to raise and form a complex.

The domain in which NP-raising is licensed is also the domain in which "scrambling" is licensed. Although "scrambling" is adjunction to IP it is, like NP-movement, licensed by head movement. Therefore the constructions where NP-movement is obligatory always show monosentential behavior.

3.2. *Optional Raising*

The next cases are those in which verb complex formation is optional. If we take a sentence like

(43)   *weil   Hans dem Kind die Sandburg   zu zerstören*
         because Hans the   child   the sand-castle to destroy
         drohte
         threatened

this sentence is ambiguous and has the two interpretations in (44):

(44) a. *Hans drohte,   daß er   dem Kind die Sandburg*
         Hans threatened that he   the   child the sand-castle
         zerstören würde
         destroy   would

   b. *Es drohte,   daß Hans dem Kind die Sandburg*
         It   threatened, that Hans the   child   the sand-castle
         zerstören würde
         destroy   would

The question is whether the two different interpretations should have two different D-structures. In any case there are two different lexical entries of "drohen," one with obligatory and one with optional verb complex formation. If no complex is formed I assume a control structure like (45)a. In this case extraposition is possible and the two verbs can be separated by an adverb marginally.

For the control interpretation with verb complex formation I will assume the same D-structure (45)b. as for the impersonal interpretation. This is possible if "drohen" in its control interpretation can select an adjunct theta role, which means that this theta role is invisible for the theta criterion and NP-raising to its position is possible. Zubizarreta (1982), who introduced this notion for the first time, makes a difference between optional and obligatory adjunct theta roles: A predicate with an obligatory adjunct theta role shows the same syntactic reflexes as a raising verb. The optional adjunct theta role can allow either a control structure or a raising structure. In the case of NP raising verb complex formation has to take place and the domain for scrambling becomes extended.

(45)

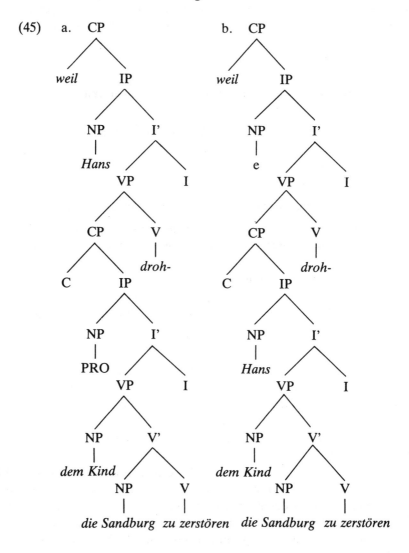

3.3. *Small Clauses*

The causative verbs and the verbs of perception take complements without the infinitival marker "zu." I will analyze these complements not as being sentential but as small clauses. A causative construction like

(46)   *weil   Peter den Paul   ihm   helfen läßt*
         because Peter   Paul:ACC him:DAT help   lets

has a structure like

(47)

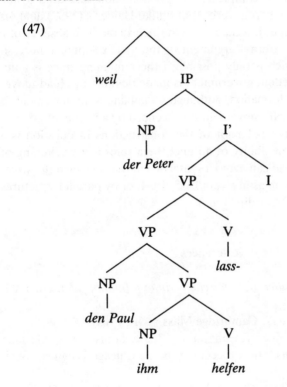

The verbs form a complex because no I node intervenes and the lower V also has to be governed by I. If the specified subject is adjoined to VP both the binding relation and scrambling out of the small clause are ungrammatical. The lack of an opacity effect when an ergative verb is embedded could be due to the fact that in this case no argument has to move out of the VP and therefore no subject in adjoined position blocks binding or scrambling. As examples like (27) show, extraction of PPs sometimes is possible which would be unexpected if the relevant condition would be antecedent government, i.e., the ECP.

5. Conclusion

In this analysis of verb complexes the phenomenon is related to the lexical structure of the triggering verbs, but unlike Haider's (1989) analysis the complex formation does not take place in the lexicon. The absence of a (full) theta-role for the external argument of the matrix sentence necessitates NP-movement, which is only possible if the remaining trace is antecedent governed. Antecedent government is made possible by Head-movement, i.e., verb complex formation. Although scrambling is no movement to argument positions, like NP-movement it is licenced by antecedent government. The monosentential behavior of the constructions in question is a reflex of this fact. The possibility of adjunct theta roles is a weakening of the theta criterion, but one can avoid a syntactic analysis in which the structure is changed (by deletion as in Evers 1975, 1984, or by parallel structures as in Haegeman & van Riemsdijk 1986).

References

Bech, G. 1955. *Studien über das deutsche verbum infinitum.* 2nd. ed. 1983. Tübingen: Niemeyer.

Chomsky, N. 1986. *Barriers.* Cambridge Mass.: MIT Press.

Ebert, R.P. 1975. "Subject Raising, the Clause Squish, and German scheinen-Constructions." In: Proceedings of the Chicago Linguistic Society 11.

Evers, A. 1975. "The Transformational Cycle in Dutch and German." Diss., University of Utrecht.

——— 1984. "Clause Union in French and German." Ms., University of Utrecht.

Grewendorf, G. 1983. "Reflexivierung in deutschen A.C.I.-Konstruktionen — kein transformationsgrammatisches Dilemma mehr." In: *Groninger Arbeiten zur Germanistischen Linguistik* 23: 120-196

————. 1989. *Ergativity in German*. Dordrecht: Foris.

Haegeman, L. & H. van Riemsdijk. 1986. "Verb Projection Raising, Scope, and the Typology of Rules Affecting Verbs." *Linguistic Inquiry* 17, 417-476.

Haider, H. 1989. *Parameter der deutschen Syntax*. Tübingen: Narr.

Koster, J. 1986. "The Relation between pro-drop, Scrambling and Verb Movements." *Groningen Papers in Theoretical and Applied Linguistics* 1.

Rizzi, L. 1986. "Null Objects in Italian and the Theory of **pro**." *Linguistic Inquiry* 17: 501-557.

Rouveret, A. and J.R. Vergnaud. 1980. "Specifying Reference to the Subject: French Causatives and Conditions on Representations." *Linguistic Inquiry* 11: 97-202.

Thiersch, C. 1985. "VP and Scrambling in the German Mittelfeld." Ms., University of Tilburg.

Webelhuth, G. 1985. "German is Configurational." *The Linguistic Review* 4: 203-246.

————. 1986. "More Diagnostics for Structure." Ms., University of Massachusetts, Amherst.

Zubizarreta, M.L. 1982. "On the Relationship of the Lexicon to Syntax." Diss., Massachusetts Institute of Technology.

The Infinitival Prefix "zu" as INFL

Arnold Evers
University of Utrecht

1. Introduction

Languages tend to make a distinction between finite and non finite verb forms. Certain languages display a variety of non finite forms, such as supina, gerundiva, gerundia, participles and infinitives. My problem in its most general form concerns the purpose or purposes served by this diversity. An interesting answer has been given for Russian by Babby (1974). He pointed out that V-projections are to be considered for a limited but prospectively universal set of deep structure options. They may either subcategorize a lexical item X, or function as adjuncts within an N or V projection, or realize an absolutive construction.

Languages differ less in these general deep structure possibilities than that they differ in ways to express these functions by means of finite verb forms, non finite verb forms and the various associated I (INFL) and C (COMP) affixes. A finite or non finite verb form and its I and C entourage are appropriately characterized if their appearance and distribution are derived from the general deep structure possibilities. Within this approach it seems reasonable to outlaw subcategorization statements that refer to verbal affixes or to I and C elements. One may further wonder whether I (INFL) and C (COMP) are separate projections. They often seem to be predictable as elements that reflect the theta functions imposed upon a V-projection by its lexical governor.

My more specific problem is which deep structure factors are reflected by the German infinitival prefix "zu."

(1)   DEEP STRUCTURE CONDITIONS ON V-PROJECTIONS
            (no reference is made to C elements, I elements or ver-
            bal categories like <+finite> or <−finite>)
            SURFACE STRUCTURE FORMS OF V-PROJECTIONS
            (the choice of C and I elements and the choice of
            <+finite> or <−finite> is derived from subcategoriza-
            tion and theta functions)

2.   Surface complement types

I would like to consider four types of verbs that are subcategorized for
a V-projection.

Verbs of control	type *hoffen*	"hope"
Sentence qualifying verbs	type *scheinen*	"seem"
Auxiliaries	type *werden*	"will"
A.c.i. verbs	type *sehen*	"see"

The auxiliaries do not allow a tensed complement, the other types do.

(2) a.   *da der Johann hofft*   [*daß er den Samba tanzt*]
          since John   hopes   that he is dancing the samba
     b.   *da es*   *scheint* [*daß der Johann den Samba tanzt*]
          since it   seems   that John dances the samba
     c. **da es*   *wird*   [*daß der Johann den Samba tanzt*]
          since it   will   that John dances the samba
     d.   *da die Marie*   *sieht* [*daß der Johann den Samba tanzt*]
          since Mary   sees   that John is dancing the samba

The complements in (3) are infinitival and they have been extraposed.
Extraposition is immediately obvious in continental West Germanic (Afrikaans, Dutch, Frisian, German, and all their dialects). The matrix verb is in
head final position in all COMP marked clauses. The extraposed complements are to the left of that head. See (3).

(3) a.   *da der Johann hofft*   [(PRO) *den Samba zu tanzen*]
          since John   hopes   to dance the samba
     b. **da der Johann scheint* [t_{NP} *den Samba zu tanzen*]
          since John   seems   to dance the samba
     c. **da der Johann wird*   [t_{NP} *den Samba tanzen*]
          since John   will   dance the samba

d. *da die Marie   sieht   [den Johann den Samba tanzen]
   since Mary   sees   John dancing the samba

The infinitival complements in (4) have not been extraposed, they have been restructured by an adjunction of the infinitive to the matrix verb. The restructuring is optional for controlled complements but obligatory for the non controlled complements. The variants in (4) do not differ in meaning from those in (3). All variants in (4) are grammatical.

(4)   a.   *da der Johann*   *den Samba* [*zu tanzen hofft*]
      b.   *da der Johann*   *den Samba* [*zu tanzen scheint*]
      c.   *da der Johann*   *den Samba* [*tanzen wird*]
      d.   *da die Marie den Johann   den Samba* [*tanzen sieht*]

Most matrix verbs allow the <+finite> complement in (2) as well as the <−finite> complements in (3) and (4). The auxiliary type *werden* "will" is a clear exception. It does not allow a <+finite> complement or an extraposed <−finite> complement, cf. (2c) and (3c). This may be explained by the circumstance that the auxiliary does not assign a theta role to the complement it is subcategorized for. Such a complement can probably not survive in surface structure. I tend to see all modal verbs within the same light. There are other verbs that do not allow a <+finite> complement or an extraposed <−finite> complement, e.g. the causative *lassen* "let." The verbs of intention, e.g. *versuchen* "try" do not allow a <+finite> complement. These verbs are certainly not auxiliaries. They theta mark their subject and their complement. A verb of intention requires a controlled complement. Further constraints bring the verbs of intention quite close to the modal verbs and the auxiliaries. See Cremer (1983) for highly relevant observations and a proposal to explain them. The causative verb *lassen* "let" is an a.c.i verb. It differs from the other a.c.i.verbs and from the verbs of intention in not allowing a nominalization of its complement.

At present I would like to leave the <+/−finite> problem and the various nominalization problems aside and concentrate on variations in the status of the infinitive. Three surface properties of the infinitive are to be considered:

(a) presence (versus absence) of the prefix "zu", the (a) and (b) variants in (3) and (4);
(b) presence (versus absence) of a lexicalized subject, the (d) variants in (3) and (4);

(c) V-to-V Raising (versus Extraposition) of the complement, the variants in (4) versus those in (3).

The (c) option (V-to-V Raising) makes the infinitive become part of a V-cluster as exemplified in (4). The phenomenon is diagrammed in (5), (6) and (7) below. A variety of arguments supports the view that deep structure (5) corresponds to a surface structure as in (6) or (7), cf. Bech (1955), Evers (1975).

(5)

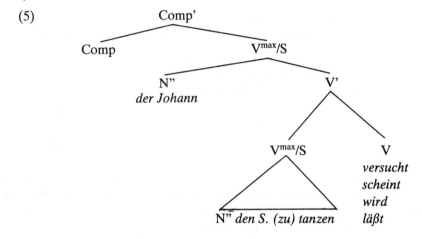

The preservation of the complement structure by means of a t_v requires that a trace headed complement not be extraposed. The result would be a word salad. One must also take care that the trace headed complement does not begin functioning as a full fledged binding category. If the Raising of the infinitive does not leave a trace, it seems reasonable that the V-projection line of the complement disappears as well. This will simplify the structure as in (7).

Favorable consequences of (7) are the impossibility of extraposing a restructured sentential complement and the absence of binding qualities. Yet these favorable consequences are minor points if compared with a downright suspicious property of (7). The derivation of monoclausal (7) from biclausal (5) is incompatible with Chomsky's Projection Principle. If *versuchen* "try" is subcategorized for a sentential complement in deep structure, the Projection Principle requires that this complement be preserved in the derived structure.

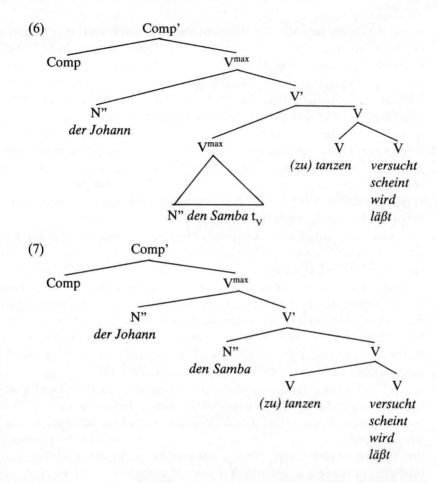

It stands to reason that the Projection Principle as a general perspective for a theory of grammar is not to be abandoned for a few language specific facts that are somewhat paradoxical. I will nevertheless defend the view that the option between (6) and (7) constitutes a major alternative. The German facts are not merely language specific, they reflect a deeper more general problem of clause union. As a consequence, the derivation of monoclausal (7) from biclausal (5) is less shortsighted than it might seem. I am guided by the following considerations.

(a) The most significant problem of clause union constructions is the ambiguous nature of the restructured complement. The arguments within a restructured complement differ in status. Some are involved in "long rules," i.e., rules that affect positions in the matrix construction. Examples of "long" rules are "long" clitic movement, "long" passive, and "long" reflexivization. Other arguments of the restructured complement are inert with respect to the long rules. The phenomenon has been discovered by the relational grammarians. They labelled the inert arguments as "chomeurs." They made it clear that the inertness is a phenomenon in core grammar. It should be anticipated by universal principles. A mirror image of the problem appears in the Government and Binding theory. The restructured complement, if still existant at all, seems to be neither fully rule transparent nor completely opaque. A barrier theory will have difficulties in drawing the appropiate distinction between the inert and the non inert arguments since they both inhabit the same domain.

(b) If the restructured complement preserves its status as a barrier, the inert "chomeurs" are no problem. The restructured complement, for example, would still block long clitic movement and long reflexivization. The problem within a barrier context is rather to save certain "long" rule phenomena. One needs additional measures to soften the barrierhood of the complement. Such measures are likely to be merely fact saving devices. This point of view leads to a criticism of the argument reindexing in Rouveret/Vergnaud (1980:161-162) and the multiple structure proposals made for German in Haegeman/Van Riemsdijk (1986:422).

(c) Instead of adding statements that weaken the barrier of a restructured complement, one may claim that the restructured complement label has been pruned as in (7), cf. Evers (1975:56), or that the structure as such has been preserved due to an empty place as in (6) but with the provision that a trace headed complement is transparent, cf. Baker (1985:79). The problem has now been inverted. The inert arguments, the "chomeurs," are the new problem, whereas the old problem, how to weaken the barriers for long rules, disappears. Again the status difference between chomeur and non chomeur has to follow from general principles. An ad hoc indexing of arguments is of no use at all.

(d) It is possible to present a unified trigger for V-to-V Raising. If the complement lacks an element that functions as INFL, restructuring by V-to-V Raising will follow. The V-to-V Raising rule serves to restore an INFL configuration for the infinitive. From this point of view it seems unlikely that different rules for clause union co-exist. If there were two clause union rules, one for controlled complements and one for the other complements, one would expect two different rule triggering circumstances. Considering two or more clause union rules, one should realize that the German clause union rules feed one another. The a.c.i. cluster [*tanzen sehen*] "see dancing" is fed into the control cluster [[*tanzen zu sehen*] *versuchen*] "try to see dancing." The control cluster [*zu tanzen versuchen*] "try to dance" is fed into the a.c.i. cluster [[*zu tanzen versuchen*] *sehen*] "see (him) trying to dance." There is a clear difference in meaning due to the different build up of the cluster. One attempts to see the dancing or one sees the attempt to dance.

The assumption that there is more than one rule with a clause union effect has been an element in the otherwise rather different clause union analyses made by Grewendorf (1987), Haider (1986) and analyses of clause union without reference to German as made by Rizzi (1978) and Marantz (1984).

Besides (6) and (7), there is a third option. Bresnan, Kaplan, Peters and Zaenen (1982: 620-624) propose that the V-cluster is base generated. This leads to a difficult problem for any lexicalist approach. The infinitives within the base generated V-cluster are in an awkward position for subcategorization. They lack a projection line of their own. The authors courageously propose that each infinitive within the V-cluster is subcategorized with respect to a VP located outside and to the left of the V-cluster. Their lexicalist theory does not allow a V-movement or a V-co-indexing between the subcategorizing complement and the infinitive in the V-cluster. Consequently the authors are forced into the position that the subcategorizing VP constituents lack any V. The implication is that the lexicalist analysis of the construction no longer captures a fundamental insight of the X-bar theory. Phrase labels come into being as projections of an endocentric head only.

In addition, but this is by comparison a minor issue, the lexicalist analysis in Bresnan and others (1982) needs the equivalent of a construction specific rule of subcategorization. It checks whether the lexical insertion of the infinitives within the verb cluster conforms with the rest of the structure. This rule is a reversal of cyclic V-to-V Raising. It eventually succeeds in relating an infinitive deep down in the V-cluster to an appropiate VP-torso somewhere to the left of the V-cluster.

The lexicalist analysis in Höhle (1978) does not offend X-bar theory, but is less radical about the V-cluster as a V^o constituent. The V-cluster as a V^o category does not really fit the lexicalist analysis. The V-cluster is no less a problem for the Government and Binding theory, as we will see below.

3.   Three surface structure properties of the German infinitive

Let me return to the four types of verbs mentioned in (2). They are all subcategorized for a V-projection and the V-projections differ among each other in three surface structure properties.

(8) | control | S-qualifying | auxiliary | a.c.i. verb |
(*hoffen*)	(*scheinen*)	(*werden*)	(*sehen*)
a.	+zu	+zu	−zu	−zu
b.	−lex.subj.	−lex.subj.	−lex.subj.	+lex.subj.
c.	+/−V-to-V	+V-to-V	+V-to-V	+V-to-V

Due to my opening statement in (1), I am not in a position to cram these properties (8a/b/c) into subcategorizing frames. Fortunately, the set in (8) offers an entrance, if one looks at the weak implications. The property $<+zu>$ unambiguously implies the property $<-$lex.subj$>$. Moreover, the property $<-zu>$ unambiguously implies the property $<+$V-to-V (Raising)$>$. I propose to frame these observations in the following hypothesis.

The prefix "zu" signals a V-projection with a matrix dependent mood value and a matrix dependent subject value. The dependent mood may be described as $<+$virtual$>$ or as $<-$actual$>$. The dancing of the samba is presented by the "zu" marked complements as intended or as envisioned or asserted by some controller present in the matrix clause. The speaker performs this "mood controller" function within the "scheinen" constructions. It is all samba dancing in a mental world, a second world in the sense of Popper (1968). The infinitival complements without "zu" present the samba dancing differently. They mark it as actual samba dancing, or at least as samba dancing that has not been marked as "virtual." If one accepts this guess, one might say that "zu" is a kind of INFL since it specifies the two INFL values, mood/M and subject/AGR. Moreover, the element "zu" presents these two INFL values as dependent from a matrix antecedent. Hence, I would characterize "zu" as an anaphoric form of INFL.

(9)   "zu" is a form of INFL since it represents the two INFL values Mood and AGR.

          "zu" is governed by the matrix verb (by percolation) and it needs co-indexing within its governing category (if any), hence "zu" is anaphoric INFL.

Assuming a theta feature <virtual mood> and anaphoric INFL, I will derive the surface properties in (8).

As for (8a), the theta role <virtual mood> requires an INFL element if it is to be assigned to an infinitival complement. The only INFL element for infinitives is "zu." The relation between <zu> and <+virtual mood> is symmetric. The presence of the INFL element "zu" requires that a mood <+virtual> be assigned. Absence of "zu" is the only possibility for an infinitival complement that will not receive a theta role <virtual mood> from its matrix verb.

Let me now turn to (8c). A V-projection without INFL is in bad shape. It lacks a Mood value and an AGR value. Hence it fails to express two crucial theta functions. In the first place, the Mood value of INFL serves to express the modal status alias the theta role of the complement. The INFL affix functions as the carrier of the complements verbal "case" (Fabb 1984). It has to be present in order to express the mood/theta role of the V-projection. In the second place, the AGR value of INFL, whether anaphoric or not, serves to express the subject function of the V-projection. A V-projection without INFL cannot realize its full interpretation since it cannot realize its subject function. I conclude that absence of INFL, e.g. absence of "zu," doubly disqualifies the V-projection as a constituent in derived structure. Here is the true cause for clause union. The lack of an immediate surface structure status triggers restructuring by V-to-V Raising.

This proposal for triggering clause union is to be seen as a prospective universal. The restructuring by V-to-V Raising restores an INFL configuration. It realizes minimal government of the infinitive by an item, in casu the matrix verb, which is fit to mark the infinitive's Mood and Subject values. The restructuring of the "zu"-less complements yields a grammatically visible point to which the complement's theta role can be assigned. This analysis of V-to-V Raising assumes like Marantz (1984:229) and unlike Baker (1985:67) that the deep structure theta relation between a head and its complement may be expressed by a cluster of the two heads in surface structure. This analysis does not yet account for the fact that V-cluster outcome is optional for some head complement pairs while being obligatory for others.

Let me turn for a moment to property (8b). I gratefully accept Haider's (1984) idea that the "zu"- affix invariably attracts the subject theta role of its verb. Since not only "zu" but also the V-cluster may realize the INFL configuration this can be generalized as in (10).

(10)

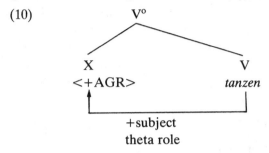

+subject
theta role

> The AGR carrier X is the minimal V-governor. X may be
> an INFL element like *zu*, or an INFL stand in such as *hofft*
> "hopes," *scheint* "seems," *wird* "will" or *sieht* "sees." The
> actual precedence relations between X and V are a matter
> of morpho-phonological rules.

In a way, we have something like Postal's NP-Raising here. None of the restructured infinitives could boast a lexicalized subject of its own. Strictly speaking, all verbs considered in (10b) are < −lexical subject>. The two infinitives without "zu" transmit their subject theta role to the element that functions as their INFL governor within the V-cluster. This item, the former matrix verb, subsequently provides a case configuration in which the subject theta role of the dependent infinitive can be realized. The auxiliary verb in *wird* "will" provides a nominative configuration. The a.c.i. verb in *sieht* "sees" is equipped with a subject theta role of its own. It has to realize the additional theta role by means of the other structural case, the accusative. This is not an additional assertion. One may assume that the accusative is a structural case in the sense that any verb, even an auxiliary verb, may assign an accusative as soon as a theta role is available.

I return now to the optional versus obligatory V-to-V Raising in (8c). Let me assume that the restructuring by means of V-to-V Raising is optional, in principle "not blocked," for any V-governed infinitival complement. This frames the problem in the following way. The control verbs in (8c), type *hoffen* "hope," are no problem, — they do have V-to-V Raising as an option —. It is the obligatory nature of V-to-V Raising for the other verb types in (10c) that needs to be explained.

I will do that in a moment, but let me face two more obvious problems first. If V-to-V Raising is a general possiblity, why does it not arise in other languages, e.g. there is no such rule in English. The basic answer must be that the surface INFL configuration in English and many other languages is "INFL + VP," whereas the German surface configuration is "INFL + V°." According to my trigger proposal, the V-to-V Raising makes sense only in languages with the former type of INFL configuration. This was a global answer to a global objection.

There is a more specific problem with optional V-to-V Raising as well. Many control verbs do not allow V-to-V Raising. Verbs that have to be sisters of a particle or an idiomatic adjunct malfunction as stand-ins for INFL, i.e., such matrix verbs block the V-to-V Raising option. The same holds for matrix verbs with a factive complement and matrix verbs that have to assign an inherent case, e.g. an NP dative, cf. Evers (1975: 39-42), also Cremers (1983). Such verbs cannot enter a V-cluster as INFL stand-ins. Matrix verbs in the form of a past participle passive do not qualify as INFL-governor either. It seems feasible to define the function of INFL-government in such a way that these exception classes fall out as an natural consequence.

Considering the amount of verbs that do not qualify as INFL stand-ins, Grewendorf (1987) raises the question whether it would not be simply better to define the V-to-V Raising class of control verbs by means of a rule feature. Some of Grewendorf's counterexamples to a general rule of V-to-V Raising are irrelevant since they fall within the exception categories just mentioned. Other counterexamples, e.g. his analysis of the verb "wünschen," can be dispelled by a different look at the original V-cluster arguments. However, the issue as such is too important for incidental remarks. It needs an exhaustive treatment. All verbs of control have to be considered and each verb that does not allow V-to-V Raising must be shown to belong to an independently motivated exception class. I cannot perform that task here, but I accept the challenge.

The sentence qualifying verbs, type *scheinen* "seem," restructure their infinitival complements obligatorily. These verbs differ from the auxiliaries, type *werden* "will," in as far as they assign a theta role to their complements, mark a dependent infinitival complement with "zu" and allow a finite complement in principle, whereas the auxiliaries, by contrast, do not assign a theta role to their complement, never allow a finite complement and do not mark the dependent infinitive with "zu." Neither the auxiliary nor the sentence qualifying verb has a subject theta role available. The

finite complement of "scheinen" is saved by a dummy subject, but the infin-
ival complement marked by anaphoric "zu" requires an antecedent within
the matrix structure. There is but one way to feed the matrix verb with a
theta role. The V-to-V Raising option should bring the sentence qualifying
verb into the structural position of an INFL element. The infinitival subject
theta role subsequently leap frogs up into the matrix construction according
to the procedure indicated in (10). The raised subject theta role will not fail
to constitute an antecedent for "zu."

(11)

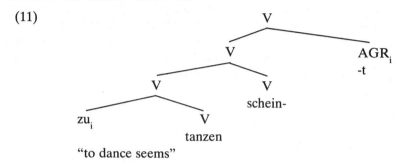

"to dance seems"

The Raising of the embedded subject obviously does not take place for
the complements of the *hoffen* "hope" group. A class like the English
"want/believe" "I want/believe John to dance the samba" is not available in
German.

(12)   *$daß$ die $Marie_i$ den Johann den Samba [zu_i tanzen $glaubt_i$]
                                                                                     $hofft_i$]
                                                                                     $versucht_i$]
          that   Mary   John   the samba   to   dance   believes
                                                                                     hopes
                                                                                     tries

It seems that an element "zu" within the V-cluster has to be subject
controlled. Why that should be, I do not know. But if so, it follows that
"zu" in (12) gets two matrix antecedents and fails to comply with the binding principles. Hence the theta leap frog sketched in (10) is obligatory for
the *scheinen* "seem" construction in (11), which needs a controller for "zu."
The theta leap frog is not applicable to the control constructions in (12).
They already contain a controller for the "zu" element.

This section argued that INFL-government is a useful notion for
verbs. It may serve as a uniform trigger for V-to-V Raising in German. Due
to this result, I will assume that the four classes of infinitival complements

mentioned in (2) are subject to the same rule of V-to-V Raising. This rule must in principle affect the transparency of the restructured complement in a uniform way. It is now time to return to the issue, whether the structure after V-to-V Raising is like (6) or like (7).

4. Chomeurs and double accusative constructions

The structure in (6) satisfies the Projection Principle. All theta relations are directly represented due to the t_V. The V-projection headed by a t_V is a fairly transparent category, be it not a totally transparent category. To see this we have to pay some attention to three variations of the direct object within a restructured clause. Among other things, the embedded object may be a clause, a clitic or a reflexive.

If the object is sentential all the restructured clauses turn out to be transparent for extraposition, cf.(11).

(13)   (extraposition out of a restructured complement)

a.   *da der Johann* [*die Leute* t_S t_V] [*sagen hörte*], *daß es*
       since John   the people   say   heard   that it
       regnete
       rained
       "since John heard the people say that it rained"

b.   *da der Johann* [(PRO) t_S t_V] [*zu sagen versuchte*] *daß es*
       since John   to say   tried   that it
       regnete
       rained
       "since John tried to say that it rained"

If the embedded object is a clitic "es" (it) or a reflexive pronoun, the a.c.i. complement is non transparent, cf. (14) and (15).

(14)   (clitic movement out of an a.c.i. complement)

a.   * *da   es der Johann* [*die Leute* t_{cl} t_V] [*beurteilen hörte*]
       since it   John   the people   judge   heard
       "since John heard the people judge it"

(15)   (long reflexivizations in an a.c.i complement)

a.   * *da   der Johann$_i$* [*die Leute   sich$_i$* t_V] [*beurteilen hörte*]
       since   John$_i$ the people himself judge   heard
       "since John heard the people judge himself"

b.   *da   der Johann$_i$ [die Leute über sich$_i$ t$_v$] [urteilen hörte]*
     since   John   the people about himself judge   heard
     "since John heard the people judge about him"

The non a.c.i. restructured complements are as transparent as possible, cf.(16) below.

(16)   (clitic movement out of a non a.c.i. complement)

a.   *da   es der Johann* [(PRO) t$_{cl}$ t$_v$] *genau   [zu beurteilen*
     since it   John   precisely to judge
     versucht hat]
     tried   has
     "since John has tried to judge it precisely"

b.   **da   es der Johann versucht hat* [(PRO) t$_{cl}$ *genau   zu*
     since it   John   tried   has   precisely to
     beurteilen]
     judge
     "since John has tried to judge it precisely"

c.   *das was der Johann versucht hat* [(PRO) t$_{wh}$ *genau   zu*
     that what John   tried   has   precisely to
     beurteilen]
     judge
     "that what John has tried to judge precisely"

d.   *da   der Johann versucht hat* [(PRO) *es genau   zu*
     since   John   tried   has   it precisely to
     beurteilen]
     judge
     "since John has tried to judge it precisely"

It might seem for a moment that restructured a.c.i. complements are non transparent for the co-indexing of a reflexive or a clitic-trace, whereas the other restructured complements are fully transparent. However, Reis (1976) made it clear that theta autonomous constituents, especially adjuncts of place and direction, may long reflexivize, cf. (15b). The long reflexives show, as Reis pointed out, that the a.c.i. complements do not comply with standard assumptions about non transparent categories.

The clitic movement from a non a.c.i. complement is possible only if the complement has been restructured. The long clitic movement is blocked if the complement has been extraposed instead of restructured. The clitic may move into the adjacency of the Comp element, but it cannot, for some mysterious reason, pass freely through the Comp into the matrix construction. There are exceptions but they are marginal. Clitic movement differs in that respect from WH-movement. See the ungrammatical clitic movement in (16b) versus the grammatical WH-movement in (16c). The factual difference between "move clitic" and "move WH" is used as an argument. If the clitic moves in the "long way" as it does in (16a), there is probably no complement barrier. If the clitic movement blocks as in (16b), the barrier seems to exist.

I claim that the restructured complement headed by a t_V, is no longer a barrier. If that is true, there are two problems. The first is how to protect the PRO in the restructured control complements against government by the matrix V-cluster, see e.g. (13b) and (16a). The second problem is what might block the long clitic movement of the object in the a.c.i. complement of (14a), and the long reflexivization in (15a). These a.c.i. complement are also restructured and as likely to be transparent as the a.c.i. complements in (13a) or (15)b.

The problem with PRO in a restructured controlled complement can be evaded. The hypothesis that "zu" represents an anaphoric variant of INFL implies that all subject functions can be attributed to INFL, cf. the notion SUBJECT in Chomsky (1981:209). Hence, there is no immediate need to assume empty elements like "PRO," "t_{NP}," or "pro." The INFL in the appearance of the infinitival prefix "zu" may carry the subject functions. A favorable consequence is that anaphoric INFL, i.e., "zu" rather than PRO, need not be protected against government by the matrix verb. Indeed, it requires that government. The stipulation of an empty COMP in front of controlled complements is no longer neccessary.

The second problem is the truly interesting one. It is clear that the embedded object of the a.c.i. construction is not accessible for the rules of long clitic movement and long reflexivization, cf. (14a) and (15a). This led Grewendorf (1987), Haider (1986) and Haegeman/Van Riemsdijk (1986) to the idea that the a.c.i. complement should somehow be preserved as an opaque category. Grewendorf proposed to apply a distinction made by Rizzi (1978) for Italian. The V-cluster for the non a.c.i. verbs would follow from "restructuring." The restructuring rule would still transform a biclausal deep structure into a monoclausal surface structure. Grewendorf (1987) further doubted whether the restructuring rule for non a.c.i. matrix verbs is that general. These verbs might form a highly restricted idiomatic class to be defined by a rule feature. This, however, is Grewendorf's minor point. His major point is that the restructuring of a.c.i. complements is different in nature from the restructuring of controlled complements. The restructuring of the a.c.i. complement is due to a different cause and takes the different effect of preserving the opacity of the a.c.i. complement.

Haider (1986) basically agrees. He somehow re-applies V-to-V Raising in different components. There is a V-to-V Raising in a kind of pre-syntax (at deep structure) and there is a comparable rule later on (between deep structure and derived S-structure). The later V-to-V Raising yields a V-cluster as well, but it applies in full syntax and the Raising now leaves a t_v in the complement structure. A clause union procedure that reappears in different components of syntax, has also been proposed by Marantz (1984).

Marantz forsees four types of restructuring and, presumably four types of trigger, corresponding to four types of syntactic representation. Restructuring may transform a biclausal set of theta relations into a monoclausal set (restructuring at deep structure). It may also turn a biclausal set of grammatical relations into a monoclausal set (restructuring at S-structure) or hide a biclausal set of grammatical relations in a monoclausal set of case assignments (restructuring at surface structure) or merely package a biclausal case structure into the phonological phrases of a simplex clause (restructuring at P-structure). The later the merger into monoclausal forms applies, the more biclausal the structure reacts. The structure pruning effect of the clause union rules makes Marantz abandon Chomsky's Projection Principle.

Baker (1985) covers the same ground but he claims there is but one merger/restructuring rule. Chomsky's Projection Principle is not abandoned. The empty place t_v, left by the V-to-V Raising, is rather used to impose a locality restriction on restructuring. However, Baker's claim (1985: 79) about the t_v is opposite to the one made by Haider (1986). According to Baker (1985) t_v enables the V-cluster to govern into the restructured complement. His prediction is that the embedded arguments will be V-cluster arguments and hence in principle "long" rule accessible.

Baker (1985) and Marantz (1984) consider various languages around the globe, but they shy away from the West European shores. This brings us in an excellent position to review their results from a new point of view, the grammar of German. The long clitic movement in (16a), the long reflexivization in (15b) and the long extrapositions in (13) are no problem if one claims that the restructured complement is transparent, cf. Baker

(1985) or for that matter Evers (1975). The transparency approach fails to anticipate the chomeur problem, such as the restrictions on the long rule accessibility of the embedded object, cf. again (14a) and (15a).

The chomeur problem leads Grewendorf (1987) and Haider (1986) to the belief that at least a.c.i. verbs are subject to a clause union rule that preserves the complement's opacity. The problems with this approach may now be clear enough. In the first place, the better the opacity of the a.c.i. complement is established, the more difficult the long reflexives become, cf.Reis (1976). This long reflexivization appears in restructured a.c.i. complements only. In the second place, the restructured non a.c.i. complements are fully transparent anyway. Consequently, one has to arrange two different types of clause union. One may assume, like Haider (1986), that all V-clusters are generated by the same rule, but since the rule operates in different components, it takes different effects. The V-clusters that are generated before the actual syntax give rise to the monoclausal structures. Other V-clusters are generated within syntax. This latter fully syntactic type of V-cluster emerges in the a.c.i. constructions and preserves the complement structure by means of a t_V. Somewhat differently one may conclude with Grewendorf (1987), that there are two completely different clause union procedures. One of them yields a V-cluster and a monoclausal string. The other clause union procedure is a "reanalysis." It does not bring about a V-cluster or a pruning of the complement label. The various arguments that generalize over apparent a.c.i and non a.c.i. V-clusters have to be reinterpreted. I am sceptic about that program, but let me take a different perspective.

None of the proposals elaborated on the trigger of the restructuring. They assumed a class of matrix verbs defined by a rule feature. If the trigger for restructuring proposed above is valid there is but one rule of V-to-V Raising. It generalizes over a.c.i. and non a.c.i. structures. Suppose now that the derived structure left a t_V as in (6). Suppose further, following Baker (1985: 79), that this t_V is governed by the raised infinitive and transmits the theta roles of the raised infinitive to the arguments in the t_V headed complement. If so, there is no difference in status between the arguments that are long rule accessible and the arguments that are not long rule accessible. Yet there is a difference in argument status, although it does not follow from the structural representation in (6). Due to the V-to-V Raising some arguments became long rule accessible whereas other became "chomeurs."

Consider now derivation (7). No t_V has been left and the structure is definitely monoclausal. It is possible though to construct a difference between the chomeurs and rule accessible arguments. Two plausible assumptions suffice.

(17) (i) Structural case is assigned by the V^o cluster.
          Verbs within the cluster do not assign structural case.
     (ii) There is no merging of theta-grids within the V-cluster.
          Only the head of the cluster projects its grid to the top.

First observe that there is a kind of correspondence between V-clusters like those in (18).

(18)   *ich glaube daß*
         I   believe that
     a. *die Marie den Johann den Samba* [[*tanzen zu sehen*]
             Mary   John   the samba dance   to see
         versuchte]
         tried
         "Mary tried to see John dance the samba"
     b. *die Marie den Johann den Samba* [*wird* [*tanzen sehen*]]
             Mary   John the   samba will   dance see
         "Mary will see John dance the samba"
     c. *die Marie den Johann den Samba* [[*tanzen zu sehen*]
             Mary   John   the samba dance   to see
         schien]
         seemed
         "Mary seemed to see John dancing the samba"

The verbs in (18a) *versuchte* "tried," in (18b) *wird* "will," and in (18c) *schien* "seemed" govern the group [*tanzen (zu) sehen*] "[dance (to) see]." They theta-determine the subject *Marie*. They do this due to the theta leap frog described in (10) above. As cluster elements they are to be considered as the INFL tag on top of the cluster. They define the subject theta role but they are not neccessarily the head of the V-cluster. For the lexical head of the cluster one should look at the highest verb that defines a non subject theta role. For example, the head of the clusters in (18) is *sehen* "see." It defines the object *den Johann*. The transitivity of *sehen* "see" derives from the procedure in (10) as well.

Suppose now, contrary to the usual assumptions, that merger of theta grids is not possible. Only the lexical head *sehen* "see" of the clusters in (18) may theta determine a non subject. It then follows that the embedded object of an a.c.i. complement, e.g. "den Samba" in (18), is no longer theta determined by the V-cluster. Its theta determiner *tanzen* "dance" got too deep down in the cluster to assign theta roles outside of the cluster. Arguments like "den Samba" in (18) continue to be case governed by the V-cluster but they are no longer theta governed by it. This is the reason that they are no longer visible for rules that turn theta representations into case representations. Under such assumptions the arguments and adjuncts singled out by Reis (1976) remain long rule accessible. They are theta-autonomous due to their specific prepositions.

5. Conclusions

The introduction of arguments that are case marked but not theta marked looks like a desperate proposal. Such arguments violate the theta criterium. However, things are not neccessarily as bad as they may seem.

5.1 *The trigger for clause union*

A general cause for clause union rules has been proposed. Clause union attempts to restore an INFL configuration in S-structure. German V-to-V Raising follows from the INFL surface configuration "V + INFL." The same holds for Afrikaans, Dutch and Frisian.

This is a much better trigger proposal than the usually tacit assumption that clause union holds for a lexical class of matrix verbs defined by a rule feature <+restructure>.

5.2 *The derivation of control*

The control problem has been clarified by the introduction of anaphoric INFL. Anaphoric INFL instead of PRO was neccessary to handle the restructuring of controlled complements.

Anaphoric INFL yields a better theory of control for English as well, cf. (Evers: 1986). It also leads to the abolishment of all empty subject elements (PRO, t_{NP} and pro). Their functions are taken over by the AGR-index of INFL. This is a simplification since AGR as a referential index was already there.

5.3 *The derivation of chomeur status*

An explanation has been provided for the emergence of arguments
that are no longer rule accessible (the "chomeur" phenomenon). Due to
the non merging of theta grids in the V-cluster, some arguments are case
marked by the V-cluster, but no longer theta determined by it. These are
the inert chomeur arguments. The problem has been outlined by the relational grammarians.

Analyses of clause union within the government and binding theory
either do not consider the chomeur problem at all (Baker 1985) or they
attempt to introduce semi-transparent categories, cf. Rouveret and Vergnaud's argument reindexing (1980: 161/162) or multiple constituent
analysis (Haegeman and Van Riemsdijk 1986, among others). These proposals are completely construction specific and as descriptive devices capable
of anything. To my mind, they destroy the explanatory value of the theory
that they attempt to protect.

Marantz (1984) may handle some chomeur problems by means of his
options for rule ordering, but the German problems are beyond the reach
of his system. Further, it must be remembered that Marantz is not a flag
waving member of the government and binding program. He abolishes t_{NP},
t_V and Chomsky's Projection Principle (Marantz 1984: 299).

5.4 *Derivational versus configurational grammar*

The temporary eclipse of a structure preserving constraint like the Projection Principle is not necessarily a disaster for syntactic insight. The local
effect of the derivational steps in syntax is obvious enough to be preserved
by some other convention. Chomsky's Projection Principle predicted the
empty places that were to be argument bound. The preference for
anaphoric INFL over empty elements like PRO, pro, and t_{NP} and the preference for (7) over (6) is compatible with the idea that such empty places
may not exist.

References

Asbach-Schnitker, Brigitte and Roggenhofer, Johannes. 1987. *Neuere Forschungen zur Wortbildung und Historiographie der Linguistik*. Tübingen: Narr.

Babby, L. 1974. "Towards a Formal theory of Parts of Speech." In: Brecht and Chvany (eds).

Baker, Mark C. 1985. "Incorporation: A Theory of Grammatical Function Changing." Diss., Massachusetts Institute of Technology.

Bech, Gunnar. 1955. *Studien über das Deutsche Verbum Infinitum*. 2nd. ed. Tübingen: Niemeyer.

Brecht, R.D. and C.V. Chvany. 1974. *Slavic Transformational Syntax*. Michigan: Michigan University Press.

Bresnan, Joan., R. Kaplan, Stanly Peters, and Annie Zaenen. 1982. "Cross Serial Dependencies in Dutch." *Linguistic Inquiry* 13, 613-635.

Chomsky, Noam. 1981. *Lectures on Government and Binding*. Dordrecht: Foris.

Cremers, C. 1983. "On Two Types of Infinitival Complementation." In: Heny and Richards (eds).

Evers, Arnold. 1975. "The Transformational Cycle in Dutch and German." Diss., University of Utrecht.

———. 1986. "Clause Union in German and French." *Groninger Arbeiten zur Linguistik* 28, 170-201.

Fabb, Nigel. 1984. "Syntactic Affixation." Diss., Massachusetts Institute of Technology.

Grewendorf, Günther. 1987. "Kohärenz und Restrukturierung." In: Asbach-Schnitker and Roggenhofer (eds.)

Haegeman, Liliane and Henk Van Riemsdijk. 1986. "Verb Projection Raising, Scope, and the Typology of Rules Affecting Verbs." *Linguistic Inquiry* 17, 417-466.

Haider, Hubert. 1984. "Was zu haben ist und was zu sein hat." *Papiere zur Linguistik* 30, 73-114.

———. 1986. "Nicht Sententiale Infinitive." *Groninger Arbeiten zur Germanistischen Linguistik* 28.

Heny, Frank and B. Richards. 1983. *Auxiliaries and Related Puzzles* Volume I. Dordrecht: Reidel.

Höhle, Tilman N. 1978. *Lexikalistische Syntax*. Tübingen: Niemeyer.

Lieber, Rochelle. 1983. "Argument Linking and Compounds in English."
    Linguistic Inquiry 14, 251-286.
Marantz, Alec. 1984. *Grammatical Relations*. Cambridge Mass.: M.I.T.
    Press
Popper, Karl. 1968. "On the Theory of the Objective Mind." In: Popper
    1974.
————. 1974. *Objective Knowledge, an Evolutionary Approach*. Oxford:
    University Press.
Rizzi, Luigi. 1978. "A Restructuring Rule in Italian Syntax." In: Rizzi
    1982.
————. 1982. *Issues in Italian Syntax*. Dordrecht: Foris.
Rouveret, Alain and Jean-Roger Vergnaud. 1980. "Specifying Reference
    to the Subject: French Causatives and Conditions on Representations."
    Linguistic Inquiry 11, 97-202.

Scrambling and Minimality

Wolfgang Sternefeld
Johann Wolfgang Goethe University, Frankfurt

This paper aims to reconstruct the clause-boundedness of scrambling in terms of Chomsky's ECP and Baker's minimality definition of barrierhood, demonstrating that the locality of scrambling in so-called "incoherent" constructions is due to a CP boundary between the target position and the source of scrambling. Contrary to what one might expect, the transparency of "coherent" constructions with respect to scrambling will not be analysed in terms of reanalysis or any other kind of CP-deletion; rather we will stick to the most strict version of the Projection Principle, showing that in cases of "long scrambling" COMP can be used as an escape hatch for movement: although the scrambled element itself cannot move directly into COMP, it can do so more indirectly via pied piping of a VP. This movement of the VP can in turn be justified on independent grounds; principles of government of "verbal Case" require movement of a VP into the governed domain of the "coherent" matrix verb.

1. Minimality

Consider the following configuration, where X, Y, and Z are lexical categories:

(1)

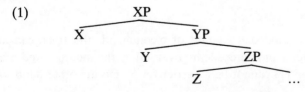

According to the intuitive concept of minimality, X cannot govern ZP or Z, because Y is a closer governor that protects ZP and Z from government by X. We shall say that Y erects a minimality barrier YP between X and Z.

The barrierhood of a category will also block antecedent government for movement. In the configuration depicted above this implies that Z cannot be moved to the X-position. Baker (1985) has shown in detail that the incorporation of lexical categories is restricted in this way. As a consequence of minimality and the ECP he can derive that X^0-movement is a local head-to-head movement (cf. Chomsky's Head Movement Constraint, *Barriers*, p. 69f). For instance, it would be impossible to incorporate a noun into a verb, as in the following modification of (1):

(2)

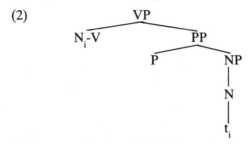

In contrast, the more local incorporation of the preposition into the verb is not blocked by minimality, as can be demonstrated by the following example from German:

(3)　a.　*als　er entlang des Zaunes fuhr*
　　　　　when he along　the fence　drove
　　　b.　*als　er den Zaun entlangfuhr*
　　　　　when he the fence along-drove

The structure of (3-b) is something like this:

(4)

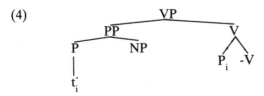

Assuming an extended definition of c-command, the trace can and must be c-commanded and antecedent-governed by the incorporated preposition. Thus, YP in (1) cannot be a barrier for Y. On the other hand, our informal discussion of the configuration (1) above implied that the PP is still a minimality barrier for the NP within PP. Intuitively, this result is incorrect, since the Case government relations change in the transition from (3-a) to (3-b): in (a) the preposition assigns genitive Case to the NP, whereas in (b) the NP receives accusative Case from the complex verb.

Phenomena of this type have been analysed by Baker (1985) with respect to government and agreement relations in a number of languages of the world. Baker has convincingly shown that incorporation (or X^0-movement) opens a barrier: if Y in (1) had been incorporated into X, YP could no longer be a barrier for ZP. If incorporation has applied in this configuration, Baker says that X is no longer *distinct* from Y. As a first approximation of Baker's more complicated definition we can conclude that

(5)   YP is a barrier between α and β iff
        (a) YP excludes α,
        (b) the head of YP is distinct from α,
        (c) the head of YP m-commands β.

Applying this definition to (4) we have to take into account that the verb is no longer distinct from the preposition. (More precisely, we should say that the complex verb is not distinct from the position occupied by the trace of the preposition.) Since condition (b) is no longer satisfied, movement of a lexical category has opened the PP-barrier so that the complex verb can now assign Case to the NP it governs.

As is clear from the context above, β in definition (5) is not necessarily lexical; it could be either a lexical or a phrasal category. Nor did we require that α be a X^0-category. The possibility of α and β being maximal projections will be discussed in the next section.

2. Barriers

In the following sections we will successively modify the above definition, so as to be able to treat some cases of antecedent government of a maximal projection. First, we observe that if α is not lexical then the head of YP is necessarily distinct from α. Thus we can drop condition (5-b) for the case of XP movement. Any attempt to apply the above definition to antecedent government in the standard cases will immediately reveal, however, that this definition must be inadequate; for instance, CP would always turn out to be a barrier for antecedent government. I do not want to go into a detailed demonstration of this fact but will immediately present a (still) simplified version of Baker's (1988) definition of a minimality barrier. The discussion of this definition will implicitly show why (5) would yield a number of unwarranted results.

(6)   YP is a barrier between α and β iff
           (a) YP excludes α,
           (b) the head of YP is distinct from α,
           (c) the head of YP selects a ZP contained in YP,
           (d) either $\beta=ZP$ or β is included by ZP.

As (a) and (b) have remained unchanged we have to comment on only (c) and (d). First note that "selection" is close to L-marking in Chomsky's *Barriers*, the motivation of which derives (in part) from the fact that adjuncts are always barriers. Baker defines selection as follows:

(7) α selects β iff either
           (a) α θ-marks β, or
           (b) $\alpha = I^0$ and $\beta = VP$, or
           (c) $\alpha = C^0$ and $\beta = IP$.

Since adjuncts are never selected, they are barriers according to the following definition of barrierhood:

(8)   YP is a barrier between α and β iff
           1. YP excludes α and includes β, and
           2. either clauses (b) to (d) of (6) hold, or YP is not selected

In this paper the barrierhood of adjuncts will be almost irrelevant. Let us therefore return to the use of selection in (6c). The effect of this condition is illustrated by (cyclic) movement "from COMP to COMP." As a consequence of the *Barriers* framework, this movement has to pass through VP, i.e., it moves an XP from the specifier position of COMP to the next VP and then moves this adjoined phrase to the specifier of the next COMP. The first step of this movement is depicted in (9):

(9)

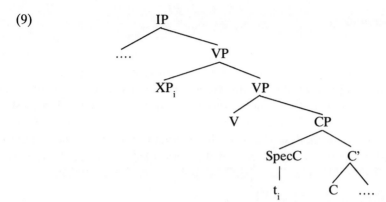

Contrary to what would be predicted by (5), this movement is legiti-
mate, since SpecC is not selected by C. If, on the other hand, a phrase *is*
selected by a category Y, it is (in general) also governed by Y, and the minimality idea of barrierhood suggests that this position be also protected by
Y, which means that Y erects the minimality barrier YP.

As another illustration of (6), consider the standard configuration of
barrierhood depicted in (10):

(10)

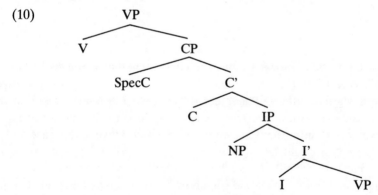

We have to establish that the subject NP (= PRO if I = [-tense]) cannot be governed by V, since C erects a minimality barrier. This can be
shown as follows: (a) clearly V is outside of CP; (b) C is distinct from V; (c)
the head of CP selects an IP; and (d) this IP includes NP. Therefore, all
conditions on barrierhood are satisfied, and C protects PRO from government by the verb.

3. Scrambling

Within the *Barriers* framework there is good reason to exclude adjunction to IP as a possible landing site for *wh*-movement. Suppose adjunction to IP were permitted. As an unwarranted consequence of (6), nothing (except lack of selection as in the second clause of (8.2)) could block successive movement through IP and VP into SpecC of the matrix COMP. To illustrate this, let us analyse the following configuration, where movement of XP did not pass through SpecC of the embedded clause (in the following trees, irrelevant nodes like SpecC will deliberately be omitted):

(11)

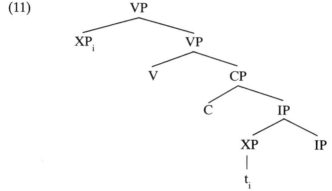

For CP to be a barrier we have to check: whether C selects IP (which it does according to (7) above); whether XP_i is outside CP (which is obvious); and whether either XP is selected by C (which is not the case), or the trace is inside IP. But as the trace is only adjoined to IP, but not included in IP, we have to infer that CP cannot be a barrier between the trace and its antecedent. Nor could IP be a barrier, because (c) and (d) of (6) would require that I selects XP. Thus adjunction to IP makes CPs transparent for movement and therefore should somehow be excluded as a possible landing site for *wh*-movement (cf. *Barriers*, p.5).

Turning next to the phenomenon of scrambling we must cope with the fact that all movement analyses of scrambling do involve adjunction to IP (and VP, see below). The above considerations should imply, however, that successive scrambling as in (12-b) be grammatical. But clearly it is beyond doubt that (b) is completely ungrammatical in German:

(12) a.   *weil   Hans glaubt   daß ihn   jeder   bemitleidet*
           because John believes that him everyone sorrows

b. *weil   Hans ihn glaubt   daß (t) jeder   bemitleidet
   because John him believes that   everyone sorrows

In order to find an explanation for the observed ungrammaticality we cannot block adjunction to IP but have to modify our definition of barrierhood. Suppose we were to replace (6-d) by:

(6)   (d') either β=ZP or β is dominated by (a segment of) ZP.

Since scrambling has adjoined an XP to IP, a segment of IP dominates the trace of XP in (12-b). From (7) we know that IP is selected by C. Clearly C is distinct from XP, and XP is outside CP. Given the extra stipulation that Scrambling cannot use SpecC as an intermediate position, it now follows from the modified definition (6') that CP is a barrier for *Scrambling*.

Although this modification correctly blocks the derivation of (12-b) it yields a problem in the case of successive COMP-to-COMP movement via adjunction to VP. As is shown in (13), *wh*-movement from VP to SpecC would be blocked because IP turns out to be a barrier between the two positions involved:

(13)

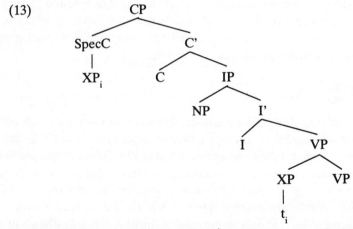

According to (6d') a segment of VP (=ZP) dominates β=XP. Therefore IP, which includes XP but excludes SpecC, must be a barrier between XP and its trace. But clearly such a movement must be licensed if an explanation along these lines can be made work at all. It now seems that we have to reach the same conclusion already drawn in Chomsky's original *Barriers* framework, namely that in certain well-defined cases it has to be stipulated that IP be exempt from barrierhood.

Let us therefore discuss the circumstances which would still allow IP to be a barrier in Chomsky's *Barriers*. Clearly an IP could inherit barrierhood from VP as a blocking category, or from the subject of IP. In the first case, the blocking character of VP can always be neutralized by adjunction to VP. Therefore we can completely disregard extractions from within VP. The second case might arise in extractions from the subject. As we are not concerned with subjacency in this theory, it will suffice to note that the subject itself constitutes a barrier for movement out of the subject.

Having shown that there seems to be no context other than (13) where the question of the barrierhood of IP could arise, we may follow Chomsky in making IP exempt from barrierhood by definition, leaving it open how this stipulation can be derived from other principles of grammar (cf. Müller 1989, for a theory of strong and weak INFLs and COMPs, which allows for such a derivation). Alternatively, our theory also allows for adjunction to IP as another way to make IP transparent for movement of phrases. Since IP should still be a barrier for head-movement, the latter option should be preferred.

As a consequence of the above modifications of Baker's definition of barrierhood we have established that *Scrambling* is clause bound. The only idiosyncratic property of scrambling, which must be stated in addition, is that — unlike *wh*-movement — scrambling cannot move a phrase into SpecC: it is genuinely a process of adjunction.

4. Infinitives

There are two kinds of infinitive constructions in German which differ with respect to scrambling and a number of other criteria not relevant in this context. The first type of infinitive behaves like (12-b) in that scrambling into the matrix clause is impossible. This kind of behaviour is already explained in analogy to the explanation given for the case of embedded finite clauses. A relevant difference between finite clauses and infinitives of this type seems to be that only in the case of (incoherent) infinitives will the matrix verb c-select an empty complementizer which in turn selects an infinitive with "to" (= *zu* in German). Note furthermore that with infinitives in German it is impossible to move into the SpecC position of the embedded clause:

(14) a.   *Max weiß   (*wie)* PRO *es* (t) *zu tun*
            Max knows   how   it   to   do

b. * *Max weiß   was* PRO *zu   tun*
    Max knows what   to do

The second type of infinitive construction does allow scrambling and is traditionally described as "coherent" in not presupposing a clause boundary between the elements of the construction. Until recently, the most promising account of these constructions has been the theory of reanalysis developed by Haegeman and Riemsdijk (1986). The theory has also been discussed in v. Stechow/Sternefeld (1988), where we tried to show that any empirically adequate theory of reanalysis has to imply an additional level of representation: reanalysis cannot apply on the way from D- to S-Structure but has to apply after principles of S-Structure have been checked, thereby creating a new level of representation with its own set of constraints (cf. Sternefeld (to appear) for a discussion of levels of representation and v. Stechow (this volume) for a discussion of "verbal Case" assignment (or status government), which has to apply after removing barriers by reanalysis).

The reason for this further multiplication of levels is that neither D-Structures nor reanalysed structures permit us to keep apart control, raising, and exceptional Case marking in the appropriate way. The differences between these constructions can, however, be represented in S-Structures of the usual type. But for rules like scrambling to apply properly, it also seems necessary to remove the CP boundary, thereby creating an additional level of representation. We therefore concluded that reanalysis must be ordered after NP-movement, Case assignment and other rules and S-Structure conditions that are sensitive to the presence of a CP. It can also be shown (cf. Sternefeld, to appear) that this ordering of rules is needed to define the required levels of representation.

Nevertheless, a multiplication of levels is unwarranted in that it (re-)introduces a kind of rule ordering that seems to have been abandoned in the course of introducing trace theory. The following analysis will show, however, that — contrary to what has been proposed by Haegeman, Riemsdijk, v.Stechow and myself — we do not have to multiply levels if we adopt Baker's theory of incorporation.

His basic idea concerning comparable cases in other languages than German is to move a VP into the embedded specifier position of C:

(15)

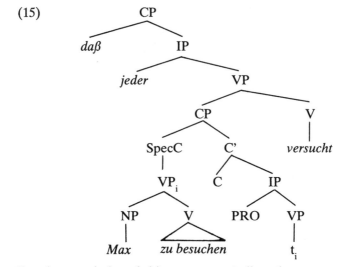

For the remainder of this paper we shall explore some of the consequences of this idea when applied to scrambling and "status government,"
i.e., the government of verbal Case in German.

As a lexical property of verbs that admit of a coherent construction, I
will assume that these verbs do not c-select an empty complementizer and
that for this reason (which presupposes, by lack of any other explanation,
essentially a doubly filled COMP filter) it is possible to move into SpecC.
This analysis should be contrasted with our remarks concerning (14) above,
which imply that movement to SpecC is impossible in incoherent constructions, because there is already an empty complementizer in COMP. On the
other hand, if no empty complementizer is selected, the verbal Case, i.e.,
the *zu*-infinitive of (15) cannot be checked by a complementizer in C but
must be selected directly by the matrix verb. As all selection relations are
local, the matrix verb must be able to govern the embedded verb. This is
the reason why the VP must move into SpecC, for otherwise CP would be a
barrier between the two verbs. We therefore have to show that CP in (15)
cannot be a barrier between the matrix and the embedded verb. But this is
easy to see: for CP to be a barrier with respect to an element in SpecC, the
head of C must be able to select SpecC. But as we have already argued
above this cannot be the case.

As a consequence of movement into SpecC, the embedded verb is in
the domain of the matrix verb, and therefore can, and sometimes must be
incorporated into the matrix (as in the analyses of Evers, Haegeman,

Riemsdijk, and others) without prompting an ECP violation and *without implying the deletion of CP*. This seems to be an important result as it shows that we do not have to assume an additional level of representation, nor do we need any tree pruning device like S-bar deletion, which has been shown to give rise to difficult problems concerning the subsequent government and deletion of PRO (cf. v.Stechow/Sternefeld, chapter 12, for an extensive discussion).

Let us now return to the issue of scrambling. In what follows we will assume that the ECP does not differentiate between adjuncts and arguments in German: all available data suggest that, contrary to what might be expected from the grammar of English, the movement of adverbials is even less restricted than that of objects (cf. Andersson & Kvam 1984 for empirical data). As it is not my concern to explain these cross-linguistic differences, I will simply assume that (in German) all traces must antecedent-governed on S-Structure. As a consequence we can also explain why scrambling of objects (and *eo ipso* scrambling of subjects and adverbials) is equally clause-bound, even if we do not try to use adjunction to IP as an escape route: If CP is a barrier for an element dominated by IP, it is irrelevant whether this element is an adjunct or an argument.

Things turn out differently for elements within CP which are not dominated by IP. Scrambling that starts from the object position in (15) is fully grammatical, as shown in (16):

(16) *daß Max*:ACC *jeder*:NOM *zu besuchen versucht*
      that Max   everyone to visit   tries

The derivation of (16) cannot proceed directly via adjunction from the object position in (15) to the IP of the matrix. Inspection of (15) will reveal that both VPs are barriers to direct movement. Suppose therefore that the NP is first adjoined to the lower VP. Whereas the object position is selected by V, the adjoined position is not, and therefore the VP can no longer be a barrier to further movement; nor can the CP above VP. To circumvent the second barrier, again we have to use adjunction to the matrix VP as an escape hatch. Not surprisingly, movement has to proceed exactly as in Chomsky's *Barriers* via adjunction to VP.

The above analysis has shown that we can explain why coherent infinitives behave as if they were mono-clausal, although we are not forced to delete CP which still protects the subject position PRO from government by the matrix verb. To get this result it is crucial to assume that IP cannot be a barrier. For assume we did not make IP exempt from barrierhood. It now follows that it is impossible to move the VP into SpecC: the IP would simply block this movement by minimality.

5. Incorporation

In v.Stechow/Sternefeld (1988) we have proposed that the preposition-like element *zu* in German is generated in INFL exactly as its equivalent "to" in English. Since INFL follows the VP in German, but *zu* precedes the verb, the preposition is generated "in the wrong place" in D-Structure. Following a GB-type approach to the INFL-verb relationship we assumed that INFL had to be incorporated into the verb. But given Baker's general theory of incorporation, we now would have to say that the preposition should remain *in situ*, for otherwise the trace of incorporation would not be m-commanded by its antecedent. Rather, it is the verb which has to be adjoined to INFL.

This assumption leads to the following problem: if we were to assume that in coherent constructions the embedded verb has to adjoin to the matrix verb, it seems that this movement must pass through INFL in order to pick up the inflectional element *zu*. But the subsequent movement from INFL to the matrix verb is blocked by the minimality barrier CP. We therefore have to assume that the verb first moves into INFL, then moves into the empty C-position (which is not "occupied" by the empty complementizer), and finally adjoines to the matrix verb, say to the right of the matrix verb as in Dutch:

(17)   *dat   Ria* [$_{CP}$ t [PRO *in   Duitsland* t t]] *probeert te blijven*
         that Ria   in Germany   tries   to stay

The problem arises from the fact that this movement opens the barrier CP, because C and V are no longer distinct. This would imply that PRO is governed by the matrix verb — a disasterous result we were just trying to avoid.

One might have to conclude that the element *zu* (or *te* in Dutch) is in fact directly selected by the matrix verb, implying that it is not generated in INFL but directly generated with the verb. Being directly drawn from the lexicon there is no problem with the derivation of the surface form of (17).

First we move the VP into SpecC and then we adjoin the embedded verb to the matrix verb:

(18)   *dat Ria* [$_{\text{CP}}$[$_{\text{VP}}$ *in Duitsland* t] [PRO t]] *probeert te-blijven*

Let us now return to the evidence that motivated our original assumption that *zu* is generated in INFL. Marga Reis was the first to point out a peculiarity of the following construction:

(19)   *ohne   ihn   haben warten zu   lassen*
         without him   have   wait   to   let

According to the hypothesis that *zu* is already an element of the lexical form of the verb, the D-Structure source of (19) must be something like (20):

(20)   *ohne* [$_{\text{IP}}$ PRO [$_{\text{VP}}$[$_{\text{IP}}$ *ihn warten*] *lassen*] [*zu haben*]]

We now have to incorporate *warten* into *lassen*, which produces the complex verb *warten-lassen*. Next we have to reverse the order of *warten-lassen* and the infinitival form of *haben*. This will produce the completely ungrammatical sequence (21):

(21)   **ohne ihn zu haben warten lassen*

Our conclusion must be that *zu* cannot be a lexical element of the verb *haben* in (19). Rather, the reordering of verbs has to be VP internal, and only after this reordering has taken place the rightmost verb can move into INFL to satisfy the subcategorization frame of *zu*.

This discussion seems to suggest that we have to provide for two different kinds of constructions. In coherent infinitives the higher verb directly selects the infinitival form of the embedded verb and therefore *zu* must be a part of the verb drawn from the lexicon. In this case of lexical incorporation the higher verb governs a "*zu*-infinitive." But in the incoherent construction, *zu* is selected by *ohne* or by the empty complementizer. This is a case for syntactic incorporation: *zu* is indeed an element of INFL which in turn selects the "infinitive without *zu*." (For a similar conclusion, see also v.Stechow, this volume.)

Alternatively, we might as well stick to our original hypothesis that *zu* is incorporated into the verb; even if such a view contradicts "the spirit" of Baker's work, there is recent evidence presented by Pollock (1988) that such a rule is also operative in English. If so, the relevant question is how to block (21) and the derivation depicted in (17).

As for (17) we may assume that the verb of an embedded clause never moves into the C position of that clause. The reason seems to be one of categorial selection: as has been put foreword at length in v.stechow/Sternefeld (1988) it is reasonable to assume a difference between verb/second clauses and complementizer clauses, the latter being nominal in character, whereas the former are more "verbal." Without going into the details of our previous work I would like to propose that the same reason that bars a verb in the C-Position in the S-Structure of an embedded sentence also blocks the intermediate use of this position as an escape hatch for V-raising.

Turning again to (21), we have already indicated that V-raising must precede *to*-incorporation. On the other hand, examples like (18) suggest that *te* must be incorporated *before* V-raising can apply. The usual way to avoid the paradox is to require cyclic rule application. Of course such a situation is not very satisfying, especially since I do not know of any other domain in syntax that would require the cycle. For the time being I have to leave matters as they stand.

6. Verb Projection Raising

In this section I will show how scrambling interacts with the adjunction analysis of V-raising. I will not go into the literature on V-raising but will immediately present an analysis of a complicated case of V-raising first discussed in Haegeman & Riemsdijk (1986). Consider the following construction of Swiss German:

(22)   *das er em Karajan will   en arie chöne   vorsinge*
        that he to Karajan wants an arie be-able sing

The D-Structure source of (22) must be something like this:

(23)   *das er* [PRO [PRO *em Karajan en arie vorsinge*] *chöne*] *will*

Although the ordering of operations in the following derivation is not essential, let us assume that we first move the infinitives into SpecC. The relevant part of the derivation will be this:

(24)

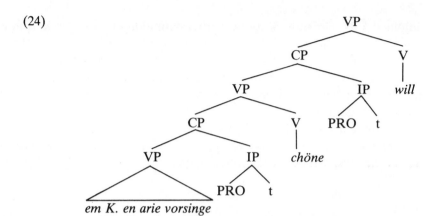

Next assume that we successively adjoin the VP to the right of the next higher VP. What we get is a string like this:

(25)   *das er will chöne em Karajan en arie vorsinge*

At this point we see that the finite verb cannot actually move to INFL, because in that case it would always have to appear on the right periphery of a clause. The only way to save the movement analysis would be to say that VP raising is adjunction to IP. Such a theory does not seem to be particularly attractive, especially as it destroys the basis for our analysis in the last section. It has therefore been assumed in v.Stechow/Sternefeld (1988) that the verbal morphology is *governed* and checked by INFL. Thus, movement of the finite verb into INFL cannot be obligatory. To get from (25) to (22) we finally have to scramble *em Karajan* to the VP headed by *will*, and *en arie* to the VP headed by *chöne*. This gives us the desired surface form (22).

A potential problem with the last step of this analysis is the following. As I have assumed in section (2) above, adjoined positions should be barriers for movement, since they are not selected. But clearly this cannot always be the case in German, since extraposed clauses are adjoined (to VP or IP) but nevertheless are transparent for movement. This is not true for adverbial clauses, whether extraposed or not. The difference is that complements are selected "on some level of representation," whereas this is not the case with adverbials. We therefore have to assume that the property of being selected will be inherited in the case of extraposition of clauses and adjoined VPs. Going back to our earlier definition of barrierhood it now follows that the adjoined VP cannot *per se* be a barrier in the sense of the second clause of condition (8.2), because we just stipulated that it is selected by INFL via the trace of movement. (The same remark also holds for the VP in SpecC, which still has to be selected by I via the trace of movement, but not by C!)

Turning again to clause (c) of definition (6), we see that none of the adjoined VPs can be barriers because they are not selected by the head of any of the VPs. The relevant configuration is this:

(26)

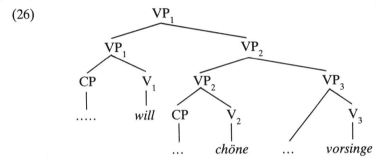

For example, VP_2 could not be a barrier for scrambling, because its head does not select VP_3. Although this seems to be a welcome result for scrambling it seems to be the wrong result when it comes to the assignment of verbal cases. If one were to assume that the verbal Cases are checked in a representation like (26), i.e., if one were to assume that the verbs govern to the right in constructions like these, we would expect that V_2 would errect a minimality barrier between V_1 and VP_3 or V_3. But we have just seen that VP_2 does not have the formal status of a barrier.

At least three reactions are possible and will be discussed in the final paragraphs.

1) First observe that scrambling could move "through VP_2" via adjunction to VP_2, even if VP_2 were a barrier for V_3. If we want to take advantage of this possibility we have to answer the question of how VP_2 could be made a barrier. To ensure barrierhood, VP_3 must be selected by V_2, which seems to be the only way to make VP_2 a barrier in (26).

At first sight it seems to be fairly obvious that the selection of VP can only be stipulated *ad hoc*. Baker's theory can work properly only if it is assumed that the verb, in this case V_2, θ-marks and *thereby* selects the CP (but not the VP). Stipulating that VP is selected by V seems to imply that the VP is θ-marked by the verb. But the only available θ-role has to be assigned to CP, for otherwise CP would not be selected and therefore should be a barrier. So it seems to me that the barrierhood of VP cannot be made to follow from our principles.

2) The second reaction is to claim that VP_2 is not a barrier and that (26) is not the relevant level on which government relations are checked. To put it in other words, the verb still governs *to the left* only, and the government of verbal Cases is government into SpecC, but not government within the part of the structure depicted in (27). In a sense, then, V_1 governs V_3, but this structural government relation cannot be relevant for Case assignment. This solution still doesn't solve the intuitive problem, namely that we would not like to predict that there could exist any relation between V_1 and V_3 in (26) that would not be blocked by V_2. For instance, we wouldn't like to predict that one could incorporate V_3 into V_1, even though an incorporation rule of this kind doesn't exist in the grammar of German.

3) As is often the case with problems of this kind a straightforward solution could reveal that we have misanalysed the structure: following Haegeman & Riemsdijk we have presupposed Verb Projection Raising (VPR), i.e., we have raised the VP. But this move is rather odd, since rightward adjunction to VP (or IP) is normally only allowed for CPs in German. Therefore we shouldn't apply the somehow exceptional mechanism of VPR, but should — as usual — simply extrapose the whole CP. Part of the relevant structure is depicted in (27):

(27)

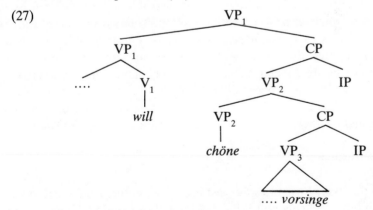

We have argued above that selection must be inherited in extrapositions. But now we see that the extraposed CP is not only selected, it is also selected by an element which could erect a minimality barrier for something within this CP! Applying definition (6) it now follows that VP_2 is in fact a minimality barrier between V_1 and V_3: Since the head of VP_2 selects its argument CP in (27), VP_2 is a barrier for any node within CP.

Let us now return to scrambling. If VP_2 is a barrier, we cannot scramble the object of V_3 directly into the matrix, but have to open the barrier by adjoining to it. Again this is of course exactly what one would expect according to the Barriers framework.

4) An obvious problem for this analysis arises from the fact that standard German does not allow VPR but only V^0-raising. If the proposed analysis should also hold for German we have to explain why scrambling is almost obligatory in standard German but not in Swiss German. Since no such explanation is in sight, we should rethink the issue, and turn back to the problem of selection. Suppose that a structure like (28) is generated by V-raising:

(28)

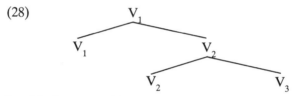

Intuitively we would want it to have that V_2 erects a minimality barrier between V_1 and V_3. The problem seems to be that selection has been largely interpreted as θ-marking. But if a lexical category assigns Case to a position it usually also θ-marks that position. Thus assignment of Case was not regarded as giving rise to selection because it usually goes proxy with θ-assignment. But now imagine that more kinds of necessary relations between items are dubbed "selection." To my mind there is nothing wrong with the idea that assignment of verbal Case — though dissotiated from θ-assignment — is a kind of selection. If this were true one problem would be solved, and another one arises: what is the nature of selection?

7.   Conclusion

In this essay I tried to solve just one small problem of a Barriers theory of scrambling and coherence, but I did not even mention the merits of previous alternative proposals that did involve "real" reanalysis instead of "structure preserving" adjunctions. I have merely indicated how Baker's theory could be made to work in a small array of facts drawn from German. Other contributions to this volume should have revealed that these proposals can only be the beginning of a theory of coherence. At present, however, the only conclusion can be that a lot of work still remains to be done.

References

Andersson, Sven-Gunnar & Sigmund Kvam. 1984. *Satzverschränkung im heutigen Deutsch*. Tübingen: Narr.

Baker, Mark. 1985. "Incorporation: A Theory of Grammatical Function Changing." Diss., Massachusetts Institute of Technology.

———. 1988. *Incorporation. A Theory of Grammatical Function Changing*. Chicago: University of Chicago Press.

Chomsky, Noam. 1986. *Barriers*. Cambridge: MIT Press.

Haegeman, Liliane & Henk van Riemsdijk. 1986. "Verb Projection Raising, Scope, and the Typology of Movement Rules." *Linguistic Inquiry* 17, 417-466.

Müller, Gereon. 1989. "Barrieren und Inkorporation." Masters Thesis, University of Constance.

Netter, Klaus & Christian Rohrer. (to appear). Proceedings of the conference on "Representation and Derivation." Dordrecht: Reidel.

Pollock, Jean-Yves. 1988. "Verb Movement, UG and the Structure of IP." Ms., Université de Haute Bretagne.

Stechow, Arnim von. & Wolfgang Sternefeld. 1988. *Bausteine syntaktischen Wissens. Ein Lehrbuch der generativen Grammatik*. Opladen: Westdeutscher Verlag.

Sternefeld, Wolfgang. (to appear). "Derivation and Representation in Generative Grammar. A theoretical Synopsis." To appear in: Netter & Rohrer (eds.).

IV. Scrambling and Ergativity

Two Classes of Intransitive Adjectives in Italian*

Guglielmo Cinque
University of Venice

1. Introduction

In the following, we shall argue that the ergative/unergative distinction motivated by Perlmutter (1978) and Burzio (1981,1986) for the class of intransitive verbs extends to (intransitive) adjectives as well.

The existence of 'ergative' adjectives (as well as that of 'ergative' nouns — cf. Giorgi 1986) would in fact seem to be theoretically expected in a theory which incorporates the so-called Lexicalist Hypothesis (Chomsky 1970). According to this hypothesis, morphologically related verbs, nouns and adjectives are represented in the lexicon as single, categorially unspecified, entries endowed with certain unique θ-marking and selectional properties (including subcategorization properties).

In this frame, one could thus expect that an adjective morphologically related to an ergative verb (e.g. *morto* 'dead' related to *morire* 'die') should in principle also be ergative, i.e., should have its subject generated in the internal object position, under A.'

This expectation is, however, not fulfilled. Quite generally, the class of adjectives which are morphologically related to ergative verbs are not ergatives themselves.

No problem for the Lexicalist Hypothesis arises, however, if, as we suggest below, the role of derivational morphology is taken into consideration vis à vis the different categorial realizations of the neutralized lexical entry (cf.sect. 4).

2. Two Theoretical Considerations

One general consideration pointing to the existence of ergative adjectives is the fact that there happen to be adjectives entering the alternation typical of strictly ergative verbs of the *affondare* 'sink' class. Thus alongside AVB / BV pairs like (1a-b) (cf. Burzio 1981,1986)

(1) a. *Il   capitano affondò la   nave*
         The captain   sank   the   boat
     b. *La   nave affondò*
         The boat sank

one finds such AAdjB / BAdj pairs as (2a-b) (noted in Longobardi 1987)[1]

(2) a. *Gianni è* $\left\{ \begin{array}{c} certo \\ sicuro \end{array} \right\}$ *[che verró]*
         G.   is certain/sure that I will come

     b. *[Che verró]   è* $\left\{ \begin{array}{c} certo \\ sicuro \end{array} \right\}$
         That I will come is   certain/sure

The same alternation is also found when the propositional internal argument is realized as a NP (if we abstract from the preposition *di* 'of' which appears, for Case reasons, in front of the NP in the 'transitive' variant of the adjective):

(3) a. *Gianni è* $\left\{ \begin{array}{c} certo \\ sicuro \end{array} \right\}$ *[di questo]*
         G.   is certain/sure of   this

     b. *[Questo] è* $\left\{ \begin{array}{c} certo \\ sicuro \end{array} \right\}$
         This   is certain/sure

As with the corresponding verbal case, these systematic alternations can be given a maximally simple account (i.e., an account which leaves the selectional / subcategorization properties intact), if one poses that with such adjectives the external θ-role can either be assigned to [NP,S] or "suspended": a minimal lexical parameter. If it is assigned, the a. cases of (2) and (3) are generated. If it is not, the b. cases are, after syntactic movement of the internal argument to [NP,S].

A second theoretical argument for the existence of ergative adjectives can be based on a derivational parallelism obtaining in English, where, differently from Italian, raising adjectives are attested.

Consider first the various uses of a verb like *happen*:

(4) a   John$_i$ happens [t$_i$ to be punctual]
     b. It never happens [that John is punctual]
     c. This never happens

As (4a-b) show, *happen* has a use in which it selects for (and θ-marks) a propositional internal argument (CP) while assigning no external θ-role to [NP,S]. (4c) naturally reduces to the same single use if we assume that a propositional argument can be realized in the general case as *either CP* (in certain cases, possibly IP) *or NP* (cf. Pesetsky 1982: Chapter 1; Chomsky 1986a: Chapter 3), and that the latter, as opposed to the former, may not remain in situ, for Case reasons. Under this unitary lexical representation of *happen*, (4a) and (4c) receive a parallel derivation (cf. (5a-b))

(5) a   NP   V   [t   X   ]

     b. NP   V   t

where the raising configuration (5a) is but a special case of the 'ergative' configuration (5b).

Now, note that adjectives like *certain* or *likely* enter the same contexts as *happen*:

(6) a. John$_i$ is $\left\{ \begin{array}{c} \text{certain} \\ \text{likely} \end{array} \right\}$ [t$_i$ to win]

     b. It is $\left\{ \begin{array}{c} \text{certain} \\ \text{likely} \end{array} \right\}$ [that John will win]

     c. This is $\left\{ \begin{array}{c} \text{certain} \\ \text{likely} \end{array} \right\}$

By parity of reasoning, they too should be characterized as having the same, unique, lexical property of selecting for an internal propositional argument, either CP or NP, where the NP is obligatorily moved to [NP,S] for Case reasons. If so, (6a-b) also enter a parallel derivation

(7) a. NP   A   [t   X   ]

     b. NP   A   t

in which the raising configuration (7a) is but a special case of the ergative configuration (7b). In other words, just as (4a) renders an ergative derivation of (4c) plausible, so does (6a) for (6c). The fact that the raising configuration with adjectives is a marked structure (cf. Chomsky 1986b: 78) is, from this point of view, immaterial.

Aside from these general considerations, a number of empirical arguments can be adduced in support of the postulation of ergative adjectives alongside the 'complement' class of unergatives. They will be considered in the next section.[2]

3. Some Empirical Arguments

The evidence discussed in this section is drawn exclusively from Italian, although it is to be expected that comparable evidence will be available in other languages. To the extent to which the different ergativity tests utilized below yield non inconsistent results when they are applied to the same adjective (not all tests will be applicable to the same adjectives, though), a good case will be made for the existence of ergative adjectives.

3.1 *Ne-Cliticization from the Inverted Subject*

In Burzio (1981,1986), Belletti-Rizzi (1981), substantial evidence is presented which motivates the following generalization (cf. (27) of Chapter 1 of Burzio 1986: 30):

(8)   *Ne*-cliticization (to V) is only possible from the structural object position

See the contrast between (9) and (10)

(9) Ne_i ha   [*affondate* [*due* t_i]]
        Of-them (he/she) sank   two

(10) a. *Ne_i ho fatto riferimento a [*due* t_i]   (obj. of P)
         Of-them (I) referred   to two

     b. *Ne_i hanno avuto successo [*due* t_i]   (inverted subj.
         Of-them had   success two   of trans. V)

     c. *Ne_i sono   rimasti [*due* t_i] *(di settimane)*   (adv. NP)
         Of-them (they) stayed two

     d. *[*Due* t_i] ne_i sono arrivate ieri   (preverbal subj.)
         Two   of-them   arrived yesterday

The exception provided by the wellformedness of *Ne*-cliticization from the inverted subject of passive, *si*-passive, and ergative verbs (see (11)) is only apparent if we consider that that NP, due to the "pro-drop" nature of Italian, may have remained in situ, in the structural object position where it was generated at D-structure (cf. Burzio 1986).

(11) a. *Ne$_i$*   *sono state affondate* [*due* t$_i$]   (inverted subj.
          Of-them have been sunk   two   of passive)

      b. *Se ne$_i$*   *sono affondate* [*due* t$_i$]   (inverted subj.
          Of-them *si* sank   two   of *si*-pass.)

      c. *Ne$_i$*   *sono affondate* [*due* t$_i$]   (inverted subj.
          Of-them sank   two   of erg. V)

Although Burzio (1981,1986), Belletti-Rizzi (1981) just mention the case of partitive *Ne*-cliticization, the generalization holds of 'adnominal' or 'genitive' *Ne*-cliticization as well:

(12) a. *Ne$_i$ ha   affondato* [*la chiglia* t$_i$]
          Of-it (he) sank   the keel

      b. *Ne$_i$ è   stata affondata* [*la chiglia* t$_i$]
          Of-it was sunk   the keel

      c. *Se ne$_i$ è   affondata* [*la chiglia* t$_i$]
          Si of-it sank   the keel

      d. *Ne$_i$ è   affondata* [*la chiglia* t$_i$]
          Of-it sank   the keel

(13) a. **Ne$_i$ ho   fatto riferimento al* [*la   chiglia* t$_i$]
          Of-it (I) referred   to the keel

      b. **Ne$_i$ ha contato* [*la   chiglia* t$_i$]
          Of-it mattered the keel

      c. **[La chiglia* t$_i$] *ne$_i$ oscilla*
          The keel   of-it swings

Generalization (8) appears to be a consequence of the Empty Category Principle (ECP), of which a number of slightly different versions are proposed in the recent literature. I adopt here the one in Chomsky (1986b) (see (14)), as it is presumably the most well-known. But the argument does not crucially rest on aspects peculiar to that frame, except possibly for its requirement of head-government over and above antecedent-government.[3]

(14) a.   α properly governs β iff α θ-governs or antecendent-governs β and

b.   β is governed by some (lexical) head

Consider first partitive *ne*, which I assume after Belletti-Rizzi (1981) to be a pro-N', a projection of the head of NP. The trace of *ne* is not θ-governed even when its maximal projection is, if θ-government fails to "percolate" from a category to its head (Chomsky 1986b: 71). Hence it needs to be antecedent-governed. This requires there to be no barrier between *ne* and its trace. When the NP dominating the trace of *ne* is in object position, as is the case in (9) and (11), it is not a barrier, since it is θ-governed and L-marked by V. But whenever it is not θ-governed, as in the cases of (10), the NP will count as a barrier, thus blocking antecedent-government of the empty N' by *ne*. Hence the contrast between (9)/(11) and (10).

Consider next adnominal *ne*. If, following observations of Kayne (1981), Longobardi (1987), we slightly modify the "Barriers" approach by assuming that only [+V] categories are able to head-govern traces whose antecedents are outside their maximal projection, we can express the fact, amply motivated in Longobardi (1987), that all movement from NP passes via the SPEC of NP (at least in Romance).

Under this assumption, an NP-internal trace will be head-governed by N only if it is also antecedent-governed within the NP (the first maximal projection that contains the trace). But if no adjunction to NP is possible (cf. Chomsky 1986b), only those constituents that can move to the SPEC of NP position (thus antecedent-governing their trace internally to the NP) will be extractable. This seems indeed to express the right generalization (cf. Longobardi 1987).[4]

This analysis of extraction from NP (and its consequences) also permits a straightforward account of why extraction is possible only from NPs which are directly θ-marked (by a [+V] category). This is so because the intermediate trace in the SPEC of NP needs itself to be antecedent-governed (and head-governed), and can be, provided that the barrierhood of the NP is "voided," i.e., that the NP is L-marked (by a [+V] category).

Let us now return to the case of adjectives.

In arguing for the descriptive generalization that *Ne*-cliticization is only possible from the structural direct object position (namely from the object of transitive verbs and the inverted subject of passive, *si*-passive and ergative verbs), Burzio (1981, 1986: 30 and passim) explicitly contrasts the case of passive verbs with the most similar of the copulative-adjective constructions: the case of "unpassive" adjectives. In opposition to verbs, their inverted subjects appear not to allow for *Ne*-cliticization (see (15b) vs.

(15a)), arguably because they fill no structural object position (cf. Burzio 1986: 31).

(15) a.　*Ne*$_i$　　sarebbero [$_V$ *riconosciute*] *molte* t$_i$ *(di vittime)*
　　　　　Of-them would be　　recognized　many　(of victims)

　　b.　**Ne*$_i$　sarebbero [$_A$ *sconosciute*] *molte* t$_i$ *(di vittime)*
　　　　　Of-them would be　　unknown　　many　(of victims)

Burzio further notes that the configuration (15b), involving *Ne*-cliticization "appears impossible with all adjectives," thus suggesting "that there are no ergative adjectives, namely no adjectives appearing in the D-structure '[e] be-Adj NP.' If any existed, they should allow Ne-Cl with respect to the NP [...]. At this point, I know of no clear theoretical reason for the non-existence of such a class of adjectives" (p.74,fn.13).

What we suggest is that such a class of adjectives does exist and that it behaves as predicted by Burzio in allowing for *Ne*-cliticization from the inverted subject. Cf. (16)-(18), which contrast with (19)-(21) containing unergative adjectives:[5]

(16) a.　*Ne*　　*sono note*　　　*molte*
　　　　　Of-them are　well-known many

　　b.　*Ne*　　*sono note*　　　*le tendenze*
　　　　　Of-them are　well-known the tendencies

(17) a.　*Ne*　　*sono certe ben poche*
　　　　　Of-them are　certain really few

　　b.　*Ne*　　*sono certe le dimissioni*
　　　　　Of-them is　certain the resignation

(18) a.　*Ne*　　*è oscura più d'una*
　　　　　Of-them is obscure more than one

　　b.　*Ne*　　*erano oscure le motivazioni*
　　　　　Of-them were　obscure the motivations

(19) a.　**Ne*　　*sono buoni pochi*
　　　　　Of-them are　good few

　　b.　**Ne*　　*sono buone le intenzioni*
　　　　　Of-them are　good　the intentions

(20) a.　**Ne*　　*sono state ingiuste molte*
　　　　　Of-them have been unjust　many

　　b.　**Ne*　　*è stata ingiusta la condanna*
　　　　　Of-them has been unjust　the condemnation

(21) a. *Ne   è assurda più   d'una
          Of-them is absurd more than one
      b. *Ne   è assurda la   dichiarazione
          Of-him is absurd   the   statement

This indeed suggests that with certain adjectives (such as those in (16)-(18)) the 'inverted' subject NP may remain in situ in the structural object position of the AP, where it is generated at D-structure. The structure conforms with Case Theory requirements by virtue of the fact that the inverted subject NP is in a CHAIN with the pre-copula subject position governed, and assigned Nominative, by INFL, just as in the corresponding verbal configurations:

(22)   [np^i copulative V [$_{AP}$ [$_{A'}$ A NP^i]]]

As to the adjectives that do not allow for *Ne*-cliticization (such as those in (19)-(21)), we conclude that they enter an unergative structure parallel to the corresponding verbal case. That is to say, they realize their subject NP as an external argument at D-structure: either in the [NP,S] of the copulative verb, or, more likely, in the SPEC of the small clause (IP) selected by the copulative verb (taken as a raising verb).[6] In either case, the inverted subject will be in an adjunction position, adjoined to VP or AP, respectively; not in the structural object position of AP:

(23) a. [np^i [$_{VP}$ [$_{VP}$ copulative V AP] NP^i]]
      b. [np^i copulative V [$_{IP}$ np^i [$_{AP}$ [$_{AP}$ A] NP^i]]

As is the case with the inverted subject of unergative verbs, *Ne*-cliticization from the inverted subject of unergative adjectives will thus also be barred.

3.2. Wh-Extraction from the Inverted NP Subject

A variant of the previous argument is provided by wh-extraction from the inverted NP subject, as wh-movement from NP in Italian appears to mirror clitic extraction from NP (Cinque 1980; Longobardi 1987). In essence, only those constituents which give rise, when cliticized, to wellformed clitic extraction from NP can be wh-extracted. Compare (16)-(21) with (24)a-b:[7]

(24) a.   *A Mario, di cui   è nota/imminente   una*
          M.,   of whom is well-known/forthcoming a
          presa diposizione sul tema,...
          statement   on the subject,...

    b.   **Mario, di cui è impossibile/ingiusta una presa di posizione*
       sul tema,...

The reason is the same: ECP. Cf. the previous section, and, for a detailed discussion of this correlation, Longobardi (1987).

    The fact that, in several cases, wh-extraction appears to yield results that are less illformed than the corresponding impossible *Ne*-extraction cases (or even quite acceptable) is argued in Longobardi (1987), Cinque (1987a: Chapter 1) to be due to the existence of parallel, non extraction, derivations for the 'fronted' wh-phrase (a possibility unavailable to *Ne*-cliticization). Cf. also Belletti-Rizzi (1986).

3.3 *Wh-Extraction from the Inverted Sentential Subject*

    A slightly different variant of the two previous arguments is represented by extraction of a wh-phrase from the inverted sentential subject of an adjective.

    As is well known, successive cyclic extraction is not possible out of genuinely extraposed sentences (inverted sentential subjects of transitive and unergative verbs). But it is allowed from the complement of ($[+V]$) heads, inverted sentential subjects of passive and ergative verbs included (given their faculty of remaining in situ in the position of the internal complement). See the contrast between (25) and (26), involving adjunct extraction, which, for ECP reasons (Chomsky 1986b), can only proceed successive cyclically:

(25) a.   *$\left\{ \begin{array}{l} \textit{In che modo} \\ \textit{Per quale ragione} \end{array} \right\}$ *vi rovinerebbe* [t' *che*
        In which way/for which reason would it ruin you that
        se ne andasse t]?
        he leaves?

    b.   *$\left\{ \begin{array}{l} \textit{In che modo} \\ \textit{Per quale ragione} \end{array} \right\}$ *conta*   [t' *che lui*
        In which way/for which reason does it matter that he
        abbia reagito t]?
        reacted?

(26) a. $\left\{ \begin{array}{l} \textit{In che modo} \\ \textit{Per quale ragione} \end{array} \right\}$ *vi   ha detto* [t' *che   se ne*

In which way/for which reason did he say   that he

andrà t]?

will leave?

b. $\left\{ \begin{array}{l} \textit{In che modo} \\ \textit{Per quale ragione} \end{array} \right\}$ *vi è stato detto* [t' *che*

In which way/for which reason was it told you   that

se ne andrà t]?

he will leave?

c. $\left\{ \begin{array}{l} \textit{In che modo} \\ \textit{Per quale ragione} \end{array} \right\}$ *potrà   succedere* [t' *che*

In which way/for which reason can it happen   that

se ne vada t]?

he leaves?

The grounds for the contrast, in a "Barriers" framework, is the need for each trace left by successive cyclic movement to be antecedent-governed (and head-governed). In (25), for example, while t is antecedent-governed by t' in the SPEC of the embedded CP, t' itself is not antecedent-governed, since a barrier (the embedded CP, owing to its non L-marked status) intervenes. The adjunct extraction in (26) is, on the contrary, wellformed since the embedded CP does not qualify as a barrier, being L-marked by the matrix verb. As a consequence of that, not only t, but t' too, will be antecedent-governed (and head-governed), in conformity with the ECP.

Restricting ourselves to the unergative/ergative pair, the crucial difference between (25b) and (26c) resides in the fact that the inverted sentential subject is found in a complement (L-marked) position in the latter (which contains an ergative verb), but not in the former (which contains an unergative verb).

This observation provides an immediate diagnostic for the ergative/unergative distinction in the domain of adjectives as well.

Successive cyclic extraction should be possible only from the inverted subject of ergative adjectives (which L-mark the inverted CP), not from that of unergative adjectives (which do not). The prediction is once again borne out. Only the class of adjectives that allow for *Ne*-cliticization from their inverted subjects also allow for successive cyclic extraction from their inverted sentential subjects.[8] See:

(27) a. $\left\{\begin{array}{l} In\ che\ modo \\ Per\ quale\ ragione \end{array}\right\}$ era   prevedibile

In which way/for which reason was it forseeable

[t' *che se ne andasse* t]?
      that he would leave?

   b. $\left\{\begin{array}{l} In\ che\ modo \\ Per\ quale\ ragione \end{array}\right\}$ è   probabile [t' *che*

In which way/for which reason is it likely   that

reagisca t]?
      he will react?

(28) a.   *$\left\{\begin{array}{l} In\ che\ modo \\ Per\ quale\ ragione \end{array}\right\}$ era   assurdo che

In which way/for which reason was it absurd   that

se ne andasse t?
      he left?

   b.   *$\left\{\begin{array}{l} In\ che\ modo \\ Per\ quale\ ragione \end{array}\right\}$ sarebbe   stato

In which way/for which reason would it have been

inopportuno [t' *che avesse   reagito* t]?
inappropriate   that he would have reacted?

3.4. *(Short Distance) Anaphor Binding into the Subject*

Some of the adjectives that allow for *Ne*-cliticization and Wh-movement from their inverted subject permit us to check a further prediction of the analysis that classifies them as ergative. The adjectives in question are adjectives taking a (prepositional) dative object.

Since (prepositional) dative objects can (marginally) bind object anaphors in Italian (see Giorgi 1986; Belletti-Rizzi 1986 for recent discussion), and since, by hypothesis, the inverted subject of an ergative adjective can occupy the structural object position of AP, which is asymmetrically c-commanded by the dative object, it is predicted that a short distance anaphor within the inverted subject of an ergative adjective should be bindable by the prepositional dative:

(29)

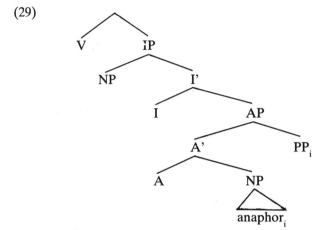

The prepositional dative object of an unergative adjective, on the other hand, is expected not to be able to bind an anaphor found within the inverted subject, since the latter is adjoined to AP. Hence outside of its c-command domain:[9]

(30)

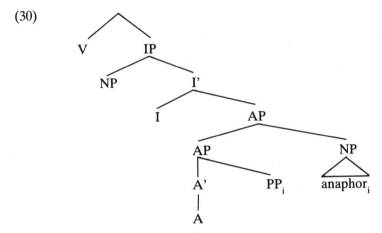

This twofold prediction is indeed fulfilled, although it can only be checked indirectly, owing to the fact that (definite) inverted subjects can remain in situ (between the A and the dative object) only very marginally (cf. (31)), just as in the case with (definite) inverted subjects of ergative verbs (cf. (32)).[10]

(31)   *? *Era noto*   *il suo libro a   tutti*
        Was well-known his book to everybody

(32)   *? *Era piaciuto il suo libro a tutti*
        Was liked   his book by everybody

The prediction can nonetheless be checked if the 'inverted' subject is moved from its in situ position either to the left, into [NP,S], by NP-movement, or to the right, into an adjunction position, by Heavy-NP-Shift. See the contrast between (33)-(34) containing the ergative adjectives *noto* 'well-kown,' *chiaro* 'clear' and (35)-(36) containing the unergative adjectives *affezionato* 'fond' and *fatale* 'fatal':[11]

(33) a.   *Il   proprio$_i$ destino era noto   solo a lui$_i$*
           His own   destiny was well-known only to him
     b.   *Era noto a lui$_i$ solo il proprio$_i$ destino*

(34) a.   *La   propria$_i$ missione era chiara a   tutti$_i$*
           Their own   mission was clear to everybody
     b.   *Era chiara a tutti$_i$ solo la propria$_i$ missione*

(35) a.   **I   propri$_i$ vicini   erano affezionati anche a Gianni$_i$*
           His own   neighbors were fond   also of G.
     b.   **Erano affezionati a Gianni$_i$ anche i propri$_i$ vicini*

(36) a.   **Il   proprio$_i$ sbaglio fu   fatale anche a Gianni$_i$*
           His own   mistake was fatal also   to G.
     b.   **Fu fatale a Gianni$_i$ anche il proprio$_i$ sbaglio*

The wellformedness of (33)-(34) is admittedly rather surprising at first sight, given that the anaphor is not c-commanded by its putative antecedent at S-structure. In the a. member of each pair, the anaphor is contained in [NP,S] and its putative antecedent is within VP. In the b. member, instead, the anaphor is contained within a NP which is higher up in the tree than its putative antecedent.

This state of affairs is in fact exactly analogous to that obtaining with the *preoccupare* class of psych-verbs analysed by Belletti-Rizzi (1986). See (37a-b):

(37) a.   *I   propri$_i$ sostenitori preoccupano Gianni$_i$*
           His own   supporters worry   G.

                                    (=(67a) of Belletti-Rizzi 1986)

     b.   *Questi pettegolezzi su di sé$_i$ preoccupano Gianni$_i$*
           This gossip   about himself worry   G.
           più di   ogni altra cosa
           more than anything else

The apparent exceptionality of (37) with respect to Principle A of the Theory of Binding is reduced by them to the standard analysis by showing via independent evidence that I) the S-structure subject of this class of psych-verbs is generated, at D-structure, in the structural object position under VP, and II) Principle A of Binding Theory need only be satisfied at some level of representation, either D-, or S-structure (or possibly LF), and that once it is satisfied at any one of those levels the sentence is deemed grammatical even though the required configuration is not met at the other levels (cf. Belletti-Rizzi 1986: sect. 2.1) for a detailed argument to this effect).

The contrast between (33)-(34), and (35)-(36) thus suggests that Principle A is satified at some level of representation (D-structure) in the former, but not in the latter, case.

Thus, Belletti-Rizzi's (1986) assumption II) above, in interaction with the ergative hypothesis for adjectives renders the wellformedness of (33)-(34) no more surprising than that of (37), and permits us to still discriminate between ergative and unergative adjectives despite the near impossibility of leaving the inverted subject in situ with ergative adjectives (and verbs). This is because only ergative adjectives have at least one level of representation in which the anaphor is appropriately A-Bound by the dative object (namely, D-structure), at which the dative object (asymmetrically) c-commands the subject anaphor.

As noted in Giorgi (1984: Appendix), an anaphor contained in the subject of a psych-verb can even receive a bound variable interpretation if the (prepositional) object is quantificational. See (38a-b):

(38)   a   *La propria$_i$ salute preoccupa [ognuno di loro]$_i$*
           His own   health worries   each   of them

       b. *Tu dici che il proprio$_i$ futuro non   interessa a*
           You say that his own   future does not interest
           nessuno$_i$
           anybody

However this is to be interpreted,[12] we may note that the same property is also found with ergative (but again not with unergative) adjectives, thus reinforcing their parallelism with psych-verbs and the hypothesis that their inverted subject originates in the structural object position of the AP. See:[13]

(39) a. *Il   proprio$_i$ destino non è noto   a   nessuno$_i$*
His own   destiny   is well-known to nobody

b. *Solo la propria$_i$ missione era chiara ad [ognuno di loro]$_i$*
Only his own   mission was clear to each   of them

3.5 *Long Distance Anaphor Binding by the Subject.*

One way to determine the ergative or unergative status of a certain V is to consider those grammatical phenomena that require the presence of a thematic subject at D-structure and check whether the verb allows for those grammatical phenomena. If it does, it is unergative. If it does not, there is reason to think that it is ergative.

Most of these phenomena, however, (such as whether it allows for impersonal passivization or for impersonal *si* in certain infinitival contexts (Cinque 1987b), whether it allows for the reflexive cliticization of an indirect object (Rizzi 1982), etc.) are inapplicable to adjectives for one reason or another. The foremost of these is the fact that such tests can usually be carried out only in configurations in which the adjective (phrase) is embedded in a full sentential structure. That is to say, in configurations in which the AP is within a small clause complement to a copulative (raising) verb whose subject is non thematic. This has the effect of neutralizing the 'derived' vs. 'non-derived' status of the adjective's subject by having it become the derived subject of the copulative/raising verb in both cases.

There is however one grammatical phenomenon which provides a test for the thematic nature of the D-structure subject and which is independent from the embedding of the AP in a full sentential structure. This is long distance anaphor Binding, according to a recent interpretation of one of its properties in Belletti-Rizzi (1986).

In discussing the contrast in (40), observed in Giorgi (1984),

(40) a. *Gianni$_i$ teme coloro che vogliono sostenere la propria$_i$*
G.   fears those who want to   support   the own
candidatura
candidature
'G. fears those who want to support him as candidate'

b. **Gianni$_i$ preoccupa chiunque dubiti della propria$_i$ buona fede*
'G. worries whoever doubts his good faith'

Belletti and Rizzi note that the ungrammaticality of (40)b can be attributed, within their analysis of psych-verbs, to a basic configurational difference between verbs of the *temere* class and verbs of the *preoccupare* class. The former, though not the latter, have a D-structure thematic subject. If one assumes that long distance anaphors can only be bound from a thematic (subject) position, the contrast is explained. As independent evidence for the proposed condition on long distance anaphor binding, they cite the following contrasts:[14]

(41) a. *Gianni$_i$ *sembra* [t *essere efficiente*] *a   chiunque sostiene*
         G.   seems   to be efficient   to whoever supports
         la propria$_i$ *candidatura*
         him as   candidate

     b. *Gianni*$_i$ *promette* [*di* PRO *essere efficiente*] *a   chiunque*
         G.   promises   to be efficient   to whoever
         sostenga la propria$_i$ *candidatura*
         supports him as   candidate

(42) a. *Gianni$_i$ *pare*   [t *intelligente*] *a   chiunque*
         G.   appears   intelligent   to whoever
         accetti   le   proprie$_i$ *idee*
         accepts his own   ideas

     b. *Gianni*$_i$ *dà aiuto a chiunque accetti   le   proprie*$_i$ *idee*
         G.   helps   whoever accepts his own   ideas

Despite the rather marked status of long distance anaphor binding phenomena in Italian, the contrasts indicated are in fact quite clear. We thus have a diagnostic to determine the thematic or non thematic status of an adjective's subject. What we need to do is embed a long distance anaphor in the complement of the adjective (so as to ensure c-command of the anaphor by the pre-adjectival subject position) and see whether such binding is wellformed or not.

The prediction is that it should be wellformed with unergative adjectives, whose external subject position is thematic, and illformed with ergative adjectives, whose external subject position is not thematic. The prediction is borne out. Once again, despite the generally marked status of the phenomenon, the contrast between ergative and unergative adjectives appears to be quite sharp. See (43) vs.(44), which contain adjectives behaving as unergative and ergative, respectively, in relation to the other tests:

(43) a. *Gianni*$_i$ *è* [*riconoscente a chiunque aiuti i propri*$_i$ *amici*]
          G.   is grateful   to whoever helps his own friends

      b. *Gianni*$_i$ *è* [*scostante con chi   non   accetta*
          G.   is rude   to   those who do not accept
          le proprie$_i$ *idee*]
          his own   ideas

(44) a. **Gianni*$_i$ *è* [*noto   solo a chi   abbia seguito*
          G.   is well-known only to those who followed
          la propria$_i$ *storia sulla cronaca cittadina*][15]
          his own   story in the local press

      b. **Un discorso*$_i$ *del genere è* [*chiaro solo a chi*
          A similar speech   is clear   only to those who
          conosce la propria$_i$ *logica*]
          know   its own   logic
          (cf. *un discorso del genere ha la propria logica* 'A similar
          discourse has its own logic')

3.6 *An Asymmetry in come-Clauses*

This argument is based on a peculiarity of the syntax of *come*-clauses
such as (45)

(45)   *Gianni è partito, come tutti   sanno*
          G.   left,   as   everybody knows

that is noted in two recent studies of this construction (and the related *as*-
construction in English) (Burzio 1987; Stowell 1987). The main properties
of the construction can be summarized as follows:

a) *The come-clause contains a CP gap.*

This is shown by the wellformedness of (46), which contains a verb that
apparently subcategorizes for CP (or IP) only, not NP (**Questo non sembra
a nessuno* 'This does not seem to anybody') and the illformedness of (47),
which contains a NP gap:

(46)   *Come sembra — , non ce la farà*
          'As it seems,he will not make it'

(47)   **Questo, come Gianni mi ha descritto — , è grave*
          This, as   G.   to me described, is serious

b) *The CP gap is bound by* <u>come</u> *moved from the sentence containing the gap.*

The relation between *come* and the gap is "unbounded" and sensitive to island conditions (Stowell 1987):

(48) a. *Come credo   che temessero —, lui alla fine si presentò*
         As   I think   they feared,   he finally   turned up

     b. **Come conosciamo chi temeva —,   Mario ha dato le*
         As   we know   those who feared, M.   resigned
         dimissioni

     c. **Come ci siamo stupiti   dopo aver saputo —, Mario*
         As   we were astonished after learning,   M.
         si è sposato
         got married

Stowell (1987) assumes movement of an empty CP operator from the position of the gap to the COMP containing *as*, but certain considerations militate against this assumption, at least in the case of *come*.

First, as Burzio (1987: fn. 2) notes, the semantics of the construction "seems to presuppose an adverbial as well, suggesting *as* [and *come*] may license both an adverbial and a [propositional] gap." This appears to be corroborated by the French analogue of the construction:

(49) a. *Comme elle vous l'avait dit, Jean est déjà parti*
         'As she had told you, J. has already left'
     b. *Comme il vous l'a été dit, Jean partira*
         As   it you it was told, J.   will leave
         'As you were told, J. will leave'

Here a pronoun obligatorily occurs in place of the gap in Italian, which suggest the presence of a distinct gap to which the wh-operator is related (an adverbal gap). That *comme* is a wh-operator binding a gap is indicated by the fact that it licenses 'stylistic inversion" (*Comme vous l'a dit Marie, Jean est deja parti.* Cf. Kayne-Pollock 1978, Kayne 1986). That it is actually moved from the clause containing the pronoun, rather than base generated in COMP, is indicated by the island sensitivity of the relation between *comme* and the pronoun. Cf. (50a) vs. (50b):

(50) a.   *Comme nous avons appris   qu'il   avait dit,   Jean*
          As   we   have   learned that he had   said, J.
          est parti
          left

     b.   **Comme nous avons connu qui   l'avait dit,   Jean*
          As   we   have   met   he who had it said, J.
          est parti
          left.

A similar conclusion can perhaps be drawn from the NP-headed use of the *as* construction in English, where a pronoun may appear (and is in fact the preferred option). See Burzio (1987), from which (51) is taken:

(51)   These are the events as John presented them to me

Now, as Giuseppe Longobardi remarked, if *come* is indeed a wh-operator occupying the SPEC of CP position, there is no "landing site" available for the putative empty CP operator.

There is in fact further evidence that the CP gap is bound by *come*, actually moved from the sentence containing the gap, rather than by an empty CP operator originating in the position of the gap.

In general, as a consequence of ECP, constituents θ-marked by a [+V] element, but not adjuncts like *come*, can be extracted from a wh-island in Italian (Chomsky 1986). See the contrast between (52a), where a CP complement of a verb is extracted, and (52b), where the adjunct *come* is extracted:

(52) a.   *?Mario, [di visitare il quale] non ricordo   chi   avesse*
          M.,   to visit   whom   I do not remember who had
          allora promesso,...
          then promised,...

     b.   **Mi comporterò come mi avevano chiesto chi si fosse*
          I   will behave as they had asked me   who had
          comportato ieri
          behaved   yesterady

Now, if an empty CP operator were indeed involved in *come*-clauses, with *come* presumably in the head of CP, we would expect the relation between *come* (actually, the empty CP operator) and the CP gap to extend over a wh-island, since the CP is θ-governed by a verb. But this is not so. Cf.:

(53)   *Gianni si interessa   di linguistica, come mi avevano chiesto
          G.   is interested in linguistics, as they had asked me
          chi   vi   avesse detto —
          who had told   you

This behavior, however, follows from ECP if what actually moves is
the adjunct *come*.[16]

c) *Come can only bind CP gaps found in the structural object position.*

See, for example, a contrast such as that between (54) and (55) noted in
Burzio (1987), and Stowell (1987) for the corresponding *as*-clauses:

(54) a.   *Come* [speravamo —], Mario si è sistemato   (object)
            As   we hoped,   M.   settled down

      b.   *Come è stato* [detto —], M. si è sistemato (inverted subject
            As   has been said,   M. settled down   of passive V)

      c.   *Come si è* [detto —], M. si è sistemato   (inverted subject
            As   si is said,   M. settled down   of *si* passive)

      d.   *Come spesso* [succede —], M. si è sbagliato (inverted subject
            As   often   happens,   M. was wrong   of ergative V)

(55) a.   *Come* [conta] — agli occhi di molti, M. ha vinto
            As   counts   for many people, M. won
                                              (inverted subject of unergative V)

      b.   *Come ha* [fatto scalpore] —, M. si è sposato
            As   made a big fuss,   M. got married
                                              (inverted subject of transitive V)

Property c) is the one relevant to our argument.

Stowell's (1987) suggestion (for the corresponding *as*-clauses) is that
the difference between the former and the latter case lies in the non properly governed status of the CP gaps of (55) at D-structure. If it is crucially
assumed that ECP holds at every level of representation, *including D-structure*, then the contrast is derived in a principled way. At D-structure, the
CP gaps of (54) are θ-governed, hence properly governed. Those of (55)
are not θ-governed, nor, obviously, antecedent-governed (given that movement has not yet applied).

Whether or not this theoretical account of the peculiar restriction of
CP gaps in *come-* (*as-*) clauses to θ-governed positions will be confirmed or
not by further research, the phenomenon represents by itself a test for
ergativity that can be applied to adjectives as well. If the CP gap needs to

be θ-governed at D-structure, the prediction is that the inverted subject of ergative, but not that of unergative, adjectives will be a wellformed gap in *come*-clauses. This prediction is indeed borne out by the facts, in a way that is consistent with the results of the previous tests:

(56) a. *Come è* [*probabile* —], *G. ce la farà*
         As   is probable,   G. will make it

   b. *Come era* [*prevedibile* —], *G. non è venuto*
       As   was foreseeable,   G. did not come

   c. *Come sembra ormai* [*certo* —], *G. ce la farà*
       As   seems by now sure,   G. will make it

(57) a. *Come è [*sorprendente*] —, *G. ha vinto*
         As   is surprising,   G. won

   b. *Come sembra [*significativo*] —, *G. è sparito*
       As   seems significant,   G. disappeared

   c. *Come era [*possibile*] —, *G. ha vinto*
       As   was possible,   G. won

The same contrast emerges in the small clause analogues of (56)-(57), parallel to the small clause case of verbs (*Come t predetto t, non verrà* 'As foreseen, he will not come'). See:[17]

(58) a. *Come noto,   la delegazione sovietica non parteciperà*
         As   well-known, the soviet delegation   will not take part
         all'incontro
         in the meeting

   b. *Come implicito in quanto è stato detto finora,*
       As   implicit   from what has been said so far,
       si dissocieranno
       they will dissociate themselves

   c. *Come prevedibile, Mario non si è piú fatto vedere*
       As   foreseeable, M.   didn't turn up any longer

(59) a. **Come deprecabile, l'incontro   non avrà luogo*
         As   deprecable, the meeting will not take place

   b. **Come ormai significativo, Mario rifiuta di farsi*
       As   by now significant, M.   refuses to be
       intervistare
       interviewed

c.   *_Come pertinente per quanto è stato detto,_   _Mario_   _si_
      As   relevant   for what   has been said, M.   will
      dimetterà
      resign

3.7 _Complementizer selection_

In Italian, only infinitival clauses which are complements of a lexical
head are, in general, obligatorily introduced by a prepositional complementizer, either _di_ 'of' or _a_ 'to,' depending on the governing head.[18] The choice
is not idiosyncratic. For present purposes, it suffices to note the following
generalizations (cf. Cinque 1987a: chapter 1 and references cited there):

(60)   _di_ is chosen when a) the lexical head subcategorizes for a _di_
            + NP complement, b) the infinitival clause is an object
            clause

(61) a.   _Lui si compiace di non avere   amici_
            He   rejoices   at not having friends
                                    (cf. Si compiace _di questo_)
                                    (He rejoices at that)

      b.   _Gli ho chiesto   di aiutarmi_ (cf. Gli ho chiesto _questo_)
            To-him-I-have asked to help me (To-him-I-have asked this)

(62)   _a_ is chosen when a) the lexical head subcategorizes for an _a_
            + NP complement, b) the infinitival clause is complement
            to certain verbs (_provare_ 'try,' _cominciare_ 'begin,' _con-_
            tinuare 'continue' etc.)

(63) a.   _Mi sono rassegnato a   partire_
            I   resigned myself to leaving
                                    (cf. Mi sono rassegnato _a questo_)
                                    (I resigned myself to this)

      b.   _Ho cominciato a fumare_ (cf. Ho cominciato _questo_)
            I began   to smoke   (I began this)

Subject clauses are never introduced by a prepositional complementizer. The (inverted) subject clauses of passive and ergative verbs, which
are (obligatorily) introduced by the prepositional complemetizer _di_, are
only an apparent exception. They can plausibly be taken to fall under (60b)
if we consider that they are generated in object position at D-stucture and

that complementizer selection operates at that level. See, for example, the contrast between (64), containing transitive or unergative verbs and (65), containing passive or ergative verbs:

(64) a. *Comporta dei rischi anche solo* [(*di) cercarlo]
          It implies   risks even only   looking for him
      b. *Non ha   contato* [(*di) essere ricchi]
          It did not count   to be   rich

(65) a. *Mi è stato chiesto* [*(di) rimanere]
          I was asked   to stay
      b. *Mi è capitato*   [*(di) assistere ad un curioso incidente]
          It happened to me to   witness   a   curious accident

Such contrast suggests that (aside from the case of complements of verbs subcategorizing for *di* + NP) only infinitival subject sentences that realize the internal object argument at D-structure can (and must) be introduced by the prepositional complementizer *di*.

This is particularly interesting in the present connection since it apparently provides a new diagnostic to determine the D-structure position of an adjective's inverted sentential subject.

What we expect is that ergative adjectives will differ from unergative adjectives in that the infinitival sentential subject of the former, but not that of the latter, will be introduced by the prepositional complementizer *di*.

Although not many of the adjectives that qualify as ergative according to the previous tests easily admit infinitival sentential subjects, those that do conform to the expectation. They require the prepositional complementizer *di* (cf. (66)), which indeed suggests that their sentential subject is an internal argument at D-structure. Unergative adjectives, instead, systematically exclude *di*, as expected (cf. (67)):

(66) a. *Non gli era noto*   *(di) essere cosi famoso*[19]
          It wasn't   known to him to be   so   famous
      b. *Non mi era affatto chiaro*   *(di) non poterlo prendere*
          It wasn't   at all   clear to me that I could not take it
      c. *Non gli era del tutto evidente* *(di) non essere all'altezza*
          It was not   at all   evident to him not to be   able
          del compito
          to face the task

(67) a.   *Mi è impossibile   (*di) aiutarti*
           It   is impossible to me to   help you
      b.   *E' pericoloso (*di) sporgersi dal finestrino*
           It is dangerous   to lean out of the window
      c.   *E' ingiustificato (*di) comportarsi così*
           It is unjustified   to behave   like that

4.   A Note on the Lexicalist Hypothesis and Derivational Morphology

To conclude, we would like to return to the question raised at the outset: why are adjectives deriving from ergative or passive verbs themselves unergative? See, for example, (68) containing cases of *Ne*-cliticization:

(68) a.   *Ne_i sembrano* [$_A$ *morte/ infrante/ abbandonate/etc.*] *molte* t_i
           Of-them seem   dead/ broken/ abandoned/etc.   many
      b.   *Ne_i sembrano* [$_A$ *morte/ infrante/ abbandonate/etc.*] *le*
           Of-them seem   dead/ broken/ abandoned/etc.   the
           speranze t_i
           hopes

Despite appearances, this state of affairs can perhaps be reconciled with the Lexicalist Hypothesis.

The latter does in fact make the right prediction with respect to pairs of morphologically related nouns and verbs. As noted in Giorgi (1986: sect. 5), there is some evidence that nouns morphologically related to ergative verbs are also ergative (in the sense that their *di* + NP subject is generated as the innermost argument position under N').

The evidence has mainly to do with the possibility for a prepositional dative to bind an anaphor in the inverted subject position of the N.[20] This possibility should be open only to nouns related to ergative verbs (if at all) since these represent the only case where the prepositional dative actually c-commands the inverted subject. With nouns related to unergative verbs, instead, the expectation is that the inverted subject under N'' should be outside the c-domain of the prepositional dative. The facts indeed conform to such expectations. See the contrast between (69a-b) and (70a-b) (the *a* cases are from Giorgi (1986)):

(69) a.   *L'apparizione   di se stessa$_i$ a Maria$_i$, in sogno*
           The appearance of herself   to Mary,   in her dreams

b. *L'apparizione   dei propri$_i$ figli   a   Maria$_i$, in·
The appearance of her own children to Mary,   in
sogno
her dreams

(70) a. **La   telefonata di se stesso$_i$ a   Gianni$_i$*
The phone call of himself to G.

b. **La   telefonata   dei propri$_i$ figli   a   Gianni$_i$*
The phone call of his own children to G.

The Lexicalist Hypothesis, which posits a single lexical entry for the pair of related noun and verb, with unique selectional properties, is thus directly supported:

(71) a. $[_{V/N}$ appar-$]$ $\diagdown$ (i)re (V)
$\diagup$ (i)zione (N)

b.   (theme, experiencer)

What is the difference, then, between the well-behaved verb/noun case and the ill-behaved verb/adjective case?

We suggest that it resides in the different way in which the two pairs are morphologically derived.

For the verb/noun case it seems reasonable to assume that both the verbal affix (whether infinitival or indicative or participial) and the nominal affix (*-zione*) are attached to an underived, category neutral, stem (*appar-*). For the verb/adjective case, instead, it seems correct to assume that the adjectival form is derived from an already morphologically derived verbal form, the past participle:

(72) $[_{V/N}$ appar-$]$ $\begin{cases} + \text{(i)re} \to \text{V (infinitival)} \\ + \text{to etc.} \to \text{V (past participle)} \\ + \text{(i)zione} \to \text{N} \end{cases}$

(73)   (ergative/passive) $[_V$ X-to$] \to$ A

In other words, the derivation of the adjective, though not that of the noun, is a category-changing morphological derivation.

Now if we assume, following Borer (1984), Levin-Rappaport (1986), that those morphological derivations which produce a change of category (and only those) necessarily affect the θ-grid of the input as well, we may draw the correct distinction between the verb/noun and the verb/adjective pairs.

The morphological derivation of adjectives from verbal past participles will now be as in (74):

(74)   (pass/erg) Vpastp → A   a) It changes category (V → A)
                                    b) It affects the θ-grid of the input
                                       by
                                       i) externalizing the internal
                                          θ-role
                                       ii) eliminating the [NP,VP]
                                           position

This will have, then, the correct effect of rendering adjectives derived from ergative or passive past participles syntactically unergative.

A quite general prediction follows from this analysis. Should there be other morphological processes deriving adjectives from ergative/passive *verbal* forms, they should also yield *unergative* adjectives, since the change of category would bring with it a consequent change in the θ-grid of the input, along the lines just indicated.

Indeed, this appears to be confirmed by the morphological derivation of -*bile* (-able) adjectives in Italian. Although they too are derived from either passive or ergative verbs (cf. Horn 1980; de Miguel 1986) for this characterization of the corresponding English and Spanish cases), they are quite regularly *unergative*. See e.g. (75a-b) involving the *Ne*-cliticization test:

(75) a. *Ne_i sono confermabili/condannabili/ desiderabili/etc.
          Of-them are   confirmable/ condemnable/desirable/etc.
          poche t_i *(di notizie)*
          few   (items of news)

      b. *Ne_i è giustificabile/perseguibile/ truccabile/etc.
          Of-it is justifiable/   prosecutable/fixable/etc.
          la   vendita t_i
          the sale

This follows, as suggested, from their category-changing nature (the suffix -*bile* attaches only to *verbs*, to yield adjectives):

(76)   (trans/erg) V + -bile → A a) It changes category (V → A)
                                      b) It affects the θ-grid of the
                                         input by
                                         i) externalizing the internal
                                            θ-role
                                         ii) eliminating the [NP,VP]
                                             position

If so, the Lexicalist Hypothesis can still be maintained, despite prima facie
evidence.

Notes

*   Earlier versions of this paper were presented at UFSAL, Brussel, in January 1985, at the
     XI Incontro Informale di Grammatica Generativa held in Rome in the February of the
     same year, and at the III Vienna Syntax Round Table in September 1987. I am indebted
     to those audiences, and in particular to Richard Kayne and Giuseppe Longobardi, for
     helpful comments and criticism.

1.   The adjective *triste* ('sad') apparently enters alternations like that in (2a-b):

     (i)   a.   ?*Lui è triste [che non possiate venire]*
                He is sad   that you cannot   come
           b.   *[Che non possiate venire] è triste*
                That you cannot   come   is sad

     Yet it qualifies as an unergative adjective with respect to the ergativity tests to be discus-
     sed below.
         It is however dubious that (ib) is the ergative variant of (ia), as the slightly marginal,
     or colloquial, character of its "transitive" use ((ia)) already suggests. Moreover, the prop-
     ositional argument in (ia), differently from that in (ib), appears not to be a theme. This is
     particularly clear in the corresponding nominal version, where the NP is introduced by a
     preposition (*per* 'for') other than that normally introducing 'themes' (*di* 'of'). Compare
     (iia-b) with (3a-b):

     (ii) a.   *Lui è triste per/* di questo*
                He is sad   for/ of this
           b.   *Questo è triste*
                This   is sad

     We, thus, conclude that (ib)-(iib) are not derived by 'Move NP' from (ia)-(iia), i.e. do not
     enter a genuine 'ergative alternation.'

2.   Our conclusion will thus differ both from that in Abraham (1983), Toman (1986), where
     it is suggested that adjectives are in the general case unaccusative, and from that in Bur-
     zio (1986), Stowell (1987), where it is argued that no unaccusative adjectives exist.

3.   Chomsky (1986b: 83) suggests that government by a lexical head is possibly required by
     antecedent-governed traces, but we may generalize it to all traces, given that government

by a lexical head is obviously met by θ-governed traces. Further evidence for an independent head-government requirement is discussed in Aoun-Hornstein-Lightfoot-Weinberg (1987), Longobardi (1987), Rizzi (1987), among others. The first suggest dissociating the (generalized) requirement of head-government from that of antecedent-government by locating the two at two different levels of representation (the former at PF, the latter, reduced to a version of Aoun's Generalized Binding, at LF).

The definition of θ-government and antecedent-government in Chomsky (1986b) are:

(i)   α θ-governs β iff α is a zero-level category that θ-marks β and α,β are sisters
(ii)   α antecedent-governs β iff α governs β and α is coindexed with β

4. Note that adjunction to N' must also be excluded. Otherwise traces of N complements would be properly governed (antecedent-governed within the NP and head-governed by N) independently of the SPEC of NP position. This might again be a consequence of the general 'defective' character of [-V] categories (vis à vis the ECP) (cf. Cinque 1987a; Longobardi 1987).

5. With other adjectives the contrast is perhaps less sharp, and some variability among speakers is occasionally found. This suggests that certain adjectives may be marginally attributed (by certain speakers) to the ergative class (cf. also fn. 19). Here I will not attempt a semantic/thematic characterization of the class of ergative adjectives, but will limit myself to listing some of the adjectives that belong to this class (according to the ergativity tests discussed in this paper):
    noto 'well-known,' *chiaro* 'clear,' *certo* 'certain,' *sicuro* 'sure,' *oscuro* 'obscure,' *probabile* 'likely,' *prevedibile* 'foreseeable,' *gradito* 'welcome,' *implicito* 'implicit,' *esplicito* 'explicit,' *evidente* 'evident,' *ovvio* 'obvious,' etc.

6. Evidence that copulative verbs are to be assimilated to raising verbs can be found in Couquaux (1979, 1981), Stowell (1978), Rizzi (1982), Cinque (1987b), among others.

7. For independent reasons (cf. Belletti 1980), it is not possible to wh-extract the constituent which is pronominalized by partitive *ne*. See, e.g.:

    (i)   *Ne   ho letto solo uno (dei suoi articoli)*
            Of-them I   read   only one (of his articles)
    (ii)   **I suoi articoli, di cui   ho letto solo uno, sono molto noti*
            His   articles, of which I read only one, are   very well-known

8. Another context admitting only successive cyclic extraction and thus providing an additional means to discriminate between ergative and unergative adjectives (as well as verbs) is extraction from preverbal subject sentences in Italian (cf. Longobardi (1987), where contrasts such as (i)-(ii), involving ergative and unergative adjectives, are explicitly noted):

    (i)   *??Gianni, con il quale   era prevedibile che [parlare t oggi] sarebbe*
            G.,   with whom   it was foreseeable that to speak today would
            stato   impossibile,...
            have been impossible

    (ii)   **Gianni, con il quale   sarebbe fastidioso che [parlare t oggi] ci*
            G.,   with whom   it would be bothering that to speak today was
            fosse impedito,...
            barred to us,...

9.   This presupposes the adoption of the strict definition of c-command (i) from Reinhart (1976):

(i)   α c-commands β iff α does not dominate β and the first branching category that dominates α dominates β

On the independent preferability of (i) over Aoun and Sportiche's (1982) definition for the purposes of Binding Theory, cf. Chomsky (1986b: 8).

10.   Cf. Antinucci-Cinque (1977) and, more recently, Belletti (1985), who suggests an account of this phenomenon within a more general treatment of the 'Definiteness Effect.' To our ears, even an indefinite inverted subject in situ gives somewhat marginal results (?(?) *Era noto qualche libro a tutti*, ?(?) *Era piaciuto qualche libro a tutti*), for reasons that are presumably related to yet poorly understood pragmatic conditions on the informational structure of the (Italian) sentence.

11.   Note that the adjectives *affezionato* 'fond,' *fatale* 'fatal' also fail to allow for *Ne*-cliticization and wh-extraction out of their inverted subjects, thus behaving consistently with the ergativity test under discussion here. See:

(i)   a.   **Ne   sono affezionati pochi (dei suoi amici)*
           Of-them are   fond   few   (of his friends)

      b.   **Ne   erano affezionati anche i   nemici,   alla sua idea*
           Of-him were fond   even his enemies, of his idea
           'Even his enemies were fond of his idea'

      c.   **?Di che   professore vi   era affezionata la figlia*
           Of which professor of-you was fond   the daughter

(ii) a.   **Ne   fu   fatale più d'uno   a Carlo (di sbaglio)*
           Of-them was fatal more than one to C.   (of mistakes)

      b.   **Ne   furono fatali gli sbagli   (di Carlo)*
           Of-him were   fatal the mistakes (of C.)

      c.   **?Di che   statua fu   fatale il   furto?*
           Of which statue was fatal the theft

12.   Cf. Giorgi (1984) for some discussion.

13.   Burzio (1981, 1986: 3.3) notes that the use of *ciascuno* 'each' as a 'floating quantifier' requires c-command by a plural antecedent at D-structure, as suggested by the relative wellformedness of (ii), in which the antecedent NP c-commands *ciascuno* at D-structure (though not at S-structure):

(i)   *Hanno assegnato [un interprete   ciascuno] ai visitatori*
           They assigned   an interpreter each   to the visitors

(ii)   *??Un interprete ciascuno fu   assegnato ai visitatori*
           An interpreter each   was assigned   to the visitors

When the antecedent NP c-commands *ciascuno* neither at D- nor at S-structure, as in (iii), the sentence is unacceptable:

(iii)   **[Un interprete   ciascuno] parlò ai visitatori*
           An interpreter each   spoke to the visitors

Although such forms as (ii) are quite marginal to begin with, some difference with (iii) is still perceptible. We can use this as a further diagnostic to distinguish ergative from unergative adjectives. Only with the former will *ciascuno* be c-commanded by the dative at D-structure. Despite the marked character of the phenomenon, as noted, it seems that a difference is again detectable in the expected direction:

(iv) ?*Una sola cosa ciascuno era   chiara/nota   a   quei   ragazzi*
      Just one thing each   was clear/well-known to those boys

(v)   *?*Un solo amico ciascuno era   affezionato a quei   ragazzi*
      Just one friend each   was fond   of those boys

14. Similar cases were observed in Giorgi (1984: 323), where an example is also noted which is at first sight problematic for the hypothesis that only thematic subjects can bind long distance anaphors. As the acceptability of (i) below shows, it would seem that the derived subject of a passive can bind a long distance anaphor:

(i)   *Osvaldo$_j$ è stato convinto t$_j$ da Gianni$_i$ del fatto   che la propria$_{*i/j}$ casa*
      O.   was convinced   by G.   of the fact that self's   house
      è la   più bella del paese
      is the nicest   of the village

      (=(50)b of Giorgi 1984)

It appears, however, that with such verbs as *convincere* 'convince,' *persuadere* 'persuade,' etc. (which arguably take an experiencer object, and an optional agentive subject) the object too can bind long distance anaphors. (ii), in fact, appears to have roughly the same status as (i) (perhaps '?'):

(ii) *Lo$_j$ avevano convinto   che la propria$_i$ casa era la più bella di tutte*
      They had convinced him that self's   house was the nicest   of all

This confirms that *experiencers* provide a systematic exception to the otherwise general condition that only *subjects* can bind long distance anaphors (see Belletti-Rizzi's (1986) remark about this property of regular psych-verbs).

If so, one can hold that in (i) *proprio* is bound by the object trace, a thematic position, not by the subject. When binding by the object fails, for lack of c-command, the result is one of unacceptability, as expected, even though the subject c-commands *proprio*. See (iii):

(iii) **Osvaldo$_i$ fu   visto [t entrarvi]   anche da coloro che dubitavano della*
      O.   was seen   to enter there even by those   who doubted   of
      propria$_i$ buona fede
      self's   good faith

15. Note that the trace in the structural object position (under A') cannot function as the thematic antecedent of *proprio* even though it c-commands it. This is due to the fact that differently from the case of the trace in (i) of the previous footnote, this trace is a theme, not an experiencer, and only experiencers can bind a long distance anaphor from a non subject position.

16. There is evidence that *as* too is an adverbial moved to initial position, like *come, comme.* As Rizzi (1987) notes following an observation of Ross's (1984), arguments but not adverbial elements can be extracted over a negation, what Ross refers to as 'inner islands.' *As*

behaves as an adverbial element under extraction over a negation. See (i) vs. (ii), taken from Rizzi (1987):

(i)   Bill is here, which they (don't) know
(ii)   Bill is here, as they (*don't) know

17.   Here, as in the case of verbal past participles, some questions arise concerning the nature of the (non Case-marked) empty categories, at D- and S-structure (cf. Burzio (1987: Appendix) for some discussion).

Also, note that not all ergative adjectives enter the small clause construction as easily as those in (58) (*?Come ormai sicuro,...* 'As by now sure,...'). Often the addition of some aspectual/temporal element is needed to render the form more natural (cf.(58)).

Stowell (1987) judges the analogues of (58) in English as totally unacceptable, indeed taking their illformedness as evidence for the non existence of ergative adjectives (in English). Although Burzio (1987: Appendix) cites forms like

(i)   The government staged a brutal repression, as well-known / as obvious from many gruesome discoveries

as wellformed, the informants I have consulted tend to agree with Stowell's judgements, even though they do perceive the same clear contrast between the English analogues of (56), (57) that is perceived by Italian speakers. I do not understand why English and Italian should differ in part concerning (58), (59).

18.   A limited exception to the otherwise obligatory presence of a prepositional complementizer in infinitival *complement* sentences is represented by the restricted class of 'verbs of willing' and few other verbs (*sapere* 'know (how),' *osare* 'dare,' etc.).

19.   Other adjectives marginally allow *di* as well as Ø, which might suggest that they may belong to either class (giving marginal results when ergative). Cf.

(i)   a.   *Non mi è gradito (??di) ricevere così tante visite*
            I am not pleased   to receive so   many visits
      b.   *E' auspicabile/augurabile (??di) non dover ripetere   quell'infausta*
            It is desirable   not to have to repeat that unlucky
            esperienza
            experience

This conjecture is strenghened by the fact that the same adjectives also yield intermediate results under the other ergativity tests (e.g. *?Ne sono gradite/auspicabili molte t; ?Ne sono gradite/auspicabili le dimissioni t*).

20.   As Giorgi (1986: 181) notes, 'ergative' nouns like *apparizione* 'appearance' seem to behave consistently also with respect to Burzio's *ciascuno* argument (cf. fn. 13 above), contrasting with such 'unergative' nouns as *telefonata* 'phone call' (even though the contrast here is in part obscured by the rather marked character of the phenomenon):

(i)   a.   *?L'apparizione   di un fantasma ciascuno agli studenti...*
            The appearance of a   ghost each to the students...
      b.   ** La telefonata di un professore ciascuno agli studenti...*
            The phone call of a professor each to the students

Bibliography

Abraham, W. 1983. "Adjektivrektion im Deutschen." Ms., University of Groningen.

Antinucci, F. and G. Cinque. 1977. "Sull'ordine delle parole in italiano: l'emarginazione." *Studi di grammatica italiana* 6: 121-146.

Aoun, Y., N. Hornstein, D. Lightfoot, and A. Weinberg. 1987. "Two Types of Locality," *Linguistic Inquiry* 18: 537-577.

Aoun, Y. and D. Sportiche. 1982. "On the Formal Theory of Government." *The Linguistic Review* 2: 211-236.

Belletti, A. 1980. "Italian Quantified NPs in LF." *Journal of Italian Linguistics* 5: 1-18.

————. 1985. "Unaccusatives as Case Assigners." MIT Lexicon Project Working Paper n.8. Cambridge, Mass.

————. and L. Rizzi. 1981. "The Syntax of *ne*: Some Theoretical Implications." *The Linguistic Review* 1: 117-154.

————. and L. Rizzi. 1986. "Psych-verbs and Th-Theory." MIT Lexicon Project Working Paper n.13. Cambridge, Mass.

Borer, H. 1984. "The Projection Principle and Rules of Morphology." *Proceedings of the North Eastern Linguistic Society* 14: 16-33.

Burzio, L. 1981. *Intransitive Verbs and Italian Auxiliaries*. Diss., Massachusetts Institute of Technology.

————. 1986. *Italian Syntax*. Dordrecht: Reidel.

————. 1987. "The Legacy of the PRO-Theorem." Ms., Harvard University.

Chomsky, N. 1970. "Remarks on Nominalization." In: Jacobs and Rosenbaum 1970.

————. 1986a. *Knowledge of Language*. New York. Praeger.

————. 1986b. *Barriers*. Cambridge, Mass.: MIT Press.

Cinque, G. 1980. "On Extraction from NP in Italian." *Journal of Italian Linguistics* 5: 47-99.

————. 1987a. *Types of A'-Dependencies*. Ms., University of Venice, to be published by MIT Press.

————. 1987b. "On *si* Constructions and the Theory of 'ARB'." Ms., University of Venice (to appear in *Linguistic Inquiry*).

Couquaux, D. 1979. "Sur la syntaxe des phrases prédicatives en français." *Linguisticae Investigationes* 3: 245-284.

————. 1981. "French Predication and Linguistic Theory." In: May and Koster 1981.

Giorgi, A. 1984. "Toward a Theory of Long Distance Anaphors: A GB Approach." *The Linguistic Review* 3: 307-361.

———. 1985. "On the Italian Anaphoric System." Diss. Scuola Normale Superiore, Pisa.

———. 1986. "The Proper Notion of C-command and the Binding Theory: Evidence from NPs." *Proceedings of the North Eastern Linguistic Society* 16: 169-185.

Horn, L. 1980. "Affixation and the Unaccusative Hypothesis." *Proceedings of the Chicago Linguistic Society* 16: 134-146.

Hornstein, N. and D. Lightfoot. 1987. "Predication and PRO." *Language* 63: 23-52.

Jacobs, R. and P. Rosenbaum. (eds.). 1970. *Readings in English Transformational Grammar*. Waltham, Mass.: Ginn & Co.

Kayne, R. 1981. "ECP Extensions." *Linguistic Inquiry* 12: 93-133. (also in Kayne (1984)).

———. 1984. *Connectedness and Binary Branching*. Dordrecht: Foris.

———. 1986. "Connexité et inversion du sujet." In: Ronat and Couquaux 1986.

———. and J-Y. Pollock. 1978. "Stylistic Inversion, Successive Cyclicity, and Move NP in French." *Linguistic Inquiry* 9: 595-621.

Levin, B. and M. Rappaport. 1986. "The Formation of Adjectival Passives." *Linguistic Inquiry* 17: 623-661.

Longobardi, G. 1987. "Extraction from NP and the proper Notion of Head Government." Ms., Scuola Normale Superiore, Pisa.

May, R. and J. Koster. (eds.). 1981. *Levels of Syntactic Representation*. Dordrecht: Foris.

de Miguel. 1986. "Sulla regola di formazione degli aggettivi in -*ble* in spagnolo." *Rivista di Grammatica Generativa* 11: 127-165.

Perlmutter, D. 1978. "Impersonal Passives and the Unaccusative Hypothesis." *Proceedings of the Annual Meeting of the Berkeley Linguistics Society* 4: 157-189

Reinhart, T. 1976. "The Syntactic Domain of Anaphora." Diss. Massachusetts Institute of Technology.

Rizzi, L. 1982. "On Chain Formation." Ms., University of Calabria.

———. 1987. "Relativized Minimality." Ms., University of Geneva.

Ronat, M. and D. Couquaux. (eds.). 1986. *La Grammaire Modulaire*. Paris: Minuit.

Ross, J.R. 1984. "Inner Islands." *Proceedings of the Annual Meeting of the Berkeley Linguistics Society* 10: 258-265.

Stowell, T. 1978. "What was there before there was there." *Proceedings of the Chicago Linguistic Society* 14: 458-471.

———. 1987. "As *So*, Not So *As*." Ms., University of California at Los Angeles.

Toman, J. 1986. "A (Word-) Syntax for Participles." *Linguistische Berichte* 105: 367-408.

Small *pro* in German*

Günther Grewendorf
Johann Wolfgang Goethe University, Frankfurt

1. The Ergative Hypothesis and Descriptive Generalizations in German

In this paper, I want to show that a series of syntactic phenomena of German, unexplained up to now, can be accounted for if we assume that the surface subject of a certain class of intransitive verbs is in fact a deep structure object.

I will suppose that the reader is familiar with Burzio's hypothesis, who made the same claim with respect to Italian. I will further assume that the reader is familiar with the sort of evidence usually adduced in support of this hypothesis ("ne"-cliticization, auxiliary selection, attributive use of past participles, impersonal passive, topicalization of verb and subject, discontinuous phrases like for example in den Besten's "subextraction"). I shall therefore limit myself to phenomena that are not so *obviously* related to the transitive deep structure of ergative verbs.

My next step will be to address the question of small *pro* in German. I will show that it actually occurs in German as an empty expletive pronominal subject, and that Rizzi's (1986) analysis of the *pro* module provides the basis for an adequate analysis of subjectless constructions in languages like German.

* This paper was presented at the Fourth Vienna Round table on Comparative Syntax in September 1987. I would like to express my gratitude to the participants of that conference for their useful contributions in the discussion. I would like to thank in particular Guglielmo Cinque, Hubert Haider, Jan Koster, Martin Prinzhorn, Henk van Riemsdijk, and Peter Staudacher for their helpful comments and critical suggestions.

Finally, I am going to discuss some critical comments on this approach
made by Haider with respect to small *pro* in German and by Shlonsky with
respect to Rizzi's analysis of the *pro* module.

Let us first consider *extraction from subject sentences* (just with infinitives). We can observe a clear difference in grammaticality depending on
whether the main verb or an auxiliary verb is in the matrix COMP, a difference that has gone unnoticed so far cf.

(1)   a.   *Was   gehört __   zu beanstanden sich nicht?*
           what:ACC befits a person to complain of   not
      b.   *Was   hat __ zu beanstanden sich nicht gehört?*
           what:ACC has   to complain of   not   befitted a person

(2)   a.   *Wessen   Beispiele   frustierte __ zu analysieren*
           whose:GEN examples:ACC frustrated   to analyse
           dich   mehr, Huberts   oder Wolfgangs?
           you:ACC more Hubert's:GEN or   Wolfgang's:GEN

      b.   *Wessen   Beispiele   hat __ zu analysieren dich*
           whose:GEN examples:ACC has   to analyse   you:ACC
           mehr frustiert,   Huberts   oder Wolfgangs?
           more frustrated, Hubert's:GEN or   Wolfgang's:ACC

It is not my intention to explain this difference. I would just like to point
out that it is related to the possibility of circumventing a blocking NP-node
by adjunction to S. In this respect, it should be noted that the same difference can be observed when we extract from a complex object NP:

(3)   a.   *Was   hat [$_S$Hubert [$_{NP}$ den Versuch __ zu fangen]*
           what:ACC has   [Hubert:NOM [the attempt:ACC to catch]
           unternommen]?
           undertaken

      b.   *Was   unternahm __ zu fangen Hubert   den*
           what:ACC undertook   to catch   Hubert:NOM the
           Versuch __?
           attempt:ACC

      c.   *Was   hat __ zu fangen Hubert   den Versuch __*
           what:ACC has   to catch Hubert:NOM the attempt:ACC
           unternommen?
           undertaken

Now it is interesting to note that the restriction in question does not apply in the case of adjunction and extraction from an object infinitive. Consider the following examples:

(4)   a.   *Wen   hat einzuladen Hans   allen Anwesenden*
           who:ACC has to invite   Hans:NOM all   present:DAT (ones)
           hoch und heilig versprochen?
           most solemnly promised

       b.   *Wen   versprach einzuladen Hans   allen*
           who:ACC promised to invite   Hans:NOM all
           Anwesenden   hoch und heilig?
           present:DAT (ones) most solemnly

As for ergative verbs, we can observe that extraction out of a subject clause does not exhibit this restriction either. So the situation with the ergative case is the same as with the object case:

(5)   a.   *Wen   ist zu besiegen dem Wimbledonsieger*
           who:ACC is to defeat   the winner of Wimbledon:DAT
           zum   zweiten Mal gelungen?
           for the second time succeeded in
           'Who has the winner of Wimbledon succeeded in defeating for the second time?'

       b.   *Wen   gelang   zu besiegen dem*
           who:ACC succeeded in defeating the
           Wimbledonsieger   zum   zweiten Mal?
           winner of Wimbledon:DAT for the second time

Note that the argument is valid only if we assume that in the ergative case, NP-movement of the D-structural object is not obligatory in German. That means that the D-structural object can remain *in situ* at the surface structure. But this is not surprising given the well-known fact that NP-movement is not obligatory with German passive either.

It should be clear that the resulting problem of Case assignment can be solved along the lines of Safir's (1985) or Hoekstra's (1984) theory if small *pro* is an available option for the subject position.

Let us now turn to the second argument, which concerns the combination of extraction and extraposition. When considering relative clauses, we can observe the following: the combination of extraction and extraposition is impossible with subject clauses, but it is not ungrammatical with object clauses:

(6) a. *Subject case:*
    *ein Mann, dem   den Peter   frustiert   hat die
    a   man   who:DAT the Peter:ACC frustrated has the
    Arbeit   zu machen.
    work:ACC to do

  b. *Object case:*
    ein Mann, den   Hans   beabsichtigte für den
    a   man   who:ACC John:NOM intended   for the
    Vorsitz   vorzuschlagen.
    chair:ACC to propose
    'a man who John intended to propose for the chair.'

Again, ergatives and passive behave like the object case:

(7) a. *eine Frau, der   dem Hans   schwergefallen*
    a   woman who:DAT (for) the John:DAT been difficult
    ist zu widersprechen.
    is to contradict

  b. *ein Spieler, den   dem Hans   gelungen ist zu*
    a   player who:ACC the John:DAT succeeded in
    besiegen.
    defeating

  c. *ein Mann, dem   von Hans   beabsichtigt wurde zu*
    a   man   who:DAT by John:DAT intended   was   to
    helfen.
    help

Putting aside the question of why the latter example is much worse when the relative pronoun is in the accusative, e.g.

(7) c.' **ein Mann, den   von Hans   beabsichtigt wurde zu*
    a   man   who:ACC by John:DAT intended   was   to
    beleidigen.
    offend

it should nevertheless be clear that in this case too, we find clear evidence for the ergative hypothesis.

    Let us now consider examples involving a secondary effect of the grammatical process in question. By this I mean the presence of *es* in cases of extraction and extraposition (I am only considering *wh*-extraction). According to Haider (1983), extraction from an extraposed clause is ungrammatical if the position of the extraposed clause is occupied by the pronoun *es*. This is illustrated by Haider with the following examples:

(8)   a.   **Welchen Polizisten   glaubst du   würde es*
           which   policeman:ACC think   you:NOM would it:NOM
           selbst   diesem Gauner   schwerfallen mit diesem
           even   (for) this   rascal:DAT be difficult   with this
           Trick   zu täuschen?
           trick:DAT to deceive

      b.   *Welchen Polizisten glaubst du würde selbst diesem Gauner schwerfallen mit diesem Trick zu täuschen?*

It should be clear that these examples contain an ergative verb, and *with respect to this particular case* Haider's generalization is correct even though it is only half of the truth. As can be seen from the following examples, the correct generalization should be that presence of *es* and *wh*-extraction from an extraposed clause is ungrammatical if that clause is an object clause, but it is not ungrammatical, or at least clearly better, if that clause is a subject clause. Compare the following examples (the examples under (9a) and (9a') illustrate the availability of an extraposition *es* with the object infinitive):

(9)   *Object case*:
      a.   *Peter   hat es   unterlassen, den Eltern   eine*
           Peter:NOM has it:ACC omitted   the parents:DAT a
           Nachricht   zu schicken.
           message:ACC to send
           'Peter neglected to send his parents a message.'

      a'.   *Peter   hat es   bedauert, den Kollegen*
           Peter:NOM has it:ACC regretted the colleague:ACC
           beleidigt zu haben.
           offended to have

      b.   **Wem   hat Peter   es   unterlassen, eine*
           who:DAT has Peter:NOM it:ACC omitted   a
           Nachricht   zu schicken?
           message:ACC to send

      b'.   **Wen   hat Peter   es   bedauert, beleidigt zu*
           who:ACC has Peter:NOM it:ACC regretted offended to
           haben?
           have
           'Who has Peter regretted offending?'

(10)   *Subject case:*
 a.   *Wen   hat   dich   mehr frustiert   zu übersetzen ...?*
      who:ACC has you:ACC more frustrated to translate...
 a'. *Wen   hat es   dich   mehr frustiert   zu übersetzen.?*
      who:ACC has it:NOM you:ACC more frustrated to translate...
 b.   *Was   hat sich nicht gehört   zu*
      what:ACC has   not befitted a person to
      beanstanden?
      complain of

 b'. *Was   hat es sich nicht gehört   zu*
      what:ACC has it:NOM not befitted a person to
      beanstanden?
      complain of

It goes without saying that Haider's halfway generalization (covering only the ergative cases) provides further support for the ergative hypothesis. Ergative as well as passive examples correspond to the object case:

(11) a. **Wem   wurde es   von Peter   bedauert*
         who:DAT was   it:NOM by Peter:DAT regretted
         geholfen zu haben?
         to have helped
     b. **Wem   ist es   dem Hans   schwergefallen eine*
         who:DAT is es   (for) John:DAT been difficult to put off
         Absage zu erteilen?

Finally, let me mention one argument taken from the field of derivational morphology. I will assume that the reader is familiar with the evidence provided by *er*-nominalizations. A similar point can be made with *-ling* suffixes in the case of deverbative derivations. This kind of suffix is not productive anymore, it occurs with transitive verbs and always identifies the θ-role of the object, as in

(12)   *Lehrling* (apprentice), *Prüfling* (examinee), *Findling* (foundling), *Liebling* (darling), *Säugling* (suckling (baby)), *Sträfling* (convict), *Schützling* (protégé).

It sometimes occurs with intransitive verbs too:

(13)   *Ankömmling* (someone who has just arrived), *Eindringling* (intruder), *Emporkömmling* (upstart), *Sprößling* (sprout).

It should be quite obvious that ergative verbs are involved here, and so it should be clear how these data can be accounted for in terms of the ergative hypothesis.

2. Empty Expletive Subjects

I have already pointed out that some of the arguments presented in support of the ergative hypothesis can only be sustained if we assume that in German, NP-movement of the D-structural object into the subject position is not obligatory. This leads to the question of what is in the subject position when the surface subject, i.e., the nominative NP, remains in the object position.

Let us put aside the problem of how an NP can receive nominative Case in a VP-internal position. With respect to this problem, I would like to refer the reader to theories of indirect Case assignment as proposed by Safir and Hoekstra. Instead we will now turn to a necessary condition for this kind of indirect assignment of nominative Case: namely the availability of an empty element — of a certain kind — in the subject position of German sentences; in other words, the availability of an empty element from which nominative Case might be inherited.

I will assume once again that the reader is familiar with Rizzi's (1986) analysis of the *pro* module. Basing his analysis on some facts concerning the Italian gerund and the availability of an object *pro*, Rizzi distinguishes between

(a) formal (structural) licensing of *pro* and
(b) interpretation of content (feature-assignment by the licensing head)

and he arrives at the conclusion that small *pro* may be structurally licensed in a language without that language being a "full-fledged" *pro*-drop language, i.e., without that language allowing for the interpretation of *pro* as a true argument.

The crucial question is as follows: *is the subject position in German available for an empty expletive pronoun (expletive small pro)*?

I will now argue that German is in fact endowed with an empty expletive pronominal subject. For the sake of my first argument, we have to recall that the big PRO i.e., the control PRO, due to the functional determination of empty categories, can only be controlled by an argument rather than by an expletive antecedent.

In addition to this theorem of the theory of government and binding, the argument is based on an empirical generalization due to Höhle (1978) which says that the subject of an infinitive introduced by *ohne zu* has to be controlled by the matrix subject.

It is then tempting to construct such an argument in the following way. One might say that if a sentence like

(14) a. ?*daß dem Trainer   der junge Spieler$_i$ aufgefallen ist,*
that the   coach:DAT the young player$_i$:NOM stricken   is
ohne   PRO$_i$ sich besonders angestrengt zu haben.
without PRO$_i$ having made a particular effort
'that the young player has been noticed by the coach without having made a particular effort.'

as opposed to

(14) b. *daß der junge Spieler$_i$ dem Trainer   aufgefallen ist,*
that the young player$_i$:NOM the   coach:DAT stricken   is
ohne   PRO$_i$ sich besonders angestrengt zu haben.
without PRO$_i$ having made a particular effort

were ungrammatical, this would be due to the empty expletive subject of the matrix sentence (which has to control PRO but cannot because of the above theorem). Unfortunately the sentence (14a) is not as ungrammatical as it should be even though there is a clear contrast with (14b). But this does not matter if we take note of the fact that the structure of (14a) is not necessarily like

(14) a'. [$_S$ pro [$_{VP}$ *dem Trainer der junge Spieler* ...]]

and it is not necessarily that way because German permits scrambling in the sense of adjunction to S, as has been shown by Thiersch (1985) and den Besten/Webelhuth (1987). We can put objects in front of the subject, left-adjoining them to IP. So the structure might be like

(14) a''. [$_S$ *dem Trainer* [$_S$ *der junge Spieler* [$_{VP}$ ...]]]

and in this case, there is no *expletive* subject controlling the PRO of the embedded sentence.

In order to make this argument really convincing, we have to look for sentences in which left-adjunction of the dative is excluded to make sure that we really have a case of an empty expletive subject. A.c.I.-constructions are a case in point, as the following examples demonstrate:

(15) a.　*Karl*　　　*sah* [_S *einen Knaben der Dame*　*helfen*].
　　　　Charles:NOM saw　a　　boy:ACC the lady:DAT help
　　　　'Charles saw a boy help the lady.'

　　b.　* *Karl*　　　*sah* [_S *der Dame*　*einen Knaben helfen*].
　　　　Charles:NOM saw　the lady:DAT a　　boy:ACC help

However, in *ergative* constructions the dative can precede the surface subject because as we know, the surface subject can remain in the D-structural object position:

(16)　　*Hans*　　*sah* [_S *dem Knaben einen Stein*　　*auf die*
　　　　John:NOM saw　the　boy:DAT a　　stone:ACC on　the
　　　　Füße　　*fallen*].
　　　　feet:ACC drop
　　　　'John saw a stone drop on the boy's feet.'

So in this case we can be sure that the surface subject is not in the subject position. As for the argument towards which I have been working, compare the following sentences:

(17)　　* *Der General*　　*ließ den Diktator*_i　*auspeitschen*,
　　　　the general:NOM let　the dictator_i:ACC be whipped
　　　　ohne　　PRO_i *eine Miene zu verziehen.*
　　　　without PRO_i a hair to turn
　　　　'The general had the dictator_i whipped without him_i turning a hair.'

(18) a.　*Hans*　　*sah den Studenten*_i　*aufstehen* [*ohne*　　PRO_i
　　　　John:NOM saw the student_i:ACC get up　[without PRO_i
　　　　die Augen　*zu öffnen*].
　　　　the eyes:ACC to open]

　　b.　*Hans*　　*ließ*　　*den Knaben*_i *aufstehen,* [*ohne*　　PRO_i
　　　　John:NOM made the boy_i:ACC get up　[without PRO_i
　　　　ein Hilfsmittel zu benutzen.
　　　　an aid:ACC　　to use]

It looks as if the accusative in the ECM-infinitive can be a controller in the ergative example (18), but not in the passive example (17). So *den Studenten* in (18) can qualify as such a controller, but not *den Diktator* in (17). What is the reason for this difference?

　　The reason is that in the passive-like A.c.I., the verb assigns accusative to its object. As we would expect, Case absorption does not apply with this kind of passive given that this kind of passive does not exhibit any morphological effects. But if the D-structural object receives Case from the verb, NP-movement cannot take place. So the ungrammaticality of example (17) can be explained if we assume that the subject is an expletive *pro*.

Now let us look at the ergative example. Because accusative is never assigned by the ergative verb in this case, we always have the following two options available: indirect Case assignment to the D-structural object *in situ*, or NP-movement into the subject position. This latter option explains the grammaticality of the ergative example.

A further argument for the existence of *pro*-subjects in German concerns parasitic gaps. It is based on an observation with respect to English made by Luigi Rizzi at a GLOW-discussion in Venice in 1987.

Although it is frequently assumed that parasitic gap constructions do not exist in German, Felix (1985) has shown that instances of parasitic gaps do in fact marginally occur in some particular constructions in German, e.g.

(19)   *Hans   hat Maria$_i$ ohne   e$_i$ anzuschauen geküßt.*
         John:NOM has Mary$_i$:ACC without e$_i$ to look at   kissed
         'John kissed Mary without looking at her.'

Although this phenomenon seems to be much more restricted in German than in English or other SVO languages, Felix demonstrates that on the basis of a structure like (20), the fundamental characteristics of parasitic gaps that are usually derived from universal principles with respect to other languages can also be established with respect to German:

(20)

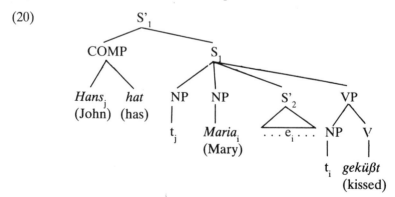

If we now compare the following examples

(21) a.   *ein Mann,   den$_i$ Hans   [ohne   e$_i$ zu kennen] t$_i$
          a   man:NOM who$_i$:ACC John:NOM [without e$_i$ to know]   t$_i$
          eingeladen hat
          invited   has*

b.   **ein Mann,   der$_i$ [ohne   e$_i$ zu kennen] t$_i$
          a   man:NOM who$_i$:NOM [without e$_i$ to know]   t$_i$
          eingeladen wurde
          invited   was*

we can develop an indirect argument for a *pro*-subject on the basis of the following consideration.

Suppose we analyse (21b) in terms of NP-movement. The anti-c-command condition for parasitic gaps would then be violated, i.e., e$_i$ would be locally A-bound by the trace in the subject position, and a violation of the θ-criterion would be the result.

We have just seen that NP-movement is not obligatory in the German passive. So we cannot rule out sentence (21b) by appealing exclusively to a movement analysis. But if there were no elements in the subject position (or no subject position at all) in the non-movement case, the relevant structure of (21b) would be analogous to that of the grammatical example (21a). In other words, if only the trace in the object position of the relative clause were relevant to the parasitic gap, the ungrammaticality of (21b) would remain unexplained: in (21a) as well as in (21b), the condition of anti-c-command would be satisfied.

So we have to conclude that there is a subject position in (21b) and that this position is occupied by an empty element which is responsible for the ungrammaticality of this example. But then it follows from the functional determination of empty categories that this empty subject can only be *pro*.

There are thus two ways of explaining the ungrammaticality of (21b). Assuming that the unification hypothesis of co-indexing is correct, the explanation would take the form similar to that of a movement case. Given that a *pro*-subject does not prevent the empty category in (21b) from being locally A-bar-bound by the relative pronoun, the ungrammaticality of (21b) could be explained by assuming that the co-superscripted trace inherits the c-commanding property from the *pro*-subject, thus violating the anti-c-command condition.

A final argument for the existence of *pro*-subjects in German is as follows. Compare the following sentences (for the descriptive generalizations see Höhle (1978: chap. (6.1.)), Eisenberg (1986: chap. (11.2.1.))):

(22)   *Wolfgang   ist glücklich,*
          Wolfgang:NOM is happy

    a.   *weil   geliebt zu werden wunderbar ist.*
        because loved to get   wonderful is
        'because it is wonderful to be loved.'

    b.   **weil   gearbeitet zu werden wunderbar ist.*
        because worked   to get   wonderful is

    c.   *weil   gearbeitet zu werden scheint.*
        because worked   to get   seems
        'because it seems that people are working.'

Why is it that the impersonal passive cannot be embedded in a control structure as in (22b), but can be embedded under a raising verb as in (22c)? Assuming the availability of an expletive *pro*-subject, we can explain the difference in the following way.

In (22c), the empty expletive *pro*-subject of the infinitive can be moved to the non-θ subject position of the matrix verb to receive Case. In (22b), this kind of movement is excluded because the subject position of the matrix sentence is a θ-position. So a *pro*-subject of the infinitive would fail to receive Case, and a PRO subject would not be available because it would fail to get a θ-role. So again we have to conclude that a *pro*-subject does, in fact, exist in German.

We are therefore led to the conclusion that German allows an empty expletive subject, which not only explains a lot of "ergative effects" in German, but also supports the claim that phenomena like the German impersonal passive, which are supposed to be "subjectless", do not contradict the Extended Projection Principle.

3.   "Subject Inversion" with Non-Ergative Verbs

In German, there is the unmarked possibility of "postposing" the subject of certain verbs like *gefallen* (to please), *helfen* (to help), *schaden* (to harm), which for this reason, e.g. in Lenerz (1977), have been considered to be ergatives. With respect to the Italian counterparts of verbs like *gefallen*, Belletti/Rizzi (1986) have tried to establish the ergative character of these verbs. However, I would like to show that these verbs are not ergative. Upon closer inspection, they turn out to be verbs that have thematic subjects; the only particular thing about these verbs is that their subjects have the θ-role *theme*.

In order to show that the verbs in question are not ergative, I will make use of some generalizations stated by Koster (1984) about postposition stranding. Koster has shown that in SOV languages, postposition stranding is only possible if prepositions are structural governors and if a condition he terms "Global Harmony" is fulfilled, that is, if the governors necessary for domain extension exhibit a uniform direction of government. However, examples of postposition stranding in a complex NP seem to contradict the condition of Global Harmony:

(23)   *Da*$_i$ *hat Hans*   [*ein Argument*   [*t*$_i$ *gegen*]]
                                    →   ←
         there$_i$ has John:NOM [an argument:ACC [*t*$_i$ against]]
         vorgebracht.
              ←
         advanced
         'Against it John has advanced an argument.'

We therefore have to assume that the PP is outside the NP, arguing that the order of NP and PP can be changed whenever that kind of postposition stranding is possible, as in

(24)   *Hans   hat gegen   Wittgenstein ein Argument*
         John:NOM has against Wittgenstein an argument:ACC
         vorgebracht.
         advanced
         'John has advanced an argument against Wittgenstein.'

Given that some kind of reanalysis is involved here, we predict that *only complex NPs within a VP* allow the postposition stranding process in question. This prediction is borne out by the following example:

(25)   **Da*$_i$ *hat* [*ein Argument*   [*t*$_i$ *gegen*]]   *den Studenten*
         there$_i$ has [an argument:NOM [*t*$_i$ against]] the student:ACC
         überzeugt.
         convinced
         'An argument against it has convinced the student.'

As we would expect, the order of NP and PP cannot be reversed in this case either:

(26)   **Gegen Wittgenstein hat ein Argument   den*
         against Wittgenstein has an argument:NOM the

Studenten   überzeugt.
student:ACC convinced
'An argument against Wittgenstein has convinced the
student.'

Let us further note another restriction for postposition stranding also
pointed out by Koster, namely that categories in derived positions are
islands. So accordingly it is the preposed PP in the following example that
prevents postposition stranding from being grammatical:

(27)   *Da$_i$ hat Hans   [t$_i$ gegen] [ein Argument]
         there$_i$ has John:NOM [t$_i$ against] [an argument:ACC]
         vorgebracht.
         advanced
         'Against it John has advanced an argument.'

We are now able to use postposition stranding in a complex NP as a test for
the position of "postposed" ("inverted") subjects. We can predict the following: this kind of postposition stranding should be possible only if the
complex NP occupies neither the subject position nor a derived position,
i.e., only if it occupies a non-derived position within the VP.

As can be seen from the following examples in (28), postposed subjects
of verbs like *gefallen* (to please) show the behaviour of NPs that occupy
either a subject position or a derived position. So irrespective of which of
the two alternatives does in fact apply, the conclusion to be drawn is that
the verbs in question are not ergative:

(28) *Postposition stranding*
     a.   *Da ist dem Professor   ein Argument   gegen*
          there is the   professor:DAT an argument:NOM against
          eingefallen.
          occurred
          'An argument against it has occurred to the professor.'
          (ergative case)

     b.   *Da hat dem Professor   ein Argument   gegen*
          there has the   professor:DAT an argument:NOM against
          gefallen.
          pleased
          'An argument against it has pleased the professor.'
          (*gefallen*-case)

NP-PP-order

c.   *weil   dem Professor   gegen Wittgenstein ein*
because the   professor:DAT against Wittgenstein an
Argument   eingefallen ist.
argument:NOM occurred   is
'because an argument against Wittgenstein has occurred to
the professor.'
(ergative case)

d. **weil   dem Professor   gegen Wittgenstein ein*
because the   professor:DAT against Wittgenstein an
Argument   gefallen hat.
argument:NOM pleased has
'because an argument against Wittgenstein has pleased the
professor.'
(*gefallen*-case)

4. Refuting some Counterarguments: Against <u>pro</u>-drop-drop and pro non-argument <u>pro</u>

In a recent paper, Haider (1987) has objected to the hypothesis advocated by Platzack (1985), Koster (1986), and myself (Grewendorf 1988) that "semi-*pro*-drop languages" like German allow an empty expletive pronominal subject. His argument runs as follows: given that constructions like the impersonal passive have to be analysed in terms of an expletive small *pro*, we would expect these constructions to occur in full *pro*-drop languages too, a full *pro*-drop language being at least as well supplied with *pros* as a semi-*pro*-drop language. However, as is generally known, a language like Italian, even though it is a full *pro*-drop language, allows neither the impersonal passive nor *Aux+da-infinitives*:

(29) a. **E' stato lavorato.*
        is been worked

     b. **Su Mario   non è da contare.*
         on Mario:ACC not is to count
         'One cannot count on Mario.'

Given that it is in fact the absence of small *pro* that prevents these constructions from occurring in a full *pro*-drop language, we should conclude, as Haider does, that expletive *pro* does not exist at all.

However, this line of reasoning is not convincing. The availability of an expletive *pro* is not alone a sufficient condition for the occurrence of impersonal passive constructions. Therefore the non-occurrence of the impersonal passive does not entail a non-existence of expletive *pro*. Let us take a closer look at the Italian examples in question. A sentence like

(29) a. *E' stato lavorato.*

literally means, because of the *masculine* ending of the participle,

(29) a'. <u>He</u> has been worked.

In other words, the above utterance has to be understood in a personal sense, i.e., as the *personal passive of an intransitive verb*, and this is the reason why this example is regarded as ungrammatical. This is exactly what Cinque (1987) points out in a recent paper on *si*-constructions. He says (Cinque 1987: 12) that a [non-argument] *si* "serves as a syntactic means to supplement personal AGR with the features able to 'identify' (in the sense of Chomsky (1982: chapter 5), Rizzi (1986)) the content of *pro* as a generic person pronominal, an interpretation that would not, otherwise, be available to the ordinary person inflection paradigm. *Dorme troppo qui* can only mean 'He/She sleeps too much here,' while *Si dorme troppo qui* acquires the meaning 'One (unspecified) sleeps too much here.'"

To test this alternative diagnosis of the Italian impersonal passive, we have to look for a *pro*-drop language that displays impersonal verb endings, and the question to be asked is whether or not such a language allows the impersonal passive. Russian is a case in point, and Russian permits the impersonal passive in exactly the same way as German does:

(30) a. *Bylo nakureno v   komnate.*
          was smoked   in the room
      a'. *weil   im   Zimmer geraucht wurde.*
          because in the room   smoked was
      b. *Bylo napisano ob   ètom v   gazete.*
          was written about this in the newspaper
      b'. *weil   darüber in der Zeitung geschrieben wurde.*
          because about this in the newspaper written   was

The account given by Cinque for the role of [non-argument] *si* as a syntactic marker for a generic person not only enables us to explain why the impersonal passive is not available in Italian, but it also carries over to *Aux+da-infinitives*, providing us with an explanation of the following difference:

(31) a. ** Su Mario non è da contare.*
          on Mario not is to count
      b. *Su Mario non c'è   da contare.*
          on Mario not there is to count

In these cases too, a syntactic marker is needed to "neutralize" personal AGR, i.e., to express generic person. Incidentally, the *pro*-analysis receives further support from the fact that these constructions are ungrammatical with ergative verbs:

(32)   ** A Roma non c'è   da arrivare.*
        at Rome not there is to arrive

Haider's own theory, according to which an INFL without a θ-role does not allow for a *pro* subject that satisfies ECP (German is supposed to be an exception because there is no VP), is not convincing in view of the fact that the following example shows such an INFL without a θ-role:

(34)   *E' stato picchiato Enrico.*
        is been beaten   Enrico:NOM

Shlonsky (1987) claims that null expletives and null arguments are subject to the same licensing conditions; that is, if they are treated by the *pro* module as elements of the same type, then it is surely not the characterization of the subject position as thematic or non-thematic that is relevant for the assignment of features.

This claim clearly contrasts with the observation made by Rizzi (1986), who suggests that an expletive *pro* need only be formally licensed, whereas an argument *pro* must be assigned feature content by the licensing head.

Let us take a closer look at the argument that Shlonsky presents in support of his claim. He points out that in Hebrew, direct objects may experience long extraction over a *wh*-island, but that a subject of an ergative or passive verb may not be extracted in the same way. This can be seen from the following examples:

(35) a. *Ma   lo yada-ta   'im   Dani hepil?*
          what:ACC NEG knew$_2$:P.M.SING. whether Dani dropped
          "What didn't you know whether Dani dropped?"
          [wh$_i$ ... [$_{CP}$ wh [$_{IP}$ Dani [$_{VP}$ dropped t$_i$]]]]

b. *? *Ma   lo   yada-ta   'im   nafal 'al ha-ricpa?*
   what:NOM NEG knew₂ :P.M.SING. whether fell   on the floor
   "What didn't you know whether fell on the floor?"
   *[wh$_i$ … [$_{CP}$ wh [$_{IP}$ *pro$_i$* [$_{VP}$ fell t$_i$]]]]

He then relates the possibility of postverbal subject extraction to the
licensing principles for null subjects, showing that the principle violated in
the ergative example (in inversion constructions) concerns the preverbal
pro and not the postverbal trace.

Given that it is precisely in the vicinity of *first* and *second* person (Past/
Fut) agreement that argument *pro* is possible in Hebrew, the following evidence is supposed to show that preverbal expletives are subject to a
requirement more restrictive than just formal licensing. Shlonsky observes
that in general, only first and second person subjects may be extracted over
a *wh*-island:

(36) a. **Xaym, af exad lo   Sa'al   lama 'azav*
        Xaym no one neg asked:3.P.M.SING. why left:3.P.M.SING.
        et ha-mesiba   mukdam.
        the-party:ACC early
        "Xaym, nobody asked why (he) left the party early."

     b. *Ani ve-at,   af exad lo   Sa'al   lama*
        I   and-you no one NEG asked: 3.P.M.SING. why
        'azav-nu   et   ha-mesiba mukdam.
        left:1.P.PLUR. the party:ACC early
        "Me and you, nobody asked why (we) left the party early."

     c. *Ata ve-Xaym, af exad lo   Sa'al   lama*
        you and-Xaym no one NEG asked:3.P.M.SING. why
        'azav-tem   et   ha-mesiba mukdam.
        left:2.P.PLUR. the party:ACC early
        "You and Xaym, nobody asked why (you) left the party
        early."

He takes this as evidence that the possibility of extracting a subject correlates with the capacity of AGR to license argumental *pro* drop. Given
that subject inversion without extraction is acceptable in Hebrew, he
arrives at the conclusion that *pro* must be associated with phonologically
overt grammatical features at the S-structure (supplying *pro* with the feature [+person]) and that under inversion, *pro*'s features are recovered or

assigned by the postverbal NP itself by being coindexed with *pro*. The non-extractability of postverbal subjects is thus due to the fact that the feature-assigning element has to remain present.

There are obvious counterexamples to this approach: consider, for example, the expletives usually associated with S'-extraposition or impersonal passives. Shlonsky, therefore, distinguishes between two kinds of *pro*: the argumental *pro* that has a specification of person and the impersonal *pro*, the "true expletive" so to speak.

Ignoring some problems with respect to Shlonsky's evaluation of the Hebrew data (cf. Müller/Rohrbacher 1989), we can raise the following objections to Shlonsky's approach.

First of all, it is not at all clear whether or not the examples in (36) — which are supposed to illustrate the argumental character of *pro* — are, in fact, cases of extraction. They look very much like instances of *left dislocation*. But if *this* is true, then these sentences merely represent the situation that we find with ordinary declarative sentences.

Secondly, if argumental *pro* and inversion *pro* were licensed by the same conditions, why should there be languages which are endowed with inversion *pro* but not with argumental *pro*?

Finally, if sentences were associated with the feature "impersonal," as is suggested by Shlonsky's analysis of extraposition *pro*, we would have to conclude that in the case of inverted *sentential* subjects of ergative verbs, as in the German example

(37) *weil   dem Hans   Maria   zu verlassen*
      because (for) the John:DAT Mary:ACC to leave
      schwergefallen ist.
      been difficult   is
      'because John had difficulty leaving Mary.'

yet another type of *pro*, namely non-argumental *pro*, occurs that differs from all the other cases. But this would entail that in this case, extraction of the postverbal subject should be possible in Hebrew, or that the subject could remain empty as with the impersonal passive. Yet this is clearly not the case.

I would therefore like to conclude that Shlonsky's objections to Rizzi's analysis of the *pro* module are not convincing, and that his own alternative approach cannot be sustained.

References

Abraham, Werner (ed). 1985. *Erklärende Syntax des Deutschen*. Tübingen: Narr.

Belletti, Adriana and Rizzi, Luigi. 1986. "Psych-Verbs and Th-Theory." Lexicon Project Working Papers 13. Center for Cognitive Science, MIT, Cambridge/Mass. In: *Natural Language and Linguistic Theory*.

Besten, Hans den and Webelhuth, Gert. 1987. "Remnant Topicalization and the Constituent Structure of VP in the Germanic SOV Languages." Paper presented at the GLOW-Conference, Venice, March 30-April 2, 1987.

Chomsky, Noam. 1982. *Some Concepts and Consequences of the Theory of Government and Binding*. Cambridge, Mass.: MIT Press.

Cinque, Guglielmo. 1987. "On 'si' Constructions and the Theory of 'Arb'." *Linguistic Inquiry* 19, 1988, 521-581.

Eisenberg, Peter. 1986. *Grundriß der deutschen Grammatik*. Stuttgart: Metzler.

Felix, Sascha. 1985. "Parasitic Gaps in German." In: Abraham (ed.).

Grewendorf, Günther. 1989. *Ergativity in German*. Dordrecht: Foris.

Haider, Hubert. 1983. "Connectedness Effects in German". *Groninger Arbeiten zur Germanistischen Linguistik (GAGL)* 23: 82-119.

———. 1987. "Pro pro-drop Drop." University of Vienna/University of Stuttgart.

Höhle, Tilman N. 1978. *Lexikalistische Syntax: Die Aktiv-Passiv-Relation und andere Infinitkonstruktionen im Deutschen*. Tübingen: Niemeyer.

Hoekstra, Teun. 1984. *Transitivity. Grammatical Relations in Government-Binding Theory*. Dordrecht: Foris.

Koster, Jan. 1984. "Global Harmony." Tilburg Papers in Language and Literature 61. University of Tilburg.

———. 1986. "The Relation between Pro-Drop, Scrambling, and Verb Movements." Groningen Papers in Theoretical and Applied Linguistics, TTT Nr.1. University of Groningen.

Lenerz, Jürgen. 1977. *Zur Abfolge nominaler Satzglieder im Deutschen*. Tübingen: Narr.

Müller, Gereon and Rohrbacher, Bernhard. 1989. "Eine Geschichte ohne Subjekt." Ms., University of Frankfurt. *Linguistische Berichte 119*, 1989, 3-52.

Platzack, Christer. 1985. "The Scandinavian Languages and the Null Subject Parameter." Working papers in Scandinavian Syntax 20.

Rizzi, Luigi. 1986. "Null Objects in Italian and the Theory of *pro*". *Linguistic Inquiry* 17: 501-557.

Safir, Ken. 1985. *Syntactic Chains*. Cambridge, Mass.: MIT Press.

Shlonsky, Ur. 1987. "Subject Inversion in Hebrew and the pro Module." Ms., Massachusetts Institute of Technology.

Thiersch, Craig L. 1985. "VP and Scrambling in the German Mittelfeld." Ms., University of Cologne/University of Connecticut.

V. Barriers and Domains

Long Movement from Verb-Second-Complements in German

Peter Staudacher
University of Regensburg

1. The problem

It is uncontroversial that in all varieties of German sentences like (1) and (2) are well-formed:

(1)   *Wen   behauptet Hans, habe   Maria getroffen*
        Whom claims   Hans has:SUBJ Mary   met

(2)   *Wie   meint Hans, habe   Maria das Problem gelöst*
        How think Hans   has:SUBJ Mary   the problem solved

Embedding such sentences in order to form indirect questions leads to unacceptable sequences, cf. (3) and (4)

(3)   **Ich weiß   nicht, wen   Hans behauptet, habe Maria*
        I   know not   whom John claims   has   Mary
        getroffen
        met

(4)   **Ich weiß   nicht, wen   Hans behauptet, Maria habe*
        I   know not   whom John claims   Mary   has
        getroffen
        met

(5)   **Ich weiß   nicht, wie er meint, habe Maria das Problem*
        I   know not   how he thinks has   Mary   the problem
        gelöst
        solved

(6)   *Ich weiß nicht, wie er meint, Maria habe das Problem
         I   know not   how he thinks Mary has the problem
         gelöst
         solved

In those varieties of German which allow wh-movement out of *daß*-complements, a comparable contrast can not be observed, cf.(7) and (8)

(7)   Wen   behauptet Hans, daß Maria getroffen habe
         Whom claims   Hans that Mary met   has

(8)   Ich weiß nicht, wen   Hans behauptet, daß Maria
         I   know not   whom Hans claims   that Mary
         getroffen habe
         met   has

It seems to be almost uncontroversial that the problem can not be solved by treating e.g. *behauptet Hans* in (1) and (2) as a parenthetical expression, with an occurrence restricted to main clauses. See Grewendorf (1988) for a listing of standard arguments against this solution, to which could be added that the acceptability of sentences like (9)

(9)   Welche Extraktionen meinst du   habe Karl behauptet
         Which extractions   do you think has   Karl claimed
         könne man iterieren?
         could one iterate

is hardly compatible with a parenthetical analysis. Assuming that this way of trivializing the problem is not viable, an analysis along the lines of Craig Thiersch (1978) suggests itself as natural: sentences like (1) have to be related with verb-second-complements like (1a)

(1) a. Hans behauptet, diesen Kerl   habe Maria getroffen.
         Hans claims   this   guy:ACC has Mary met

which would mean that the relevant S-structural properties of (1) have to be represented as in (1')

(1')   wen$_i$ behauptet$_k$ Hans e$_k$ [t$_i$ habe$_j$ Maria getroffen e$_j$]

If we assume, following Den Besten (1977), that the landing site of moved finite verbal elements (as e.g. *habe$_i$* in (1')) is the position occupied by complementizers like *daß* in verb-final sentences, thus accounting for their complementary distribution, a solution for the problem posed by (3) could look as follows: the last step of the wh-movement exemplified in (1)

requires that the two connected positions (occupied by *wen*$_i$ and t$_i$ in (1'))
be of the same kind. In the case of (3), so the argument would go, the final
position of *wen* is structurally different from its in termediate 'prefield'-
position before *habe*. The same structural difference could be used to
account for the general impossibility of embedded verb-second questions,
cf. (10)

(10)   ** Ich weiß, wer hat Maria angerufen*

The contrast between (1) and (3) could thus be seen as due to the structural
difference of wh-landing sites in direct and indirect questions.

2.   Haider's solution

Hubert Haider (1984), in his reply to Marga Reis (1983), has tried to
formally reconstruct this solution within a general theory of verb-second
phenomena. He assumes that the German COMP-position is basically
characterized by two feature complexes which normally can not be realized
in the same position, cf. (11).

(11)

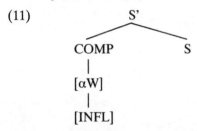

INFL-features have to be realized as verbal affixes. αW-features can
be realized by so-called "basic COMP-elements," e.g. a complementizer
like *daß*, causing the INFL-features to leave COMP and to be attached as a
suffix to the verbal head, cf. (12).

(12)

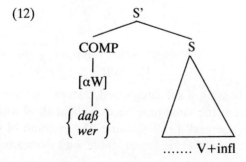

The same happens, if wh-phrases move into the COMP-position, an option open to them, but not to non-wh-phrases. αW-features can always be realized in a position adjoined to COMP, optionally in the case of [+W]-phrases and obligatorily with [-W]-phrases, with INFL attracting the verbal head of S. The result is a verb-second structure, cf. (13).

(13)

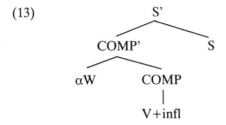

Wh-phrases are thus free to occupy both positions. In the case of indirect questions, though, they are forced to occupy the 'basic COMP-position' which, being the head of S', is required by general principles of subcategorization to bear the [+W]-features selected by the matrix predicate.

The relevant part of the S-structure of (3) would thus have to be represented as in (14):

(14)

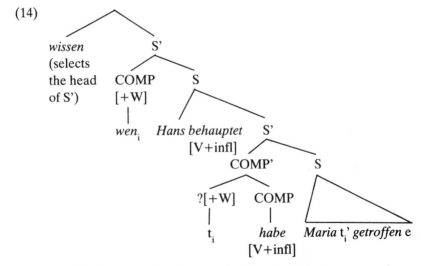

According to Haider, wen_i, bearing a subcategorized feature, occupies a 'structural' [+W]-position and at the same time heads a chain all of whose members have to bear this 'structural' [+W]-feature. The position of the intermediate chain-member t_i, however, is incompatible with its bearing a

[+W]-feature, because *behaupten* in its turn selects a complement-clause without [+W]-features, (3) being correctly ruled out as ill-formed.

Leaving aside some problems connected with the chain-concept used by Haider, I would make two objections:

1) If the COMP-features selected by *behaupten* rule out the presence of an intermediate trace in COMP left by a moved wh-phrase on its way into a subcategorized position, sentence (8) from above

(8)   *Ich weiß nicht, wen Hans behauptet, daß Maria getroffen habe*

should also be ruled out. For Haider's account implies an intermediate trace in COMP for (8) too. Otherwise the strong deviance of (4) and (6), in which the intermediate COMP-position obviously has been skipped, remains unexplained, feature-clash as a factor not being available. But it would be observationally inadequate to treat (3) and (8) on par.

2) In view of the general principles Haider uses in deducing the existence of 'structural' [+W]-chains, one would expect that their effects could also be observed in other languages with wh-movement. But the acceptability of e.g.

(15)   *I don't know, who John believes Mary loves*

is hardly reconcilable with this new concept.

In a modified version of his proposal (Haider 1989), Haider tries to take account of deviant cases like (16),

(16)   * *Wen   meint sie,   daß du glaubst,*
         Whom does she think that you believe
         hätte man einladen sollen
         one should have invited)

which is not ruled out by the version just mentioned, since *wen*, the head of the relevant chain, does not occupy a [+W]-position selected by a higher predicate. Assuming that the complementizer *daß* can be coindexed with a wh-phrase moved over it, he analyzes (16) as (16'),

(16')   * *Wen$_i$ meint sie [daß$_i$ du glaubst [t$_i$ hätte man einladen sollen]]*

thus reducing the deviance of (16) to a violation of a wellformedness condition on chains which forbids the mixing of specifier- (*Wen$_i$*) and head-positions (*that$_i$*) in a Non-A-chain.

But this can not be entirely correct, since now the acceptability of (7) or of (17)(coindexed according to Haider's proposal)

(17)   *Wann$_i$ meinst du,   daß$_i$ er eintreffen wird*
         When do you think that he will arrive?

remains unaccounted for.

3. The problem reconsidered in the framework of Barriers

In the following, I will reconsider the problem in the framework of
Barriers (Chomsky 1986).

Chomsky's Extension of the X'-system in its strict form to the nonlexi-
cal categories INFL and COMP, illustrated in (18),

(18)   'Subject-Aux-Inversion' according to *Barriers*:

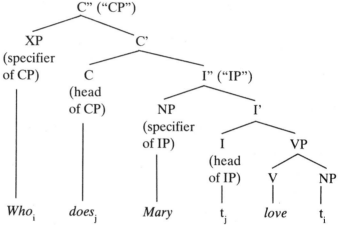

together with his theory of movement precludes moving wh-phrases into
the head-position of S'. For substitution has to obey among others the following structure preserving restrictions:

i.   "Only X^0 can move to the head position."
ii.   "Only a maximal projection can move to the specifierposi-
           tion."

Similarly adjunction is no longer free to adjoin phrases e.g. to COMP, since
in order to ensure visibility for θ-marking the following principle holds:

           "Adjunction is possible only to a maximal projection
           (hence, X") that is a nonargument."

Movement to COMP now being replaced by movement to the specifier of
CP, the relevant part of the S-strucure of (3) is as given in (19)

(19)   =   *Barriers*-structure of (3)
       Ich weiß nicht $[_{C''}$ *wen*$_i$ $[_{C'}$ C° $[_{I''}$ *Hans behauptet* $[_{C''}$ t_i'
       $[_{C'}$ *habe*$_j$ $[_{I''}$ *Maria* t_i *getroffen* $t_j]]]]]]$

It follows that the complementary distribution of finite verbs and Wh-elements in the COMP-region of German dependent clauses, sometimes
adduced in favor of their positional identity, is an epiphenomenon which
should not lead to hasty conclusions.

But why is (3) not acceptable, and why, on the other hand, is (1), with
its structure given in (20), unexceptionable?

(20)   =   *Barriers*-structure of (1)
       $[_{C''}$ *wen*$_i$ $[_{C'}$ *behauptet*$_j$ $[_{I''}$ *Hans* t_j $[_{C''}$ t_i' $[_{C'}$ *habe*$_k$ $[_{I''}$ *Maria*
       t_i *getroffen* $t_k]]]]]]$

The superficial and yet crucial difference is the position of *behauptet*: in the
acceptable structure in (20), it has been moved to the head of CP, in the
unacceptable one in (19), it remains in sentence-final position. The question why *behauptet* can not be moved in (19) will be resumed later.

It seems that this difference of the verb position can only be relevant
for the relation of the wh-phrase *wen*$_i$ to its intermediate trace t_i', since the
relation of the intermediate trace t_i' to the trace in the extraction site, t_i,
seems to be the same in the two structures.

Traces must be properly governed. Are all traces in (19) properly governed? The relevant definition of *Barriers* is as follows:

Proper Government:
    α properly governs β iff α θ-governs β
                                   or α antecedent-governs β.

θ-government:
    α θ-governs β iff   (1) α is a zero-level category
                         (2) α θ-marks β
                         (3) α and β are sisters.

The trace t_i in basic position is clearly θ-marked by its sister *getroffen*, a
zero-level category, hence it is θ-governed. The intermediate trace t_i' obviously is not θ-governed. Is it antecedent-governed? The definition of antecedent-government is:

Antecedent Government:
  α antecedent-governs β iff (1) α governs β;
                              (2) α and β are coindexed
                                   (members of a chain).

Coindexation obtains. So we need the definition of government:

Government:
  α governs β iff (1) α m-commands β;
                   (2) there is no Γ, Γ a barrier for β,
                        such that Γ excludes α.

The auxiliary notions inclusion, exclusion, and m-command are defined as follows:

Inclusion:
  α includes β iff every segment of α dominates β.

Exclusion:
  α excludes β iff no segment of α dominates β.

(Adjoined elements are thus neither excluded nor included by their mothers).

m-command:
  α m-commands β iff (1) α does not include β ;
                           (or alternatively: α excludes ß)
                      (2) every maximal projection Γ
                           that includes α includes β.

wen_i obviously m-commands its intermediate trace t_i' in (19). It remains, then, the question whether there is a barrier excluding wen_i and interrupting the chain between wen_i and t_i. The definition of the central concept is as follows:

Barrier:
  A maximal projection Γ is a barrier for β iff (a) or (b):
      a. Γ immediately includes δ, δ a blocking category for β;
      b. (i) Γ is a blocking category for β and
          (ii) Γ ≠ IP.

The first maximal projection which includes t_i' and excludes wen_i is the CP-sister of *behauptet*. Not being an IP, it would be a barrier according to alternative b of the definition, if it could be shown to be a blocking category

Blocking Category:
    A maximal projection Γ is a blocking category for β
                iff (1) Γ includes β
                     (2) Γ is not L-marked.

L-marking:
    α L-marks Γ iff (1) α is a lexical category
                          (2) α θ-governs Γ.
                             (more generally: there is a β, such that α θ-governs β and Γ agrees with the head of β)

Since *behauptet* is subcategorized for a complement clause, it is natural to assume that it θ-governs and consequently L-marks its CP-sister, which therefore cannot be a blocking category for t_i'. And since this CP immediately includes the trace t_i', it cannot be a barrier by 'inheritance' and thus it cannot be a barrier for t_i' at all.

The next potential barrier is the maximal projection of the Verb *behauptet*. Assuming that it is a VP, it could only be a barrier for t_i' qua blocking category, the CP immediately included not being a blocking category as just shown. But the VP's eventual blocking effect can surely be voided, either by adjunction to VP or some other mechanism which must be effective also in simple cases of short extraction like (21)

(21)   *es ist unklar, was$_i$ Hans* $[_{VP}$ t_i *behauptet*$]$
          it is unclear, what Hans   claims

But if the VP of *behauptet* is not a blocking category, the dominating IP cannot be a barrier either. It seems, then, that the strong deviance of (19) cannot be explained by the interrupting effect of a barrier.

But before drawing this conclusion, another possibility to induce barriers should be examined, namely barriers to government by "minimality" which in the core cases prevent the anarchy of multiple government.
Minimality:
    Γ is a barrier for β, if   there is a δ, such that
                                  1. Γ is a projection (the immediate projection) of δ,
                                  2. δ is a zero-level category distinct from β.
                                  3. Γ includes β

(the third clause has been added, it is tacitly assumed as a matter of course in *Barriers*)

Assuming that barriers by minimality are induced at a structural level where CP's are still sisters of their governing verbs, a trace inside such a CP could be protected against antecedent-government by the verb governing the CP, that is in (19) the VP-projection of *behauptet* would be a barrier by minimality for t_i' as indicated in (19a)

(19)   a.

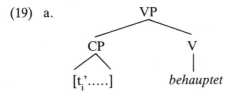

Since the specifier position of the complement clause is not θ-governed, t_i' would be a trace not properly governed, unless some mechanism for voiding the barrier were available. Let us postpone the question whether adjunction to VP would be such a possibilty and assume for the sake of the argument that it is a minimality effect that discriminates (19) against (20). Is it possible that the verb-second movement in (20) neutralizes this effect?

The paradigm case of removing a barrier induced by minimality is the treatment of passive and raising in ch.11 of *Barriers*. Considering the structure of

John seems to be intelligent

as given in (22)

(22) $[_{I''}$ *John*$_i$ $[_{I'}$ *seem*-I$_j$ $[_{VP}$ t$_j$ $[_{I'}$ t$_i$ $[_{I'}$ *to be intelligent*]]]]]

Chomsky argues as follows: VP is a barrier for t_i by the Minimality Condition. Voiding the barrier by adjunction to VP, an option open in cases of wh-movement, is not possible; it would be a case of "improper movement" ruled out by condition C of the binding theory, as in the "super-raising" case (23)

(23)   *John seems that it appears* [t *to be intelligent*]

which is, therefore, correctly excluded as an ECP-violation.

In (22) *seem* is moved into the head-position of IP, where it enters into the relation "SPEC-head agreement" with *John*, conceived of as the sharing of an abstract feature F. Assimilating feature sharing to chain coindexing, SPEC-head agreement implies the identification of two chain-indices, i.e., the index of *John* is identified with the index of *seem*-I, i=j. In (22), then,

t_i is governed by and coindexed with t_j, the trace of the raised verb. In order to fulfill the conditions of antecedent-government, it must be possible to treat t_j and t_i as members of the same chain. Therefore the concept "extended chain" is introduced according to which ($seem$-I_j, t_j, t_i) forms a chain in the extended sense. Being governed by a chain-comember, t_i is now, as required, properly governed.

As pointed out by Chomsky, the relation of SPEC-head agreement as sharing of an abstract feature, ultimately indistinguishable from a chain index, does not only hold between specifier and head of an IP but also between specifier and head of CP.

Applying this concept to (20), the structure of (1), repeated below,

(20) $[_{CP}$ wen_i $[_{C'}$ $behauptet_j$ $[_{IP}$ $Hans$ t_j $[_{CP}$ t_i' $[_{C'}$ $habe$ $[_{IP}$ $Maria$ t_i $getroffen]]]]]]$

we can say that being moved by verb-second movement to the head of CP, $behauptet_j$ enters into the index-sharing relation of SPEC-head agreement with wen_i. The resulting index-unification identifies the indices i and j, t_i' becomes a member of the extended chain ($behauptet_j$, t_j, t_i'), in which it is antecedent-governed and consequently properly governed by t_j, the minimality barrier being voided.

But let us come back to the question why (3) with its structure (19) is ungrammatical at all. If the intermediate trace is protected against antecedent-government by minimality, this should, according to *Barriers*, not have any deteriorating effects, because the trace t_i in the basic position is θ-governed and therefore properly governed by *getroffen*. Intermediate traces are subject to the ECP only if they have to be present in LF. This aspect of the approach of Lasnik and Saito (1984) has been fully integrated into the system of *Barriers*. But intermediate traces of items whose basic position is θ-governed don't appear to have any LF-functions, so they are non-existent for the ECP. They have only to be members of chains whose links are not interrupted by barriers against movement, thus obeying subjacency. Minimality, however, induces only barriers against antecedent-government.

The point is illustrated by the contrast of the following examples of *Barriers*:

(25)   *how_i did John announce $[_{NP}$ a plan $[_{CP}$ t_i^2 $[to$ $[_{VP}$ t_i^1 fix the car $t_i]]]]$

(26)   which car did John announce $[_{NP}$ a plan $[_{CP}$ t^2 $[to$ $[t^1$ fix $t]]]]$

In (25), *plan* induces by minimality a barrier against antecedent-government of the intermediate adjunct trace t_i^2, resulting in an ECP-violation. In (26), the same configuration has no effect, the trace t^2 being nonexistent in LF.

Thus (3) ought to be completely unexceptionable, what is more, there should be a sharp contrast between (3) and (5), repeated below.

(3)   * *Ich weiß nicht, wen_i Hans [behauptet [t_i habe [Maria t_i' getroffen]]]*

(5)   * *Ich weiß nicht, wie_i er [meint [t_i habe [Maria t_i' das Problem gelöst]]]*

4. Two alternative solutions

The strong deviance of both sentences and the lack of any contrast between them suggests the following alternative ways of solving the problem:

1. The intermediate trace before *habe* which is the offending one occupies a special position — the German 'prefield.' It has to obey the ECP already at S-structure and can thus not be absent at LF. The barrier protecting the trace could then either be 'normal' or induced by minimality, causing in both cases an ECP-violation.

2. The intermediate trace before *habe* can be treated along the lines of Lasnik and Saito, i.e., owing to the different levels at which the ECP becomes effective for traces of adjuncts and arguments, the offending trace is present in the LF-structure of (5), but absent and thus exempted from antecedent-government in the LF-structure of (3).

4.1 *First alternative: the German 'prefield' is exceptional*

Let us consider the first alternative: The importance of the German 'prefield'-position in verb-second complements for the assessment of the proposal of Lasnik and Saito has already been demonstrated by H.Haider (1986). He observes that the expletive *es*, the obligatory default-filler of the 'prefield' or specifier of CP in verb-second sentences, as exemplified in (27),

(27)   *Er sagte zu ihr, *(es) sei dem Prüfer kein Fehler aufgefallen*
          'He said to her that the examiner did not notice any error'

can not be inserted, if the 'prefield' is used as an escape hatch for wh-movement, cf. (28) and (29):

(28)   *Wem$_i$ sagte er zu ihr (*es) sei e$_i$ kein Fehler aufgefallen?*
        'Who did he say to her did not notice any error'

(29)   *Warum$_i$ sagte er zu ihr, (*es) sei dem Prüfer kein Fehler e$_i$
        aufgefallen?*
        'Why did he say to her the examiner did not notice the
        error?'

This is unexpected in the complement-extraction case (28), if we assume, following Lasnik and Saito, that semantically inert items can be inserted freely into empty positions and that traces not needed for antecedent-government can be deleted or omitted in S-structure before the ECP takes effect for arguments at S-structure level. Again, no difference between adjunct- and complement-extraction can be observed.

In the framework of *Barriers*, it does not seem that we are forced to allow free insertion into trace positions not needed for antecedent-government. We might take the option that trace-deletion takes place not earlier than in LF. But the lack of contrast beween adjunct- and complement-extraction remains to be explained.

If we assume, following Chomsky in ch.11. of *Barriers*, that θ-government without antecedent-government is not sufficient for proper government, the lack of contrast mentioned would not be unexpected, provided that adjunction to VP is ruled out in German. And that could be motivated as follows: Again following the analysis of raising and passive in *Barriers*, we could say that movement of the head of VP into the head of IP (INFL) results in L-marking of the VP, voiding its barrierhood, but simultaneously barring adjunction to VP because of visibility for θ-assignment.

Chomsky does not take the last step for English, but we might motivate it for German by observing that the German INFL, unlike the English one, does not have independent d-structural representatives, like the English modals which, not being lexical, can not L-mark their VP-sister. Thus, whereas according to *Barriers* English VPs are sometimes L-marked, sometimes not, the same would not have to be assumed for German, since filling the head of IP by a verbal head originating from the VP is always necessary.

We might even add that moving VP-heads (except *be* and *have*) is doubtful for English in view of the fact that lexical verbs do not appear in the head of CP, cf.(30).

(30)   *[*Which boy*$_k$ [*loves*$_i$ [*she* t$_i$' [t$_i$ t$_k$]]]]]

So it might be asked whether VP-adjunction is possible in English because English VPs are never L-marked. Otherwise the lack of iterated head-movement of lexical verbs would have to be accounted for.

To sum up: If antecedent-government is necessary also for argument traces and VP-adjunction is not available, then the specifier of CP is the first position from which traces inside IP can be antecedent-governed. Skipping this position would thus violate the ECP, the CP becoming a barrier by inheritance. The lack of contrast in Haiders examples and also between (4) and (6), repeated here,

(4)   *_Ich weiß nicht, wen   Hans behauptet, Maria habe_
         I   know not   whom John claims   Mary   has
         getroffen
         met

(6)   *_Ich weiß nicht, wie er meint, Maria habe das Problem_
         I   know not   how he thinks Mary has   the problem
         gelöst
         solved

could thus be explained without modifying the framework of "Barriers," provided that we could rule out deleting *es* in LF and inserting an appropriately indexed trace instead, thereby incorrectly allowing (29). By stipulating that traces can only be created by movement we can effect this.

What still has to be explained, is the lack of contrast between (3) and (5), repeated here.

(3)   *_Ich weiß nicht, wen_$_i$ _Hans_ [_behauptet_ [t$_i$ _habe_ [Maria t$_i$'
         getroffen]]]

(5)   *_Ich weiß nicht, wie_$_i$ _er_ [_meint_ [t$_i$ _habe_ [Maria t$_i$' _das Problem_
         gelöst]]]

Assuming as above that the offending trace is protected by minimality, we can only rule out (5), because the intermediate trace of *wie*$_i$ must be antecedent-governed, but not (3), since the extraction site of *wen*$_i$ already possesses the government-feature $[+\Gamma]$ by assignment at S-structure level. What seems to be required, is that the intermediate trace t$_i$ of *wen*$_i$ gets assigned a government-feature at S-structure level too, which would be $[-\Gamma]$ because of minimality. In other words, traces in CP-specifiers functioning as 'prefields' have to be treated on par with traces in A-positions. That would mean that the class of traces subject to the ECP already at S-structure level can not be specified only on the basis of the Projection Principle. It is unclear how to avoid a stipulative solution.

A minor problem resulting from our ruling out adjunction to VP in German is connected with the present formulation of the Minimality Condition. If antecedent-government is necessary for proper government and barriers by minimality cannot be voided by adjunction, then every extraction out of VP would violate the ECP. Assuming, that there are no cases in which it is necessary to protect complement- or adjunct-positions by minimality-barriers induced by their sister-heads, which seems to be correct, we can add the following clause to the Minimality Condition:

(31)   Addition to *Minimality*: β does not m-command δ.

In the System of *Barriers*, but not in our presently considered modification of it, the addition could be used to cancel the restriction of the Minimality Condition to non-IP-heads, since if adjunction to VP is available, adjoining an item to VP causes it to be no longer included by the respective VP and thus to m-command the next higher IP-head, as shown in (32):

(32) $[_{IP}...[_{I'}$ I $[_{VP}$ α $[_{VP}...]]]]$ (α is not included in VP, α m-commands I).

So adjunction to VP would not only void a VP-barrier, but simultaneously also an eventual I'-barrier induced by INFL.

The addition can be motivated, apart from our special needs. For without it the following example, borrowed from Grewendorf (1986),

(33)   *eine Frau,* [*die   zu küssen*] *Hubert* [[$_{NP}$ *den Versuch* t]
        a   woman which to kiss   Hubert   the attempt
        unternommen] *hat.*
        made.
        'a woman which Hubert tried to kiss.'

would incorrectly be ruled out, if we would stick to antecedent-government. For then the noun *Versuch* would protect the trace t against government by [*die zu küssen*]. Conversely, the example (34)

(34)   **Welche Frau$_i$ hat Hubert* [$_{NP}$ *den Versuch* [$_{CP}$ t$_i$ *zu küssen*]]
        unternommen?

starred by Grewendorf, could be excluded by assuming that *Versuch* by minimality protects the trace in the specifier of the infinite CP against gov-

ernment. As above, it would be necessary to assume, that the extraction's
site being θ-governed does not cancel the offending character of the intermediate trace. But since the judgements are not stable in this case, it is
perhaps not necessary to rule out (34) by the ECP.

Example (33) poses a problem in that the verbal head *unternommen*
unexpectedly does not induce a barrier by minimality, suggesting that
adjunction to VP is indispensible in German after all. But the contrast of
(33) with (35)

(35)   **eine Frau,*   [*die   zu küssen*] *Hubert* [[*den Versuch* t]
         a   woman, which to kiss   Hubert the attempt to kiss
         getadelt hat
         reprimanded has

shows that adjunction to VP can not be the solution, since it would incorrectly allow (35). Considering that *den Versuch unternehmen* in contrast to
den Versuch tadeln functions as a simple verb (*versuchen*), we might say
that the argument-status of the NP den Versuch in *den Versuch unternehmen* is obliterated and that it is therefore licit to adjoin to this NP,
thereby leaving a trace which m-commands the verbal head *unternommen*
und thus voids the minimality barrier. But that is only possible if our addition to the definition of Minimality is adopted.

4.2 *Second alternative: head-marking instead of L-marking*

Let us now consider the second alternative mentioned above, i.e., to
rule out (5), but not (3),

(3)   **Ich weiß nicht, wen$_i$ Hans* [*behauptet* [t$_i$ *habe* [*Mari t$_i$'*
         getroffen]]]

(5)   **Ich weiß nicht, wie$_i$ er* [*meint* [t$_i$ *habe* [*Maria* t$_i$' *das Problem*
         gelöst]]]

as an ECP-violation and to explain the deviance of (3) by a lack of subjacency, adopting the approach of Lasnik and Saito along the lines of *Barriers*. As remarked above, this is only possible if the barrier protecting the
intermediate trace is not erected by Minimality, but either by a blocking
category or by inheritance.

Now, if the VP is a blocking category, it can surely be voided, as is tes-
tified by simple short distance movements like (36)

(36)   *Ich weiß nicht, warum Hans nicht gearbeitet hat*
         I   don't know why   Hans did not work

It remains, then, that in (3) and (5) the CP which depends on *behauptet* is
a blocking category. That would mean that θ-marking by a lexical head in
sister-position (i.e., L-marking) is not sufficient for ruling out a blocking
category. We would thus have to alter the relevant definitions.

As seen above, in ch.11 of *Barriers* an attempt is made to get rid of the
disjunctive character of proper government and to create a unified concept
by restricting proper government to antecedent-government. The dependence of the concept of proper government on θ-marking is still not completely eliminated, θ-marking figuring as an ingredient in L-marking and
thus in the concept of barrier, which in its turn is used in defining government. A consequence of this remaining dependence of government theory
on θ-marking is the exceptional status of IP which, being never L-marked,
is always a blocking category and must therefore be excluded from the class
of inherent barriers by stipulation, in order to cope with wh-movement.

If IP could be included in the class of potential inherent barriers, new
light could be thrown on a number of verb-second phenomena. For suppose
that IP is a barrier, if its sister CP-head does not harbor any features, but is
completely empty. Then any movement into the specifier of CP would be
stigmatized, as indicated in (37) (direct question reading)

(37)   a.   *$[Welches Buch_i [[][_{IP} er\ t_i\ geschrieben\ hat]]]$
       b.   *$[Which book_i [[][_{IP} he\ has\ written\ t_i]]]$.

Verb-second movement, conceived of as head to head movement into the
head of CP, would then result in voiding the IP-barrier, in the same manner
in which in *Barriers* (ch.11) movement of a verb into the head of IP is
analysed as voiding the inherent barrier of VP, cf. (37')

(37') a. $[Welches Buch_i [[hat_k][_{IP} er\ t_i\ geschrieben\ t_k]]]$
       b. $[Which book_i [[has_k][_{IP} he\ t_k\ written\ t_i]]]$

What counts, is the configuration after, not before movement.

The asymmetries of dependent and matrix clauses with respect to verb-
second phenomena could be treated as follows: the heads of subcategorized
CPs, e.g., indirect questions, bear features, therefore the sister-IP is not a
barrier, wh-movement being possible without verb-second. That verb-second is not only unnecessary, but in some languages also impossible under
such circumstances, e.g., Sub-Aux-Inversion in English dependent ques-

tions and related constructions in other languages, would have to be accounted for by feature incompatibilities.

For the case of German verb-second complements, we will assume that their heads are empty in the base, otherwise verb-second would not be possible. So here we have the surely marked possibility of subcategorized, hence θ-marked, complements without selected head-features. And this marked property, so we assume, qualifies them as barriers qua blocking categories. The contrast in (38)

> (38) a.   *mein Glaube, mir werde eine Lösung einfallen*
>   b.   ** my belief I would find a solution*

could be seen as supporting this analysis: as the English example seems to show, nouns are too weak as governors to licence the English null-complementizer (cf.Stowell 1981, Longobardi 1987), which has features requiring head-selection, but, as the German example shows, nouns are strong enough to admit featureless CP-heads which can be filled by verb-second.

The requirements just pointed out can be fulfilled by modifying the Barrier-system as follows:

Head-marking:

> α head-marks β iff   1. α is a non-empty zero-level category
>
> 2. There is a Γ, Γ a sister of α, such that α selects or is coindexed with the head of Γ and β agrees with the head of Γ.

In normal cases, we have:

> α head-marks β, in case
>
> 1. α is a non-empty zero-level category
> 2. α is a sister of β that selects or is coindexed with the head of β.

Blocking Category:

> Where Γ is a maximal projection,
> Γ is a blocking category for β iff
>
> 1. Γ includes β;
> 2. Γ is not head-marked

Barrier ("BM"):

> Where α is a maximal projection,
> α is a barrier for β, β included by α, iff (a) or (b):
>
> a. β does not m-command the head of α
> b. α is a blocking category for β.

Note that we do not assume, as in the second alternative above, that adjunction to VP is excluded in German. Otherwise we would have to alter clause a. of our barrier-definition.

The relation between the original definition in *Barriers* and the modified one ("*BM*" for short) is as follows: Every barrier by inheritance is a barrier according to *BM*, clause a. For assume that Γ is a barrier by inheritance for β. Γ, then, immediately includes δ, δ a blocking category for β. Hence, δ must be a maximal projection including β. So β, being included in a maximal projection included in Γ, cannot m-command the head of Γ. Hence, Γ is a barrier according to *BM* a. too.

The converse does not hold, however, for there are barriers according to *BM* which are not barriers according to the original definition. A case in point is (39) (= (72)(a) in *Barriers*)

(39)   *which book$_i$ did John hear* [$_{NP}$ *a rumor* [$_{CP}$ t$_i$' *that you read* t$_i$]]

where a violation of subjacency has to be assumed, yet no barrier is crossed according to the original definition (cf. *Barriers* p.35.). According to the modified version *BM*, the NP *a rumor* is a barrier for the intermediate trace t$_i$', since this trace does not m-command the head of *a rumor*.

On the other hand, the contrast between (40) and (41), correctly predicted by the original definition (cf. *Barriers* p.26), is not predicted by the modified version, unless adjunction to *qué traducciones* in (41) is allowed.

(40)   **esta es la autora* [*de la que*]$_i$ [$_{IP}$[*varias traducciones* t$_i$] *han ganado premios internacionales*]

(41)   [*de que autora*]$_i$ *no sabes* [$_{CP}$ [*qué traducciones* t$_i$] *han ganado premios internacionales*]

The strict locality of head-movement is correctly predicted by our modified version. In *Barriers* (p.68) the illicit long head-extraction in (40)

(40)   [*how tall*]$_j$ *be*$_i$ [$_{IP}$ *John* [$_{I'}$ *will* [$_{VP}$ t$_i$ t$_j$]]]

is ruled out because the VP is not L-marked, *will* not being lexical. According to our modified version, IP is a barrier for t$_i$, because the trace does not m-command the head of IP (i.e., *will*).

Let us come back to the examples (3) and (5), repeated below:

(3)   **Ich weiß nicht, wen*$_i$ *Hans* [*behauptet* [$_{CP}$ t$_i$ *habe* [*Maria* t$_i$' *getroffen*]]]

(5)   *Ich $wei\beta$ $nicht,$ wie_i er [$meint$ [t_i $habe$ [$_{CP}$ $Maria$ t_i' das $Problem$ $gel\ddot{o}st$]]]

In both examples the most deeply embedded CP is a barrier by lack of head-marking resulting in a violation of subjacency in the case of (3) and a violation of the ECP in (5). In the case of (1) with its structure (20), repeated below,

(20)   [$_{CP}$ wen_i [$_{C'}$ $behauptet_j$ [$_{IP}$ $Hans$ t_j[$_{CP}$$t_i$' [$_{C'}$ $habe_k$ [$_{IP}$ $Maria$ t_i $getroffen$]]]]]]

the index j of the chain headed by $behauptet$ is identified with the index i of the chain headed by wen because of SPEC-head agreement, which is made available by verb-second movement, as pointed out above. The index i has been unified by SPEC-head agreement with the index k of $habe$. So, by transitivity, the index j of $behauptet$ is ultimately unified with the index k of $habe$ and the CP is now head-marked.

References

Abraham, W.(ed.). 1985. *Erklärende Syntax des Deutschen.* Tübingen: Narr.

Chomsky, N. 1986. *Barriers.* Cambridge, Mass.: MIT Press.

den Besten, H. 1977. "On the Interaction of Root Transformations and Lexical Deletive Rules." Ms., University of Amsterdam.

Grewendorf, G. 1986. "Relativsätze im Deutschen: Die Rattenfänger-konstruktion." *Linguistische Berichte* 105:409-434.

———. 1988. *Aspekte der deutschen Syntax. Eine Rektions-Bindungs-Analyse.* Tübingen: Narr.

Haider, H. 1984. "Topic, focus, and V-second." *Groninger Arbeiten zur Germanistischen Linguistik* (25): 72-120.

———. 1986. "Affect α: A Reply to Lasnik and Saito, "On the Nature of Proper Government"." *Linguistic Inquiry* 17: 113-126.

———. 1989. *Parameter der deutschen Syntax.* Tübingen: Narr.

Lasnik, H. and M. Saito 1984. "On the Nature of Proper Government." *Linguistic Inquiry* 14: 554-561.

Longobardi, G. 1987. "Extraction from NP and the Proper Notion of Head Government." Ms. Scuola Normale Superiore, Pisa.

Reis, M. 1983. "Satzeinleitende Strukturen im Deutschen." Ms. University of Cologne. (Revised version in: Abraham (ed.)).

Stowell, T. 1981. "Origins of Phrase Structure." Diss., Massachusetts Institute of Technology.

Thiersch, C. 1978. "Topics in German Syntax." Diss., Massachusetts Institute of Technology.

Interpretive Islands: Evidence for Connectedness and Global Harmony in Logical Form*

Josef Bayer

Max-Planck-Institute for Psycholinguistics, Nijmegen

0. Introduction

The goal of this article is to show how certain problems of German syntax can find a natural solution in a theory which has become known over the last few years as Connectedness Theory (CT). I want to make clear from the very beginning, however, that CT is used here in a rather loose sense, to refer to a class of theoretical developments. It should therefore not be expected that the analyses presented in this paper can be cast in any one fixed version of CT. The common core of these theoretical approaches is that non-local dependencies should be derived from local dependencies.

The problems that I will address arise from cases of ungrammaticality, which are prima facie unexpected from the viewpoint of standard Government and Binding Theory. My starting point in approaching the phenomenological array is the behavior of so-called "scalar" or "quantificational" particles like *only* and *even*. While these words have attracted a great deal of attention by semanticists, they have received very little attention from syntacticians. As I hope to show in this article, the lack of con-

---

* For their theoretical advice and/or discussion of my blurred data I would like to thank the following colleagues: Manfred Bierwisch, Melissa Bowerman, Ad Foolen, Liliane Haegeman, Hans Peter Kolb, Ewald Lang, Andreas Lötscher, Janet Randall, Henk van Riemsdijk, Arnim von Stechow and Craig Thiersch. Thanks also to Yves Fuchs who has worked on various versions of the text, Inge Tarim for the graphics and Lee-Ann Weeks for checking my English. First and foremost, however, I am indebted to Wolfgang Sternefeld whose comments on the entire chapter led to various improvements. Needless to say that all remaining errors are mine.

tributions from recent developments in syntax may be understandable only insofar as CT is left aside. The gist of my arguments will be that the syntax and logical form (LF) of particles is constrained by largely the same principles that constrain overt syntactic movement; principles which themselves derive from such basic notions as "direction of government," "g(overnement) projection," etc.

Most of the empirical problems to be treated here were brought to the attention of linguists working on German by Jacobs (1983). As should become clear, I owe a lot to this work, although I disagree with certain conclusions drawn by Jacobs.

The article is organized as follows: Section 1 introduces a number of problems that arise when we make the natural assumption that *only, even*, etc. may adjoin to any major syntactic category. Section 2 introduces the relevant part of the theory of Jacobs (1983). Section 3 contains the major arguments of the article. In 3.1 several conditions are discussed under which the islandhood of PPs for proper scope assignment can be dissolved. In 3.2, complex-NP constructions are dealt with, which are also islands for the scope assignment of *only* and *even*. Sections 3.1 and 3.2 are close in spirit to CT in the sense of Kayne (1983); the most important issue there is how an illicit path can connect to a licit path. In 3.3 we will have a close look at directionality of government and the formation of extraction domains in the sense of Koster (1987). Section 3.4 is a slight deviation from the general course of this article. It will be argued there that certain ill-formed coordinations involving particles can possibly be ruled out on quite independent semantic grounds. Section 3.5 deals with constraints on rightward movement. The instances of rightward movement are basically extraposition and verb raising. The article ends with a brief comparison of German and English with respect to the scope of scalar particles such as *only* and *even* in rightward movement.

1.   Some Problems with Particle-Adjunction

I want to argue — in agreement with traditional grammar — that particles like *only* and *even* may adjoin to any major constituent. This constituent then counts as the syntactic domain of the particle. There are two possibilities: Either the domain coincides with the focus of the particle, or the focus is a proper part of this domain. This is exemplified in the following two examples.

(1) a. *John loves [only [MARY]]*
     b. *John would [only [go to ENGLAND]]*

In (1a), *only* adjoins to an NP which is both its domain and the only focus constituent within this domain. In (1b) *only* adjoins to the VP *go to England*, but the focus constituent is *England* — a proper part of the adjunction domain.

One of the most reliable facts about German syntax is the "V-second constraint" or simply "V2." It means that in a root sentence there should be one and at most one constituent before the verb. V2 serves in various ways as a test for constituency in German syntax. We will use it here to argue that the combination [Particle + XP] forms a single syntactic constituent. If such a string can occur before the finite verb in a root sentence, it must be a single constituent at some level of representation. If it cannot occur there, we have good evidence that this string only appears to be a constituent. The following examples clearly show that [Particle + XP] is a constituent.

(2) a. *[Nur den Hund] hat Hans gefüttert*
         only the dog:ACC has Hans fed
         'It was only the dog that Hans had fed'

     b. *[Nur gefüttert] hat Hans den Hund*
         'Hans had only fed the dog (... he hadn't done anything else with the dog)'

     c. *[Nur den Hund gefüttert] hat Hans*
         'Hans had only fed the dog (... he hadn't done anything else)'

     d. *[Nur daß der Kanzler   zu dick sei] hat Hans gesagt*
         only that he chancellor too fat is   has Hans said
         'The only thing Hans said was that the chancellor is too fat'

In the following section we will address some problems with the adjunction account as pointed out in Jacobs (1983).

1.1 *Extraposition*

A problem for the adjunction account becomes obvious from the following set of data.

(3)   *weil Hans nur gesagt hat* [*daß der Kanzler   zu dick*
        since Hans only said   has that the chancellor too fat
        sei]
        is

(4)   [*Nur daß der Kanzler   zu   dick sei*] *hat Hans gesagt*
        only that the chancellor too fat   is   has Hans said

(5)   **weil Hans gesagt hat* [*nur daß der Kanzler   zu   dick*
        since Hans said   has only that the chancellor too fat
        sei]
        is

In (4), *nur* adjoins to a CP which is also the focus of *nur*. (3) is unproblematic as well, because *nur* may adjoin to VP and select its focus (i.e., CP) within VP. This is shown in (6).

(6)

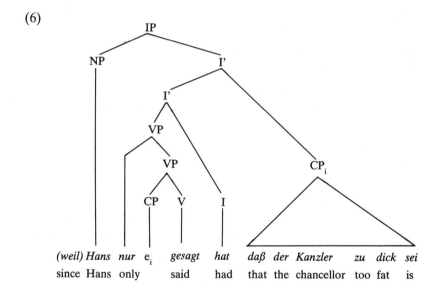

The question is: Why does extraposition of a *nur*-adjoined CP lead to ungrammaticality? This fact is unexpected, because the grammar must allow for [particle + CP] constituents, as shown in (4).

1.2 *NP in PP*

Another problem that was noticed by Jacobs (1983) is the following: If [particle + NP] is a constituent of type NP, it should be able to appear in the governing domain of a preposition. As the following data show, this holds in English but not in German:

(7)   a.   *John would <u>only</u> go to* ENGLAND
      b.   *John would go <u>only</u> to* ENGLAND
      c.   *John would go to <u>only</u>* ENGLAND

(8)   a.   *weil   sie   <u>nur</u>   mit   dem* OPA   *plaudert*
          since she   only with the   grandfather chats
      b. **weil   sie   mit   <u>nur</u>   dem* OPA   *plaudert*
          since she   with only the   grandfather chats

(9)   a.   *weil   sie   <u>sogar</u> von der* KÖNIGIN *träumt*
          since she   even   of   the queen   dreams
      b. **weil   sie   von <u>sogar</u>   der* KÖNIGIN *träumt*
          since she   of   even   the queen   dreams

1.3 *Genitive-NPs*

A similar problem appears in genitive constructions. The position NP__ is an environment into which in German genitive Case is assigned. Thus if [particle + NP] is a constituent, it should be able to appear in this environment. The facts again contradict this expectations.

(10)   a.   *weil   sie   <u>nur</u>   den Sohn des*   GRAFEN *liebt*
           since she   only the son   (of)the count   loves
      b. **weil sie den Sohn <u>nur</u> des* GRAFEN *liebt*

(11)   a.   *weil   sie   <u>sogar</u> die Schuhe der*   KINDER   *putzt*
           since she   even   the shoes   (of)the children   polishes
      b. ?**weil sie die Schuhe <u>sogar</u> der* KINDER *putzt*

1.4 *Coordination*

Judgements on the following examples are less clear cut, but it is still surprising that [particle + NP] cannot freely undergo coordination with a bare NP.

(12) a.   *weil nur Peter und Luise spazieren gehen*
          since only Peter and Luise for a walk go
     b. ?? *weil Peter und nur Luise spazieren gehen*

(13) a.   *weil Gerd sogar Peter und Luise traf*
          since Gerd even   Peter and Luise met
     b. ?? *weil Gerd Peter und sogar Luise traf*

Of course, the a-sentences are well-formed because the syntactic domain of
nur and *sogar* may be the coordinate NPs, i.e.,

(14)

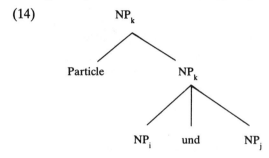

In the b-sentences, however, a bare NP is coordinated with a [particle +
NP]-type NP. Free adjunction of the particles generates such cases.

I will argue below that in spite of the problems mentioned in sections
1.1 through 1.4, the adjunction analysis can be maintained in full general-
ity, and that the problem cases can be ruled out on independent grounds.
Although we will argue for a solution which is totally different from the one
proposed by Jacobs (1983), it should be clear that Jacobs' major insights
will be maintained. In order to make this transparent, it is necessary to give
a brief introduction to the syntax part of Jacobs' work.

2.   Jacobs' (1983) Account

Jacobs distinguishes three notions which are essential for any sound
theory of particles. These are *syntactic domain, scope* and *focus*. The syntactic domain of a particle X is the (sub)tree Y with which X forms a constituent; that is, another (sub)tree Y.

(15)   *John only [goes to England]*

In (15), the bracketed phrase is the syntactic domain of the particle *only*.
Scope is determined by the "logical" properties of the particles in question.

Only and *even* clearly have quantifier properties. Thus, like all quantifiers, they select the entire proposition (corresponding to the sentence) as their semantic domain. In this sense, (15) would translate into something like

(16)   Only x, x = go to England (John does x)

Finally, the selection of focus determines which constituent (within the syntactic domain) is particularly "affected" by the particle. (See Jackendoff, 1972:section 6.5). If the focus is on *England*, for example, (16) may be such that *only* binds the focus or that the focus constituent gets raised in LF along with *only*.

(17) a.   Only (John goes to ENGLAND)
      b.   Only x, x=England (John goes to x)

The novelty in Jacobs' account is that — for the various reasons alluded to in sections 1.1 through 1.4 — the syntactic domain for particles is confined to V-projections. Jacobs adopts a (transformationally slightly enriched) categorial syntax along the lines of Montague's PTQ. The sentence is the highest projection of V, and particles adjoin exclusively to a projection of V. Thus, in terms of X'-theory particles can adjoin either to V^0, V', V" or V"'. The following example should suffice to show how this works.[1]

(18)   *(daß) Luise <u>nur</u> ihrem   ARZT   ein Auto vermachte*
          that   Luise only (to) her doctor a   car   donated

Instead of assigning (18) a phrase structure in which *nur ihrem* ARZT forms a constituent, the representation is the following.[2]

(19)

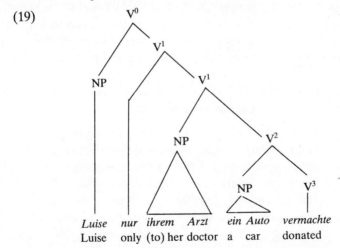

Luise	nur	ihrem	Arzt	ein Auto	vermachte
Luise	only	(to) her doctor		a car	donated

In (19), the syntactic domain of *nur* is V^1, a traditional VP. Notice that within such a framework each step in the syntactic composition corresponds to a step in the semantic composition. This may be seen as a well-motivated aspect of such an approach in that *nur ihrem Arzt* cannot be associated with a meaning in the same way as *ihrem Arzt* can. On the other hand, there is a less favorable consequence for the overall theory of German syntax, which Jacobs discusses in detail.[3] This has to do with the fact that the under-lying structure (18) can surface as (20).

(20)   *Nur ihrem ARZT vermachte Luise ein Auto.*

Now, if *nur* can only adjoin to a V-projection, the representation of (20) must be as follows.

(21)

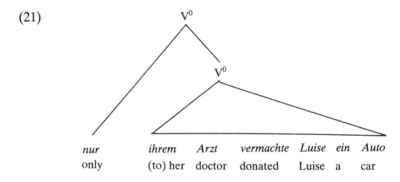

nur	ihrem	Arzt	vermachte	Luise	ein	Auto
only	(to) her	doctor	donated	Luise	a	car

In (21) the finite verb *vermachte* is preceded by two constituents, *nur* and *ihrem Arzt*, that is, we get the verb as the third constituent in the sentence. Jacobs is willing to accept this consequence and treat cases with particles preceding the finite verb in root sentences as exceptions to the V2-con-straint. Certain deviations from this general proposal have to be allowed, however, specifically cases where the particle is in fact inside a non-V-pro-jection; examples in which the particle serves what Jacobs calls an "ad-pre-dicative" and "ad-article" function are given below.

(22) a.   *Peter gilt   als nur MÄSSIG   intelligent*
            Peter counts as only moderately intelligent

      b.   *Peter ist ein nur WENIG begabter Komponist*
            Peter is a   only little gifted   composer

      c.   *Die meisten der   Prüfer   hielten   Gerdas*
            (The) most of the examiners considered Gerda's
            Leistung   für nur DURCHSCHNITTLICH
            achievement as only mediocre

(23) a. *Die Polizei geht von nur EINEM bewaffneten Täter   aus*
          The police goes from only one armed   criminal out
          'The police assume that only one armed criminal was
          involved'
      b. *Die Sanierung nur   EINER Altbauwohnung machte*
          The renovation (of)only one old-apartment   made
          ihn zum   Millionär
          him (into a) millionair

The interesting thing in the above examples is that *nur* must select the
immediately following word as its focus. Otherwise the examples are
severely ungrammatical.

(24) a. ** Peter gilt als nur mäßig INTELLIGENT*
      b. ** Die Polizei geht von nur einem BEWAFFNETEN Täter aus*

Moreover, the constituents that serve as the focus of *nur* are consistently of
a special type. They are, themselves, quantifiers[4]. For example, *ein*, which
in German is ambiguous between the indefinite article and the numeral
'one,' can only have the numerical interpretation in this particular context.

   Although Jacobs' work covers a lot of interesting ground and provides
us with some insights into the operation of quantificational particles, e.g.
that they must have access to the V-projection, this work nevertheless
leaves us with a distorted picture of German syntax. The largest problem is
the violation of the V2-constraint. My feeling is that this constraint (or
whatever it derives from) should only be abandoned in the face of the
strongest sort of counterevidence. Jacobs' list of problems with unlimited
adjunction that were mentioned in sections 1.1 through 1.4 is impressive,
but considering the amount of exceptions he is forced to allow into the syntax it is certainly not enough to abandon the V2-constraint. Let us therefore
see how the problem cases can be accounted for under a description of German syntax in which particles can freely adjoin to any major syntactic category.

3.   An alternative consistent with adjunction to X^n

   In the following I will adopt a level of syntactic representation which
became known as "Logical Form" (LF). LF provides a structure that can be
interpreted semantically and provides information which is not available
from either the D-structure or S-structure levels of representation, in other

words, a structure from which structural ambiguities and scope options can directly be read off. I will show that an LF-account of the phenomena noted in sections 1.1 through 1.4 covers a much wider range of data than considered up to this point and that LF as a level of linguistic representation is therefore given additional empirical support. I will adopt the rule of quantifier raising (QR) as proposed by May (1977, 1985). QR is a sub-rule of the rule move-alpha which applies in the derivation of S-structures. As the name says, QR moves a quantified (or other scope-sensitive) expression to a place where it c-commands its semantic scope. To take one familiar example, QR raises the quantified NP in

(25)   *John saw everyone*

and adjoins it to the highest node (which we take, following Chomsky (1986) to be a maximal projection of I(NFL)):

(26) $[_{IP}$ Everyone$_i$ $[_{IP}$ John saw e$_i]]$

Only, even, are quantifiers in the sense that they map the entity that corresponds to their focus constituent on some mental scale. Thus, a sentence such as

(27)   *Even JOHN smokes cigars*

induces a scale onto which people may be mapped with respect to their likelihood of cigar-smoking. What (27) then says is that John ranges low on such a scale. Take another example,

(28)   *John smokes even CIGARS*

Here the ontological domain of *even* consists of things that are being smoked. In the ordering of these things, cigars range very low. The LF-representations for (27) and (28) are roughly as follows:

(29) $[_{IP}$ Even John$_i$ $[_{IP}$ e$_i$ smokes cigars]]

(30) $[_{IP}$ Even cigars$_i$ $[_{IP}$ John smokes e$_i]]$

Since I am not concerned here with the lexical semantics of *only* and *even* etc., I will not delve any deeper into the issues of the properties of such scales.[5]

Let us now look back at the problems with free adjunction of particles which were addressed in sections 1.1 through 1.4.

3.1 NP in PP

As we have seen in the discussion of Jacobs' work, quantificational particles can, in principle, appear inside a PP. In an earlier proposal, Bayer (1985), I argued that the difference between (31) and (32):

(31)   *weil sie mit <u>nur</u> dem OPA   plaudert
          since she with only the   grandfather chats

(32)   weil sie mit <u>nur</u> EINEM Opa plaudert
                                       one

can be derived from Case theory. A filter was invoked which said that in PPs the Case assigner has to be adjacent to the head of the assignee in the sense that it should not be separated from the head by a non-inflecting category. Since *nur* does not belong to an inflecting category, it breaks the Case assignment process in (31), the structure being

(33)   ... [$_P$ mit [$_{NP}$ nur [$_{NP}$ dem Opa]]]

In (32), things are different, since *nur* adjoins to an inflecting category which is again adjacent to the head.

(34)   ... [$_P$ mit [$_{NP}$ [$_{DET}$ nur [$_{DET}$ einem]] Opa]]

A problem with this account is that it does not extend to all the other cases. Take the particle *ausgerechnet* ('exactly'). The following example does not sound bad to me, and yet a noninflecting particle intervenes between the NP and the Case-assigner.[6]

(35)   ?weil sie mit <u>ausgerechnet</u> dem OPA   plaudert
          since she with exactly   the   grandfather chatted

In any case, (35) is not bad enough to invoke a system as central to syntactic theory as Case Theory to handle it. Now, the interesting thing here is that *ausgerechnet* is not quantificational or "scalar" in the sense of *only* and *even*. *Ausgerechnet* has more the flavor of an attitude marker, although it is sometimes subsumed under the scalar particles.[7] On the other hand, uncontroversial scalar particles cannot be used in PPs, if they cannot adjoin to a quantificational determiner. The proper distinction to be drawn seems to be that only those particles that are affected by the rule QR lead to ungrammaticality when they are c-commanded by a preposition. This may suggest that PPs are islands for QR. However, as this statement stands, it is immediately falsified by the fact that other types of quantifier NPs inside PPs can undergo QR.

(36)   *Bill played with every kid*

(37)   [$_{IP}$ Every kid$_i$ [$_{IP}$ Bill played with e$_i$]]

We may speak of *all, every, both*, etc. as "primary quantifiers" because their lexical semantics is not context dependent in the sense that *only* and *even* are. Another reason to distinguish them from scalar particles is that they are not — like the particles — parasitic on a focus constituent. A third distinction appears only in inflecting languages like German or Russian. This is that *all, every, both* etc. inflect and thus may function as autonomous NPs, whereas *only, even* etc. to my knowledge never inflect even in inflecting languages. Let us therefore call quantificational or scalar particles "secondary quantifiers." Provided that particles like *ausgerechnet* may not be quantificational at all, we can state the following constraint, at least for the grammar of German:

(38)   (to be revised)
         PPs are islands for QR affecting secondary quantifiers

The constraint expressed in (38) rules out cases like (31), but it allows for cases like (32). The reason for the latter is that *nur* in (32) is parasitic on a primary quantifier. QR can raise *nur* together with the "primarily quantified" NP *einem Opa*.

Now I would like to turn to cases like (22c) which, for convenience, is repeated as (39).

(39)   *Die   meisten der   Prüfer   hielten   Gerdas*
         (The) most   (of)the examiners considered Gerda's
         Leistung   für nur DURCHSCHNITTLICH
         achievement as   only mediocre

Since *für* heads a PP and there is obviously no primary quantifier involved which could give *nur* a free ride as QR takes place, (39) seems to constitute a counterexample to the constraint in (38). This is, however, only an impression. *Durchschnittlich* denotes a property that induces a scale. Thus, there are reasons to assume that in such cases *nur* can range over this scale and does not need to be raised out of the PP. An analysis along these lines is supported by other examples in which *nur* focuses on NPs whose referents can easily be plotted on a scale. In such cases, the particle can always appear inside the PP, for example *Sie ist mit nur einem ARBEITER verheiratet* ('She is married with only a worker'). In this use, *nur* induces a prestige scale for professions and suggests that workers range low on such a scale.

As we will see below, the particle and its focus-NP cannot be raised out of the PP for good reasons. This does not do any harm here, however, because the particle can be interpreted in situ. It does not need the property expressed by the VP in order to quantify over a set of entities. A set of entities is already inherent in the scale induced by the NP-meaning.

Let us now return to those cases in which the syntactic domain of the particle does not contain a constituent that could by itself induce such a quantificational domain. Notice that *halten* in (39) in the sense of 'consider' is a lexical item which strictly subcategorizes for a *für*-PP. Although things in this area are far from settled, the overall effect of strict subcategorization of a specific P seems to be that the barrierhood of P is markedly reduced in such cases. Other examples are *denken an* ('think about'), *sich erinnern an* ('remember'), *achten auf* ('take notice of'). As the following examples show, particles are not completely impossible in these contexts:

(40) a. *Hans dachte nur(noch) an   den Käsekuchen*
          Hans thought only   about the cheese-pie
          'The only thing Hans still thought about was the cheese pie'
      b. ?? *Hans dachte an nur(noch) den Käsekuchen*

(41) a. *Emma erinnerte sich   sogar an   den   Urlaub*
          Emma remembered(refl.) even(prep) the   vacation
          'Emma remembered even the vacation'
      b. ?? *Emma erinnerte sich an sogar den Urlaub*

(42) a. *Der Gefangene achtete   zumindest auf den Polizisten*
          The captive   took-notice at least   of the policeman
          'The captive took at least notice of the policeman'
      b. ?? *Der Gefangene achtete auf zumindest den Polizisten*

The (b)-examples can be considerably improved if they are followed by *noch* ('still') or something similar. In order to account for the (b)-sentences as they stand, however, we assume that the lexicon specifies in one way or the other that P here is "in construction with" V. That is, we have a case that is very similar to the various reanalysis processes that have been proposed to account for cases of preposition-stranding.[8] Given this, the constraint in (38) should be changed to that in (43), where we leave — for the time being — the notion "in construction with" deliberately vague.

(43)   (to be revised)
          PPs are islands for QR affecting secondary quantifiers
          unless P is in construction with a governing V.

I would now like to draw attention to an observation that to my knowledge has never been addressed in the literature. I owe this observation to Ad Foolen (personal communication). There are cases where (43), as stated, makes wrong predictions. Note the following contrasts.

(44) a. *Das schafft   ein Normalbegabter   <u>nur</u> mit*
This achieves a   normally-gifted(person) only with
Studieren
studying
'A normally gifted person can achieve this only if (s)he studies'

b. **Das schafft ein Normalbegabter mit <u>nur</u> Studieren*

(45) a. *Das schafft   ein Normalbegabter   <u>nur</u> mit*
This achieves a   normally-gifted(person) only with
Studieren   nie
studying   never
'A normally gifted person will never achieve this with studying alone'

b. *Das schafft ein Normalbegabter mit <u>nur</u> Studieren nie*

Interestingly, the presence of the adverb *nie* makes (45b) acceptable. Recall now that something similar was found to be true for the (b)-examples of (40) through (42) above in connection with the presence of the particle *noch* ('still'). What might be the reason for this? Two things seem to be crucial. First, *nie* is itself a quantifier, meaning something like 'for no time t.' Thus, *nie* itself must undergo QR. Second, *nie* appears at S-structure lower in the tree and to the right of the problematic PP. Since V2 is irrelevant in this case, we will represent the S-structure of (45b) with the finite verb in its D-structure (end) position.

(46)

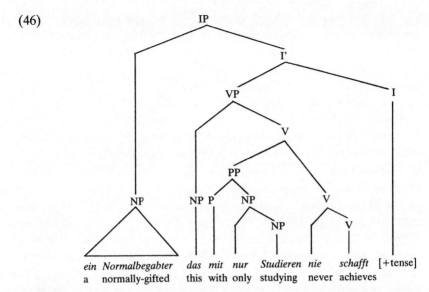

The syntactic domain of *nie* is *schafft*. German, however, also allows such adverbs to select a larger domain. An example is given in the next tree representation.

(47)

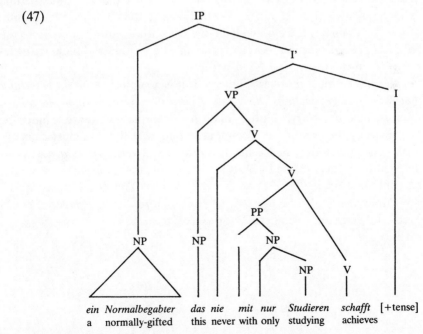

For me and some of my informants, (47) is markedly worse than (46). Given that in both cases QR moves *nie* and adjoins it to IP, the difference may be attributed to its position relative to the annoying PP. While the raising of *nie* crosses the PP in (46), it fails to do so in (47). This is reminiscent of Kayne's (1983) Connectedness Theory.

The essence of Connectedness Theory (CT) is that certain geometrical properties of phrase structure trees can account for the binding of empty categories by an antecedent or for the linking of WH-elements in situ to other such elements. A universal principle of government projection ("g-projection") together with a parameterized option for directionality of government defines an accessible path through a tree. A g-projection is started by the projection of a lexical head in the sense of X'-syntax. It can be extended above the XP-level if there is a maximal projection Z of a g-projection of X^o, and Z is in a canonical government configuration with some sister W. In languages like English and the Romance languages, where the verb governs to the right, W has to precede Z in order to fulfill the requirement; in languages like Dutch or German, where the verb governs to the left, W has to follow Z. The latter prediction causes problems, as pointed out in Grewendorf (1988). We will, however, not address these problems here. Kayne's definition of g-projection captures the fact that certain extractions in English lead to ECP-violations. In the complex NP *a picture of (e)*, for example, the empty element e can form a g-projection up to the NP-level. This projection, however, can only be continued if there is an element W which governs the NP canonically. A situation like this is given if the NP is the object of a verb, but not if it is a subject: *Who do you think that Mary bought pictures of?* versus **Who do you think that pictures of were bought by Mary?* Notice that the ill-formed sentence cannot be explained by the usual ECP-account according to which an empty category must be properly governed, since it is properly governed in *both* cases. As the tree-diagrams (48) and (49) show, however, the g-projection can only be continued up to the WH-antecedent in (48). This is indicated by the wavy line. In (49), the wavy line ends before the antecedent-WH is reached, because the subject-NP is on a left branch.

(48)

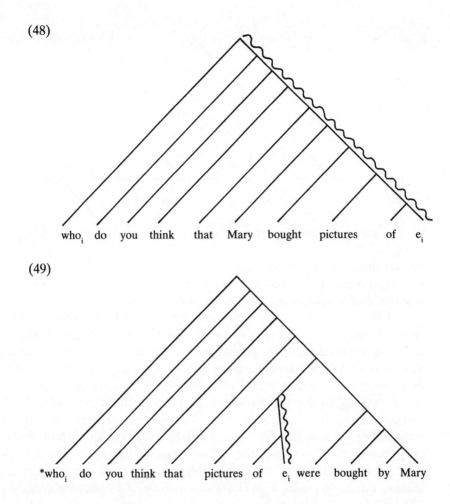

who$_i$ do you think that Mary bought pictures of e$_i$

(49)

*who$_i$ do you think that pictures of e$_i$ were bought by Mary

Most important for our observation is the fact that deviant examples of this kind can be "rescued" by the g-projection of another empty element, when the path of this second g-projection spans the offending subtree. This situation is exemplified in (50).

(50)

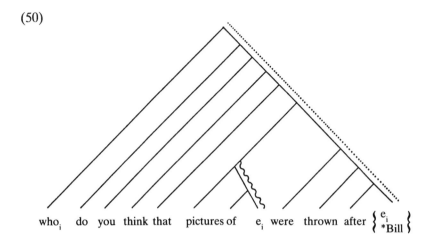

who$_i$ do you think that   pictures of   e$_i$ were thrown after $\left\{ \begin{matrix} e_i \\ *\text{Bill} \end{matrix} \right\}$

The maximal set S of empty categories $e_1,\ldots,e_n$ together with an antecedent A defines a tree T. Kayne's Connectedness Condition (CC) requires that any subset of S together with A form a subtree of T.

In (50) the path marked with the dotted line can, of course, only be created if the object of *after* is an empty category. If it is a lexical NP, no path will be created and, as a consequence, the path that stops due to its being locked on a left branch cannot reach the antecedent. The reason is that it does not connect to a tree which is spanned by a licensed path.

As the CC is formulated in order to deal with ECP-violations and parasitic gap constructions, it is of little help for our purposes. The reason is that all the gaps in question share one index with the antecedent. However, Kayne (1983) extends the CC in order to capture connectedness effects also in cases where different indices play a role, for example connectedness effects in multiple WH-questions. Note the following contrast: *Which man said that which woman was in love with him? versus ?Which man said that which woman was in love with which boy? The idea, which makes multiple interrogation accessible to CT, is the following: The WH in situ must be linked to the WH in COMP in order to be interpretable. Notice that the WH-phrase must have scope over the embedding verb *say* because this verb does not tolerate WH-complements. Linking a WH-item from a left branch seems to be impossible, however, as the ill-formed example shows. But once there is another WH-item from which a g-projection can be built to the WH in COMP, the problematic phrase ceases to be annoying. The CC, as it stands, is not in a position to deal with these cases, because each WH-phrase has a separate index. Kayne therefore reformulates the CC in such a way that the set $\{e_1,...,e_n\}$ of empty categories is replaced by a set of categories that are uniformly bound by some antecedent A. In the case of multiple interrogation the WH in operator position would "bind" a set of WH-phrases (in situ). It is evident that Kayne's generalization of the CC provides a framework in which an explanation for the contrast between (46) and (47) could be found.

Before we proceed to applying the CC to our examples, however, a word of caution is necessary: Kayne's original proposal introduces the directionality parameter only at the level of *extended* g-projections, but not at the level of X'-syntax. Although the orientation of the verb is suggested as the key factor in determining the canonical government direction of a language, the CT allows lexical governors to deviate from the canonical orientation. As Koster (1984,1987) has shown, and as we will demonstrate independently below, the orientation of lexical governors must also conform to the general orientation that holds in a language. Under this assumption, a g-projection would stop in a German PP in which P governs to the right. The reason is that rightwards government does not conform to the general leftward orientation of German governors.

With this in mind, (46) and (47) will get LF-representations, created by raising the quantified focus phrase and the temporal adverb to sentence-initial operator positions. If we assume that S-structure encodes potential operator positions and the CC applies at S-structure, as suggested by Kayne, (46) and (47) should be as follows:

(46')

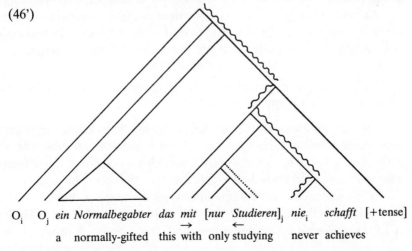

O_i O_j *ein Normalbegabter das mit* [*nur Studieren*]$_j$ *nie*$_i$ *schafft* [+tense]
          a   normally-gifted this with only studying   never achieves

(47')

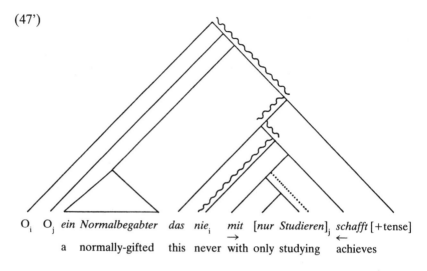

O$_i$ O$_j$ *ein Normalbegabter* *das* *nie*$_i$ *mit* [*nur Studieren*]$_j$ *schafft* [+tense]
                         →
      a   normally-gifted   this never with only studying achieves
                                    ←

As signalled by the paths through the trees, the g-projection of *mit* along which *nur Studieren* has to be raised is a subtree of the g-projection of the verb and the INFL-element along which the adverbial can raise in (46'), but not in (47'). In both of these representations, the PP is an island for QR affecting secondary quantifiers. This is not due to the PP's sitting on a "wrong" branch,[9] but to its being an island in the sense of the constraint expressed in (43). The difference lies in the fact that only in (46') the path of *nur Studieren* is connected to the path of *nie*. Let us thus summarize that a PP-barrier can be neutralized if it is connected to an LF-path spanning it.

Nur imposes quantificational proporties on *Studieren* and therefore the whole NP must be assigned scope. Now that the PP-barrier is neutralized, QR can affect the quantified NP and the desired LF-representation of (46) can be derived. Ignoring irrelevant details this may be as follows.

(46")   [$_{IP}$ *nie*$_i$ [$_{IP}$ *nur Studieren*$_j$ [$_{IP}$ *ein Normalbegabter das mit* e$_j$ e$_i$ *schafft*]]]

We may now ask whether the CC, as it stands, makes the right predictions in all possible cases of an LF-element licensing an otherwise illicit path. Kayne's theory is not specific enough to determine what happens when paths with separate indices are created. However, his application of the CC to sentences with multiple interrogation suggests that the WH-binder, which is in the matrix-COMP at S-structure, "absorbs" the WHs in situ at LF in the sense of Higginbotham and May (1981). A proposal that is more specific in this respect is Pesetsky's (1982) Path Theory. Elaborating on an earlier proposal by Fodor (1978), Pesetsky claims that structures with intersecting paths are only well-formed if one path is properly contained in the other one. This has become known as the "Path Containment Condition" (PCC). Given the reading in which the negative takes widest scope, the path [*nur studieren*]$_j$,e$_j$] in (46') is properly nested in the path [*nie*$_i$,e$_i$]. This raises the question of whether we are dealing with a general requirement of "path containment".[10] I will show that such a generalization may be premature and that — given certain qualifications — other scope options do not necessarily violate the PCC. Consider the following contrasts.[11]

(51) * *weil Hans sich unter <u>nur</u> dem BETT sicher fühlt*
         since Hans REFL under only the bed safe feels
         'since Hans feels safe under only the bed'

(52) ? *weil Hans sich unter <u>sogar</u> dem BETT <u>nicht</u> sicher fühlt*
         since Hans REFL under even the bed not safe feels
         'since Hans doesn't feel safe under even the bed'

If our explanation of the contrast between (46) and (47) is reasonable, then it should also capture the contrast between (51) and (52). It should be noted that the stress pattern of the sentences under investigation is a strong cue for proper scope assignment. In (45b), *Das schafft ein Normalbegabter mit nur Studieren nie*, both *studieren* and the adverb of negation *nie* have stress peaks, and a small pause may be inserted between the two stressed items. The stress on *nie* seems to signal that it has to be assigned wide scope. In (52) (*?weil sich Hans unter sogar dem Bett nicht sicher fühlt*), on the other hand, there is only one stress peak, namely on *Bett*. *Nicht* remains unstressed and may even cliticize onto the following adjective. The S-structure order is retained for the assignment of LF-scope. As a result, the negative remains in the scope of the *even*-phrase. Assuming that *nicht* is an LF-sensitive element that has to undergo raising,[12] a reasonable LF-representation of (52) is the following.

(52') [$_{IP}$ *sogar dem Bett*$_i$ [$_{IP}$ *nicht*$_j$ [$_{IP}$ *Hans sich unter* e$_i$ e$_j$ *sicher fühlt*]]]

Any occurrence of neg before *sogar*, irrespective of whether it is due to some requirement on S-structure order or to a deeper principle of scope, is excluded. Whatever the reason for this may be, the paths in (52') are not nested;[13] they intersect.

May (1985) makes similar observations with respect to an application of the ECP at the level of LF. If both quantified NPs are assigned absolute scope over S (IP) and if the ECP holds at LF, wide scope of *every student* in the sentence *Every student admires some professor* would violate the ECP. May adopts the definition of c-command by Aoun and Sportiche (1983) according to which the two operators c-command each other (because they are adjoined to S, which counts here as a non-maximal projection). This enables the quantifiers to freely convert with respect to their relative scope without violating the ECP. May points out problems with an ECP-account of scope phenomena and these lead him to abandon it and instead adopt the PCC. Unfortunately, the discussion of quantification other that WH is too sketchy to say anything conclusive.[14] Further elaboration on path theory would lead us off the track. Thus, we will conclude with the remark that particles can escape PP-islands if there is some path which neutralizes the barrier. We hope that future research will clarify in which way issues of relative scope can precisely be accommodated in CT or in Path Theory.

The licensing LF-elements in the sentences used above were all negatives. This may superficially give the impression that quantificational particles embedded in PPs are negative polarity items. The crucial characteristics of negative polarity items, however, is that they can only appear in the scope of negation in LF.[15] As (52) and (52') showed, however, the negative may also be in the LF-scope of the expression to be licensed, a disqualification of this particular syntactic construction as a negative polarity item under any of the current theories. In addition, there seem to be data which do not involve negation and still exhibit a subject/object asymmetry. Among the following examples, I clearly disfavor (53b) and (53c):

(53) a. ?*weil Hans hinter* <u>*sogar*</u> *dem* KLEIDERSCHRANK *jemanden*
         since Hans behind even   the   closet   someone
         gesehen haben will
         seen   have   wants
         'Even behind the closet Hans wants to have seen someone'

    b. ?**weil Hans jemanden hinter* <u>*sogar*</u> *dem* KLEIDERSCHRANK *gese-*
        hen haben will
        (same gloss as in (53a))

    c. ?**weil jemand Hans hinter* <u>*sogar*</u> *dem* KLEIDERSCHRANK *gesehen*
        haben will
        'Even behind the closet someone wants to have seen Hans'

It is obvious how the connectedness explanation given above would account for the contrasts in (53).

Let us turn now to a major complication for the proposal presented so far. It has been observed by many generative grammarians that syntactic movement to operator positions and movement in LF share certain properties. As the examples in footnote 10 have shown, English WH-movement seems to interact with QR in such a way that traces on both levels of representation, S-structure and LF, count in the determination of path geometries. We have seen that the ban against intersecting paths cannot be upheld in German syntax. The least we could expect, however, is that WH-movement in German can license LF-sensitive particles inside PPs. The prediction would be that (54a) below is well-formed while (54b) is not.

(54) a. α_i ... $[_{PP}$ ... particle ...] ... e_i
      b. α_i ... e_i ... $[_{PP}$ ... particle ...]

Testing this prediction is difficult, because it is not entirely clear what the underlying position of the PP should be. A plausible assumption would be that questioned NPs must have rhematic status and that, in the unmarked case, rhematic elements are placed as near as possible to the verbal complex. The problem stems from the fact that the PP in question must itself be rhematic because it bears the focus-sensitive particle. This is exemplified with the following pair of sentences involving WH in situ.

(55) a.   *Wer hat gesagt, daß man welchen deutschsprachigen*
          who has said   that one which   German
          Aufsatz sogar in LINGUISTIC INQUIRY   abdrucken wollte?
          article even   in Linguistic Inquiry print   wanted
          'Who said that they wanted to print which article in German even in Linguistic Inquiry?'
      b.   *Wer hat gesagt, daß man sogar in LINGUISTIC INQUIRY welchen deutschsprachigen Aufsatz abdrucken wollte?*

Under the assumption that (55a) is a well-formed input for WH-movement, but not (55b), CT predicts that all sentences of type (54) should be ungrammatical in German, that is, no subject/object asymmetries should be observed. The following examples present strictly subcategorized as well as adjoined PPs in relevant question contexts:

(56) subcategorized:

   a. *[Welchen Jungen]*$_i$ *hat man* [e]$_i$ *auf* <u>*nur*</u> *den* BODEN *gesetzt?*
       ACC   NOM
       'Which boy was placed only on the floor?'

   b. *[Welcher Junge]*$_i$ *hat* [e]$_i$*sich auf* <u>*nur*</u> *den* BODEN *gesetzt?*
       NOM   ACC
       'Which boy placed himself only on the floor?'

(57) adjoined:

   a. *[Welchen Aufsatz]*$_i$ *hat man* [e]$_i$ *in* <u>*sogar*</u> LINGUISTIC INQUIRY
       ACC   NOM
       abgedruckt?
       'Which article was printed even in Linguistic Inquiry?'

   b. *[Welcher Artikel]*$_i$ *hat* [e]$_i$ *in* <u>*sogar*</u> LINGUISTIC INQUIRY
       NOM
       Aufsehen erregt?
       'Which article created excitement even in Linguistic
       Inquiry?'

Although one cannot "see" traces, if our argument concerning (55b) above is correct, the WH-trace is never to the right of the illicit PP. Thus, the path induced by the projection of the WH-trace does not cross the PP, and the sentences should all be ruled out. A number of speakers who I consulted for judgements found similar sentences odd, but not entirely bad. Subject/ object asymmetries were hardly ever reported. Moreover, a few speakers found some of the (b)-sentences less ungrammatical than the (a)-sentences. I will return to the issue of WH-movement in the next section. The only conclusion to be drawn at this point is that there is no reason to expect any interesting interactions between WH-movement and LF-movement of particles such as *nur* and *sogar* out of PPs in German. Given that the above argumentation can be maintained, CT would, of course, rule out all the examples in (56) and (57) because in none of them would the WH-path span the offending PP.

To summarize, we have found still another condition under which quantificational particles ('secondary quantifiers') can escape PP-islands without depending on primary quantifiers. The condition is that they must lie in some path induced by LF-movement. The constraint in (38) will therefore need to be revised a second time along the following lines.

(58)   PPs are islands for QR affecting secondary quantifiers if neither
   (i)   P is in construction with a governing V
         nor
   (ii) the LF-path of the secondary quantifier connects to a licit (LF-)path.

Before turning to some less construction-dependent considerations about bounding effects in LF, let us take a closer look at the problems presented in sections 1.3 and 1.4.

3.2 Particles Inside NP

What we have said in 3.1 about the circumvention of constraints on LF-movement can be extended to the case of complex NPs. For convenience, I will repeat examples (10) and (11) (here numbered (59) and (60)) from section 1.3:

(59) a.   *weil sie nur den Sohn des   GRAFEN liebt*
          since she only the son   (of)the count loves
     b.   **weil sie den Sohn nur des GRAFEN liebt*

(60) a.   *weil sie sogar die Schuhe der   KINDER   putzt*
          since she even the shoes (of)the children polishes
     b.   ?**weil sie die Schuhe sogar der KINDER putzt*

We can start by saying that NPs are islands for QR whenever secondary quantifiers alone are involved. Once there is a primary quantifier involved, which the particle can adjoin to, the (b)-sentences above turn out to be acceptable. As we have seen above, the same is true for particles in PPs. With respect to particles in PPs we have found two ways in which the PP-barrier could be crossed in LF: (i) reanalysis of P as part of the verb, such that the particle has immediate access to the verbal projection and does not have to cross a barrier; (ii) licensing the LF-path induced by the particle by connecting it to a path which is induced by LF-movement of some other element; "connecting" means that the licit path has to start to the right of the offending phrase. We could not, however, find evidence that the stronger condition of path containment needs to hold in German. It was also not possible to determine whether or not particle-induced paths can be licensed by syntactic movement.

It is immediately clear that in German we cannot expect a circumvention of the NP-barrier by means of mode (i), reanalysis; there is no way to lexically attach the NP-head to the verb.[16] Thus, the NP-barrier cannot be removed by a lexical operation. The examples given below demonstrate, however, that licensing by mode (ii), connecting, is as operative here as we have found it to be in the PP-cases. In (61) are examples in which the negative adverb *nie* ('never') is assigned LF-scope over the secondary quantifier.

(61) a. ?*weil Hans den Sohn nur des   GRAFEN NIE   geschlagen*
       since Hans the son   only (of)the count never beaten
       hat
       has
       'Since it was never the case that it was only the son of the count that Hans has beaten (Hans has beaten other people's sons as well)'

    b. ?* *weil Hans NIE den Sohn nur des GRAFEN geschlagen hat*

As expected, it is also not essential here that the LF-raising element take scope over the problematic NP. This is shown by the following contrast in (62). Note that in (62a), *nicht* remains in the scope of the *nur*-phrase.

(62) a. ?*weil Hans den Sohn nur des   GRAFEN nicht geschlagen*
       since Hans the son   only (of)the count not   beaten
       hat
       has
       'Since it was only the son of the count who was not beaten by Hans (everybody else's son was beaten by him)'

    b. ?* *weil Hans den Sohn nur des GRAFEN geschlagen hat*
       'Since it was only the son of the count who was beaten by Hans (nobody else's son was beaten by him)'

The following pair of examples is designed to show that LF-sensitive elements other than negatives can license particles in NPs as well, e.g. quantified NPs.

(63) a. ?*weil der Sohn nur des   GRAFEN jeden Jungen schlagen*
       since the son   only (of)the count every boy   beat
       will
       wants
       'It is only the son of the count who wants to beat every boy (nobody else's son would possibly want to do that)'

b. ?* *weil jeder Junge den Sohn nur des* GRAFEN *schlagen will*
'It is only the son of the count whom every boy wants to beat (and nobody else's son)'

I must admit that the judgements above are my own and that it is unlikely that every other speaker of German will agree on the observed contrasts in these highly marked constructions. A further complication is that some speakers show a higher tolerance for particles in NPs than for particles in PPs. For example, a particle may be disfavored in a PP and nevertheless less disfavored in an NP that is part of a PP. Furthermore, once an LF-path is licensed by a crossing quantifier, depth of embeddedness in virtual bounding nodes seems to be irrelevant. My own intuitions are perhaps not reliable enough in these complex cases, and therefore I again asked native speakers for judgements. The marks on the following sentences represent the average for eight raters.

(64)   *Bei starken Regenfällen ärgert sich der Hofbibliothekar darüber, daß der Lakai...*
during heavy rainfall, the royal librarian gets mad that the servant...

a. ?? *unter* <u>*nur*</u> *das Dach der*   BIBLIOTHEK <u>*keine*</u> *Eimer*   *stellt*
under only the roof (of)the library   no   buckets puts

b. * *alle* <u>*Eimer*</u> *unter* <u>*nur*</u> *das Dach des*   *fürstlichen*
all buckets under only the roof (of)the royal
SCHLAFZIMMERS *stellt*
bedchamber puts

c. *unter das Dach* <u>*nur*</u> *der* BIBLIOTHEK <u>*keine*</u> *Eimer stellt*

d. ? *alle* <u>*Eimer*</u> *unter das Dach* <u>*nur*</u> *des fürstlichen* SCHLAFZIMMERS *stellt*

The difference between (64a/c) on the one hand and (64b/d) on the other is, of course, that in the former but not in the latter QR moves a quantified NP across the offending category. There is, however, another remarkable difference, namely that (64c/d) are felt to be less ungrammatical or even perfectly acceptable when compared to (64a/b). Thus, in the end NP does not seem to be as strong a bounding node for QR affecting secondary quantifiers as PP. What might be the reason for this? In order to answer this question we must turn to a concept which plays a role in Kayne's original CT, but which received a lot more attention in Koster (1987). This concept is "directionality of government."

In Kayne (1983), a rather crude distinction was made between languages in which the (transitive) verb seeks the object-NP to its right and languages in which the verb governs to its left. As we indicated in the brief introduction to CT in section 3.1, English verbs govern to the right. According to Kayne, this property parameterizes the canonical extraction site for English in such a way that above the X^0-level of a structural governor, extraction is only possible from a right branch but not from a left branch, unless a subtree can be connected to a g(overnment)-projection, which itself is subject to the direction parameter. Kayne's CT has been developed in various ways in the recent literature,[17] and one of the most interesting proposals is by Koster (1984), which is also a substantial part of Koster (1987). A full presentation of Koster's theory would go beyond the scope of this chapter and therefore I will confine myself to only those aspects of the theory which most immediately touch upon the issues being discussed here.

One goal of the theory is to replace the notion of subjacency with a unified theory of binding and bounding. We will not discuss the binding theory here, but keep in mind that within the theory, binding and bounding are ruled by the same core principles. Koster proposes that minimal maximal projections like NP, PP, AP, S' are bounding nodes for movement. An empty category can, however, be licensed within such a category if it fulfills the condition of "Global Harmony." This condition is an extension of Kayne's notion of directionality of government. What it says is that a local domain like a PP can be extended upwards when governed by a series of governors, a so-called "dynasty," in which all of the governors have a uniform orientation. The most interesting testing ground for such a proposal are languages with a mixed rather than uniform orientation of governors. Dutch and German are such languages, because they happen to have prepositions i.e., rightward governors and verbs that govern to the left. According to the Condition of Global Harmony, extraction out of prepositional PPs should be impossible in Dutch and German. This prediction is borne out.

(65) a.   *Who$_i$ did he play [with e$_i$]?*

b.   **Wat$_i$ heeft hij [mee e$_i$] gespeeld?* (Dutch)
     what has   he with   played

c.   **Was$_i$ hat er [mit e$_i$] gespielt?* (German)

English exhibits preposition stranding effects simply because the Condition of Global Harmony (CGH) is fulfilled: The local domain of the preposition can be extended upwards because it is governed by an element that also governs to the right, the verb. In Dutch and German, however, the PP cannot be extended because it is governed by a verb that is oriented to the left. In other words, the formation of a dynasty is blocked. However, Dutch and German also have a small number of postpositions. These are mostly lexical PPs consisting of pronominal+P; for example *waar+onder* ('where under') or *da+mit* ('there with'). In these cases, P is a postposition and therefore the CGH is met. Under these conditions, P-stranding should be allowed. Again, this prediction is borne out by Dutch and various dialects of German.

(66) a. *Waar$_i$ slaapt hij* [e$_i$ *onder*]? (Dutch, from Koster (1987))
         what sleeps he   under

  b. *Waar$_i$ heeft hij* [e$_i$ *mee*] *gespeeld?* (Dutch)
         what did   he   with play

  c. *Who$_i$ hat er* [e$_i$ *mit*] *gespielt?* (various German dialects)

Notice that P-stranding is forbidden in Standard German, probably due to a rule of prescriptive grammar. But even Standard German has a limited number of postpositions that allow P-stranding and as a consequence fulfill the CGH. *Entlang* ('along') is one of the most interesting cases; it can be used either as a preposition (with the Genitive Case following) or as a postposition (with the Accusative Case preceding). In fact, the following contrast is exactly as expected in Koster's theory.

(67) a. *Den Zaun$_i$*   *hat er* [e$_i$ *entlang*] *die Bäume gefällt*
         the fence:ACC has he   along   the trees   cut
         'He cut the trees along the fence'

  b. **Des Zaunes$_i$ hat er* [*entlang* e$_i$] *die Bäume gefällt*
         GEN

The same effect has also been demonstrated for other languages, such as Swedish. In Swedish, as in German and a number of other languages, adjectives can be Case assigners. In German, the NP-complement of A appears on the left side e.g., *ihm treu* ('him (dat) faithful'), whereas PP-complements appear on the right side of A. In Swedish, NP-complements of A appear generally on the right side, but in some cases also on the left side e.g., *överlägsen sin motstandare* ('superior (to) his opponent') versus *honom kär* ('(to) him dear'). Koster presents data indicating that in

Swedish — a language with rightward orientation of the verb — extraction is indeed possible from APs as long as A governs an NP to its right.[18] In German, the situation is exactly the reverse, as predicted by the CGH.

(68) Swedish:

    a. *Vem$_i$ var han [överlägsen e$_i$]?*
       who was he superior

    b. **Vem$_i$ var hon [e$_i$ kär]?*
       who was she dear

    c. *Vem$_i$ var hon [kär [för e$_i$]?*
       who was she dear for

(69) German:

    a. *Wem$_i$ war er [e$_i$ treu]?*
       who was he faithful

    b. *[Zu wem]$_i$ war er [treu e$_i$]?*
       to whom was he faithful

    c. **Wem$_i$ war er [treu [zu e$_i$]]?*

The German equivalent of (68b) is (69a), which is fully grammatical. (69b) is substandard, but not ungrammatical. And (69c) involves preposition stranding, which is not an option in German, but allowed in Swedish as demonstrated in (68c).

Given this syntactic movement evidence supporting the CGH, we may now ask whether it is also operative on the level of LF. We are again treading on slippery ground, however, because there is evidence both for and against the association of overt gaps with "gaps" produced by LF-movement. Koster, whose version of CT I adopt, suggests that LF can be dispensed with entirely. His argumentation is based for the most part on multiple interrogation sentences, languages lacking overt WH-movement, and problems that arise in connection with the Empty Category Principle (ECP) as proposed by Chomsky (1981) and subsequent work. It would go beyond the scope of this article to discuss the pros and cons concerning LF. For the time being, I will remain neutral on the issues. I do maintain however, that LF as a level of syntactic representation can hardly be excluded on conceptual grounds, and — more importantly — that there are independent empirical reasons which invite a thorough comparison between the syntax of overt movement and LF. As will be shown in the following there are indeed constraints on LF which appear to be similar to constraints on S-structure.

3.3 *Harmonious LF-Paths*

We have observed in the previous section that NPs seem to count as bounding nodes for the movement of secondary quantifiers to a lesser extent than PPs. It would be difficult to account for such a difference in CT when the original Chomskyan proposal is adopted according to which N is a governor in the same sense as V, A, and P are governors.[19] As a matter of fact, it is completely unclear just what kind of lexical governor a noun that does not subcategorize for a complement would be. For example it has been stated over and over again in the recent generative literature that nouns do not assign genitive or possessive Case to the NP that follows; rather Case is assigned to a structurally determined position. Given this state of affairs, it is not surprising to see that N as a lexical governor also misbehaves to some extent in Koster's theory of Global Harmony. Koster (1987) quotes the following Dutch example from van Riemsdijk (1978).

(70)   *Waar heeft hij [een argument [e tegen]] verworpen?*
          what has he an   argument   against rejected

If *argument* is a rightward-looking governor, the CGH predicts the ungrammaticality. On the other hand, there are fully grammatical cases where the same constellation seems to hold, as in the following examples.

(71) a.   *Waar$_i$ heeft hij [een collectie [e$_i$ van]] gezien?*
           what has he a   collection of   seen
      b.   *Waar$_i$ heeft zij [een boek [e$_i$ over]] geschreven?*
           what has she a   book   about written

It is not clear how to account for these conflicts. One way out may simply be to say that there are lexical reasons that is, certain nouns and semantically related pre-/postpositions may be "more closely linked" than usual and therefore an apparent bounding node can get skipped. It is, however, difficult to see why this line of reasoning should not also pertain to (70). After all, "arguments" are also inherently linked to the relations "for" or "against." One alternative, which needs further exploration, might be that nouns are neutral with respect to the direction of government, or more radically, that most nouns do not lexically govern at all. NPs lacking an explicitly governing head would then only weakly block extraction. Whether the barrier can be removed or not would depend entirely on lexical overuse and not on the CGH. Example (70) would then be ruled out on the rather trivial ground that the N and P are not encountered frequently enough in the language to justify the process of barrier-removal. When the NP lacks a governing head, no conflict in direction of government arises and the extraction process does not violate the CGH. Applying this suggestion to our findings in (64) above, the contrasts would get accounted for in the following manner: (64a) violates a PP-barrier, but given that there is a second LF-path, the barrier is removed. In (64c) the particle is closer to the focus-constituent — which may be desirable for completely different reasons — and it therefore locally fulfills the CGH; a second LF-path then becomes available and the barrier that may still be involved gets removed. Example (64b) involves a local violation of the CGH, *nur* being in the immediate domain of a preposition, and there is also no LF-path to span the offending phrase. The same is true for (64d), although in this case the CGH-violation is reduced by the fact that *nur* is embedded in a category (NP), the head of which may not observe the directionality constraint. If this suggestion gains further support, it might account for the observation that for LF-movement NPs seem to be weaker bounding nodes than PPs in which the P has a rightwards orientation.

Let me now turn to the predictions which the CGH makes for LF-movement out of PPs. As we have seen above, preposition phrases seem to be severe obstacles to the extractability (raising) of secondary quantifiers. For postposition phrases, however, the CGH predicts that they will lead to much milder violations. Testing this prediction is unfortunately accompanied by a complicating factor. In German, *nur* ('only'), *sogar* ('even') and a number of other particles can not only precede their focus constituent but also follow it i.e., adjoin to the right of it. This is a stylistically marked option. There are conversational situations in which a postposed particle is felt to be stylistically inappropriate. On the other hand, if postpositions are taken into consideration the choice of this marked option is necessary. Notice that the string in (72a) below could always be analyzed according to the unproblematic option (72b). In this case, the interesting option, (72c), would most likely not be tested at all. What we need is then a postposition with an NP-complement that shows the stylistically marked option of particle attachment as in (72d).

(72)   a.   *nur   den FLUSS entlang*
           only   the   river   along
           'only along the river'

      b.   [*nur* [*den FLUSS entlang*]]   (*nur* adjoined to PP)

    c.   [[*nur den* FLUSS] *entlang*] (*nur* adjoined to NP)
    d.   [[*den* FLUSS *nur*] *entlang*] (*nur* adjoined to NP)

Thus, we have to make use of the marked option which enables us to insert the particle between NP and P. But even with this prerequisite, the postpositional PPs fare better than the prepositional ones.[20]

(73) a.   postpositional *entlang*:
        ??*weil er die Bäume den* FLUSS *nur/sogar entlang gefällt hat*
         since he the trees   the river only/even along cut has
        'since he had cut the trees only/even along the river'
    b.   prepositional *entlang*:
        *weil er die Bäume entlang nur/sogar des FLUSSES *gefällt hat*

(74) a.   postpositional *gegenüber*:
        ??*weil Hans seiner* MUTTER *nur/sogar gegenüber aggressiv*
         since Hans his   mother only/even against   aggressive
        wurde
        became
        'since Hans got aggressive only/even against his mother'
    b.   prepositional *gegenüber*:
        *weil Hans gegenüber nur/sogar seiner MUTTER *aggressiv*
        wurde

(75) a.   postpositional *wegen*:
        ??*weil der* COMPUTER *nur wegen die Temparatur gesenkt*
         since the computers only for   the temparature reduced
        wurde
        was
        'since the temperature was reduced only for the computers'
    b.   prepositional *wegen*:
        *weil wegen nur der COMPUTER *die Temparatur gesenkt wurde*

Notice that the (b)-sentences conform to the stylistically unmarked positioning of the particles. In spite of this, however, the (a)-sentences are still more acceptable. We can attribute this to the fact that in German, postpositions establish a dynasty of successive canonical governors, whereas prepositions fail to do so.

I have already drawn attention to the fact that some German adjectives govern complements to their left. For the sake of completeness, I want to show now that the CGH also makes the correct predictions with respect to adjectives and their complements. In the following, I will present adjectives governing an NP-complement. In German, this is only possible if the NP appears to the left of A. I will also present adjectives with PP-complements, which are not constrained in the same way, because the NP is not Case-marked by the adjective but by the preposition. One should also be aware that the prenominal use of APs is constrained by an adjacency requirement by which the category adjacent to N must be an inflecting A. This rules out cases like *ein [beliebt(-er) [bei allen Menschen]] Mann ('a man, liked by all people') versus ein [[bei allen Menschen] beliebt-er] Mann. With this independent restriction in mind, the data pattern as follows.

(76) a.   *weil das Gericht [dem KRANKEN sogar] bekömmlich war*
           since the meal   the   patient even   suitable   was
           'since the meal was suitable even for the patient'

      b.   *ein [dem KRANKEN sogar] bekömmliches Gericht*
           a   the   patient even   suitable   meal
           'a meal suitable even for the patient'

(77) a.   *weil er [nur auf die SPORTSCHAU] gespannt war*
           since he only for the sportnews   curious   was
           'since he was curious only for the sportnews'

      b.   *?weil er [auf nur die SPORTSCHAU] gespannt war*

      c.   *ein [nur auf die SPORTSCHAU] gespannter Mann*
           a   only for the sportnews   curious   man
           'a man curious only for the sportnews'

      d.   *?ein [auf nur die SPORTSCHAU] gespannter Mann*

(78) a.   **weil er gespannt [nur auf die SPORTSCHAU] war*
           since he curious   only for the sportnews   was
           'since he was curious only for the sportnews'

      b.   **weil er gespannt [auf nur die SPORTSCHAU] war*

The examples in (76) are entirely as predicted by the CGH. The adjective *bekömmlich* governs the NP-complement canonically and therefore the AP does not count as a bounding node for QR. In (77), (b) and (d) are worse than (a) and (c), although they are not ungrammatical. At first glance, one might conclude that (77b,d) should be excluded entirely. After all, the CGH is violated by the fact that the leftwards looking governor *gespannt* meets with a rightwards looking governor, the preposition. Recall, however, that it was concluded in section 3.1 that something like reanalysis must be allowed in the grammar. The APs in question here are exactly this type of phrase. *Gespannt*, for instance, allows for an *auf*-PP and nothing else. As far as I can see, this holds in general for adjectives governing a PP; the associated preposition is as predictable as the Case assigned by NP-taking adjectives. The crucial difference between the two sets of examples therefore seems to be entirely reducible to the Case Filter. If reanalysis or some equivalent operation can be motivated, it is obvious how to account for the weakening of the PP-bounding-node in (77b,d).

Let us turn now to the completely ungrammatical examples in (78). One may at first think that the canonically governed PP has been extraposed from the AP; but extraposition in German always attaches a node to the right of the finite verb. In (78), however, the PP stays in the so-called "Mittelfeld" i.e., it does not move across the INFL-boundary. I have suggested that there is a unique reason for distinguishing NP- and PP-complements of adjectives: NPs are subject to the Case-Filter while PPs are not. This means that PP-complements can appear on either side of A, although canonical government of the PP is only achieved on the left side. We will henceforth assume that government is independently guaranteed by the presence of a c-commanding relationship between a lexical head and a complement. The directionality requirement enters in as an independent factor. We will turn to this in more detail in section 3.6 below. For the time being it is sufficient to draw attention to the following: The cases of reanalysis presented so far all involve constituents in a canonical government configuration. Although this is not so obvious in cases of V2 (cf. examples (40) through (42) of section 3.1 above) at D-structure the verb occupies a position in which it canonically governs the PP and, as Koster (1987) has independently pointed out, the D-structure position seems to be critically involved in dynasty formation. In (78) the situation is entirely different, however. As I have argued above, the appearance of PP at the right side of A is not likely to be the result of movement. Rather the PP is most likely base generated to the right of A and the CGH cannot find a level of representation at which to build a dynasty. The result is that reanalysis cannot apply and the AP becomes an island for QR. In (78a) it is only the AP; in (78b) it is the AP and the PP embedded in it. Native speakers found both examples in (78) ungrammatical and could hardly detect a difference between (a) and (b). It seems that once the competence system is pushed to its limits, the calculation of possible violating factors is not an issue anymore.

If the analysis presented above is not completely misguided, we are now in a position to generalize the construction-specific condition (58) of section 3.1 in such a way that specific bounding nodes for LF-movement need not be mentioned. As I, following Jacobs (1983), have pointed out, the particles under investigation *must* have access to the verbal projection. If this is impossible, then a well-formed LF cannot be derived from S-structure. A natural consequence of this is that the German V- and/or INFL-projection does not lead to a bounding node for the LF-movement of a secondary quantifier. As we have seen, the maximal projections of lexical categories other than V i.e., NP, PP and AP, show island effects for secondary quantifiers. We also saw that NPs seem to impose less stringent constraints than PPs and APs, and I speculated that this may be because the head of NP does not have directionality properties for government. LF-movement out of PPs and APs is subject to the CGH (Koster, 1984;1987). However, if a dynasty of successive governors can be built, then particles can occur inside PPs and APs as a marked option and LF-movement is licensed. That is, contrary to Koster's claims we have found fairly broad agreement between the grammar of overt gaps and the grammar of "LF-gaps." General conclusions may be premature, however, because the overall evidence in favor of LF as a syntactic level of representation is still littered with unpleasant asymmetries between syntactic movement and LF-movement. Leaving this difficult problem unsettled, we can still consider a generalization of condition (58) in section 3.1.

(79)   XP is a bounding node for QR affecting secondary quantifiers if none of the following conditions holds:
         (i)   X = V or X = INFL
         (ii)   X is part of a chain of successive uniformly oriented governors or X is in construction with a canonical governor
         (iii) a licit (LF-)path spans XP.

Conditions (i) and (iii) of (79) should be clear by now. Assuming that "in construction with" is the result of an abstract lexical process, we may still want to supplement (ii) with the following:

(80)   A (head) category Y can be in lexical construction with an absorbing head category X iff Y or the projection of Y is canonically governed by X, the direction of canonical government being a matter of crosslinguistic parametrization.

In German and Dutch, (80) automatically excludes parts of complements from being absorbed into a governor if the part to be absorbed does not appear to the left of the governor in D-structure. We will see in section 3.6 that this relates to a set of highly interesting facts about rightward movement in German and closely related languages/dialects. Before we turn to this, however, a few words should be said about the fact that particles also cannot freely appear in coordinate constructions.

3.4 Coordination

In this section I want to address the problems with coordination that were pointed out in section 1.4. As the reader will see, this section turns out to be a digression from the main topic of this chapter because I do not refer to CT in my analysis of the restrictions on coordinate constructions.

For the sake of convenience, I will repeat below the data from section 1.4. ((12), (13)) which were brought up in Jacobs (1983).

(81) a. *weil* <u>nur</u> Peter *und Luise spazieren gehen*
          since only Peter and Luise for a walk go
      b. ??*weil Peter und* <u>nur</u> *Luise spazieren gehen*

(82) a. *weil Gerd* <u>sogar</u> *Peter und Luise traf*
          since Gerd even Peter and Luise met
      b. ??*weil Gerd Peter und* <u>sogar</u> *Luise traf*

Recall that Jacobs used these data as support for an analysis in which scalar particles must have access to the V-projection throughout a derivation (or a Montagovian process of sentence composition). I have assumed that particles of this kind are quantifiers and therefore have to undergo raising in order to provide an interpretable LF. Under such an assumption one can argue that the (b)-sentences in (81) and (82) are simply ruled out by a constraint on the syntax proper, namely Ross' (1967) Coordinate Structure Constraint (CSC). This constraint says that no conjunct of a coordinate structure may be moved. Ross adopted it in order to block the derivation of sentences like *What sofa will he put the chair between some table and?* or *Whose tax did the nurse polish her trombone and the plumber compute?* We could argue that something parallel goes on in the derivation of LF. Indeed, many cases could be captured by extension of the CSC, as indicated in (83) below.

(83) a. *John and everybody would go to Mary's party
      b. *Hans und jeder würde auf Marias Party gehen

Unfortunately, this account has turned out to be too simplistic. More recent studies have shown that coordination is constrained in a variety of ways, including some which seem to be semantic in nature. Gazdar, Pullum, Klein and Sag (1985, chapter 8), for example, point to the possibility of coordinating categories which are not syntactically alike, e.g. NP and AP, ADV and PP. In a sentence such as the following (=their (10))

(84)   She walked slowly and with great care

both conjuncts express a manner property which may, for instance, correspond to the question morpheme how.

However, semantic likeness of the phrases to be coordinated is not a sufficient condition either. As Lang (1984) shows, even the informational structure (i.e., theme-rheme organization) can be a filtering factor. Finally, although such a semantic homogeneity constraint would rule out coordination of quantified and unquantified expressions (e.g. the examples in (83)), such a constraint is still too simplistic, as we will shortly see.

Barwise and Cooper (1981) have developed a theory of natural language quantifiers in which they distinguish between monotone increasing and monotone decreasing quantifiers.[21] In dealing with what they call "NP-conjunction," they argue that increasing quantifiers can combine with other increasing quantifiers and decreasing quantifiers with other decreasing quantifiers; mixing the two, however, is not allowed. The reasoning was as follows: While two increasing/decreasing quantifiers undergoing and-conjunction would produce another increasing/decreasing quantifier expression, mixing the two would produce to a hybrid. This proposal would successfully rule out the examples in (83) and given that nur ('only') has the properties of a monotone decreasing quantifier,[22] (81b) would also be ruled out. The example in (82b) seems to be more problematic. Sogar ('even') clearly gives rise to a conventional implicature, but it differs from nur ('only') in that its implicature does not involve a generalized quantifier. The Barwise and Cooper account simply does not pertain to (82b).[23] There are other cases which also show that this condition on quantifier conjunction is not sufficient. Take German alle ('all') and jeder ('every'). Although both are increasing quantifiers, they still behave differently with respect to NP-coordination.

(85) a. *Hans und <u>alle</u>   Mädchen spielten im   Garten*
         Hans and all the girls   played   in-the garden
    b. ** Hans und <u>jedes</u> Mädchen spielte(n) im Garten*

Notice that whatever the difference between (85a) and (85b) will be, it would also be a threat to an application of the CSC in LF. Thus, neither of the approaches discussed so far seems to be quite capable of providing the appropriate constraints. Trying to develop the details of an account for these murky cases myself would lead me too far afield. Let me therefore conclude this section with only a speculation about NP-conjunction.

It was noticed quite some time ago that natural language *and* does only partially correspond to the truth-functional connective '&.' As Gazdar (1980) has pointed out, this may have been a strong reason to derive NP-coordination from sentence-coordination. Gazdar, Partee and Rooth (1983) and other linguists attempt to stick to strict base-generation of all coordinate constructions and develop a theory of generalized conjunction. As far as I understand this work, however, it does not provide a solution for the problems of quantifier coordination. A somewhat different picture emerges from Link's (1983) logical analysis of plurals and mass-terms. Link adopts concepts from the mereological logics of the forties, assuming that natural language *and* denotes a relation that fuses individuals. Once it is acknowledged that *and* may denote a relation between individuals or material substances, it becomes ontologically necessary to constrain fusion in such a way that individuals can only be fused with other individuals, substances can only be fused with other substances, properties of a given order with properties of the same order, etc. Given this, we must then ask in which sense a quantified NP can be combined with a name i.e., with an individual constant. The name can not be type-lifted in such a way that it matches the quantified expression. I suspect therefore that some quantified expressions can be treated as if they were on a par with individual constants. For instance, *all girls*, may refer to a group exhausting the girls of a domain of discourse. To the extent that *all girls* can be understood as a finite set of individuals (in mereological systems, another individual) there would seem to be no objection to combining this set with another set containing only one individual. The NP *every girl* does not allow for a comparable group reading. When it enters into a [NP VP] construction, it works exclusively as a function from individuals into truth values. Thus, according to Link's theory we should not get coordination with an NP denoting an individual. This does not, however, preclude the possibility that an expression like *every girl* receives an interpretation as [+specific]. In German, for example, *jedes Mädchen* can be used in much the same way as the explicit partitive construction *jedes der Mädchen* ('each of the girls'). An open question then is why NP-coordination can occur only with a name when an explicit partitive construction is used (*Hans und jedes der Mädchen spielte(n) im Garten*), and not simply with a partitive reading of *jedes Mädchen* (cf.(85b)).

Returning to Jacobs' examples in (81) and (82), it seems to me that the deviant examples are not as deviant as one might expect them to be, and that a mereological semantics would be hard pressed to rule them out in some straightforward way. The adjunction of *only* to an NP does not destroy its referential nature; *only* simply adds an implicature and NP-conjunction could therefore still proceed according to Link's semantic analysis. The deviant character of both (81b) and (82b) would then have to be attributed to a violation of an independent parallelism requirement as proposed in Lang (1984). I would suggest furthermore, that it must follow from a general parallelism constraint on coordination that a constituent giving rise to a conventional implicature can only combine with another constituent giving rise to a compatible conventional implicature. Naturally, two NPs with the same particle would observe this requirement as long as one implicature does not cancel out the other. Conversely, two NPs with different particles may easily violate the parallelism requirement. Let me briefly demonstrate this with some examples.

(86)   a. ?? *Only John and only Bill came to my party*
       b.   *Bei uns gibt es nur Spatzen und nur Ratten*
            with us there are only sparrows and only rats
            'Here we have only sparrows and rats'
       c.   *Even John and even Bill came to my party*
       d.   *Hans und auch Fritz kamen zu meiner Party*
            Hans and also Fritz came to my party
       e. ?* *Only John and even Bill came to my party*

Example (86a) is odd because the implicature of the first conjunct says that nobody except John had the property expressed by the VP. The second conjunct informs the hearer that the implicature does not hold in full. In addition, it gives rise to an implicature that is incompatible with the fact that John has the same property that Bill has. In the German example (86b) things are quite different. As is well known, *nur* can map entities on "prestige" scales; the implicature created is that the entity in question does not range high in prestige. Example (86b) gives rise to two implicatures (sparrows are low-prestige animals, rats are low-prestige animals) which, of course, do not cancel each other out. Example (86c) is also well-formed because both conjuncts trigger parallel implicatures which do not contradict each other. John's ranging low on a likelihood scale does not seem to exclude the possibility of Bill's ranging low on such a scale as well. Example (86d) does not contain parallel conjuncts, but the meaning triggered by *auch Fritz* is fully compatible with the first conjunct. [[*auch*[NP]] VP] means that some x has the property denoted by VP and it carries the implicature that there is some entity y which has this property too. The conjunction in (86d) leads one to automatically understand Hans as the y-individual. Notice that the reverse order *auch Fritz und Hans* implicates that there is a third unmentioned individual i.e., *auch* has the entire conjunct in its focus. Similar effects have been observed over and over in the linguistic literature; so I will not dwell on the phenomenon here. In (86e), as in all the other examples, nothing seems to block a summation of the two NP-referents in the sense of Link (1983). The problem seems to be that the same reasoning as in (86a) applies, and that the implicatures simply make reference to different scales e.g., a "prestige scale" for John and a "likelihood scale" for Bill. As Lang (1984) has shown, such cases must be ruled out by any reasonable theory of coordination.

The above remarks are not more than a sketch of a solution to Jacobs' coordination problem. One thing, however, should have become clear: The problem cannot and should not be solved in syntactic theory. The introduction of semantic features, which can block certain X'-configurations, would complicate the overall organization of phrase structure enormously. Furthermore, those principles that determine the phrase structure of a language are entirely different from those that determine entailment, implicature, semantic compatibility, etc. (In fact, a substantial part of the progress in syntactic theory can be ascribed to the exclusion of semantic, conceptual, and pragmatic aspects.)

To summarize my general arguments up to this point: I have argued that we must allow the phrase structure component to adjoin particles to all major syntactic categories and not only to V-projections. A theory of bounding should then be developed, which is articulate enough to filter out at the level of LF the many overgenerations that free adjunction would produce. And finally, the above remarks on coordination were intended to show that certain other cases of overgeneration can then be filtered out by independent interpretive and pragmatic mechanisms. In the next section I would like to return to the strictly syntactic aspects of quantifying particles.

3.5 Rightward Movement

In this section we will look at a number of phenomena, which are best referred to with the fairly theory-neutral term "rightward movement." It should become clear that the notion "movement" is not intended to have any serious theoretical connotations. Subsumed under the heading "rightward movement" are Extraposition, Heavy-NP-Shift, and cases of Verb Raising in which the underlying word order gets reversed.

3.5.1 Extraposition

If we assume, contrary to Jacobs (1983), that [particle + XP] form a syntactic constituent irrespective of the categorial nature of X, the following problem arises.

Given that the preverbal-position in German is transformationally derived, the following sentence (87) below must be derived from the D-structure given in (88).

(87)   [*nur daß der Kanzler   zu dick sei*] *hat Hans gesagt*
         only that the chancellor too fat   is   has Hans said

(88)   *(weil) Hans [nur daß der Kanzler zu dick sei] gesagt hat*

The problem is that although the quantified CP can move to the pre-verbal (A')-position, it cannot move to the right periphery of the illustrated clause. This is shown in (89).

(89)   **weil Hans gesagt hat [nur daß der Kanzler zu dick sei]*

At the same time, however, extraposition of finite clauses is almost obligatory in German (and absolutely obligatory in Dutch). Notice that this has led some linguists to argue that sentences like (88) are ungrammatical and should be ruled out by principles of the grammar.[24]

As soon as the extraposed form is used, the only possibility is to leave the particle to the left of the verb:

(90)   *weil Hans nur gesagt hat [daß der Kanzler zu dick sei]*

From a D-structure like (88), however, only (89) could be derived. In order to derive (90) from a structure which preserves the fact that the CP is the syntactic domain of *nur* and its focus, we would have to postulate something like the following D-structure.

Moving the CP to the right by a transformation would violate the A-over-A-priciple. Given the weak status of this principle, this is probably not a serious problem. Nevertheless, an analysis that does not invite reference to the A-over-A principle at all would be preferable. We can achieve this by assuming that the input-structure for extraposition is not (91), but rather (92); that is, *nur* is not adjoined to its focus constituent, CP, but to the VP inside which it selects CP as its focus constituent.

(91)

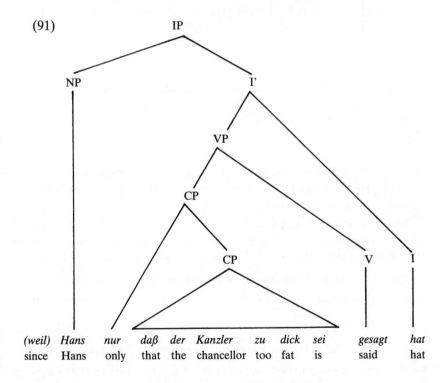

(weil)	Hans	nur	daß	der	Kanzler	zu	dick	sei	gesagt	hat
since	Hans	only	that	the	chancellor	too	fat	is	said	hat

(92)

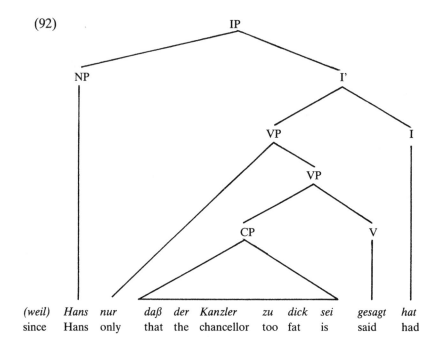

(weil)	*Hans*	*nur*	*daß*	*der*	*Kanzler*	*zu*	*dick*	*sei*	*gesagt*	*hat*
since	Hans	only	that	the	chancellor	too	fat	is	said	had

Although this solution would help us to avoid an A-over-A violation, it does not provide a very interesting answer to the question of why it is impossible to move the entire [$_{CP}$*nur* CP] in (88) to the right.

In order to arrive at a solution that rests on more than a pure phrase structure stipulation, we will need to broaden our data base somewhat. In (93) below, for example, the *nur*-clause is not offending at all.

> (93)   *weil Hans hereingekommen ist [nur wenn alle*
>   since Hans entered   has only when everybody
>   *schliefen]*
>   slept
>   'Since Hans entered only when everybody was asleep'

The difference between (89) and (93) is, of course, that in (89) CP is an argument of the verb and thus must be governed, while the adverbial CP in (93) is an adjoined structure. The restriction observed in (89) moreover not only occurs with lexically governed clauses but also with other argument-clauses. In (94) for example, a subject-sentence is involved.

(94) a. *weil* [*nur ob   Desdemona untreu   war*] *Othello*
         since only whether Desdemona unfaithful was Othello
         interessiert hat
         interested has
         'Since Othello was only interested in whether Desdemona
         was unfaithful'
     b. [*Nur ob Desdemona untreu war*] *hat Othello interessiert*
     c. *weil Othello interessiert hat* [*nur ob Desdemona untreu war*]

Thus, the free placement of a quantifier-adjoined CP seems to be possible
only if this CP is not selected as an argument. If the CP is selected i.e.,
licensed by a governor and/or by a θ-grid, the quantifier must stay to the
left of the verb. Given this and the fact that the verb governs leftwards in
German and Dutch, the principles of CT would appear to play a role here.

Let us therefore explore the possibility that QR can only affect positions that are canonically governed. In a structure like (88) this would be
guaranteed. QR would raise the quantified CP and adjoin it to IP. The LF-
representation would then be something like the following.

(95) $[_{IP}[\underline{nur}$ daß der Kanzler zu dick sei$]_i$ $[_{IP}$ Hans e_i gesagt hat]]

In order to explain (90) along these lines, we could assume the following S-
structure in which — according to standard assumptions — the extraposed
CP leaves a trace.

(96) $[_{IP}$ *Hans* $[_{I'}$ $[_{VP}$ *nur* $[_{VP}$ e_i *gesagt*]] *hat*] $[_{CP}$ *daß der Kanzler zu*
            dick sei$]_i$]

Here, *nur* is adjoined to VP and seeks a focus-constituent within VP, which
is the CP under the reading intended here. Let us assume a coindexation
relationship (superscripts) between the particle and its focus. This is always
necessary when the syntactic domain and focus of the particle are not identical. The extraposed CP would then get related back to its canonically governed D-structure position by its trace and QR could affect the quantifier
nur because — as we have argued — it is on a left branch with respect to the
verb governing the clause with which the quantifier must be coindexed.

(97) $...[_{I'}$ $[_{VP}$ *nur*^{j} $[_{VP}$ e_i *gesagt*]] *hat*] $[_{CP}$ $...]_i^j...$

Given that (96) has the assignment specified in (97), its LF after QR will be
precisely the one given in (95). The only difference between (88) and (90)/
(96) therefore seems to be functional in nature, namely that (88) is harder
to process due to center embedding. Moreover, to argue against cases such

as (88) on the basis of principles of core grammar (see also note 24) is probably premature. Processing constraints, however, should not concern us here.

Recall Koster's proposal that dynasties are built from successive governors at D-structure. It would be difficult to do it otherwise, if one does not want to adopt a completely different framework. After all, reference to the D-structure position of the verb is necessary in simple cases of WH-extraction in German.

(98)   *Wen   sah Hans?*
         whom saw Hans
         'Who did Hans see?'

If the finite verb is identical to the lexically governing verb, the verb as a whole moves to the C(OMP)-position. But then how can extraction of the WH-item be licensed when the verb does not canonically governs it? Notice that one step in the derivation of (98) would be the following.

(99) $[_{XP}$—$]$ $[_{V/I}$ *sah*$_i]$ $[_{IP}$ *Hans* $[_{I'}[_{VP}$ *wen* e$_i]]]$

If the underlying V/I-position were not accessible, it would be unclear how the argument-NP *wen* could be extracted. Assuming that Case is never assigned to an A'-position, such as $[_{XP}$—$]$ in (99), but must be inherited, it would also be unclear how the WH-item could acquire its Case. Thus, it seems reasonable, as Koster assumes, to take D-structures (or base generated trace positions in annotated S-structures) as the level of representation at which dynasties are to be formed. In (96) and (97), therefore the extraposed CP could be "relocated" into the trace position and, because the particle is thereby in the canonical government domain of the verb, particle+focus could be raised in LF. But notice now the following problem: The same could be claimed for ungrammatical cases like (89). Although the particle is not within the reach of the verbal governor at S-structure, it is within its reach at D-structure. And if D-structure is the level at which dynasties are built, then (89) should be just as acceptable as (88) or even more acceptable because it does not involve an unpleasant center embedding. Nevertheless, (89) is severely ungrammatical while (88) is acceptable.

As a solution to this problem, I will propose that extraposition is not an instance of move-alpha and that it does not leave a trace; rather, extraposition is very likely to be a grammaticized result of the parser's response to certain processing difficulties.[25] There is increasing linguistic evidence suggesting that at least certain cases of extraposition should indeed be distinguished from move-alpha. These are mostly extrapositions of PPs, appositive NPs and relative clauses from NPs. For example, Koster (1978) presented numerous subjacency violations in connection with extraposition and concluded that these cases must be considered the result of "stylistic movement" (a conclusion that we will show below cannot be maintained). Baltin (1981) does assume traces for rightward movement, but observes that rightward movement must be distinguished from leftward movement because the bounding conditions are different in the two cases. Baltin (1987) reports an observation by May in which the extraposition of a relative clause with a null-VP leads to a violation of the i-within-i Condition.[26] Other possible problems are mentioned also (e.g., problems relating to the ECP).

Relative clauses are not licensed by the Projection Principle, and there is thus little motivation to postulate traces for them in an underlying position. They should rather be treated like adjuncts. Craig Thiersch (pers.comm.) has pointed out that the postulation of traces for extraposed relatives, PPs, and other appositives is also unmotivated from a parsing point of view. In a left to right parse there is no plausible strategy for hypothesizing a gap as long as there is no obvious filler. This predicts, of course, that leftwards movement leads to the expectation of a gap, whereas rightward movement does not.

Culicover and Rochemont (forthcoming) argue for a conceptualization of extraposition from NP without traces. They propose, instead, a base-generation account in which the extraposed phrase is linked to its antecedent by what they call the "Complement Principle." I do not need to go into the complicated issue of extraposition in any more detail here. What I do need to show, however, is how a much less obvious case of rightward movement can be explained without reference to a trace/binder relationship, namely the extraposition of arguments.

In the above, I have argued that on parsing grounds there are reasons for not postulating traces for rightward movement if the moved constituent is not felt to be missing until the string constituting a minimal clause is processed. Rightward movement of arguments seems to set the stage in a completely different way, however: The parser could postulate a gap as soon as an obligatory constituent is found to be missing. But, as we have argued above, insertion of a trace to the left of a German verb selecting a clausal complement would destroy the asymmetry between leftward and rightward movement. This asymmetry is necessary, however, if the non-occurrence of secondary quantifiers to the right of the finite verb is to be explained. In the following I will give two straightforward reasons for why rightward moved constituents with argument status should not be related to a trace in German. I will also show this to be unnecessary in English.

3.5.2 What Gets Case Where?

It is common knowledge that German object-NPs can precede the subject-NP under certain conditions. This is particularly the case in V2-clauses, where the pre-verbal position is an A'-position. As I have already mentioned in my discussion of (98) and (99) in section 3.5.1, Case cannot be assigned to this position directly. Since it can be assigned to a canonically governed variable, however, a coindexed NP in the A'-position is licensed and will not be ruled out by the Case Filter. Let us then assume that rightwards moved categories with argument status are related to a trace to the left of the verb. The prediction would, of course, be that something like Heavy-NP-Shift exists in German. However, it does not exist at all and to my knowledge there is no exception to this. The examples in (100) should illustrate that the "heaviness" of the NP cannot outweight this law.

(100) a. *weil   Karl den Hund, der   so laut   bellte, geschlagen*
          since Karl the dog   which so loudly barked beaten
          hat
          has

    b. *weil Karl den Hund geschlagen hat, der so laut bellte*

    c. * *weil Karl geschlagen hat den Hund, der so laut bellte*

In this respect German differs significantly from English, and also from Italian where extraposition moves the head of the relative clause along.[27] Under the standard assumption that Case is assigned by a verb in German exclusively to canonically governed positions (to the left of the verb) and the assumption that in general rightward movement does not leave a trace, the data in (100) can be explained. With these assumptions it is also explained why certain other constituents which do not require Case may well be extraposed.[28] An argument-CP must be governed but it does not require Case. Thus, it is free to occur on either side of the verb.

My conclusion is that we keep the notion "government" as it has been used over the years (e.g., according to the definition by Aoun and Sportiche, 1983), and that we reserve "canonical government" for those instances of government in which a lexical item or morphological feature (e.g., AGR) governs a category in the direction that has been parametrized as canonical for the language in question. We can assume, furthermore, that θ-assignment is not subject to the canonicity requirement, while Case assignment certainly is.[29] This may ultimately follow from the structure of the lexicon where the θ-grid of a verb is probably represented as an unordered set of θ-roles. Under this analysis and our previous processing explanation for rightward movement, a picture emerges in which grammar and processor conspire with respect to the (non-)extraposition of clauses and NPs roughly as follows: The grammar licenses argument-CPs as long as they are governed. The processor disfavors CPs in intraposed position due to some constraint on the linguistic working memory, which is not our primary concern here. The processor could in principle shift heavy NPs but the requirement of a canonical government relation for Case assignment blocks such movement.

One problem for our account may arise from the fact that in many German dialects constituents can be moved out of finite clauses with a lexical complementizer by COMP-to-COMP movement. If the COMP-position of the embedded clause must be canonically governed, this would in our theory be an unexplained phenomenon. Nothing, however, forces us to such a conclusion. Clauses are not assigned Case and therefore they can stay in non-canonically governed position. According to standard assumptions following from the ECP, the trace in COMP should be governed by the matrix verb. But the matrix verb does not Case- or θ-mark this trace under any current theory. Thus, unbounded leftwards movement in German should be unaffected by the canonicity requirement. We may, however, go even further and see what predictions would be made by adoption of such a requirement for the licensing of WH-complements. We would expect that at least long movement out of CPs canonical position is possible. Although intraposed CPs are tolerable in German, WH-movement out of intraposed CPs leads to ungrammaticality (e.g., *Er $wollte$ $wissen,$ wen_i der $Franz,$ $daß$ wir e_i $einladen$ $sollten,$ $gemeint$ hat 'He wanted to know who Franz thought that we should invite.' Whatever the reason for this effect may be, it shows that extraction via COMP seems to be independent of canonical government restrictions. Another piece of evidence is that the external argument of a bare infinitival clause gets Case-marked by the governing verb in intraposed position in German, but never in extraposed position. Conversely, in English the external argument of a non-finite clause gets Case at the right side of the verb because this is the standard position

for Case assignment. We conclude that the government of clauses is not
necessarily ruled by the same devices as the government of NPs.

In the following I hope to show that clauses can indeed be governed in
extraposed position without the availability of traces. One must not assume
that I is a node in German (as AUX seems to be in English) but rather that
it is parasitic on the verb.[30] This is clearest in cases where the lexical governor itself is inflected (i.e., where no AUX-verb is present to carry the I-
morphology). Once the I-feature becomes the head of a V-projection, it
will become I', and once the external argument is added it will become IP.
This is illustrated in (101) below. Furthermore, it is not necessary for the
VP to be completed before IP is completed, as shown in (102) below. The
projections of V and I can proceed independently. One major reason for I
to stick to the V-projection is that it is a subword unit and thus needs a lexical host.[31] In the following representations one can see that non-terminals
can be bundles of categories i.e., that a single node may represent more
than one level of projection for each category present. This is expressed by
[X/Y], where X is a projection other than Y and both X and Y may range
from the zero-level to the maximal projection level.

(101)

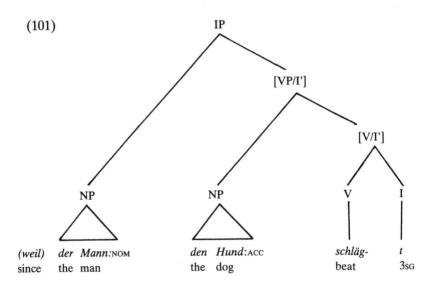

(102)

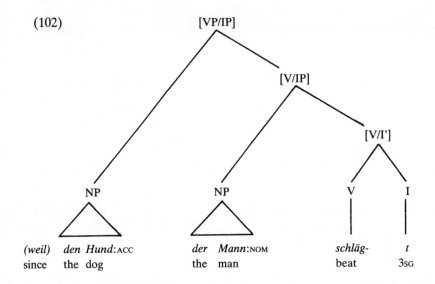

(weil)	*den Hund*:ACC	*der Mann*:NOM	*schläg-*	*t*
since	the dog	the man	beat	3SG

Notice that extraposition in German moves material to the right of I i.e., the situation is not as simple as in English where I is to the left of VP and thus the extraponendum can straightforwardly be adjoined to VP. If I always governs a maximal V-projection, extraposition of an object-CP could only be licit with a trace to the left of the verb; the verb (being locked in a maximal projection) would fail to govern its argument. According to my suggestion above this problem simply does not arise. As shown in (103) below, V will govern CP according to the Aoun/Sportiche definition of government, although it is intertwined with the I-projection.[32] In order to simplify the analysis somewhat, we assume here that auxiliaries, which govern a main verb, can be represented by I alone. (This may turn out to be untenable, but should suffice for the moment).

(103)

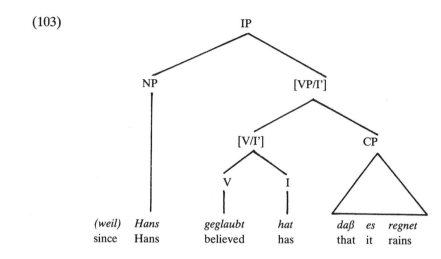

| | *(weil)* | *Hans* | *geglaubt* | *hat* | *daß* | *es* | *regnet* |
| | since | Hans | believed | has | that | it | rains |

To sum up, I have shown that the notion of government should be distinguished from the directionality (canonicity) requirement, which may be
superimposed on government. While Case is assigned by the verb only
under canonical government, argument-CPs are ruled by the weaker
requirement that they be governed by V. I have sketched one way in which
V can naturally govern across an I-projection by arguing that V and I form
syntactically independent projection lines, although I is a morpheme parasitic on V. Most important, for present purposes, is that extraposition and
other cases of rightward movement can be stated without the involvement
of traces. Put more strongly, under an account involving traces the absence
of NP-shift in German would remain quite a mystery.

3.5.3 *Complementation with Pronominal Adverbs*

German has an interesting type of complementation involving a postpositional PP, the so-called "pronominal adverb." In such cases, the PP
consists of a pronominal *da* and a postposition; for example *da+mit* ('therewith'), *da+für* ('there-for'), *da+gegen* ('there-against'), *da+zu* ('there-to')
etc. Many German verbs which do not subcategorize for a clausal argument, nevertheless do subcategorize for such a PP. These PPs can then, in
turn, license a clausal argument. I assume an analysis in which the pronominal *da* is coindexed with a CP as shown in (104).

(104) $[_{PP} \, da^i + P] \, \dots \, [CP]^i$

V2-sentences reveal that PP and CP can form a constituent, which is itself most likely a PP. This is shown in (105b) below, which we assume derives from (105a) i.e., a representation in which the complex PP is in the "Mittelfeld." In (105c) this PP is extraposed, which leads to severe ungrammaticality. Interestingly enough, if the pronominal adverb remains to the left of the verb and the CP is extraposed, as shown in (105d) below, we get a fully grammatical structure.

(105) a. *weil Hans [dafür daß Nicaragua unabhängig bleibt]*
since Hans for   that Nicaragua independent remains
gekämpft hat
fought   has
'since Hans has fought for Nicaragua to remain independent'

b. *[dafür daß Nicaragua unabhängig bleibt]$_i$ hat Hans e$_i$ gekämpft*

c. **weil Hans gekämpft hat [dafür daß Nicaragua unabhängig bleibt]*

d. *weil Hans dafür gekämpft hat [daß Nicaragua unabhängig bleibt]*

In (105a,d) the complement-linking PP is canonically governed by the verb. And the complex preverbal PP in (105b) can be relocated into a canonically governed D-structure position. However, under the assumption that extraposition does not involve traces, (105c) must be ruled out. The PP is not canonically governed or may not be governed. That is once the PP-link is detached from the verb, it fails to license the CP.[33]

If this analysis is correct, we have found yet another reason for not assuming traces in the rightward movement of arguments. It is very likely that with more careful analyses, even more asymmetries between the left and the right periphery of the sentence in German could be found. In the next section I will present evidence from a completely different case of rightward movement, namely verb raising. It will be shown that we are indeed dealing with a fairly pervasive phenomenon and that it is therefore highly unlikely that we have been trapped by a spurious generalization.

3.5.4 *Verb Raising and the Rearrangement of the Verb Cluster*

Verb Raising (VR) is an operation which lifts a non-finite verb from an embedded clause to the matrix clause where it is adjoined to the governing

verb. According to Evers (1975), the differences in the order of verbs
between Dutch and German are produced by the selection of different
adjunction sites. German cyclically adjoins the raised verb to the left of the
matrix verb, while Dutch adjoins it to the right. As a result, Dutch shows a
mirror image of the German verb order. The standard analysis assumes that
the Dutch "inverted" order is derived from a canonical (German type)
order i.e., VR applies in both languages in the same way, but the order of
verbs is changed into a mirror image only in Dutch. Anyone familiar with
the extensive literature on VR can see that this very brief characterization
is nothing but a skeleton. My goal, however, is not to discuss VR per se,
but to look at some of its effects. I will be concerned with constructions in
which inversion (or whatever process one may assume) has applied and the
raised verbs end up on a right branch with respect to their governor. Naturally, the languages we have to look at primarily are Dutch and Swiss-German. Let us first consider a Swiss-German example from Lötscher (1978).
Following VR, the D-structure represented in (106) below will surface as
(107).

(106)   *wil   de Joggel s'gottlett   ässe welle   hät*
         since the Joggel the cutlet eat wanted has
         'since Joggel has wanted to eat the cutlet'

(107)   *wil de Joggel s'gottlett hät welle ässe*

Lötscher observed that in such constructions the appearance of *sogar*
('even') and other particles is not entirely free. Assume, for instance, that
sogar is adjoined to a verb which undergoes VR e.g., *ässe*. Then an otherwise well-formed sentence as in (107) would result in the ungrammatical
string represented in (108).

(108)   ** wil de Joggel s'gottlett hät welle <u>sogar</u> ÄSSE*

In Swiss-German as well as in some other Germanic dialects, it is possible
that not only V° raises but also V-projections.[34] Thus, (106) may also surface as the following.

(109) a.   *wil de Joggel hät welle s'gottlett ässe*
      b.   *wil de Joggel hät s'gottlett welle ässe*

According to Lötscher (pers.comm.), a particle like *sogar* must always precede the finite verb. Thus, if it is adjoined to an NP, which it selects as its
focus constituent, and VPR then applies, the resulting construction will be
ungrammatical. This is shown in (110).

(110) a. *wil de Joggel hät welle <u>sogar</u> s'GOTTLETT ässe

    b. *wil de Joggel hät <u>sogar</u> s'GOTTLETT welle ässe

While the judgements on (108) are fairly stable across different speakers and also across different languages with V(P)R, the judgements on (110) are less stable. For example, one of my Swiss-German informants, Henk van Riemsdijk (pers.comm.) accepts both sentences in (110). The Dutch dialect spoken in West-Flanders also allows for VPR in about the same way as Swiss-German. The data in (111) (provided by Liliane Haegeman, pers.comm.) show basically the same distribution as the Swiss-German data; focussing on an NP governed by V with the element *en kier* ('even') is, however, possible in VPR constructions.

(111) a. *omda Jan t'vlees   heet willen <u>en</u> <u>kier</u> ETEN

         since Jan the meat has wanted even   eat

         'since Jan even wanted to EAT the meat'

    b. *omda Jan t'vlees heet <u>en</u> <u>kier</u> willen ETEN

    c. omda Jan heet willen <u>en</u> <u>kier</u> t'VLEES eten

       'since Jan wanted to eat even the MEAT'.

    d. omda Jan heet <u>en</u> <u>kier</u> t'VLEES willen eten

Standard Dutch does not have VPR but in its VR-constructions the effect can be seen very clearly, as the following pair of examples demonstrates.

(112) a. omdat Jan het boek [slechts LEZEN] wil

         since Jan the book only   read   wants

         'since Jan wants to only READ the book'

    b. *omdat Jan het boek wil [slechts LEZEN]

There is evidence that particle+V can form a constituent in Dutch. But then, VR plus inversion (or Evers' raising rule for Dutch) will affect the finite verb and the infinitival verb, to which the focussing particle *slechts* ('only') is adjoined and the phrase structure component will thus generate ungrammatical strings. Note, however, that the Dutch order of verbs is not always as rigid as one may conclude from the literature. If the V-cluster is not very complex, the German (uninverted) order can occasionally be observed. Interestingly, adjunction of a particle to a focussed V is fully acceptable under these circumstances. This can be seen in (113), which is identical to the D-structure provided in (112a).

(113)   *omdat Jan het boek* [*slechts* LEZEN] *wil*
          since Jan the boek only   read wants

Another observation comes from German. It should be noted that the canonical order of the verbal complex in German is often rearranged when the V-cluster becomes too complex. The difference between the Dutch and the German V-cluster is roughly that inversion only takes place in German when two or more infinitival verbs precede the finite verb in D-structure and that the canonical order of the shifted verbs is then retained. This inversion operation can be characterized by a rule like (114):[35]

(114)   V   V   V/I
          3   2   1 $\rightarrow$ 1   3   2

The examples in (115) show that *nur* can take the verbal complex or part of it as its focus, and that it can also be shifted to the right of the finite verb.

(115) a. *weil Hans das Buch* [*nur* LESEN] *wollen   hat*
                                      $\leftarrow$ $\leftarrow$
          since Hans the book only read   wanted has

     b.   [*nur* LESEN]$_i$ *hat$_j$ Hans das Buch* e$_i$ *wollen* e$_j$
                                          $\leftarrow$ $\leftarrow$

     c.   *weil Hans das Buch nur* [*hat* LESEN *wollen*]
                                  $\leftarrow$ $\leftarrow$

     d.   *weil Hans das Buch hat* [*nur* LESEN] *wollen*
                          $\leftarrow$ $\leftarrow$

Of course, (115d) represents a marked construction, but the canonical order of verbs is retained in the German double infinitive construction and the quantified verb *lesen* therefore remains in the canonical government domain of *wollen*. The quantified element is excluded from the government domain of the auxiliary *hat*.

We can give an account of these facts along the same lines as we did for extraposed clauses. The rightward movement of verbs or verb projections would lead to governed, but not canonically governed positions i.e., the CGH would be violated. As a result, extraction of a secondary quantifier in LF would be impossible. I believe that this analysis is basically correct. But as we have seen above, VPR can move particle-adjoined NPs to the right of the finite verb and the results are not necessarily ungrammatical, at least not for all speakers. In (110a,b) as well as in (111c,d) the offending phrase is outside the canonical goverment domain of the finite verb, but it is in the canonical government domain of a non-finite verb. In (110a), *sogar s'GOTTLETT* is canonically governed by the Case-assigner *ässe*. In (110b) the same is true, but here *ässe* has undergone reanalysis with the modal *welle*. While *ässe* is not in the canonical government domain of the modal, we can assume that it discharges its Case regularly and that it can license the presence of the particle-adjoined NP. Let us therefore assume for (110b) a phrase structure such as the following.

(110b')   IP

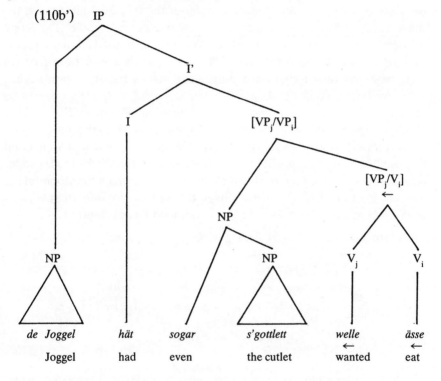

de Joggel	hät	sogar	s'gottlett	welle	ässe
Joggel	had	even	the cutlet	wanted	eat

As indicated by the arrows for the direction of canonical government, one can see that V_i is not canonically governed. V_j governs V_i, however, and projects as VP_j. Since V_i is still unsaturated, VP_j has a "hole." We must assume that the syntactic types of a daughter must be visible at the mother node as long as it is not maximal. After the NP is found at the canonical government site, V_i can project into VP_i. At this point it can be dropped from the nodes induced by a new projection line. The failure of V_j to canonically govern V_i does not have negative consequences, because the governed element does not require Case and is not quantified. So far, the assumptions made in section 3.6.1 with respect to extraposition seem to be sufficient. A problem, however, could arise when we want to maintain standard assumptions regarding LF-raising. If LF-raising must raise any scope-taking element to the IP-level and if there are no traces available for reconstructing the canonical sentence form, cases like (110a,b) and (111c,d) should be excluded. As we have already seen, however, this would not be the right consequence for at least a subset of the speakers questioned; for them, these sentences are marked, but nevertheless acceptable. The scope of *sogar/en kier* + NP cannot reach the IP-level due to the fact that it is part of a rightward moved constituent. Thus far, our theory of trace-free (in fact, base-generated) rightward movement makes the right predictions. What we now need is a concept of "relative scope." Relative scope can be obtained when LF-raising applies in a domain smaller than IP. As May (1985: Chapter 3) points out, there are empirical as well as theoretical motivations for QR towards VP.[36] If we relax QR in such a way that adjunction to a predicate phrase is possible, we can account for the marked cases under consideration. QR is then confined to the domain in which the scope-taking element is canonically governed. Given the basic orientation of governors in West-Germanic, the LFs of (110a,b) will then be as follows.

(116) a.   *wil de Joggel hät* $[_{VP}$ *welle*$_i$ $[_{VP}$ e$_i$ $[_{VP}$ *sogar s'gottlett*$_j$
$\qquad\qquad\quad \leftarrow \qquad\qquad \leftarrow$

$[_{VP}$ e$_j$ *ässe*]]]]
$\;\; \leftarrow$

   b.   *wil de Joggel hät* $[_{VP}$ *sogar s'gottlett*$_j$ $[_{VP}$ *welle*$_i$ $[_{VP}$ e$_i$
$\qquad\qquad\qquad\qquad\quad \leftarrow \qquad\qquad\qquad\; \leftarrow$

$[_{VP}$ e$_j$ *ässe*]]]]
$\;\; \leftarrow$

It is unclear why some speakers seem to disfavor the relative scope reading; similar examples of relative scope are widely accepted. Haegeman and van Riemsdijk (1986) observe that VPR leads to certain scope restrictions, which are not observed unless a quantified NP has been affected by VPR and inversion. Scope effects can also be observed in the following examples from West-Flemish (WF) and Züritüütsch (ZT).

(117) WF

   a.   *da   Jan vee   boeken hee willen   lezen*
        that Jan many books has wanted read
                                  (Q-NP<modal or modal<Q-NP)

b.   *da Jan hee willen vee boeken lezen*   (modal<Q-NP)

(118) ZT

  a.   *das de Hans vili   büecher hät welle   läse*
     that the Hans many books   has wanted read
                        (Q-NP<modal or modal<Q-NP)

  b.   *das de Hans hät welle vili büecher läse*   (modal<Q-NP)

Both of the (a) examples in (117) and (118) are ambiguous. Under one reading, the quantified NP *many books* has scope over the modal *want* and in the other *want* has scope over *many books*. Interestingly, both of the (b) sentences exhibit only this second reading i.e., narrow scope of the Q-NP. VPR has created a phrase structure in which the modal c-commands the Q-NP, but not vice versa. In their definition of c-command Haegeman and van Riemsdijk follow Muysken (1982). According to this definition, it is required that the crucial node g which dominates both a (here *vili büecher*) and b (here *welle*) is either X^{max} or X^{o}, but never X^{n} ($0<n<max$). Any newly created V counts as V^{o}. This can be seen in the following phrase structure trees of (118a,b), which are the outputs of VR/inversion and VPR/inversion respectively.

(118a')

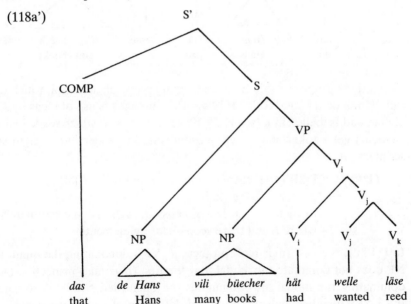

(118b')

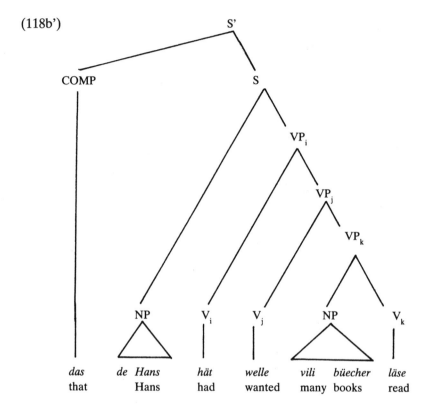

| das | de Hans | hät | welle | vili büecher | läse |
| that | Hans | had | wanted | many books | read |

The authors propose a rule for clause-bound scope phenomena, which they call "Unmarked Scope Rule" (USR). This rule makes use of ideas by Lars Hellan and Isabelle Haïk (see Haïk 1984) according to which scope bearing elements get a token index (left subscript) and a binder index (right subscript).

(119)   USR (=Haegeman and van Riemsdijk's (86))
         $_i a \ldots {}_j b \ldots \rightarrow {}_i a \ldots {}_j b_i \ldots$
         iff there is a D, D a dimension, such that $_i a$ c-commands $_j b$;
         where a and b are scope-bearing elements.

In (118b'), the first (maximal) projection (VP_k) dominating the quantified NP does not dominate the modal, but the first (maximal) projection (VP_j) dominating the modal also dominates the quantified NP. Unfortunately, the USR (together with the proposed definition of c-command) does not yield the desired result in the case of (118a). As one can see in (118a'), the

Q-NP c-commands the modal, but the modal does not c-command the Q-NP. According to our own proposal the modal can raise up to the IP-level (= S-level) because it is not subject to the requirement of canonical government. The leftward orientation of the auxiliary *hät* excludes elements to its right side that are in need of a dynasty of governors for raising to IP-level. The difficult thing is to determine which elements are in need of such a dynasty and which are not. Obviously Case-assigned elements and secondary quantifiers are prevented from raising in LF, but there are other problems. According to Haegeman and van Riemsdijk, incorporated *WH*-items can get wide scope out of VPR-contexts, while incorporated sentential adverbs cannot. This is, of course, not exactly what we would expect because *wh*-items can be Case-marked NPs while sentential adverbs, given that they are neither Case-marked nor selected as obligatory constituents, should be free of directionality constraints.

Since standard German lacks VPR, I have to confine myself to some remarks about the scope of adverbs. When VR and inversion apply in German, an adverb may be shifted to the right of the finite verb i.e., occur on a branch to the right of its governor. My observation is that adverbs requiring IP-scope are typically banned in these contexts, but can sometimes be rescued by putting stress on the scope taking adverb. This is not always possible, however. For example "attitude" adverbs such as *vielleicht* ('perhaps') and *sicherlich* ('certainly') rarely get stressed, while time adverbs must always get stressed in this environment.

(120) a.   *weil   sie   den Hans das Lied vielleicht/sicherlich/gestern*
           since they the Hans the song perhaps/certainly/ yesterday
           haben singen hören
           have   sing   hear
           'Since they have perhaps/... heard Hans sing the song'

      b.   *weil sie den Hans das Lied haben *vielleicht/*sicherlich/*
           GESTERN *singen hören.*

Obviously, stress is an important means for certain LF-sensitive elements to overcome barriers induced by the language-specific direction of government.

Haegeman and van Riemsdijk (1986) argue that QR alone cannot differentiate between the cases in which the assignment of wide scope is either permitted or forbidden. They therefore propose the USR as a device to assign relative scope. My feeling, however, is that once the directionality parameter is fully applicable for issues of LF, additional devices like USR may become unnecessary. QR (or the assignment of absolute scope) would then be naturally constrained by bounding theory and certain additional assumptions about argument/non-argument status, Case-assignment, intonation, etc.

There are three points at which our investigation of V(P)R and inversion has yielded stable results: First, it was shown that V(P)R is constrained with respect to LF-movement in the same way as extraposition i.e., both of these superficially rather different constructions interrupt the formation of dynasties, as proposed in Koster (1987). Second, it was shown that V(P)R cannot be an instance of real syntactic movement involving traces; otherwise, a D-structure level of representation with proper dynasty formation would be available and lead to well-formedness in circumstances where the S-structure is clearly unacceptable.[37] A third result is that inversion of the verbal complex is sensitive to aspects of LF. This rules out any account which ascribes inversion to the PF-level or to some stylistic component. That is, neither the T-model nor the L-model of van Riemsdijk and Williams, (1981) (which is adopted by Haegeman and van Riemsdijk, 1986) can account for the bounding constraints induced by inversion. In both models, LF is determined independently of the PF-component. My conclusion is that inversion as an operation at PF does not exist. This leaves us with two possibilities: Either inversion applies before scope assignment or the inverted orders are base generated. I tend to believe that the second option is more promising. The details of such an account have to be left for future examination.

3.6 A Comparison with English

In this section I will show that a wide range of English data contrast sharply with the West-Germanic data, which have mainly concerned us here. While the equivalents of *only* and *even* are mostly unacceptable inside PPs in German, they are inoffensive in English.

(121) a.   *John finds even the sonatas by* BEETHOVEN *boring*
      b.   *John finds the sonatas even by* BEETHOVEN *boring*
      c.   *John finds the sonatas by even* BEETHOVEN *boring*

(122) a.   *weil Hans sogar die Sonaten von* BEETHOVEN *langweilig findet*
      b.   ?? *weil Hans die Sonaten sogar von* BEETHOVEN *langweilig findet*
      c.   * *weil Hans die Sonaten von sogar* BEETHOVEN *langweilig findet*

(123)   *Since John had surgery last week,*
   a.   *he can <u>only</u> eat with a TOOTHPICK*
   b.   *he can eat <u>only</u> with a TOOTHPICK*
   c.   *he can eat with <u>only</u> a TOOTHPICK*

(124)   *Da Hans letzte Woche operiert wurde,*
   a.   *kann er <u>nur</u> mit einem ZAHNSTOCHER essen*
   b.   **kann er mit <u>nur</u> einem ZAHNSTOCHER essen*

The explanation for these differences is straightforward under our account. Inserting the particle in the governing domain of P leads at the level of LF to a violation of the CGH in German, but not in English. This is because in English P falls in the canonical direction of government by the verb. It is less clear what happens with NP as a bounding node. If the PP in (121b) and in (122b) fails to be governed by N i.e., if PP is adjoined to NP, we would predict the absence of a bounding violation and the weak effect in the German example would have to be accounted for some other way.

One of our major observations was that *nur* and related particles cannot be adjoined to extraposed complements in German. Under our account we would expect things to be different in English. The following data indicate that adjunction of *only* to the VP is preferred, although adjunction to CP is nevertheless a possible marked alternative.

(125) a.   *John <u>only</u> asked me whether the LIBRARY would be closed (he didn't ask me about other buildings)*
    b.   *John asked me <u>only</u> whether the LIBRARY would be closed (...)*

In (125b), *only* must be adjoined to the CP, inside which it selects its focus constituent. Since the CP is canonically governed the example is expected to be well-formed, which it is.

Turning to complex NPs, however, it can be shown that subjacency violations are present in both languages.

(126) a.   *John would report <u>only</u> the fact that Mary MISBEHAVED*
    b.   **John would report the fact <u>only</u> that Mary MISBEHAVED*

(127) a.   *weil Hans <u>nur</u> die Tatsache daß sich Maria nicht gut BENAHM berichten würde*
    b.   **weil Hans die Tatsache <u>nur</u> daß sich Maria nicht gut BENAHM berichten würde*

We can conclude from this that even the formation of a chain of uniformly oriented governors is not always sufficient to permit LF-raising. The complex-NP-constraint seems to apply independently. But what about the possessive constructions examined in sections 3.2 and 3.3? As we have seen, German disfavors adjoining particles to a genitive NP inside an NP. English does not have a postnominal genitive or possessive and therefore it is impossible to directly compare the two constructions. However, when a PP is used, intrusion of the particle seems to be possible in English. This is shown in the following contrasts.

(128) a. *weil sie die Schuhe sogar der KINDER   putzt
         since she the shoes even   the children:GEN polishes
         (=(60b) from section 3.2)

     b. ?weil sie die Schuhe sogar von den KINDERN putzt
                                        of

     c. She polishes the shoes even of the CHILDREN

We can tentatively say that the genitive NP in (128a) is governed by the N *Schuhe*, and that therefore the NP is not canonically governed. The PP *sogar von den Kindern* in (128b), on the other hand, is adjoined to the NP *die Schuhe*. In this case, government ceases to play a role. Therefore, the genitive NP but not the PP is an island. This contrast also shows up when the possibilities for syntactic movement are examined.

(129) a. *Der Kinder/wessen$_i$ hat sie die Schuhe e$_i$ geputzt
         the children/whose has she the shoes   polished

     b. ?Von den Kindern/von wem$_i$ hat sie die Schuhe e$_i$ geputzt
         of   the children/ of   who

Since English uses postnominal PPs, the prediction is that the particles should be able to intrude. This prediction is correct, as shown in (130) below.

(130) a. The dean admits only children of RICH people to this university

     b. The dean admits children only of RICH people to this university

     c. Even children of RICH people sometimes fail their exams

     d. Children even of RICH people sometimes fail their exams

Assuming that *of*-insertion in English results in PPs which are canonically governed, a purely direction based theory of bounding would predict that particles can occur before *of*-PPs. This prediction turns out to be wrong as shown in (131).

(131) a.   *Even* the destruction of this small VILLAGE was recorded by
           Plinius

   b.   * *The destruction* *even* of this small VILLAGE was recorded by
           Plinius

   c.   *The destruction of* *even* this small VILLAGE was recorded by
           Plinius

A theory in which it is separately stated that NP counts as a bounding node
in English could account for (131b), but as shown in (131c) there is a
residual problem, which was also found to characterize some German constructions. Namely, once the offending phrase falls into the domain of a
canonical governor, the violation is drastically reduced or completely
removed. I take this to be indicative of a general problem, which cannot be
accounted for even within the most recent developments in bounding
theory.

   Let us now look at another category, namely APs. In section 3.3. it was
shown that whenever the complement of A is not canonically governed,
German does not tolerate particles inside APs. In English APs, the (PP-)
complements are to the right of A. Given that the orientation of governors
is to the right, particles should be allowed in this context. As (132b) and
(133b) below indicate, this seems to be true.

(132) a.   *The composer was* *only* *proud of his* OPERAS
   b.   *The composer was proud* *only* *of his* OPERAS

(133) a.   *Mary was* *even* *unaware of the fact that her husband was*
           LEFTHANDED
   b.   *Mary was unaware* *even* *of the fact that her husband was*
           LEFTHANDED

Finally, let us turn to extraposition and other instances of rightward
movement. As our investigation in section 3.5 has shown, rightward-shifted
constituents are subject to severe restrictions in OV-languages like Dutch
and German. I have argued that these restrictions can be derived quite simply from the directionality parameter: If right branches at S-structure cannot be related to D-structure left branches, rightward movement leads to
positions that are — at most — governed, certainly not canonically governed. The observed island effects can then be explained, as well as the
absence of pronominal adverbs in extraposed position and the absence of
Heavy-NP-Shift in German and Dutch. For English, the situation is just the
reverse: Rightward movement does not result in a destruction of the canon-

ical VO-branching pattern and therefore neither island effects nor problems
with Case-assignment or the licensing of clausal complements should occur.
The following examples demonstrate that our theory correctly predicts
these facts. Take, for example, Heavy-NP-Shift.

(134) a. *John invited Mary for dinner*
      b. *John invited for dinner a dynamic young actress*

(135) a. *weil Hans Maria zum Abendessen einlud*
      b. **weil Hans zum Abendessen einlud eine dynamische junge
          Schauspielerin*

If "rightward movement" does not leave traces i.e, if sentences like (134b)
are base-generated, Case must be assigned to the heavy NP in a non-stan-
dard way. I assume that (134b) has a structure in which the adjacency
requirement for Case assignment is violated, but which conforms to the
requirement for canonical government.

(134b')

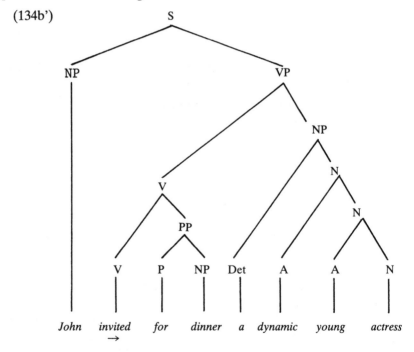

There is no reason to believe that V loses its power to canonically govern its
complement after a PP has been adjoined to it. The only factor that must be

taken into consideration, therefore, is the adjacency requirement i.e., it needs to be relaxed. Let us say therefore that adjacency can be violated under the condition that the complement is rhematic. What makes (135b) bad, then, is the fact that the verb's orientation is ←. Any NP that is not itself in the domain of ← or related to ← via a trace will violate the Case Filter.

Heavy-NP-Shift is also a good example for demonstrating that a particle can travel along with an NP.

(136) a. *John called [even MARY] up*

    b. *John called up [even his oldest friends from COLLEGE]*

As should be obvious by now, German does not have an equivalent to the English construction, although extraposition of clauses and PPs is possible in both languages. Our expectation is that English allows for extraposed particle+XP whereas German does not. The following sets of examples show that this expectation is fulfilled.

(137) a. *John even asked me yesterday [whether I would lend him my TOOTHBRUSH]*

    b. *[Even whether I would lend him my TOOTHBRUSH] John asked me yesterday*

    c. *John asked me yesterday [even whether I would lend him my TOOTHBRUSH]*

(138) a. *The criminal will only admit to the judge [that he ROBBED the victim] (but not that he has KILLED him)*

    b. *[Only that he ROBBED the victim] will the criminal admit to the judge (...)*

    c. *The criminal will admit to the judge [only that he ROBBED the victim] (...)*

In the (a)-sentences the particle adjoins to a VP containing an extraposed clause and this clause can be the focus of the particle. The (b)-sentences, which are admittedly highly marked, show that the particle can form a constituent with the clausal argument. And the (c)-sentences show that extraposition of particle+CP yields grammatical results in English. The reason for this is that extraposition leaves the quantified phrase on a right branch with respect to the governing verb. As we have seen, the situation is drastically different in German. In German, only (137a,b) and (138a,b) have grammatical correlates.

(139) a.   *weil   mich Hans gestern   sogar gefragt hat* [*ob   ich*
           since me   Hans yesterday even   asked   has whether I
           ihm meine ZAHNBÜRSTE *leihen   würde*]
           him my   toothbrush borrow would

     b.   [*Sogar ob ich ihm meine* ZAHNBÜRSTE *leihen würde*] *hat mich
          Hans gestern gefragt*

     c.   **weil mich Hans gestern gefragt hat* [*sogar ob ich ihm meine*
          ZAHNBÜRSTE *leihen würde*]

(140) a.   *weil   der Kriminelle nur   zugeben wird* [*daß   er   das*
           since the criminal   only admit   will that he   the
           Opfer AUSGERAUBT *hat*]
           victim robbed   has

     b.   [*Nur daß er das Opfer* AUSGERAUBT *hat*] *wird der Kriminelle
          zugeben*

     c.   **weil der Kriminelle zugeben wird* [*nur daß er das Opfer*
          AUSGERAUBT *hat*]

The same effect can be demonstrated for the extraposition of PP from NP. Consider the following English examples and their German correlates.

(141) a.   *Only women* [*with* RED *hair*] *can apply for this job*
     b.   ?*Women* [*only with* RED *hair*] *can apply for this job*
     c.   ?*Women can apply for this job* [*only with* RED *hair*]

(142) a.   *John would hire* [*even someone without a* HIGHSCHOOL DIPLO-
          MA] *for this job*
     b.   *John would hire someone for this job* [*even without a* HIGH-
          SCHOOL DIPLOMA]

(143) a.   *weil sich   auf diese Stelle nur   Frauen* [*mit* ROTEN
           since(refl.) for this job   only women with red
           Haaren] *bewerben können.*
           hair   apply   can

     b.   ?*weil sich auf diese Stelle Frauen* [*nur mit* ROTEN *Haaren*]
          bewerben können

     c.   **weil sich auf diese Stelle Frauen bewerben können* [*nur mit*
          ROTEN *Haaren*]

The (a)-sentences show NP+PP with the particle preceding the NP and the focus on the PP (or part of it). Only in English, however, can the particle be extraposed with the focussed PP. The examples marked with ? are slightly problematic, but we can assume that this derives from a weak subjacency violation induced by the presence of the NP. What can otherwise be seen is that English tolerates the extraposition of a quantified PP, whereas German does not. The only possible way of shifting the PP out in German is to leave the particle in front of the NP *Frauen*, as shown in (144) below.

(144)   *weil sich auf diese Stelle <u>nur</u> Frauen bewerben können [mit*
         ROTEN *Haaren]*

The phrase structure for (144) shows that *nur* can be adjoined to a constituent containing the extraposed PP.

(145)   [IP/VP]

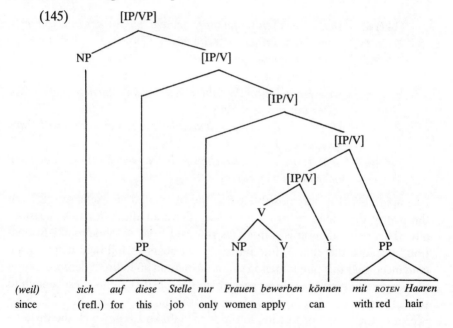

(weil)	sich	auf	diese	Stelle	nur	Frauen	bewerben	können	mit ROTEN Haaren
since	(refl.)	for	this	job	only	women	apply	can	with red hair

In (145) *nur* is adjoined to an IP containing an unsaturated V. And as long as we assume that the extraposed PP is adjoined to IP, it is guaranteed that the particle can select this PP, or part of it, as its focus.[38]

This comparison between English and German has shown a remarkable difference with respect to the rightward movement of LF-sensitive elements. The difference can be derived from the independently motivated directionality parameter, which fixes the canonical pattern of phrase structure as right branching in English and left branching in German.

Let me add that the set of constructions constrained by this parameter is not confined to particles such as *only* and *even* and their counterparts in German, but also includes other elements e.g., scope sensitive coordinators such as *either...or, neither...nor*. While the entire *(n)either...(n)or* phrase can be moved to the right in English, this is never possible in German. As the following data show, the first member must remain in a position where it is canonically governed by the verb. While extraposition observes this trivially in English, it fails to do so in German.

(146) a.   *John will either go out with his DOG or with his CAT*

    b.   *John will go out (tomorrow) either with his DOG or with his CAT*

(147) a.   *weil Hans [entweder mit seinem HUND oder mit seiner*
          since Hans either   with his   dog   or   with his
          KATZE] spazierengehen will
          cat   walking   wants

    b.   *weil Hans [entweder mit seinem HUND] spazierengehen will [oder mit seiner KATZE]*

    c.   *[Entweder mit seinem HUND oder mit seiner KATZE] will Hans spazierengehen*

    d.   **weil Hans spazierengehen will [entweder mit seinem HUND oder mit seiner KATZE]*

Example (147d) is only possible when the bracketed phrase is set off from the rest of the clause by prosodic means. German allows for this occasionally. This phenomenon is sometimes referred to as "Doppelpunkt-Intonation" because the clause, intonationally, appears to follow a colon. I am convinced that this phenomenon is not more than an indirect demonstration of the general picture according to which LF-sensitive items must remain to the left of the governing verb. In any case, the disjunctive PP must have access to the verbal projection in order to yield an LF in which the disjunction has (semantic) scope over the IP.

4.   Conclusion

Starting from a criticism of Jacobs' (1983) syntactic account of German scalar (or quantificational) particles, I hope to have shown that most if not all of the problems pointed out by Jacobs can quite naturally be solved within a theory that calls upon principles of tree geometry and the directionality-of-government parameter. Jacobs correctly argued that particles cannot be adjoined to non-verbal projections because they must take semantic scope over the entire proposition. His mono-stratal categorial syntax, however, was not flexible enough to provide solutions for the surface linguistic facts. The most important of these facts is that particles adjoin to almost any major syntactic category with which they can form a single constituent. The present account can be seen as an attempt to provide a semantically plausible analysis, which nevertheless respects the distributional facts of the language.

It was observed that maximal projections that are not headed by V or I(NFL) e.g., NPs and most PPs, are islands for quantificational particles like *nur* ('only') in German. In terms of a level of Logical Form this means that the particle and its focus constituent cannot raise out of the domain in which they are generated. Semantic interpretation, however, requires that these elements obtain scope over the V/I-projection i.e., over IP (or at least VP). It was then shown that under certain conditions these islands could be "opened." This is always the case when another raising element in the S-structure tree crosses the island. I chose to express this crossing in terms of Kayne's (1983) Connectedness Theory. It was next shown that non-verbal categories with a leftward orientation of their governing head fail to be islands for particle/focus-raising in German and Dutch. Under the assumption that languages such as German and Dutch are parametrized for leftwards orientation of the governor, this fact follows naturally. I adopted Koster's (1987) theory of Global Harmony in order to capture this observation about canonical government. Koster argues in his work against a level of LF on the basis of the observation that LF-movement (quantifier-scope assignment) usually does not observe the same bounding constraints as the grammar of visible/audible "movement." It appears, however, that not all scope sensitive elements behave alike with respect to the bounding conditions of the grammar of movement; particles were shown to conform quite closely to the bounding conditions of the grammar of movement.

The final major finding was that in German, Dutch and various related dialects, rightward movement systematically leads to positions that are islands for the raising of the particle and its focus in LF. Such an analysis can, however, only be maintained, if rightward movement is differentiated from leftward movement. It was argued that an optimal differentiation can be achieved by assuming that rightward movement does not leave traces, whereas leftward movement does. Along with Koster, we have argued that scope is co-determined by D-structure/A-positions. If in cases of rightward movement the D-structure/A-position were to be recovered via a trace, certain scope relations could be assigned and an explanation in terms of interpretive islands would fall apart. There is, moreover, increasing evidence for the absence of traces in operations such as extraposition. It is also becoming less apparent that traces play a role in the rearrangement of the verb-cluster in Germanic. Inverted verb-clusters, however, exhibit all the islandhood properties observed for extraposition. In general, rightward movement should be seen as an operation (probably the parser's response to certain complexities that are a consequence of the grammar of OV-languages) leading to a violation of the canonical direction of government in German and Dutch. Of course, this is not the case in a language such as English. In English, rightward movement leads to positions that can be assumed to still be in the range of a rightward-looking governor; leftward movement, however, leaves a trace, which enables moved elements to get relocated whenever necessary; as was seen, in English rightward movement such as extraposition and NP/PP-shift simply does not lead to islands for the interpretation of *only* and *even*.

Notes

1.   This is taken from Jacobs (1983: 40-42).

2.   The superscripts in this notation refer to the valency of the V-category. V^3 means that V seeks three arguments, V^2 that V seeks two arguments, etc.

3.   See Jacobs (1983: 49).

4.   With the exception of *durchschnittlich* ('mediocre'). We will return to this issue below.

5.   It should be noted that there is a vast literature on these issues. The only work that links the semantic aspects to modern syntactic theory is, to my knowledge, Rooth (1985).

6.   Another reason why this may be wrong is that there are arguments according to which the determiner is the head of the NP (see Fukui 1986).

7.   See König (forthcoming:5), but also his remarks on p. 40.

8.   See Hornstein and Weinberg (1981). Due to the word order of German, it would not be possible to simply resort to a process of reanalysis which converts $V[_{PP} \text{ P NP}]$ into $[_V \text{ V} + P]$ NP. Obviously, the matter is far more abstract than a local operation like this would suggest.

9.   In fact the PP is on a left branch with respect to the verb.

10. Pesetsky discusses some problems that his theory has with QR on pp. 683-687. See, however, the application of Pesetsky's theory in May (1985). As May points out, intersecting paths are banned in English. One of his examples is the following contrast involving a quantified NP and a WH-item. Notice that the former is moved in LF, while the latter is moved in the syntax:

(i)   What did everyone buy for Max?
(ii) *Who bought everything for Max?

The following simplified LFs show that the paths intersect in (ii), but not in (i):

(i') what_i [everyone_j [e_j ... e_i...]]
(ii') who_j [everything_i [e_j ... e_i ...]]

As far as I can see, contrasts of this sort cannot be observed in German. This is reminiscent of the absence of superiority effects in this language.

Notice, however, that due to the "Scope Principle" and to adjunction to operator position, as assumed in May (1985), n LF-moved quantifiers (n>1) can choose any relative scope without necessarily inducing violations of the PCC. Take for example *Every student admires some professor* with wide scope on the object-NP. May's analysis suggests the following LF

(iii)

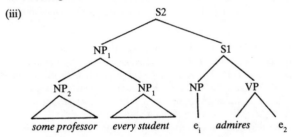

Considering the branching nodes through which the dependency has to be traced, the paths are: For 2: {VP,S1,S2,NP2} and for 1: {S1,S2,NP2}. Thus, this reading is consistent with the PCC.

11. *Only* and *even* are chosen in these examples to arrive at pragmatically appropriate meanings. They could, in principle, also be exchanged.

12. This is less obvious in the example given, than in examples where *nicht* appears as term negation. Semantic interpretation needs an input in which *nicht* has scope over the projection of the verb.

13. König (forthcoming) suggests that so-called "additive" particles cannot be in the scope of negation for pragmatic reasons. Notice that even in English where *not even* is allowed, *even* must take wide scope.

14. Pesetsky's theory crucially involves a path between INFL and COMP in order to derive the *that*-trace effect. In cases like *that every student admires some professor*, the INFL-COMP-path would always intersect with the quantifier-variable-paths in a way which violates the PCC. May has noticed that. He therefore has to stipulate that the INFL-COMP-path is only relevant at S-structure, but not at LF. See May (1985:139).

15. For further refinements, see Linebarger (1987) and related literature.

16. Notice that German has a lexical process of N°-incorporation which produces verbs like *kuchen+essen* (cake eat), *bier+trinken* (beer drink). NPs cannot be incorporated. This is shown by the fact that N°-incorporating verbs can be recategorized as N°, as in *sein Bier-trinken* ('his drinking (of) beer'), whereas NP-objects have to stay outside the verb to be recategorized: **sein [das Bier] Trinken* versus *sein Trinken [des Biers]*. The requirement seems to be that only pure lexical categories can be incorporated; that is, even non-maximal projections are not allowed to participate in the word formation process: **sein Kuchen-vom-Bäcker-essen* ('his eating of cake from a bakery'), **sein Bier-aus-dem-Fass-trinken* ('his drinking of beer from the barrell'). It is not entirely clear to me what the phrase structure of German genitive constructions is, but even if they were such that the genitive NP attaches to N° to form an N', N'-phrases like *Haus [nur [seines Vaters]]* ('house (of) only his father') could never be incorporated by a verb.

17. For instance, Longobardi (1985) or Bennis and Hoekstra (1985); see also Haverkort (1986), where some of the literature is critically evaluated and a 'Relativized Connectedness Condition' is proposed.

18. A detailed discussion of Swedish transitive adjectives is provided in Platzack (1982). The Swedish data reported here (originally due to Platzack) are taken from chapter 4 of Koster (1987).

19. See Chomsky (1981,163ff). N was taken to be a lexical governor in cases like **They gave me a vase [PRO broken]*. In this example, *vase* would govern the unprotected PRO of the adjunct small clause, violating the PRO-theorem. This is problematic in the light of well-formed examples like *They gave me the vase [PRO broken]*, where it would be difficult to argue that the use of the definite article has an influence on the governor. Let me just mention that Chomsky's example can be accounted for without recourse to government by something like the Rhythm Rule of metrical phonology. See Bayer (1989) for more details.

20. Notice that there may be even a third factor involved which affects postpositional uses. For some unclear reason, postpositions in German do not seem to favor "long" NPs as their complements. Compare, for instance:

(i)   weil entlang des Flusses, der   stark verschmutzt war, Kinder   spielten
      since along   the river   which very polluted   was children played

(ii) ??weil den Fluss, der stark verschmutzt war, entlang Kinder spielten

Whatever the nature of this constraint may be, it must be kept in mind that it will most likely also apply to particles intervening between NP and postposition. In any case, the (b)-examples in (73) through (75) sound more natural when the focus bears heavy stress and the particle plus postposition attach to the NP in an enclitic fashion.

21. For expository reasons, I would like to give a rough idea of what these concepts refer to: A quantifier Q is *increasing* if for any quantified noun-phrase QP and a pair of VPs such that the denotation of VP1 is a subset of the denotation of VP2, [QP VP1] entails [QP VP2], while the reverse does not hold. Examples of increasing quantifiers are *some, every, most, many*, and also NPs such as definite NPs and proper names, which are normally taken to be quantifier-free. A quantifier is *decreasing* if the same holds as what is

stated above, but [QP VP2] entails [QP VP1], while the reverse does not hold. Examples are *no, few, neither*, etc. The following examples should illustrate what is intended.

(i) *increasing*

    a. If many men entered the race early, then many men entered the race

    b. * If many men entered the race, then many men entered the race early

(ii) *decreasing*

    a. * If few linguists entered the race early, then few linguists entered the race

    b. If few linguists entered the race, then few linguists entered the race early

22. See also de Jong and Verkuyl (1984).

23. One should be aware that some of the allegedly well-formed conjunctions in Barwise and Cooper (1981:4.10) do not sound quite natural e.g., *No man and few women could lift this piano*.

24. See, for example, Hoekstra (1984) where a new condition is proposed, the "Unlike Category Condition," which is intended to rule out "Mittelfeld"-clauses in Dutch (and German). The UCC stipulates that no category of type [αV,βN] may (canonically) govern a category of type [αV,βN]. Under the assumption that S' is a projection of INFL and therefore of V, it follows that S' cannot remain in intraposed position. Hoekstra's proposal, however, gives rise to a number of problems. German *zu*-infinitives i.e., clauses with an INFL are quite acceptable in intraposed position, and even finite clauses are if they are short enough. Furthermore, if the UCC is intended as a universal, the handling of strict OV-languages like Japanese is unclear.

25. There is a psycholinguistic literature on extraposition and other instances of rightward movement, which I cannot review here. A useful overview is found in Frazier (1985). Frazier criticizes theories that attempt to explain extraposition in terms of changing a complex left-branching structure into a less complex right-branching structure. She proposes, instead, a measure of syntactic complexity in which the number of terminal nodes is divided by the number of non-terminal nodes in a phrase structure tree. Unfortunately, this measure predicts that intraposed clauses should be easier to process than extraposed ones, a prediction that in German lacks any intuitive appeal.

    Another problem may be that node counting alone is not enough. Some of the research reported by Frazier use adjunct clauses, which are not subcategorized. It is therefore not surprising that their placement before or after the main clause shows little or no effect on the processing load.

26. Baltin discusses the following sentence.

(i)   Bill [$_{VP}$ hit the man e$_i$] [who asked him to ___]$_i$

If the VP is copied into the empty VP of the extraposed relative clause, this VP will contain the trace of the relative clause itself. This violates the i-within-i Condition as stated in Chomsky (1981:212).

27. See Cardinaletti (forthcoming). Curiously, Cardinaletti observes German data like (100c), but does not conclude that traces may legitimize such constructions. The same applies to Fanselow (1987:chapter 6).

28. We may be forced to assume that governed PPs have Case. This is shown in examples (i) and (ii), where *stehen* subcategorizes for a PP while *rauchen* does not.

(i) a. *weil er hinter   dem Haus geraucht hat*   (adjunct-PP)
         since he behind the house smoked has
     b. *weil er geraucht hat hinter dem Haus*

(ii) a. *weil er hinter   dem Haus gestanden ist*   (governed PP)
         since he behind the house stood   has
     b. **weil er gestanden ist hinter dem Haus*

29. Chomsky (1986) has introduced a notion of "θ-government," which requires sisterhood between governor and governee. If this concept were to be called upon here, it would certainly need to be relaxed, as we will shortly see.

30. This is also the analysis of Kratzer (1984) and Reuland (1988).

31. There may be languages where I is a clitic and therefore quite independent of the verb. Klavans (1985) gives examples from Ngiyambaa, an Australian language, where the tense feature attaches to the verb, but the person and Case feature attach as clitics in second position to whatever category precedes it.

32. In a GPSG-framework, V would be a slash category which loses the slash as soon as the argument is found. Because GPSG presumably expresses leftward movement with the same device, the distinction that we want to derive is not available.

33. The situation is slightly more complicated because one can, in spoken German, observe sentences in which the pronominal adverb appears to the right of I.

    (i)   *weil Hans gekämpft hat dafür [daß Nicaragua unabhängig bleibt]*

    In these cases, however, there is a very clear prosodic break between the PP and the extraposed CP, and the PP must not receive stress. This kind of requirement is absent in cases such as (105b). We can thus be quite sure that PP and CP do not form a constituent in rightward movement. On the other hand, the PP would fail to be canonically governed i.e., it would simply be governed. From these considerations it follows that the [PP+CP]-constituent is adjoined at a height where the VP is already "closed," (perhaps to the IP). My main point remains unaffected by these details.

34. See Lötscher (1978), den Besten and Edmondson (1983), and Haegeman and van Riemsdijk (1986). Haegeman and van Riemsdijk speak about Verb Projection Raising (VPR).

35. Of course, this issue is much more complex than it appears to be here, as shown in the work of Kohrt (1979), Edmondson (1980), den Besten and Edmondson (1983), and a number of other researchers.

36. One reason to assume adjunction of a quantifier-NP to VP is that in contexts of VP-deletion such as

    (i)   *Some student admires every professor, but John doesn't Ø*

    the wide scope reading of *every professor* cannot be obtained, while it can be in the single ˙clause

(ii)   *Some student admires every professor.*

The non-ambiguity of (i) can be explained if the Q-NP *every professor* is adjoined to the deleted VP. See Sag (1976) and Williams (1977). There are other reasons, which are more closely bound to issues of weak crossover. (See Koopman and Sportiche, 1982). May (1985) assumes VP-adjunction in LF but argues that "predicate level scope" would be difficult to maintain for semantic reasons. He adopts a principle, which says that an operator which minimally c-commands a predicate must c-command all of its thematic arguments. It is difficult to see how this proposal would lead to the desired results. Since most natural languages center LF-sensitive items around the V- or INFL-projection, one may conclude that adjunction to VP is semantically equivalent to adjunction to IP without making any assumptions about c-command, etc.

37.   Notice that traces are otherwise essential for verb movement. If they were not available, it would be difficult to check at the S-structure of V2-sentences whether a given item is in the domain of a displaced verbal governor. Thus, the syntax of verbs presents yet another parade example for a difference between leftward and rightward movement.

38.   Notice that in English the situation is different. The particle preceding the NP from which a PP (or a relative clause) is extraposed can take material from the extraposed phrase only if it is adjoined to the VP, but not if it is adjoined to the NP. The reason is obvious: If the particle adjoins to the NP, its syntactic domain is the NP and nothing else. This is shown in the following examples:

(i)   John will [only[cut wood tomorrow [from BEECHES]]] (...but not from ELMS)
(ii)   John will cut [only[wood[from BEECHES]]] tomorrow (...)
(iii)   ?*John will cut [only[wood]] tomorrow [from BEECHES] (...)

(i) and (ii) are unproblematic because *only* adjoins to an XP in which it finds the PP *from BEECHES* as a focus constituent. Example (iii) is ruled out by the fact that the syntactic domain of *only* fails to include the focus constituent. I take this to be another piece of evidence against the presence of traces in extraposition. If there were a trace after *wood* in (iii), the sentence would not be so much worse than the "in situ" version given in (ii).

References

Abraham, W. (ed.) 1983. *On the Formal Syntax of the Westgermania.* Amsterdam: Benjamins.

Aoun, J. and D. Sportiche. 1983. "On the Formal Theory of Government." *The Linguistic Review* 2, 211-236.

Bäuerle, R. Ch. Schwarze. and A. von Stechow. (eds.) 1983. *Meaning, Use, and Interpretation of Language.* Berlin: De Gruyter.

Baker, C.L. and J.J. McCarthy. (eds.) 1981. *The Logical Problem of Language Acquisition.* Cambridge, Mass.: MIT Press.

Baltin, M.R. 1981. "Strict Bounding." In: Baker and McCarthy (eds.).
———. 1987. "Do Antecedent-Contained Deletions Exist?" *Linguistic Inquiry* 18, 579-595.

Barwise, J. and R. Cooper. 1981. "Generalized Quantifiers and Natural Language." *Linguistics and Philosophy* 4, 159-219.

Bayer, J. 1984. "COMP in Bavarian Syntax." *The Linguistic Review* 3, 209-274.

———. 1985. "Adjazenz und Kettenbildung: Bemerkungen zur Syntax der deutschen Gradpartikeln." Ms., Max-Planck-Institut für Psycholinguistik, Nijmegen.

———. 1989. "A Note on Alleged PRO-government." In: D. Jaspers, W. Klooster, Y. Putseys and P. Seuren (eds.).

Bennis, H. and T. Hoekstra. 1984. "Gaps and Parasitic Gaps." *The Linguistic Review* 4, 29-87.

van Benthem, J. and A. ter Meulen. (eds.) 1984. *Generalized Quantifiers in Natural Language*. Dordrecht: Foris.

den Besten, H. and J. Edmondson. 1983. "The Verbal Complex in Continental West Germanic." In: Abraham (ed.).

Cardinaletti, A. (forthcoming) "Aspetti Sintattici della Regola di Estraposizione della Frase Relativa." *Rivista di Grammatica Generativa*.

Chomsky, N.A. 1981. *Lectures on Government and Binding*. Dordrecht: Foris.

———. 1986. *Barriers*. Cambridge Mass.: MIT Press.

Culicover, P. and Rochemont, M. (forthcoming). "Extraposition and the Complement Principle." *Linguistic Inquiry*.

Dowty, D., L. Karttunen. and A. Zwicky. (eds.) 1985. *Natural Language Parsing*. Cambridge: Cambridge University Press.

Edmondson, J.A. 1980. "Gradienz und die doppelte Infinitivkonstruktion im Deutschen." *Papiere zur Linguistik* 22, 59-82.

Everaert, M., Evers, A., Huybregts, R. and Trommelen, M. 1988. *Morphology and Modularity*. Dordrecht: Foris.

Evers, A. 1975. "The Transformational Cycle in Dutch and German." Diss., University of Utrecht.

Fanselow, G. 1987. *Konfigurationalität*. Tübingen: Narr.

Frazier, L. 1985. "Syntactic Complexity." In: Dowty, Karttunen and Zwicky (eds.)

Fodor, J.D. 1978. "Parsing Strategies and Constraints on Transformations." *Linguistic Inquiry* 9, 427-473.

Fukui, N. 1986. "A Theory of Category Projection and Its Applications." Diss., Massachusetts Institute of Technology.

Gazdar, G. 1980. "A Cross-Categorial Semantics for Coordination." *Linguistics and Philosophy* 3, 407-409.

———. E. Klein, G. Pullum, and I. Sag. 1985. *Generalized Phrase Structure Grammar*. Cambridge Mass., Harvard University Press.

de Geest, W. and Y. Putseys. (eds.) 1984. *Sentential Complementation*. Dordrecht: Foris.

Grewendorf, G. 1988. *Aspekte der deutschen Syntax: Eine Reaktions-Bindungs-Analyse*. Tübingen: Narr.

Haegeman, L. and H. van Riemsdijk. 1986. "Verb Projection Raising, Scope and the Typology of Verb Movement Rules." *Linguistic Inquiry* 17, 417-466.

Haïk, I. 1984. "Indirect Binding." *Linguistic Inquiry* 15, 185-223.

Haverkort, M. 1986. "Parasitic Gaps: Multiple Variable Binding, Connectedness, ATB or Chain Composition." M.A. thesis, University of Nijmegen.

Higginbotham, J. and R. May. 1981. "Questions, Quantifiers and Crossing." *The Linguistic Review* 1, 41-80.

Hoekstra, T. 1984. "Government and the Distribution of Sentential Complementation in Dutch." In: de Geest and Putseys (eds.).

Hornstein, N. and A. Weinberg. 1981. "Case Theory and Preposition Stranding." *Linguistic Inquiry* 12, 55-94.

Huck, G. and A. Ojeda. (eds.) 1986. *Syntax and Semantics 20: Discontinuous Constituency*. New York: Academic Press.

Jackendoff, R. 1972. *Semantic Interpretation in Generative Grammar*. Cambridge Mass. MIT Press.

Jacobs, J. 1983. *Fokus und Skalen. Zur Syntax und Semantik der Gradpartikeln im Deutschen*. Tübingen: Niemeyer.

Jaspers, D., Klooster, W., Putseys, Y. and Seuren, P. 1989. (eds.), *Sentential Complementation and the Lexicon. Studies in Honour of Wim de Geest*. Dordrecht: Foris.

de Jong, F. and H. Verkuyl. 1984. "Generalized Quantifiers: the Properness of their Strength." In: van Benthem and ter Meulen (eds.).

Karttunen, L. and S. Peters. 1979. "Conventional Implicature." In: Oh and Dinneen (eds).

Kayne, R. 1983. "Connectedness." *Linguistic Inquiry* 14, 223-249.

Klavans, J.L. 1985. "The Independence of Syntax and Phonology in Cliticization." *Language* 61, 95-120.

König, E. (forthcoming.) "Gradpartikeln." To appear in: von Stechow, A. and D. Wunderlich (eds.). *Handbuch der Semantik*. Frankfurt: Athenäum.

Kohrt, M. 1979. "Verbstellung und "doppelter Infinitiv" im Deutschen." *Leuvense Bijdragen* 68, 1-31.

Koopman, H. and D. Sportiche. 1982. "Variables and the Bijection Principle." *The Linguistic Review* 2, 139-160.

Koster, J. 1978. *Locality Principles in Syntax*. Dordrecht: Foris.

———. 1984. "Global Harmony." *Tilburg Papers in Language and Literature* 61.

———. 1987. *Domains and Dynasties: The Radical Autonomy of Syntax*. Dordrecht: Foris.

Kratzer, A. 1984. "On Deriving Syntactic Differences between German and English." Ms., Technical University Berlin.

Kroch, A. and A. Joshi. 1986. "Analyzing Extraposition in a Tree Adjoining Grammar." In: Huck and Ojeda (eds).

Lang, E. 1984. *The Semantics of Coordination*. Amsterdam: Benjamins.

Linebarger, M. 1987. "Negative Polarity and Grammatical Representation." *Linguistics and Philosophy* 10, 325-387.

Link, G. 1983. "The Logical Analysis of Plurals and Mass Terms: a Lattice-Theoretical Approach." In: Bäuerle, Schwarze, and von Stechow (eds).

Lötscher, A. 1978. "Zur Verbstellung im Zürichdeutschen und in anderen Varianten des Deutschen." *Zeitschrift für Dialektologie und Linguistik*, 45, 1-29.

Longobardi, G. 1985. "Connectedness, Scope, and C-Command." *Linguistic Inquiry* 16, 163-192.

May, R. 1977. "The Grammar of Quantification." Diss., Massachusetts Institute of Technology

———. 1985. *Logical Form: Its Structure and Derivation*. Cambridge Mass., MIT Press.

Muysken, P.C. 1982. "Parametrizing the Notion 'Head'." *Journal of Linguistic Research* 2, 57-75.

Oh, C. and D. Dinneen. (eds.) 1979. *Syntax and Semantics 11: Presupposition*. New York: Academic Press.

Partee, B. and M. Rooth. 1983. "Generalized Conjunction and Type Ambiguity." In: Bäuerle, Schwarze, and von Stechow (eds).

Pesetsky, D. 1982. "Paths and Categories." Diss., Massachusetts Institute of Technology.

Platzack, Ch. 1982. "Transitive Adjectives in Swedish: a Phenomenon with Implications for a Theory of Abstract Case." *The Linguistic Review* 2, 39-57.

Reuland, E. 1988. "Relating Morphological and Syntactic Structure." In: M. Everaert, A. Evers, R. Huybregts and M. Trommelen (eds.).

van Riemsdijk, H. 1978. *A Case Study in Syntactic Markedness: The Binding Nature of Prepositional Phrases.* Dordrecht: Foris.

————. and Williams, E. 1981. "NP-structure." *The Linguistic Review* 1, 171-217.

Rooth, M. 1985. "Association with Focus." Diss., University of Massachusetts, Amherst.

Ross, J.R. 1967. "Constraints on Variables in Syntax." Diss., Massachusetts Institute of Technology.

Sag, I. 1976. "Deletion and logical form." Diss.,Massachusetts Institute of Technology.

Stowell, T. 1981. "Origins of Phrase Structure." Diss., Massachusetts Institute of Technology.

Williams, E. 1977. "Discourse and Logical Form." *Linguistic Inquiry* 8, 101-140.

Issues in the Theory of Inheritance

Jindřich Toman
University of Michigan

1. Some Background Assumptions

The following paper deals with the mechanism of inheritance, or percolation, of morphological and semantic features. Among other things, it discusses basic types of inheritance proposed in the literature and raises the question as to how these basic types are motivated and appropriately characterized. The paper itself is in part an outgrowth of the author's earlier work, in particular Toman (1983), and in part a discussion of issues raised in work by T. Höhle, R. Lieber, E. Selkirk, E. Williams and others in the late 70's and early 80's.

The overall goal of the program expounded in these studies is an assimilation of the principles of word-formation, to the set of general principles of grammar, and hence of the so-called word-formation component of the grammar, and an eventual dissolution of this component. In our own work, the intention has been to show that a large, in fact considerably large, number of properties believed to be typical of word-structure can be deduced from general principles of grammar, i.e., principles which are nonspecific with respect to the component. We have suggested that there ultimately are no specific word-formation rules and that there is no particular word-formation component of the grammar.

Among the assumptions entertained in this research program is the idea that the structure of complex words can be accounted for by general principles of phrase structure (usually referred to as X-bar theory) and a part of their semantics by principles of θ-theory as well as by principles of semantic interpretation not specific to the domain of words (for the latter point see Fanselow 1985). We have also suggested that word structure is not the proper domain of Case Theory. If this program could be carried out in its most radical form, the only substantial difference between syntax and the theory of complex words — what we have called "word syntax" — would thus be located in the domains of Case and Phonological Form. Furthermore, the whole system is assimilated to the model of grammar assumed in *Lectures on Government and Binding* (Chomsky 1981):

(1)

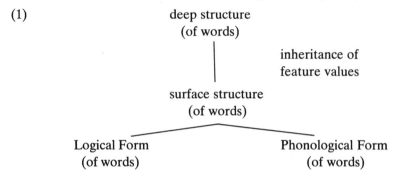

                     deep structure
                     (of words)

                                       inheritance of
                                       feature values

             surface structure
               (of words)

Logical Form   Phonological Form
(of words)   (of words)

Facts pertaining to productivity, to the "passive mode of operation" of rules accounting for words, using an expression by Morris Halle (1973), are not seen as a proper domain of the word-formation theory in our sense. In particular, it is hoped that the fact that words are often, perhaps even typically, memorized, whereas sentences are not, is to be derived from principles which are not necessarily principles of grammar. We have also stressed that not every item that counts as a word should necessarily be subject to the theory of word-syntax. In this sense the theory is not seen as responsible for any arbitrary item recognized as a word. There are numerous alternative ways of creating words beyond word-syntax, e.g. by analogy, by creating abbreviations, etc. Although this position may perhaps sound somewhat unorthodox to the reader, the latter might be the only mechanisms that actually deserve the name of word-formation rules. But even here we tend to the view that a large part of these alternative modes need not necessarily relate to core grammar but might result from the fact that certain complex patterns can be represented as having internal structure as well as from the fact that there are general ways of storing, recalling, comparing and producing structured items independently of the grammar.

Before reviewing some of the more technical concepts, we should stress that the system was primarily conceived on the basis of German material. And although we should certainly be happy to see the principles of word syntax extended in some non-arbitrary way to languages as diverse as Arabic or Eskimo, we shall for obvious reasons not commit ourselves to any particular claims in this area.

These being some general (and possibly wrong) assumptions, we should now mention at least one technical point that may perhaps appear more vital to the understanding of the present paper than the general statements above, namely the interpretation of affixes in word-syntax. Among other things, we regard derivational affixes as bound occurrences of lexical categories; i.e., an affix such as *-able* is a bound adjective, a nominalizing suffix such as *-ion* a bound noun, etc. (See also (9) below). This approach makes it possible to extend the rule schemata of X-bar theory to word syntax and to define the head-category in a more or less unified manner. These bound nouns etc. are assumed to have all the morphological properties free nouns etc. have.

Another technical concept is that of inheritance, or percolation. In the remaining part of this paper we shall discuss this concept in detail.

2. On the Status of Inheritance

2.1. *The Conceptual Basis of Inheritance*

It has generally been accepted in the literature that one way of accounting for the fact that a morphologically complex word may be complemented by a constituent which is semantically dependent on a subpart of this complex word consists in saying that the relevant properties of the subconstituent have been transferred to the whole word. Thus the fact that, say, a nominalized form of a verb may under certain conditions preserve the argument structure ("θ-structure," "semantic valency," "deep cases") of the verb has not been typically interpreted as an instance of a "long distance" assignment of a θ-role:

(2)

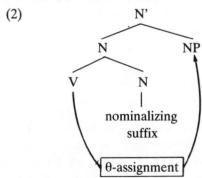

but as an instance of θ-role assignment mediated by θ-feature inheritance:

(3)

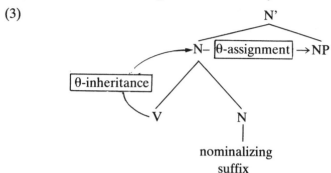

nominalizing
suffix

Sytems of inheritance were suggested by various authors around 1980, whereby the acceptance of this mechanism perhaps profited more from its intuitive appeal than from rigid definitions. However, an example of a more formal approach is also available. Consider Selkirk's final version of the definition of inheritance offered in her book on *The Syntax of Words*:

(4) a.   If a head has a feature specification $[\alpha F_i]$, $\alpha \neq u$, its mother node must be specified $[\alpha F_i]$, and vice versa.

b.   If a non-head has a feature specification $[\beta F_j]$, and the head has the feature specification $[uF_j]$, then the mother node must have the feature specification $[\beta F_j]$.

(Selkirk 1982:76)

(α, β stand for specified feature values, u for unspecified feature value.)[1]

The statement has two clauses: the first defines the priority of the "head-projection line," the second defines a "fill up" procedure which makes it possible to specify empty feature values on the head line with feature values from the non-head line:[2]

(5) $X \{\alpha A, \beta B, \delta C\}$

$Y \{\delta C, \tau L\}$ $X \{\alpha A, \beta B, uC\}$

$Z \{\beta B, \gamma M\}$ $X \{\alpha A, uB, uC\}$

It is important to stress that under this interpretation, feature inheritance is actually the inheritance of feature *values*. It consists in filling the blanks (u's) for feature values rather than in shifting the features themselves. By this token an important restriction is embodied in the system: it is not possible to inherit arbitrary features, it is only possible to fill in feature specifications in independently existing feature sets, i.e. in sets that define nodes. In other words, values of features L, M in (5) will not be inherited by the relevant mother nodes simply because the mother nodes in question are not defined by these features. This property has been informally termed "structure preserving property" of inheritance in Toman (1983).

Selkirk's statement is in some sense redundant, however, because both clauses of (4) repeat the requirement that underspecified mother nodes must receive appropriate feature specifications from their daughters. Presumably a more elegant formulation might keep apart the requirement that a mother node have the feature specification of its daughters and the statement of how this requirement is to be executed. The first requirement would essentially be in the spirit of some variant of the so-called Projection Principle, i.e., of a requirement that lexical properties be satisfied throughout all levels of representation, whereas the statement of execution would seem to be a particular instantiation of the Elsewhere Condition: if the more specific mode of application fails, i.e., if appropriate feature specifications cannot be obtained on the head-line, they will be obtained "elsewhere," namely on the non-head line.

In fact, we shall assume that from the conceptual point of view this is the proper perspective and view inheritance phenomena henceforth as resulting from some variant of the Projection Principle and the possibility of stating a priority relation between the head-line and the non-head line. As far as the exact formulation of the projection principle we have in mind is concerned we shall leave it intentionally vague. In particular, we shall say nothing about its relation to the Projection Principle in Chomsky (1981) which focuses on the preservation of the subcategorization frame. Clearly there is an open issue here, but we assume that something close to the following must be involved:

(6)   The main projection line must be functionally complete.

For clarification we add that "main projection line" is to be understood as "head line that receives inflection" in categories that can be inflected. This is a minor, but nevertheless relevant point. Note that in a compound such as:

(7)

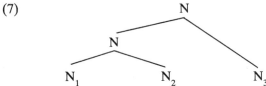

it strictly speaking does not matter whether morphological properties will project from N_2 or not — a language learner will never have any positive evidence that they do — whereas they certainly must project from N_3.

The literature has not always been quite explicit as to whether θ-features represent a special case or whether they should be treated on a par with morphological features. Referring to our own work, we have taken the latter position. Under this approach, θ-role transmission (called "argument inheritance" in Toman 1983) from a subconstituent on to a larger constituent was treated in the same manner as the inheritance of morphological features. Given this approach, there emerges a grammatical system which includes the following principles:

(8)   *Fragment of Grammar A*
   K)   [...]
   L)   θ-role Assignment: θ-assigner assigns a θ-index to its sister.
   M)   Feature Inheritance: a mother node receives/duplicates/has feature specifications of the daughter node.
   N)   Head-Projection-Line Priority: if more than one daughter is a candidate for (M), the one on the head-line has priority.
   O)   [...]

Assuming that θ-roles are represented as features and associated with lexical items, (8) represents a grammar in which θ-roles will be distributed by two distinct mechanisms, L and M.

2.2. *Status of Inheritance along the Non-Head Line*

The approach outlined above, which nearly represents the current standard, claims that both head-lines and non-head-lines may contribute to the feature content of the mother node. It is a curious fact, however, that in languages such as German it is little short of impossible to find instances of morphological inheritance from the non-head branch. Recall that given the well-motivated assumption assigning derivational suffixes the status of bound nouns, adjectives, etc., there will be no morphological inheritance from the non-head branch in structures such as:

(9)

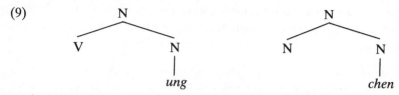

In these examples of derived nominals, the affixal heads count as morphologically fully specified, hence the possibility of feature inheritance along the non-head line cannot arise.

As far as the few deverbal verbs in German formed by means of suffixes are concerned we must conclude the same. The fact that the suffix changes the class and creates weak verbs from strong ones should be described in analogy to (9) above:

(10)

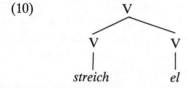

(Note: streich-en / er strich, but *streich-el-n / er streichelte,* not *er strichelte;* cf. Plank 1986.)

Apart from questions posed by the status of regular inflection (see section 2.4), the only prominent candidate for morphological inheritance from the non-head branch in word syntax is formed by certain instances of prefixed verbs. It is a well-known fact that verbal prefixation typically results neither in a change of word-class nor of morphological properties, although it may often induce a change in the argument structure of the verb:

(11) a. *spend*   past tense: *spent*
        outspend   past tense: *outspent*
    b. *schreiben*   past tense: *schrieb*
        beschreiben   past tense: *beschrieb*

The examples show that these verbs of English and German remain strong verbs after prefixation.

Current analyses tend to the view that the (causative) prefixes involved here function as heads of the verbs shown. Under this view one must assume that these heads are morphologically impoverished in that they are not specified for verbal categories such as weak/strong distinction. These specifications must then be supplied by the "real" verb, i.e., by the non-head constituent, which would seem to result in a rare instance of morphological inheritance from the non-head position:

(12)

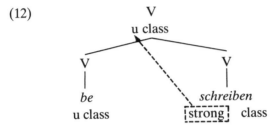

Clearly, if we want to maintain that the prefixes involved in verbs of this type are heads at the level of phrase structure, we need morphological inheritance from the non-head position. It should of course be acknowledged that an analysis which claims that these prefixes are heads poses a number of problems. One obvious drawback consists in the fact that a consistent positional definition of the head cannot be given for German (or for a number of other languages in which this type of verb occurs). There is also no generalization within prefixes: some may obviously function as heads, cf. the case under discussion, others may not (e.g., nominal prefixes).

The overall scarcity of morphological inheritance from the non-head branch as well as the not particularly clear status of the prefixal deverbal derivations might in fact provide an incentive for alternative analyses: for instance, one might assume a distinction between a semantic and a morphological head and argue for a description according to which verbal prefixes such as above are semantic, but not morphological heads. This would be insofar interesting as it would make one rare instance of morphological inheritance from the non-head branch disappear. Nevertheless the details of such an analysis are not clear to us. The question posed at this point is thus: are there radical asymmetries with respect to head/non-head status? Can an analysis of prefixal verbs be worked out which makes morphological inheritance from the non-head branch superfluous?

To anticipate the answer, we refer to our earlier work in which a suggestion was made to the effect that certain instances of syntactic heads function as non-heads at the level of Logical Form (the term being used in the sense of Chomsky 1981). In particular we have argued that a reanalysis is possible which deprives numerals and numeral-like expressions of their head-status in syntax and makes them function as non-heads at the level of Logical Form (see Toman 1986b). The question thus is whether reanalyses of a comparable kind can be argued for with prefixal verbs, or, in general, in all cases of apparent inheritance from the non-head branch in word-syntax.

The second case of inheritance from the non-head branch with which we are familiar is no less complicated and is equally susceptible to alternative analyses. It relates to the phenomenon called Pied-piping. Recall that inheritance is actually seen as non-specific with respect to word-formation. It is assumed to apply both in word-syntax and in regular phrasal syntax, i.e., it is not constrained to minimal projections only. If this is maintained, the process involved in Pied-piping could conveniently be seen as involving inheritance from the non-head branch:

(13)

(See Riemsdijk 1985 for this kind of approach.)

Assuming that the features involved are definable in morphological terms, i.e., assuming that we are dealing with a kind of morphological "letter diacritics" for pronominal roots (wh-words in English, w-words in German, k-words in Slavic),[3] the phenomenon in question would seem to involve inheritance. That is, the wh-feature is associated with the non-head branch and becomes accessible to wh-movement on the mother node dominating both the head and non-head. Consequently, the entire constituent is moved, not only a subpart of it:

(14) a.   Whose letters did you read?
     b.   *Whose did you read letters?

The problem that arises here concerns the proper generalization. Is the generalization formulated in terms of "letter diacritics" really a genuine one? Clearly, there is a competing generalization which might claim that the proper domain of analyses is a "Grammar of Scope." We note that it is a general property of certain quantifiers that they may "look" from the constituents within which they are embedded and take scope which must be described as an extension of their locally defined domain. To take an example from English, we see that both (15a) and (15b,c) equally satisfy one of the requirements for the distribution of *any*, namely that it be in the c-command scope of a negative item:

(15) a.   [Nothing]$_{NP}$ was really *any* good.
      b.   [No paper]$_{NP}$ was really *any* good.
      c.   [Nobody's papers]$_{NP}$ were really *any* good.

Should we maintain an inheritance analysis, negative quantifiers on nonhead branches (*no*, *nobodys*) would also have to be inherited in order to define the scope domain from the maximal head projection involved.

Whereas one might perhaps tolerate the idea that wh-words and negwords form a natural morphological class, not many readers would accept an extension of this class such that degree words of the type *too*, *so* would also be included in it:

(16) a.   Joey is *too* clever *to talk*.
      b.   She saw *so* many bad pictures *that she decided to leave*.

(Variants of this type of construction are familiar from a number of languages; cf. *so....daß...*(German), *si...que...*, *assez...pour* (French)).

Here, of course, there is no overt evidence for morphological feature-inheritance, although the scope properties relevant for the construction of an adequate representation at the level of Logical Form (LF) should be in crucial aspects similar to those of the wh- and neg-specifiers briefly introduced above.

What conclusion can be made at this point? Leaving aside the question of quantifier movement at LF, we see that only a small subset of quantifier words, namely wh-words, shows behavior that might be interpreted as morphological inheritance in syntax. (We assume that Pied-piping itself provides the evidence for claiming so.) The rest, which is the majority, does not involve movement in syntax and hence there is no strong reason for saying that, for instance, features of *so* are shifted to the AP by the process of inheritance. In addition, it would of course be awkward to say that *so, too, wh-words* and *neg-words* form a natural morphological class.

To conclude, we enumerate some further points which indicate that inheritance involved in Pied-piping has a number of properties which make it difficult to subsume this process under morphological inheritance from the non-head branch without reservations. The process is not always obligatory in English:

(17)   Who bought [which pictures]

Since wh-movement does not affect the phrase *which pictures* in syntax, there is no safe indication of inheritance in syntax.

In cases in which inheritance plausibly applies, maximal projections are involved:

(18)   .... persons letters of whom we should intercept

And finally, there still is an open question as to whether wh-features should form a natural class together with features such as "gender," "number," "conjugation type," "non-native morpheme" and the like. Independent evidence is hard to come by, yet considerations about scope properties involved suggest that something different is at issue. Note that a scope feature seems to be inherited "in order" to make Pied-piping possible, not necessarily to "fill up" the blanks on the head-line thus rendering the head-line functionally complete in the sense of (2b).

We thus tend to the view that the process involved is quite different from the inheritance of morphological features such as gender etc. But since we would not like to claim that we fully understand the process under discussion, we close with the following question rather than with an authoritative closing statement: in the case of Pied-piping, are we dealing with the same kind of inheritance from the non-head branch as in the case of "standard" morphological inheritance, or not? Are the scope properties of quantifiers the crucial properties involved and the syntactic Pied-piping just an accident?[4]

To summarize, we see that morphological inheritance from the non-head branch is not as common as expected and that the tentative instances are rather too complicated to provide clear and convincing examples.

2.3. *Substantive Restrictions on Feature Inheritance?*

Considering the possibility of there being no argument for morphological inheritance along the non-head branch, one might of course wonder about the status of θ-inheritance from the non-heads. Recall that it is gener-

ally assumed that in such formations as (3) the θ-content of the whole complex word is supplied by its "lexical" part. This would appear to be a good
case of inheritance from the non-head branch.

But even if there were convincing arguments in favor of morphological
inheritance along the non-head branch, what would be the exact status of θ-
inheritance after all? As we have seen above (cf. (8)), the grammar under
consideration has two mechanisms which apply to θ-roles. A logical question is whether this system is redundant or not. At first sight this might
seem to be the case.

Other questions also arise. If both morphological features and θ-features can be inherited from the non-head branch, the system treats all kinds
of features alike. Hence no substantive definition of the class of features
which may be inherited would seem to be available: whenever some property is realized "at a distance," an inherited feature must be involved. One
question which comes to mind at this point consists in considering the possibility of a substantive definition of features involved in inheritance. For
instance, the following statement which claims that these features form an
independently defined natural class seems to be worthy of consideration:

(19)   Only morphological features can be inherited.

Clearly, whatever the substance of θ-features might be, they are not morphological features even under a liberal interpretation of the term morphological. But should we adhere to (19), θ-features could not be inherited
and another mode of instantiating them would have to be considered. What
choice is there at this point?

Before we embark upon this question, we recall that, irrespective of
the technical details of θ-inheritance, the mechanism of θ-marking
(synonymously: "θ-role assignment," or for short, "θ-assignment"), must
always be available in the grammar. In addition, we know that the
mechanism is local: θ-marking involves local environments, i.e., it proceeds
among sisters only, and should it be possible to claim that all branchings are
binary, the number of sisters would of course always be limited to two.
Elsewhere we have exploited this idea and tried to argue that this is exactly
the mechanism that is also operative inside words, i.e., must be accessible
to word-syntax (Boase-Beier & Toman 1986). One of the results of this
study was that it is desirable to assume θ-marking in such instances as:

(20)

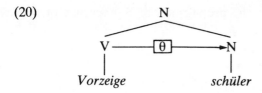

Vorzeige   *schüler*

('show pupil,' i.e. "excellent, exemplary pupil"), but not in cases such as:

(21)

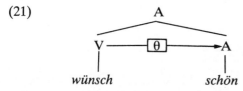

wünsch   *schön*

(Literally, 'wish-beautiful,' ungrammatical on the attempted reading "beautiful, such that one wishes (for s.o.) to be beautiful.")

The former example involves nominal targets of θ-assignment, the latter involves a non-nominal category. It was therefore suggested that categories such as V, A, P be disqualified as targets of θ-assignment:

(22)   Arguments are nominal:
          Only [+N, −V] elements can be θ-marked.
          (Boase-Beier & Toman 1986:336)

In thus restricting the recipients of θ-roles to real nominal categories (nouns, nominal phrases) and to clauses introduced by complementizers, we appealed to Kayne (1982), and may now add Taraldsen (1981) for the same point. Bearing these results in mind, what would it then mean if we abandoned θ-inheritance, a process tied to the non-head branch, and accepted θ-marking between, say, verbs and verbal affixes, roughly along the following lines:

(23)

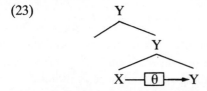

In this example, X θ-marks its sister Y, the assumption being that θ-marking is non-directional (Boase-Beier & Toman 1986:324), and the Projection Principle defined for the head-line automatically ensures the visibility of θ-properties everywhere along the head-line. (Note that the latter mechanism will also ensure the propagation of θ-properties of the verb within the VP in regular syntax.)

Whereas it is relatively clear how this mechanism may work with structures in which Y is a nominal head, it is somewhat less clear how it might work in such cases as deverbal *bar*-adjectives:

(24)

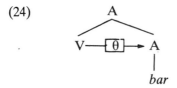

Note that the recipient of the θ-role would here be an adjective. Besides saying that the adjective itself gets θ-marked, one might entertain the idea that it is not the adjective but its argument features that actually get θ-marked (and their values then propagate along the head-line). However, both approaches lead into a conflict with the results of the study of θ-marking reported above. If θ-marking applied to such suffixes directly, a number of compounds with adjectival and verbal heads which are neither attested nor seem to be possible, would be generated.[5]

A preliminary conclusion thus runs as follows: it is not particularly clear what it would mean for a verb to θ-mark an affix such as -*bar*. Consequently, it does not seem possible to interpret θ-inheritance from the non-head in terms of θ-marking. θ-inheritance must thus be kept in the grammar.

This conclusion does not however answer the question about the nature of θ-inheritance itself. In particular, it remains unclear why morphological inheritance is so problematic along the non-head branch whereas θ-inheritance is actually "the best case." In order to answer this, tentatively at least, we return to Pied-piping. Recall that we concluded that the inheritance of the wh-feature is functionally somewhat different form the inheritance of a regular morphological feature. Asking the question about the functional nature of θ-inheritance we may also conclude that the process is not necessarily comparable to morphological inheritance in that it does not specify the head-line with a feature by which the head-projection must necessarily be characterized. The "reason" for θ-inheritance is to extend the scope domain of a θ-assigner.

2.4. *Inheritance and Inflectional Affixes*

A reader familiar with the literature may have noted that one set of facts has not been dealt with yet, namely inheritance in inflected forms. Are not words derived by inflectional affixes a good, perhaps even the best, example of inheritance from the non-head branch?[6]

The only condition which would make inheritance from the non-head work would consist in equipping inflectional affixes with all the necessary features in the unspecified form, i.e., with u's. Consequently, all the relevant properties would be free to percolate from the non-head line. Let us call this the "Empty Theory of Inflection" and illustrate it with the following schemata:

(25) a.

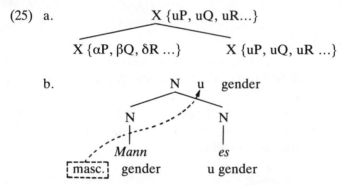

b.

(*Mannes* in (b) being genitive singular of *Mann* 'man.')

Although this description of inflection may at first sight appear to be a kind of trick, it will be recalled that under the approach outlined above no additional principles are necessary: affixes are bound instances of lexical categories. Hence we expect to encounter exactly the same set of properties that we find with non-bound, i.e., free tokens of the category in question.

It is unfortunately very difficult to find convincing positive evidence for or against this approach. Our impression is that it is entirely based on consistency considerations rather than on particular instances of evidence pointing to the nature of inflectional affixes themselves.

An alternative to the Empty Theory of Inflection is known. It consists in seeing inflectional suffixes not as sisters of words but as phrasal affixes:

(26)

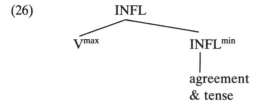

INFL

V^{max} $INFL^{min}$

|

agreement
& tense

and having them merged with lexical heads in phonology rather than in syntax. An extension of this treatment of verbal inflection to nominal inflection would require to interpret CASE in analogy to clausal INFL:

(27)

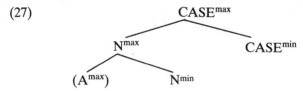

$CASE^{max}$

N^{max} $CASE^{min}$

(A^{max}) N^{min}

Here, Case is represented as a structural position and the NP is reinterpreted as a maximal projection of the Case node. An analogous treatment of APs should be possible, too.

A potentially relevant case of phrasal affixation is the German present participle, the *end*-participle. Note that if it is assumed that this form is an adjective inflected with *-end*, roughly:

(28)

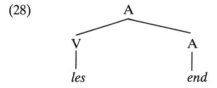

A

V   A

| |

les   *end*

it is very hard to explain how it is possible that this form can assign accusative to its direct object as in:

(29)   *der eine Zeitung   lesende Mann*
          the a   newspaper reading man

If phrasal affixation is assumed, on the other hand, roughly along the following lines (cf. Toman 1986a for details):

(30)

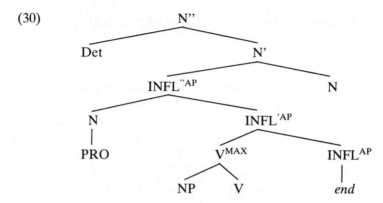

the verb will case mark the direct object with no difficulty. The ending and the verb root will then merge at the level of Phonological Representation (PF). This treatment thus accounts for the fact that these participles preserve all subcategorizational properties of verbs as well as the verbal θ-structure without any changes. The construction essentially behaves as an inflected non-finite active clause.

The question to be raised here is whether there is a strong empirical evidence for phrasal affixation across languages and how phrasal analyses can be reconciled with such approaches as Kiparsky's lexicalist phonology. In any case, a theory of phrasal inflection would seem to correctly preserve the fact that inflection does not block θ-assignment and that it is neutral with respect to such characteristics as the distinction between external and internal arguments. At the same time, phrasal treatment of inflection is compatible with X-bar theory in that it permits of treating inflectional affixes as heads at a higher level in the phrase structure (and not as heads of words).[7]

3. Summary

The reader will have noticed that the discussion in this paper has in fact centered around the question as to whether inheritance from the non-head branch could be abandoned. Among other things, we have seen that the status of inheritance is more complicated than would at first appear: besides inflection, which might plausibly require a different approach, namely phrasal affixation, morphological inheritance from the non-head line is rare and involves cases whose analysis is by no means simple (Pied-piping, prefixal verbs). It is rather probable that accounts of these phenomena might be formulated in such a way that no morphological inheritance would be involved.

θ-inheritance along the non-head would seem to remain necessary, however. It is at least not quite clear how θ-marking, a potential candidate that could take over its function, could be formulated so as to apply to affixes. Upon closer examination, however, it seems difficult to compare θ-inheritance with morphological inheritance since the former performs an operation somewhat different from the specification of unmarked features on the head-line. Its assimilation to the "fill-up" format assumed for inheritance from the non-head branch would thus require empty argument features on the head line. Although this might be a viable possibility in unifying the system of morphological and semantic inheritance, it is not clear whether an interesting generalization would be expressed in such a unified system. Note that θ-inheritance basically represents an extension of the domain in which θ-roles can be assigned. In this sense it shares certain properties with Pied-piping rather than with morphological inheritance.

The picture which emerges is hence one suggesting that the mechanism of morphological inheritance, in the standard sense, may perhaps not be needed. θ-inheritance would thus be the only "foot feature" and the rest would be taken care of by Projection Principle (6), a requirement on the well-formedness of the head-projection line.

Notes

1.   Note that despite numerous arrows in Selkirk's illustrations, the definition is formulated as a well-formedness condition on adjacent nodes, not as a processual statement of "feature movement" or the like.

2.   Throughout we shall be using the following terminology: head-projection line, or, for short, head line (branch), and non-head-projection line (branch), for short non-head line (branch). This supersedes the often-used labels "rigth branch" and "left branch," both of which apply to, and are appropriate in, situations specific to a particular language.

3.   Analogous considerations might apply for certain types of reflexive pronouns (see the discussion of "foot features" in Gazdar & al. 1985 in this context).

4.   Again, alternative analyses might be considered. Note that some of the recent theories of NPs structure argue that the head of NP is the determiner (Hellan 1986). If so, wh-inheritance in the above case would be rendered as inheritance along the head-line. Although this might well be the proper line of analysis, there are no consequences for the theory under discussion. The inheritance of other morphological features would now have to fol-

low from the non-head line. And as far as wh-inheritance itself is concerned, we shall still find instances of wh-inheritance along the non-head branch outside NP structure:

(i)   [How deep]$_{A\,P}$ is this well?

It seems implausible to say that the specifier of AP is the head of AP.

5.   The problem is familiar from other systems. We draw the reader's attention to Roberts (1985) in which the idea is expounded that the passive affix in English passive participles is actually θ-marked by the verb from which the participle is formed. Without discussing the points we are here adducing, Roberts assumes that the affix in question is actually a subject clitic and can hence be θ-marked (and perhaps also case-marked). We shall say nothing here about whether this analysis is adequate or not; it should only be noted that treating the affix as a nominal is probably the only way of ensuring that it be θ-marked. That is, as far as θ-marking is concerned, Roberts' analysis complies with (22).

6.   Selkirk (1982) treats inflected words as showing inheritance from the non-head branch. Her provision for percolation from the non-head branch in the definition (2) is in fact motivated by facts of inflection.

7.   The compatibility with X-bar theory is an important feature of the system. Recall that Selkirk (1982) also rejects the idea that inflectional affixes are heads of words. It is however unclear whether this is compatible with the principle of X-bar theory.

References

Boase-Beier, Jean. and Jindřich Toman. 1986. "On θ-role Assignment in German Compounds." *Folia Linguistica* 20, 319-340.

Chomsky, Noam. 1981. *Lectures on Government and Binding*. Dordrecht: Foris.

Chomsky, Noam. 1986. *Knowledge of Language. Its Nature, Origin, and Use*. New York: Praeger.

Fanselow, Gisbert. 1985. "What is a Possible Complex Word?" In: Toman (ed.).

Gazdar, Gerald, Ewan Klein, Geoffrey Pullum, and Ivan Sag. 1985. *Generalized Phrase Structure Grammar*. Oxford: Blackwell.

Halle, Morris. 1973. "Prolegomena to a Theory of Word Formation." *Linguistic Inquiry* 4: 3-16.

Hellan, Lars. 1986. "The Headedness of NPs in Norwegian." In: P. Muysken and H. van Riemsdijk. (eds). *Features and Projections*, Dordrecht: Foris.

Kayne, Richard. 1982. "Predicates and Arguments, Nouns and Verbs." *GLOW Newsletter* 8: 24.

Perlmutter, David M. 1978. "Impersonal Passives and the Unaccusativev Hypothesis." *Proceedings of the Berkeley Linguistics Society* 4: 157-189.

Plank, Frans. 1986. "Das Genus der deutschen *Ge*-Substantive und Verwandtes (Beiträge zur Vererbungslehre 1)." *Zeitschrift für Phonetik, Sprachwissenschaft und Kommunikationsforschung* 39: 44-60.

Riemsdijk, Henk van. 1985. "On Pied-Piping Infinitives in German Relative Clauses." In: Toman (ed.).

Roberts, Ian G. 1985. "The Representation of Implicit and Dethematized Subjects." Diss., University of Southern California, Los Angeles.

Selkirk, Elisabeth O. 1982. *The Syntax of Words*. Cambridge, Mass.: MIT Press.

Taraldsen, Tarald. 1981. "The Status of S in Germanic and Romance." In: Th. Fretheim and L. Hellan (eds.). *Proceedings of the 6th Scandinavian Conference on Linguistics*. Trondheim: TAPIR.

Toman, Jindřich. 1983. *Wortsyntax. Eine Diskussion ausgewählter Probleme deutscher Wortbildung*. Tübingen: Niemeyer.

———. (ed.) 1985. *Studies in German Grammar*. Dordrecht: Foris

———. 1986a. "A (Word-)Syntax for Participles." *Linguistische Berichte* 105: 367-408.

———. 1986b. "Cliticization from NPs in Czech and Comparable Phenomena in French and Italian." In: Hagit Borer (ed.). *The Syntax of Pronominal Clitics*. Orlando: Academic Press.